Date Due

JUN 5 82			
JUL 10 1989			
SEP 28 1989			
OCT 2 1989			
OCT 20 1989			

Thrilling, D.
Mrs. Harris

Mrs. Harris

Mrs. Harris

THE DEATH OF THE SCARSDALE DIET DOCTOR

Diana Trilling

Harcourt Brace Jovanovich, Publishers
New York and London

Library of Congress Cataloging in Publication Data
Trilling, Diana.
Mrs. Harris: the death of the Scarsdale diet doctor.
1. Harris, Jean S., 1923–   .   2. Tarnower, Herman.
3. Trials (Murder)—New York (State)—White Plains.
I. Title.

| KF224.H26T74 | 345.73'0252 | 80-81991 |
| ISBN 0-15-176902-8 | 347.3052523 | AACR2 |

Printed in the United States of America

First edition

B C D E

CONTENTS

LOOKING BACK

When I first decided to write about Mrs. Harris—it was shortly after she'd been charged with the murder of Dr. Tarnower—I'd have had no trouble explaining either my bias in the case or my fascination with it. The two were in fact inseparable. My initial response was one of unqualified sympathy for the headmistress, and I conceived the book in a spirit of partisanship. Yet six months later, at the pre-trial hearings, it became more and more difficult for me to recapture and comprehend this earlier reaction. It was one that had been widely shared not only among my friends but by casual acquaintances in all walks of life, part of what can only be called a great upwelling of feeling for the long-time mistress of the Scarsdale doctor. What, I now had to ask myself, had been the source of this sympathy? From the start, ideology had of course attached itself to the story of Jean Harris and Herman Tarnower—ideology is the sterner face of myth and we're a myth-making people. To many women, newly sensitized by doctrinaire women's liberation to the mistreatment of women not merely in public life but in all relations of the sexes, it had only to be known that Tarnower had replaced his mistress of fourteen years with a woman twenty years her junior and more than thirty years younger than himself for Jean Harris to be regarded as embattled female spirit. But ideology didn't exercise a controlling influence on female sentiment. Whoever had known sexual jealousy, that most destructive of emotions—and this would be so for men no less than for women—had known madness and had now to know sympathy for someone who had been carried by jealousy this one terrible step too far, to murder. It's also more than a common worry among women, it's virtually a universal female fear that as their sexual attractions diminish, they'll have to cede, officially or unofficially, to women younger than they are—to be alone and to advance in years is different for a woman than it is for a man. But equally with women, men responded with strong feeling to Mrs. Harris's passionate action. At a time in our culture when violence was achieving a new legitimacy as a form of public assertion, there was perhaps a special pathos in the idea of a woman so obviously foreign to extreme behavior, whose life had been dedicated to respectability and convention, being suddenly driven to such desperate conduct. Mrs. Harris's action spoke of depths of suffering and despair far beyond what most of us are pushed to though surely of the same basic stuff as the everyday pain that's woven into our experience. It forced upon us a fresh realization that behind the contained and orderly lives we lead as members of the respectable middle class there's a terrible human capacity that may one day overwhelm any of us.

But why had I lost this earlier tenderness? Why did my previous response now seem so distant that I had trouble even in recollecting it? There was more to it than merely the passing of half a year. With the beginning of the hearings in October, I felt there had to be a new beginning to everything I'd thought about the case. It was not only that I could no longer think of Mrs. Harris as a symbol of our capacity for hurt and rage but that I had to acknowledge the possibility that along with the rest of the public I had been misled in my view of her relation to her lover and her motive in coming to Purchase on the night of the shooting, even perhaps in my fundamental perception of her character: In short, I had now to restore this mythical person to her actuality. I had already drafted a book and had expected only to add a summary of the trial, perhaps having to correct a few sentences or paragraphs that might prove inaccurate to the courtroom evidence. Now it became clear that a basic revision was necessary—and even this troubling awareness was soon superseded by the recognition that revision wouldn't do but that the entire early manuscript had to be discarded. Was I a child of my ideological times? Maybe, but not to the extent of allowing any system of ideas or feelings to obscure immediate truths.

Certainly I was of my time in my dependence on the press for my knowledge of Mrs. Harris's case. In coming to my conclusions about her tragic situation I had of necessity relied upon the only sources of information available to the public, newspaper reports and a scattering of magazine articles. These accounts, it was now apparent, had themselves been mistaken and they had led me into fundamental error. Many of my earlier emotions and opinions were not only unsupported by fact; they were unwarranted, even contradicted. Through no fault of the people who wrote these early stories—from the standpoint of Mrs. Harris's defense, through no fault of anyone—I had been responding to a figure in public relations rather than to the woman who had shot Herman Tarnower. When Mrs. Harris had been charged with murder in the second degree, now the most severe charge possible in New York State except in the killing of a police officer or a prison official on duty, Westchester County's District Attorney Vergari had commented that now at last the public would be reminded that there was a victim in the Harris case, Dr. Tarnower. For Joel Aurnou, Mrs. Harris's lawyer, the case had a different victim: it was Mrs. Harris. At the time it seemed to me that both of them were wrong; there were two victims, Dr. Tarnower *and* Mrs. Harris—there usually are in crimes of passion. Yet with the start of the pre-trial hearings I began to understand what the District Attorney meant: the public, in its concern with Mrs. Harris, had lost sight of certain realities, including the reality that Dr. Tarnower had been deprived of life. Some of the newspaper errors were insignificant: could it matter, for instance, that Tarnower had died in blue pajamas rather than beige, as was regularly reported? But others were crucial in the reading of Mrs. Harris's character and of her relation to her lover. The situation had all to be looked at again; or perhaps what was asked for wasn't review but a first effort of free inquiry. At best—which is to say, even where our knowledge of a case comes to us only through courtroom evidence—it is difficult for the legal process to keep us at a sanitizing distance from crimes of passion. They make reference to emotions of which we tend to be unaware, invite identifications which aren't always as accurate as they may appear to be. And Mrs. Harris's case, located as it was in the familiar suburban middle class, was peculiarly tempting to this kind of self-intrusion and therefore to prejudice.

Here then, in all its carelessness of evidential fact, is the story as it first came to us:

On Monday, March 10, 1980, Mrs. Jean Harris, the fifty-six-year-old headmistress of the Madeira School in McLean, Virginia, a

5

woman of unimpeachable standing in the social and educational community, had driven to the Westchester home of her lover, Dr. Herman Tarnower, author of the famous Scarsdale diet. She had let herself into the house and gone to his bedroom. In one hand she carried a Harrington and Richardson .32-caliber revolver which she had bought in Virginia two years earlier; in the other, a bouquet of flowers. Tarnower's cook had heard a shot and called the police. As the patrol car approached the house the headmistress was leaving the driveway, but she readily turned back. Her empty gun was in the car. Dr. Tarnower was found dying on the floor between the twin beds of his bedroom; he was wearing beige pajamas. There were four bullets in his body. Mrs. Harris had admitted to the first officers on the scene that it was her gun that had shot the doctor but she was unable to remember pulling the trigger. She was arrested and taken to the Harrison police station.

In the following hours, Joel Aurnou, a former Westchester judge now in the practice of criminal law in White Plains, had been engaged to defend her and, the next day, Mrs. Harris had been released on $40,000 bail in the care of her family and friends and placed under psychiatric supervision. After felony and Grand Jury hearings, she was charged with murder in the second degree. The defense position, as Mrs. Harris's lawyer outlined it in the next weeks, was that the headmistress had recently been in a deeply troubled state of mind but she still loved the doctor and had come to his home that night not to kill him but to commit suicide. Tarnower had been killed by accident, in a struggle for possession of the gun. At her arrest Mrs. Harris had a visible bruise on her mouth and she was reported to have another on her arm. A young member of the Harrison police force, Patrolman Daniel O'Sullivan, one of the first police officers to appear on the scene, testified at the felony hearing of March 15 that the headmistress had said "that she had driven up from Virginia with the intention of having Dr. Tarnower kill her." He also testified that in reply to the question, who had shot the doctor, put to Mrs. Harris on the scene by Detective Arthur Siciliano, she had replied, "I did it." She said that he had slept with every woman he could and that she had "had it."

As background to the shooting, the press told us what it could

6

about the two chief characters in this drama. Of Dr. Tarnower we learned that he was a highly regarded internist and cardiologist who had begun his professional career in New York City but then decided to practice in the Westchester suburbs. In Scarsdale, which gave its name to his famous reducing regime, he had helped found the Scarsdale Medical Center, a successful group-practice clinic. In 1979 he'd published *The Complete Scarsdale Medical Diet,* an elaboration of the program he'd for a long time been recommending to his overweight patients; the book had immediately become a great best seller and the doctor had achieved worldwide celebrity. He lived on a handsome "estate" in the expensive suburb of Purchase in the township of Harrison. Physically an active man, he golfed, he fished for trout, even for salmon. He shot birds and went on safari. He was a gourmet as well as a fitness freak—the contradiction is perhaps not as acute as it sounds. He world-travelled; he consorted with the influential and wealthy, and gave elegant little dinners at which Mrs. Harris had often been his hostess. These were occasions of estimable talk; it seems that Dr. Tarnower—"Hi" to his intimates—had but a minimal aptitude for lightheartedness; his amusements were as consequential as his work. High on the list of his entertainments were women: at sixty-nine still a bachelor, he apparently didn't have to curb that appetite. His health was excellent and much as he firmed up his body, though presumably with less exercise of discipline, he'd in recent years firmed up an alliance with Mrs. Lynne Tryforos, a good-looking young divorcée who was his nurse-secretary at the Scarsdale Clinic. In the last year he'd taken two winter holidays, the first in Palm Beach with Jean Harris, the second in Montego Bay in Jamaica with her thirty-seven-year-old replacement. Although Mrs. Harris had herself not alluded to Mrs. Tryforos at the time of her arrest but spoke of infidelities abstractly, in the plural, the public at once saw in the shooting of the Scarsdale doctor a familiar triangle, the climax of an older woman's jealousy of a younger rival. The only thing that distinguished the Harris-Tarnower story from usual crimes of passion was its social location and the repute of its leading characters.

Jean Harris's career seemed also to have been a fortunate one. The former Jean Struven was said to have been born in Cleveland, educated at private school in Shaker Heights and at Smith

7

College, from which she'd graduated with high honors in 1945. In 1946 she'd been modestly married and in 1965 divorced without scandal—James Harris, her former husband, a man of no notable social position or financial success, had since died. Alone, she had reared two sons, one of whom now worked in a bank in Yonkers; the other was a Marine officer. Not long before the shooting, the Yonkers son had married and Dr. Tarnower, *in loco patris,* had given a wedding dinner for him. On graduating from college, Jean Harris had started at the thin end of the academic profession in elementary teaching in a private school in Grosse Pointe, Michigan, the proud retreat of Detroit's millionaire business leaders and "best families," but had since, for financial reasons, gone into school administration: in 1966 she moved to the Springside School in Philadelphia where she was head of the Middle School. After that, in 1971, she became head of the Thomas School in Rowayton, Connecticut, where she stayed until the school disappeared in a merger which she didn't initiate but seemed to approve. In the interval between 1975, when the Thomas School closed and 1977, when she applied for and got the position of headmistress at Madeira, Mrs. Harris worked in New York for the Allied Maintenance Corporation, a large upkeep company—Madison Square Garden was among its clients—where she was an executive at a reputed salary of $32,500. This was the position she left to become the head of the noted day and boarding school for girls in Virginia, not far from Washington. The move to Madeira had coincided with, perhaps reflected and even aggravated, the growing break, far from a clean one, in her relation with Tarnower.

That the headmistress was pretty, one knew from her pictures. She was said to be intelligent, conscientious, industrious, and markedly ambitious. She was a strict disciplinarian by present-day standards. Report had it that when the girls were supplied with fruit for healthful between-meals snacks, and orange peels appeared on the grounds, she had the fruit withdrawn. Another Madeira report was that she had expelled a girl, or perhaps it was a group of girls, for drinking beer in a public bar. She walked in the footsteps of the founder of Madeira, Miss Lucy Madeira, whose rousing motto for her girls, "Function in disaster, finish in style," had the reassuring ring of Victorian female fortitude once so much cherished in the education of young women. She talked a great deal about integrity; in fact, the students referred to her as "Integrity Jean." There were those who remembered her as "nervous" even in her pre-Madeira days. Lately her strain had been observed by both students and colleagues.

A few other details appeared with some regularity in the early accounts of the shooting. We learned that when Mrs. Harris came to the doctor's bedroom with her gun and asked him to kill her, he'd told her to get out, that she was crazy. She said he had hit her "a lot"—the bruise to her mouth, that is, was the result of an intended blow by Tarnower; it hadn't been sustained in the struggle in which Tarnower had tried to take away her gun. At the time of her arrest she had with her the names and telephone numbers of people who were to be notified of her death; and from The Hill, her residence on the Madeira campus, the police retrieved various documents that were said to bear upon her relation with Tarnower. Probably the most weighty indication of her state of mind when she drove to Purchase that March evening was a long letter she'd posted the morning of the 10th from Greenway, the local Madeira post office. Addressed to Tarnower at the Scarsdale Clinic, it had been sent by certified mail—it was supposed to have been signed for by the doctor himself. If Mrs. Harris intended to kill Tarnower or, at any rate, if she had the intention that morning in Virginia, it was of course unlikely that she'd have sent him a letter for which he'd have to sign. In a decision by the local Westchester postal authorities, the undelivered letter was returned to the defendant and was in the hands of Mrs. Harris's lawyer. The decision to return it to the sender was vigorously protested by the District Attorney, and Justice Rubin, Chief Justice of Westchester County, ruled that he would have to read the letter to determine if the defense was required to share its contents with the prosecution before the trial. But the trial began without the disposition of the Scarsdale letter (as it came to be called) having been settled.

We were told that on the night of the shooting, while Mrs. Harris had been en route from Virginia to Purchase, a five-hour drive, Tarnower had had three guests at dinner: his sister Mrs. Pearl Schwartz of Larchmont, who was chief beneficiary of his will, Mrs. Schwartz's married daughter, Deborah Raizes, and Lynne Tryforos.

I remember thinking that the combination of these three women, two of them the doctor's closest relatives and the third the new mistress, indicated that Mrs. Tryforos must be in good standing with his family; and I even surmised that Mrs. Harris had telephoned before she left Virginia to say she was coming to Purchase and therefore the dinner was an impromptu meeting of his kitchen cabinet to advise the doctor on strategy for the forthcoming encounter. At 9:00 the women left and Dr. Tarnower retired to his bedroom. The meal had been prepared and served by the van der Vrekens, Suzanne and Henri, a couple long in the doctor's employ and, by his description, as close to him as members of his own family. It was Suzanne who'd heard the shot and called the police.

This, in effect, was the story given the public in advance of Mrs. Harris's trial, and I suppose that for many people it's the story they still stay with though by now the correction of its errors has been well publicized. Mrs. Schwartz was not at dinner at her brother's house the evening of his death; only Lynne Tryforos and Debbie Raizes, whose husband is a doctor at the Scarsdale Clinic, were there and the two young women were friends. Whether or not Tarnower knew that Mrs. Harris was coming to Purchase that night was in dispute throughout the trial. Mrs. Harris wasn't leaving the doctor's driveway when the police arrived; she was at the Community Center a short distance down the road from Tarnower's house, where she says she had been going to the pay phone to call for help; she turned back when she saw the approaching police car. Although Mrs. Harris did bring flowers to the bedroom, they hadn't been picked or bought as a gift for the doctor; she had taken with her into the house a bouquet of daisies that a friendly Madeira colleague had left for her in her car earlier that day. Dr. Tarnower had four bullet wounds, but only three bullets were found in his body; how this was to be accounted for was also in extended dispute during the trial—it was of central importance, indeed, in trying to determine whether there had been conscious intent in the shooting of Dr. Tarnower, which of course had to be established in the charge against Mrs. Harris of second-degree murder. One of the facts not reported—it emerged only in the pre-trial hearings and was ruled out of evidence so that it never became known to the jury—was that, besides the five bullets with which Mrs. Harris had loaded her gun, she had an additional thirty-four rounds of live ammunition and two spent shells in her car. At the trial we would learn that Mrs. Harris had brought at least five more rounds into the house with her—for suicide this surely constitutes a considerable overkill.

Yet even these new facts, or newly corrected facts, were of but minor importance in altering my first response to the case compared to the revision Mrs. Harris made in what had been reported to be her original statement of why she'd come to Dr. Tarnower's house that evening. At the felony hearing of March 15 Patrolman O'Sullivan testified that he had heard Mrs. Harris say that she came to Purchase to have Dr. Tarnower kill her, and this statement of the young police officer had not been publicly corrected by either Mrs. Harris or her lawyer, Joel Aurnou. It was at the end of July, four months after the shooting, that the reporter for *The New York Times* asked Mrs. Harris's lawyer about the rumor that he'd heard, that Mrs. Harris was telling her friends she hadn't come to Purchase for Tarnower to kill her—that would have been "stupid"—but to kill herself unless he could dissuade her. Aurnou's reply was printed in the *Times* of July 27: "She has consistently maintained that she came here to do away with herself. Once you go beyond that simple fact, you get into everybody's version. She objects to the original version because it makes her sound like an idiot. What she's charged with is being more than stupid." Very true. But if as far back as March a mistaken account of her purpose in coming to Purchase was attributed to her, why hadn't Mrs. Harris said so? Why this delay in discovering that her first explanation had been "stupid," and why, other than because he was caught off guard, did someone as skilled in formulation as Aurnou describe what his client regarded as a serious misrepresentation as an "original version" rather than as false? I telephoned Aurnou to ask if Mrs. Harris had perhaps changed her story without his knowledge. I made note of his careful answer: "She came up with no reason to anticipate brutality. She came to kill herself on his premises. But in the course of the encounter, after she was struck, she wanted him to kill her." He told me that in court he would establish the inaccuracy of O'Sullivan's early testimony. What Aurnou actually tried to do in court was to discredit the whole of the Harrison police force, not O'Sullivan in particular, certainly not the particular statement that O'Sullivan said he had heard Mrs. Harris make to Detective Siciliano in Tarn-ower's house the night of the doctor's death. It fell to Mrs. Harris herself—and she said she was glad of the opportunity—to explain from the witness stand how it was that the early well-circulated story of her purpose in coming to Westchester had got started: before the struggle with Tarnower, after he'd struck her, when she was sitting on the guest bed, she'd asked him to hit her again, hard enough to kill her. Mrs. Harris testified that she came to Purchase for a few moments of peaceful talk with the doctor; she didn't mean him to know that she was about to kill herself. This change in the account of her purpose, though it may have rid Mrs. Harris of the charge of stupidity, suggested that we were indeed dealing in "versions." For me, as far back as July, before the trial, it had not only seriously reduced her credibility but robbed her story of much of its original impact. It's hard for me to suppose that a young patrolman would invent a tale about someone bringing a gun to her lover in order to have him kill her with it. It was the very oddity of the original explanation—this and its psychological justness—that for me had given it its authenticity. The plan, as Mrs. Harris was said to have first described it, realized the emotional intent of murder without the legal intent; if Mrs. Harris persuaded Tarnower to shoot her, he'd be shown to the world as in actual deed the killer she thought him. He had killed her emotionally; let him kill her physically so that everyone in the world would recognize him for the kind of person he was, and judge him accordingly. It was a wholly unrea-sonable plan, a "sick" plan, but we assume of people who wish to end their lives that they're sick. Like all symptomatic behavior it incorporated the two essential ingredients of emotionally dis-ordered conduct, gratification and punishment: the gratification lay of course in the damage Mrs. Harris would have done Dr. Tarnower by exposing him to the censure of the world; the pun-ishment would have been her own death. I'm not suggesting that Mrs. Harris would have been conscious of what she hoped to ac-complish with such a plan, but only that it perfectly coincided with how I supposed that she unconsciously felt about Tarnower. At any rate, this was my early picture of the headmistress and by the end of the trial I hadn't very much altered at least this part of it: I still saw her as a woman who thought she loved a man whom she deeply hated—it's not an unfamiliar phenomenon. The motive first given for the trip would also explain how Mrs. Harris, distraught as she would surely have been if she were bent on ending her life, had managed to drive for five hours without running her car over an embankment or ramming it into a tree. She had something more than her own death to achieve by her suicide.

In the early spring, soon after the shooting of Dr. Tarnower when I first decided to write about the case, a noted criminal lawyer with whom I was talking about Mrs. Harris's situation had cautioned me against my ready acceptance of the defense story. Why, he asked, was I so convinced that the four wounds in Dr. Tarnower's body had been sustained in a struggle for the gun? It was easy enough to imagine one shot being fired in a struggle, but four? That sounded to him like rage. He hoped that in starting my book before the trial I was prepared to write it again from the beginning when the trial was over. The important thing, he said, was that I attend the trial every day and keep my eye on the defendant. Since this conversation I've often remembered the soundness of his comments, but I'm afraid that at the time I hadn't enough experience to know how right he was. Mine was the fervor of ignorance.

Although not all the stories we read had their source in Joel Aurnou he is vital here: the first picture we were given of Mrs. Harris and of the events in Purchase that March night, and the one that many people have stayed with, is not to be understood apart from the activities of her gifted lawyer. If we rate the various characters in the Harris case in the order of their interest to the public, it's not Herman Tarnower who is second to Mrs. Harris; it's Joel Aurnou, a lawyer little known outside Westchester until Mrs. Harris carried him with her into the national headlines. At the time of the shooting, the Scarsdale doctor was the "celebrity" of the case: his name attached to the diet. But by the start of the trial, he'd all but disappeared from his own story. There came a moment when George Bolen, the young Assistant District Attorney who prosecuted the case, made an effort to reconstitute Dr. Tarnower as a major figure in a drama that by now centered almost wholly in Mrs. Harris. At the sentencing Bolen spoke of the loss the community had suffered because of Dr. Tarnower's death but his attempt to revive the importance of Mrs. Harris's lover was patently futile. Whatever one's judgment of Mrs. Harris's guilt or innocence, or one's reactions to her as an individual, she was the person in this story who unmistakably had a fate, like a character in fiction. Dr. Tarnower hadn't a fate; he had only an outcome, a conclusion to his life. The family of Dr. Tarnower must surely have mourned him. His pleasant sister, Pearl Schwartz, was in court each day, sometimes with her husband, often with a daughter; I wondered what Mrs. Schwartz felt, devoted to her brother as she'd obviously been, as she watched Mrs. Harris commanding the courtroom as she did— there was no doubt that the discarded mistress now had the dominance she'd not had while he was alive; hers was the last word. The doctor's death must have been very terrible for Lynne Tryforos too; the temptation to testify on both her behalf and Tarnower's must have been great but she had the good sense never to appear in court; Aurnou was in wait for her. Perhaps Tarnower's patients missed him though it was scarcely the impression I'd received from the few I'd canvassed. Although they all spoke with respect of his medical abilities, there was no personal affection—this man so much sought after by women seems not to have been very likable. There was a moment in the trial, toward the close of Henri van der Vreken's testimony, when Aurnou put a blistering question to the doctor's houseman: "Did you ever make the statement that you hated the doctor and you remained there only because Suzanne forced you to?" Bolen objected and was sustained. Flushed, obviously disconcerted, van der Vreken had shaken his head in mute denial of this imputation of treachery—Tarnower, after all, had described his servants as virtual members of his family, and in his even-handed will, as precise as his diet, he'd left each of them, both Suzanne and Henri, $2,000 for each year in his employ, which meant that each had received $32,000. Even before I encountered the van der Vrekens in Purchase, and certainly after I had that first brief sight of them the day I'd tried to see Dr. Tarnower's house, they'd struck me as not being an easy pair to read. They didn't appeal to me much more than did their former employer. In the trial we would discover that a certain ambiguity was perhaps natural in the relation of the van der Vrekens to Tarnower. For instance, in their sixteen years of employment they'd had no regular days off from work, no stated vacation periods. The doctor travelled and when he was away from home Suzanne and Henri were presumably at liberty. Still, the arrangement wasn't a usual one. Even in his conduct with his servants it seemed to be only his own convenience that counted with Dr. Tarnower, not that of the people he relied upon for his comfort.

In terms of public notice another man's destiny, Aurnou's, was more closely tied than Tarnower's to that of the defendant—Mrs. Harris's lawyer not only had a considerable native size but from the start took size from the case. So far as I know, before her trial Mrs. Harris never spoke directly to the press, not even in such off-the-cuff comments as she later made in the courtroom. It was Aurnou who spoke for her, and while on closer scrutiny his statements didn't hide a certain mechanical contrivance and a too-ready appeal to female sympathy, he did a striking job of winning pre-trial support for his client. The most puzzling exception to this record of successful public relations was the inept interview he gave a writer for *Ms.* magazine; it was strange for a man of his seeming worldliness, asked by the magazine of women's liberation what he'd be looking for in prospective jurors, to answer, "Nice legs," and say that the difference between men and women was that "guys just like to fuck." I spoke to Aurnou again after that interview to ask if he'd been correctly reported. Without contradicting any specific statement—but I didn't press him—he denied that the article was an accurate one. He was mocking and harsh about the circumstances. He'd spent five minutes, he said, with its author.

I myself had two so-called interviews with Mrs. Harris's lawyer, both in his office—I asked questions but I took few notes. The first was in May, some two months after the shooting, at six in the evening when the working day of even an over-worked lawyer is presumably over, the other on a Saturday morning in June; although on the second occasion Aurnou seemed somewhat strained, I liked him very much both times. His law firm was then Aurnou, Rubenstein, Morosco and Kelligrew; since that time Joel Martin Aurnou is listed alone—in the *Martindale-Hubbell Law Directory,* he's rated AV, the highest grade for diligence and ethical standards. The name Aurnou, he explained to me, was of recent origin: East European, his father had changed the name in Paris from Aronowicz before coming to New York in the twenties. Joel had been born in 1933 and had graduated from City College and from the New York University Law School.

It wasn't until the trial that we'd learn how it happened that Aurnou was suggested as Mrs. Harris's lawyer; before that we knew only that after the shooting the headmistress had phoned a friend and that by early morning Aurnou was on the case. The friend was Leslie Jacobson, partner in a large well-known law firm with offices in New York and Washington. The husband of a childhood acquaintance of Jean Harris, Mr. Jacobson had also been a friend of Dr. Tarnower; the Jacobsons had in fact introduced Tarnower to Mrs. Harris. By Wednesday, March 12, an associate of Aurnou had retrieved from the local postal authorities the long letter Mrs. Harris had sent Dr. Tarnower by certified mail the morning of her trip to Purchase. It would turn out to be of small benefit to Mrs. Harris that Aurnou rather than the prosecution had got this letter, but when the defense retrieved it from the post office Aurnou could not have known what the consequences would be. Even in the trial he didn't seem to recognize how calamitous the letter was for his client. It was spelled out for him in the verdict. Winning the postal decision for Mrs. Harris was Aurnou's first public coup in the case and ·brought him much credit with Mrs. Harris's partisans who also had no notion of the letter's tone or content.

What does it propose about Mrs. Harris's lawyer that his history in the Harris case is one of a series of grand victories culminating in defeat? It could be the story, I suppose, of any gambler, and there's no doubt that Aurnou gambled heavily in going for his client's acquittal instead of having her plead mental incompetency as she had many opportunities to do. But to think of Aurnou as only, or even primarily, a gambler does him an injustice. I think he is first and foremost a man of his profession, an *advocate*—I use the word that emphasizes the passion of commitment that he brings to his practice of law, or that he surely brought to the Harris case. More than it was an undertaking to which he put himself with devotion, it was a *cause,* and if he didn't at all give the impression of fanaticism —anything but—he in fact had the same kind of dedication that one finds in a religious or political zealot. Indeed, it could be a zealot's inflexibility of mind that might account for Aurnou's inability to see more than one aspect of his client and her situation and for some of his miscalculations in planning Mrs. Harris's defense. Most serious of his misjudgments was the fact that from the first he saw Mrs. Harris as "a very fine lady, of the kind you don't see much any more," and that he never seemed to adjust this view even to accommodate the idea that she was human, subject to bitterness and jealousy like the rest of us, let alone to include the interesting truth that she was often neither fine nor ladylike. The defense took her to be all of a piece, which she distinctly is not. Too, Aurnou addressed his legal adversaries not as lawyers like himself, doing the jobs required of them, but as legal enemies, which underscored his client's manifest paranoia about the legal process and its agents and inevitably stimulated the haughty disdain with which she responded to the prosecution in her trial—he should not have allowed her arrogance toward Bolen or her injudicious and unwarranted displays of grievance under cross-examination. Monolithic in his own commitment, he seems unable to think of other people except as monolithic too, either all with him or all against him, and this presumably caused the all-or-nothing attitude he took with some of the writers at the trial, myself included—for instance, he failed to understand that I was available to persuasion, and that even in a situation in which I had an early bias I still kept an open mind. I had come to his office as a Harris sympathizer and if, as the trial progressed, questions arose in my mind, this wasn't out of personal hostility to either him or his client, as he apparently took it to be. As someone who was trying to write seriously about the case, it was my job to raise questions and be carried wherever their answers might carry me; but for Aurnou questions seemed to be an attack rather than a challenge he must try to meet. In his office, before our relation had turned hostile (as he interpreted it) he'd received me as someone whose concern in the case he didn't perhaps fathom but whose support he was glad to accept. For each of his presumed allies he had—I gather—a sugarplum. Mine was the parodic poem that Mrs. Harris wrote for Hi and their friends, the Schultes, at the last Christmas that the four of them had spent together. He cautiously took a large Christmasy-looking card from the safe in his office and holding his hand over all but a few lines, let me quickly glance at it. Reduced in this way, the greeting was only funny and it also reassured me, should I need reassurance, of Mrs. Harris's continuing devotion to Tarnower.

I never again quite recaptured the impression of a canny Texas oil or cattle man that Aurnou made on me when I saw him in his office; in court he seemed more studiedly an actor, an old-fashioned movie-style lawyer. A canny Jewish Texas cattle man isn't to be met with every day of the week, not even in White Plains where the architecture prepares one for anything. (Trying to reach Aurnou's building through the maze of one-way streets, non-streets, and streets under desperate construction, I'd passed what was for all the world the tomb in *Aïda*: surely it must be the farewell duet of Radames and his Ethiopian princess that I was hearing over the noise of the traffic!) I was charmed by Mrs. Harris's non-city lawyer; on my second visit he even becomingly wore a ranger's plaid shirt. He was of medium height, stocky, balding. He looked older than his forty-seven years, yet he was boyish, even with a hint of youthful naughtiness. I was especially taken by his lack of ostentation: like his office, he was relaxed and modest. I recognized of course that behind the show of casualness there was a spring of tension ready to uncoil. The simplicity of Aurnou's office in its functional four-story building in the White Plains business section was especially attractive to someone whose mind was full, as mine now was, of the social and esthetic claims that Tarnower's Purchase "estate" made for itself—by the time I came to my first interview with Aurnou, my abortive attempt to see Tarnower's house was already behind me; I'd viewed it only from the outside but even that had filled me with distaste. At Aurnou's, one came into a waiting area carpeted in a sturdy gray carpeting, with comfortable plain black leather sofas and chairs. At the desk was a chatty receptionist of whom I happily felt that the next time we met she'd invite me into the kitchen to taste the chicken soup. Aurnou's own well-lighted office, looking down over a street that was in the process of being shredded, was crowded with evidence of work, an orderly mess. Not only his desk but his file cabinets were piled high with papers which one knew he could securely navigate. He smoked a thick cigar that stayed decently dry and never dropped ashes on his clothes. The telephone rang endlessly even at this hour; Aurnou wasn't made nervous by the interruptions as I'd have been but answered everyone patiently and as if with enjoyment. Noting all this, I didn't fail to warn myself against assessing Mrs. Harris's lawyer for less than the person he'd be under pressure; one doesn't choose the practice of criminal law from a preference for the unbuttoned life. Through both of my visits I faced a name-plate on the desk: under Aurnou's name was the legend, "I've made up my mind. . . . Don't confuse me with the facts." While the irony was light, it shot off in too many directions at once to be as disarming as he no doubt meant it to be. How simple can a man be who makes himself out to be this simple?

It was on the first of these visits, the one after work hours, that I listened to Aurnou's end of an enthusiastic telephone conversation about plans for a day of fishing: times of departure and return, food, drink, rods, bait, everything was gone into. When the call was over, he told me that the outing was to include his eleven-year-old son. I suspected that Aurnou found the call a relief from talking with me; while he was impeccably polite, I don't think he could imagine that anything I wrote could be of service to him. I was too far outside his experience with the press to be interesting to him, he had no suitable niche for me, and anyway the purpose of my visit—as he saw it and would persist in seeing it—had been accomplished in its first minutes: I wouldn't be calling my book by the name that I'd first announced, *A Respectable Murder*. Repeat as I might that I'd come to our meeting already resolved to find a new title—my reasons were only legal—Aurnou didn't hear me. He told me that the old title had made Mrs. Harris shake for two days: about that I was sorry. He took credit or, much the same thing, credited me with the most generous friendliness for the promise that it would be changed; not only in the two visits at his office but whenever we spoke on the phone, he'd again thank me for this kindness I'd shown him. Once he'd got my consent to the change of title, it was my impression that he really saw nothing further to be gained from spending time on me. He told me that the one day of fishing with his son would be the whole of his summer vacation. From the conversation I overheard, I understood that it was deep-sea fishing he had in view, not the trout stream or the salmon river—these Westchester sportsmen came in nice variety. I began to talk with Aurnou about the difference between East European Jews and German Jews, and about the part that a Gentile mistress might have played in Tarnower's social advance: with this overture I perhaps made the visit a bit less tedious for him. I also spoke of having just come from looking at Mrs. Harris's little house in Mahopac. Situated about a quarter of a mile off Bullet Hill Road—the location was of course now incredible—on a private road that ended in a dirt lane, it was in dramatic contrast to Tarnower's Purchase Street residence: a tiny shingle cottage sunk in a slight hollow, shaded by hickory trees and surrounded by woods. It was the kind of house that a city person, a writer or artist, might rent for a summer of isolated work. No house on Bullet Hill Road would be beyond the means of anyone in a steady job in a lower-middle-income bracket. Aurnou told me that it was Mrs. Harris's sole piece of property. He didn't mention, I would learn it only in the trial, that she had never lived in it.

Mrs. Harris's lawyer told me that in twenty-one years of practice he'd never lost a murder case—he didn't say how many he'd tried. As we talked, it occurred to me that he probably had no temperament for failure. The next time I saw him—this was a month later—he seemed in a less affable mood and I ascribed the change to the fact that he'd recently lost a litigation; a Westchester friend had told me about it. It wasn't a murder case: his client was a woman whose married son had left his wife, or perhaps been thrown out by her, and the mother had gone with a truck to the daughter-in-law's house to remove the belongings which she felt were hers, on family loan to her son. I don't know whether the daughter-in-law sued for their return or whether the case had another basis—I wasn't enough interested to inquire. For a lawyer about to make his debut on a world stage, it was not a dignified case to lose. But was the case Aurnou had won earlier in the year a dignified case to win? As I heard that story, also through friends, he'd won the acquittal of a young man who'd killed a child while driving very drunk. It was never denied that the client was drunk; the defense based its case on the inadequate marking of the road where the death occurred. Aurnou was known in Westchester for his success in the use of physical evidence.

It was from Mrs. Harris's lawyer that most of our knowledge of the shooting of Dr. Tarnower had emanated. Aurnou couldn't have been more prompt and assiduous in his attention to the public-relations aspect of the Harris case: he worked a forty-eight-hour day, was never too busy for interviews. To the best of his ability—and he was very able—he created the original wholly sympathetic public image of the Madeira headmistress. If he didn't correct the errors of fact in the newspaper accounts of the shooting, this, after all, wasn't his duty; he had only the single duty to give his client the best possible defense and he discharged this responsibility according to his lights. Whatever our pieties about not trying a case in the newspapers in advance of a trial, we none of us deny the usefulness of a friendly public. Not until the preliminary hearings in Mrs. Harris's trial, when Aurnou moved that the press be excluded from the courtroom on the ground that it had so distorted the truth about the shooting that it was now impossible for Mrs. Harris to get a fair trial, did he lose me, and it's my sense that with this motion he lost many other people in the press rows as well. For the man who had so generously given his statements to the papers in advance of Mrs. Harris's trial now to turn this righteously against the press was uncomfortably disingenuous.

Recently a leading American novelist whose books sell in vast quantity but who has nonetheless retained his prestige in the community of advanced intellectuals—this is unusual although it happens more frequently today than it did in earlier decades of the century—was interviewed in his new home in the country, bought from his sizable literary earnings. Talking of a critic who had been hard on his work, also of a novelist with whom he competed for fame, he asked if the former had a house like his and whether the latter could serve as good a lunch. The exchange was published to no comment from anyone I know who read it.

If the charge of vulgarity is not to be brought against someone who lives by sensibility and who, as an artist, is among the legislators of mankind, is it fair to bring it against a doctor in Westchester the whole of whose claim to cultural distinction is that he wrote a diet book? The criterion of bad taste is, I know, no longer permitted the socially conscientious. Anyone who makes the judgment is accused of asserting a right of birth or class and, in consequence, is thought to be indulging in snobbery. But surely the way in which taste is exercised—every kind of taste: in art and architecture and decoration, dress, food, manners, speech—is the firmest clue we have to how someone pursues his life in culture and therefore to the style of moral being he would legislate for us, if he had the power. Merchandising recognizes this when it presents our choice in jeans or in running shoes as a choice in moral style. In her trial Mrs. Harris was at considerable pains to consolidate her own social and cultural position by the way she pictured Dr. Tarnower, her social companion of so many years. She made him into a fitting partner of the superior intellectual life she led as a member of the academic profession. She told us that when she first met him, Tarnower talked with her of Russia and instructed her in Jewish history. She said he was the kind of man who "read Herodotus for fun" and that the two of them had never argued except "over the use of the subjunctive." (This last statement, by the way, is disputed by the report I've had that they constantly argued in public. They're supposed to have been known for it.) In the Scarsdale letter she vied with the doctor—and proclaimed herself the hands-down winner—as to which of them owned more books; her father-in-law, she wrote, had left her a library of more than five thousand volumes, many of which she had donated to school libraries. (A large number of the books Tarnower had given her over the years she had also donated to school libraries, offering him the tax deduction on them.) If Mrs. Harris's intellectual preferences and presumably those of Dr. Tarnower could be put on record as they were, with the force of a character reference, why shouldn't Dr. Tarnower's style of living be

22

submitted to similar appraisal? In adducing a moral style from a style of life, I was perhaps more generous with Mrs. Harris than with Dr. Tarnower: although I was embarrassed by her intellectual boasts, her gifts of mind were sufficiently striking so that I could at least suppose she had a better foundation for her cultural vanities than he had. I'd now seen Dr. Tarnower's house if only from the outside, and I'd read his book. Expanded from a two-page diet sheet, the book spoke more than a volume's worth of social pretension to anyone who was willing to read it as something other than just a guide to weight loss; and the house, expanded from a pool house that was once the property of the Pforzheimer family, was to my eyes a small monument to cultural inflatedness. As a famous diet doctor, Tarnower was one of our hidden tyrants of culture who, as far as he was able, dictated the way in which we were to conform our bodies to an arbitrary consumer ideal. What other standards Mrs. Harris's lover lived by—his standards of middle-class respectability and the esthetics he thought appropriate to his class situation—were as much a reflection of his society as they were his own creation. While his style of life and being did indeed represent a personal choice, it went beyond personal preference to provide a substantial portrait of present-day American middle-class establishment.

My visit to Purchase had been made in heavy rain but, weather apart, I was thoroughly uncomfortable. I'd never before viewed the scene of a crime and it troubled me that people might think this was my morbid occupation. Yet if I wasn't a curiosity seeker, I also wasn't by profession an investigative reporter—so what was I? The friendly reporter who'd given me directions for finding the Tarnower place had told me what I might do—which is to say, what *he* would do—if the caretakers wouldn't let me in. What he'd do, he said, was ask if he could use the phone to call the doctor's sister for permission to view the premises; once he got into the house, he'd have a good look around—of course, he added sadly, that wouldn't get me upstairs. His apology for this frustration that awaited me was in itself confusing: I didn't know how to explain that I was interested in the kind of furniture and pictures the doctor had in his house and not in the room where his blood had been spilled. In the event, I was too rattled to follow the advice the reporter gave me. I asked the van der Vrekens whether I could come in and, when they

23

refused, I left. Driving to Purchase that afternoon in the downpour, the insistent sound of the windshield wipers in my ears, I thought of James Agee and Walker Evans's *Let Us Now Praise Famous Men*, their brilliant study of the plight of the Southern sharecroppers in the Depression, and of Agee's agonizing sense of impropriety in intruding upon other people's lives for his own literary purposes. When I'd first read this American classic, it had been my suspicion that if Agee had been writing about the rich he'd not have been this worried by his act of literary appropriation; it was because he looked upon such poor scraps and stubs of possession that he'd felt he was thieving. But I was in the land of the well-to-do and I felt guiltily intrusive. The rich might have better protection than the poor against literary pre-emption, but that didn't spare me my disquieting emotions.

The friendly reporter who had given me my directions to the Tarnower house had said that if I passed the Knopf driveway, it meant that I had gone too far and must turn back. In the heavy rain, I went too far. So this was the home of the doyen of American publishing—not that I could see anything! Taking advantage of a single meeting many years before, I'd phoned to ask Mr. Knopf if I could drop by to talk with him about Dr. Tarnower while I was in the neighborhood. Courteous, wholly alert at close to ninety, he'd refused my request. It was understandable: he and Tarnower had been intimates, gourmets together and travel companions. He spoke of his grief at his friend's death: "My doctor for twenty years, my friend for thirty." He didn't mention Jean Harris or voice an opinion about the shooting. He wanted to know who was my publisher. In the avalanche of print loosed by the death of the Scarsdale diet doctor his home in Purchase had been always referred to as an "estate," as were the neighboring houses on Purchase Street. I'd expected manorial country and it was disappointing to discover that the imposing nomenclature meant no more, though also no less, than that these houses had enough land, five, six, seven acres, to shield them from passing motorists. The Tarnower driveway was unmarked except for an improvised "T" painted in red on a telephone pole; the paint had largely washed away. A sign warned of dogs. I turned in and moved slowly along what seemed to be the border of a neighbor's property until I pulled up in the graveled area where Mrs. Harris must have parked her car on the night of the shooting. Before stepping into the wet, I slightly opened my car door to peer out at the doctor's house. The single evidence that it was occupied was a car in the open ground-level garage to my right—it had an MD license plate. I had the certainty I was being watched. I stepped out. Water dripped from my plastic hood off the tip of my nose. My vision was blurred. It was only April, this "cruelest month" that Aurnou would refer to with me as he also did with his *Ms.* interviewer and that Mrs. Harris would cite in her Scarsdale letter—why had these people moved in on Eliot this way?—but there was a chill in the air as of a winter rather than a spring rain. What I was looking at was a low two-storied house, not large but large enough to make a sizable bad impression. I saw a Japanese—Japanoid—manifestation, a sort of domestic pagoda. The façade was incoherent with terraces; every terrace seemed to be backed by glass. It was a small busy statement of deference to the serenity of the East. I was puzzled by what, in connecting the inner and outer activity of this house, would constitute a front door and decided that the terrace that would be the most logical substitute for a porch was the one to the left of me; it was approached by a short flight of stairs. The guess was correct: I mounted the steps and a pane of glass slid open; I was confronted by Henri, Tarnower's houseman, husband of the doctor's now-famous gourmet cook, Suzanne. I knew that when Mrs. Schwartz had inherited the estate, she'd retained the van der Vrekens as care-takers; it was Henri, of course, who'd been watching me. He was a rather handsome man in a soft self-conscious way; probably he was older than he looked—close to fifty. He was Belgian, I'd read; his wife was Belgian too but of French extraction. The little he said to me was spoken with a marked foreign inflection.

I didn't think I made an impressive sight. I introduced myself and was fumbling in my bag for my credentials when it occurred to me that it was a waste of time to present them: Tarnower's servant would suspect my letter as he obviously did me. Dropping the journalist's approach that I'd rehearsed with someone who was more experienced than I in making it work for him, I explained that I was writing a book about the shooting of Dr. Tarnower and that I'd like to see the house. Short of that, I'd like to come in out of the rain—I'd stand in the entrance and look around from there. For an instant I thought I could perceive a faint glimmer of trust in Henri. Then, like a severe mother, his white-haired wife came out of the surrounding shadows and murmured something that put iron in him—later, when I thought about it, I decided that Suzanne was probably no more reluctant than Henri to be helpful but was just more frightened about breaking the rules of their employment. She was alert like a French concierge and as concerned to do the "right thing." "No!" he said sharply; the sliding door closed on me with enough decisiveness to have doubled as a guillotine. Those were the days of what I would now call my *a priori* sympathy for Mrs. Harris. The conduct of the van der Vrekens on the night of the shooting had left little doubt in my mind of their disapproval, perhaps even their dislike, of the doctor's former mistress. When Officer McKenna had first come into the house and been told that the doctor had been shot, he'd asked Suzanne who had done it. Suzanne hadn't referred to Mrs. Harris by name; indicating her, she'd replied, "His girl-friend." And later, when Mrs. Harris asked Henri whom the doctor had had at dinner that night—the question was of course intolerable in the circumstances—Henri had demanded that she be immediately removed from the house. What threatening witnesses this couple could be, I thought as I was turned away by them, and how disadvantaged a woman like Mrs. Harris would have been in a relation with people who were as marginal to the middle class as the van der Vrekens were in their special European way, in it and yet not of it. As I saw the situation, the headmistress would be too soft but too superior, too vulnerable and yet too uppity, not to tempt aggression. And servants were of course unduly invested with authority in anything that pertained to the people who employed them. I thought of my own devoted cleaning woman who had worked for me for twenty-seven years without ever telling a lie but also without ever telling the truth with entire accuracy. What would it be like to be at her legal mercy? She knew every-thing about my work, my marriage, my health, my friends, my finances, my domestic arrangements. Surely there weren't jurors to be found in this world who would believe that my bedroom curtains were regularly washed at home if she took it into her head to tell them, as she'd recently told me, that they were always done by the Loyal Laundry whose name was in fact the Royal Laundry and which had never washed anything of mine except the table-cloth I used once a year at Thanksgiving. It is an interesting fact of life that people should be so much more wary of family members than they are of servants of long standing.

With what dignity I could muster, I sloshed back to the car and sat looking around me, thinking of the van der Vrekens, thinking of Mrs. Harris, thinking of Dr. Tarnower alive and now dead. Through the dripping car window I once more took note of the gardening that I'd seen as I arrived at the house: no doubt it was this same Henri who'd just been so ungracious to me who got credit for the attractive plantings near the house, the carefully random shrubs and flowers in the upper driveway, here a great clump of forsythia in bloom, a burst of lovely yellow against the dark of the house, casting its spring light even through the downpour, there young shoots of green, young narcissus and even younger jonquils pushing up through the grass. I wished I had brought a spy-glass. I'd read about Dr. Tarnower's pond but I couldn't really see it as I wished to. It was just visible from where I sat brooding, depressed to a degree I couldn't have explained at the time and still don't ade-quately understand. I couldn't make out the little island in the pond or see whether the Buddha to which the doctor was said to have liked to row was bronze or stone, sat on its island or stood, whether it was a fat Silenus of a deity or flat-bellied as befitted the object of a diet doctor's reverence. Imagine one's private pond in Westchester with a private Buddha to row to—it was absurd! A Westchester pagoda was absurd, this expensive trumped-up seren-ity was absurd. This was what came of our winning the war in the Pacific: America now had rights on the peace of the Orient! Suddenly, as I started away, Dr. Tarnower's little lake dissolved from view, as in a film, and was replaced by the vision of a swim-ming pool on which floated the body, not of Tarnower dead, but of Gatsby dead. I began to think of F. Scott Fitzgerald, the only writer this country had ever produced who knew to the last dollar and cent the moral worth of money.

When I left Dr. Tarnower's house I drove around Scarsdale in the rain. Then I went home and re-read *The Great Gatsby*. It's not only a better book than I'd remembered but a very great American novel with a considerable bearing on the Harris-Tarnower story or any story in which social idea and social reality, spirit and money, are understood in their relation to each other. Herman Tarnower, a reputable suburban physician, wasn't Jay Gatsby, the bootlegger. There was no question of the respectability in which he'd been reared. The family history was not an unfamiliar one. His father had come to America in 1906, a period when the repressive measures of the governments of Middle and Eastern Europe, especially of Russia, had forced a vast Jewish migration to this country: in that one year, 152,000 Jewish immigrants had come through Ellis Island. On his naturalization papers Harry Tarnower had given his birthplace as Warsaw, which was then in Russian Poland, but probably the name Tarnower indicated that his forebears had come from the Galician town of Tarnow. Harry Tarnower had married an East European immigrant like himself; her place of origin was unclear, possibly it was Rumania. With various members of his family who were already engaged in the largely Jewish occupation of hat-making, he'd settled on the lower East Side and gone into the manufacture of ladies' hats; or he may have made artificial flowers or other ornaments, even braids, which were then required in women's millinery. This was perhaps the firm of Tarnower Brothers, still remembered in the New York millinery district for its past success. I doubt that Harry Tarnower's business continued to prosper as mightily as he might once have expected: it's fair to guess that with the new vogue for felt hats—its literary signpost was Michael Arlen's *The Green Hat*—there'd been a considerable falling-off in the family fortunes by the time Herman was growing up. The Tarnowers had lived in Bensonhurst, a solid but not upcoming section of Brooklyn; though Herman had begun high school at Erasmus Hall, he graduated from the new James Madison High School in his home district. It was possible, however, for him to go out of town to college: he did an accelerated six-year course as an undergraduate and medical student at Syracuse; then, on fellowship, he'd continued his medical studies abroad. From this point forward both his professional and social achievement were due to his own efforts.

And yet which, I wondered, had finally been the more impressive climb, that of Jay Gatsby, the unrooted gangster who rose from his meager beginnings as James Gatz to his lonely kingdom on Long Island, or that which took Herman Tarnower, a respectable and respected first-generation Jewish-American, from Brooklyn to the company of the millionaires of Westchester and the Caribbean? The question wasn't a frivolous one; it was a question in American social history. Gatsby was a bootlegger. Dr. Tarnower was a reputable suburban physician, a connoisseur of wines. Tarnower didn't give lavish parties such as Gatsby had given to which the rich, or those who only wanted to be among the rich, swarmed so anonymously; the guests at his table had names one kept in mind. But Tarnower with his dry strivings and worldly salvations, his best seller and his reputation which had travelled as far as China, his angry suffering mistress and his senseless violent death, was perhaps as representative of his moment in history as Gatsby, with his impossible dream named Daisy, she of the thrilling voice that was "full of money," had been representative of the American twenties. A half-century ago, Fitzgerald's aspiring gangster was already inventing American society although he mistakenly supposed that it existed and that it was Daisy and Tom Buchanan. What defined his life was not our present-day belief that money buys class but the far more radical conviction that if money was legitimately come by, it *was* class, and that class conferred moral stature. When he died Gatsby was still seeking not only a means of self-realization but a means of social incarnation as well. No such imaginative leap had been asked of Tarnower. The illusory mountain was there for him to climb, its paths were marked. His hunting, his fishing, his membership in the Century Country Club, his travels, his Herodotus, his Buddha, all blessed him and conferred moral authority on him. Every foot of his Purchase Street frontage represented his American dream. "He was a son of God," Fitzgerald had said of Gatsby, "and he must be about his Father's business, the service of a vast, vulgar and meretricious beauty." Fitzgerald was unafraid of the word "vulgar." I wanted his courage to speak in such clean terms of Tarnower's house and the kind of life it stood for. Could he or Mrs. Harris have known, could they have endured to know, how inglorious were the social heights to which they'd attained?

The Japanese used rain so quietly in their painting that it was like another downpouring of light, but upon Dr. Tarnower's Japanese house it was now beating without pity. I turned back into Purchase Street and headed toward Scarsdale and Dr. Tarnower's Medical Center. It's a pleasant-enough little nondescript building, set among trees in a hollow. I think it would be comfortable to go to if one were ill, but I don't know about the individual offices because I didn't penetrate that far. Perhaps I should have made believe I'd just been stricken with stomach cramp: was that what an experienced investigative reporter would have done? During the trial, I sent my assistant into the Clinic to ask a question for me while I remained in the car. He'd had only to mention my name for everyone to fall silent; he caught a glimpse of Lynne Tryforos's handsome legs as she fled from the room. It was plain that I was indeed an ally of neither side in this case, neither the side of the Tarnower family nor of the defense.

I spent my early childhood in Westchester before my family, too, moved to Brooklyn. The Westchester with which I was acquainted was Larchmont and New Rochelle. I had heard of Rye, Mamaroneck, White Plains, even Pelham, but I never knew of Purchase or Scarsdale; these were out of my parents' orbit. This was long ago at a time when we were allowed to raise chickens in our back yard, and when, if there was heavy snow, the bell tolled at the firehouse so we'd know that there would be no school that day. Many years later I became related to Scarsdale by marriage—my husband had family there—and it became my Middletown, which is not to claim sociological authority for what I learned from it but only to recall that in the child-oriented life of the forties and fifties, and again in the revolutionary sixties when the children of hope so often became the children of despair, it was largely from Scarsdale that I got my idea of changing attitudes in American family culture. But it was about American *family* culture that it taught me—that's the important difference between Scarsdale and Purchase.

Recently a young man told me that his sense of the Scarsdale diet came from its name: he thought that it had to be an expensive and upper-class diet because of its place of origin. This startled me. I thought of Scarsdale as far from elevated but now I discover that it always had a wider social range than I knew. To me it was the very heart and nerve-center of progressive middle-middle-class American life, especially Jewish middle-middle-class American life. Two things still come to mind when it's mentioned: the schools which, in the period when I knew it best, made the chief boast of its home owners, justifying their high taxes, and the vividness with which its family culture revealed its contradictions.

If no one speaks of Scarsdale "estates," this isn't simply because Purchase is the richer or Scarsdale the more crowded suburb. It's because they have different notions of community. Even in the most rural areas of Scarsdale the houses are in view of each other and of the public. Free-standing, they're connected by that strongest of bonds: the life of the children. Where there are children, people become neighbors; they don't merely hold property adjacent to one another. Children at play in the suburban outdoors cut paths from house to house, parents meet parents *as* parents. The absence of young children in Purchase is palpable, like all emotional emptiness, as palpable as Tarnower's bachelorhood—there are no doubt wealthy unmarried men in Scarsdale too, but bachelorhood and Scarsdale are a contradiction in terms. Tarnower found the right place in which to settle: one feels it at once. Purchase exists for people who are either beyond their child-bearing years or whose realms, like Tarnower's, are co-terminal with their lives.

The young Scarsdale residents from whom I drew my view of mid-century middle-class parenthood were all of them either the children or grandchildren of immigrants, usually East European. Themselves the product of America's famous upward mobility, they didn't intend for the progress to stop with them. The instrument of mobility is of course education but, as everyone knows, every American generation has to make a new America; one of our instituted means of accomplishing this is by altering the way in which we rear and teach our young. In the forties and fifties in Scarsdale the chief emphasis of the new pedagogy was something called "social adjustment," the ability to live with others in harmony by bringing into balance the liberal duty to tolerate the vagaries of others and the divine human right to do as we please. Much more than by the study of "subjects," it was by instruction in living within one's own peer group that the well-schooled Scarsdale youngster, this much-privileged much-loved middle-middle American child, was educated as an individual and citizen in the years following the Second World War. What this meant, in brief, was that one had to be popular before clever. The trouble was that inevitably the years rolled by and soon it was time for college, and popularity didn't necessarily guarantee that one's son got into the right college that would get him into the right law or medical school by which he'd be prepared to earn the solid professional living that was basic to his class expectation. I'm not implying that disappointed hope was unique to Scarsdale parenthood. In the bad sixties, when drugs came into widespread use among adolescents and when Scarsdale mothers developed the habit of not asking about each other's children for fear of what they'd hear, one knew that they were speaking—or not speaking, keeping their unhappy silence—on behalf of stricken motherhood everywhere in the country.

Until the death of Dr. Tarnower it hadn't occurred to me to look for a cultural connection between Scarsdale as I knew it and the doctor whose diet was associated with it. It was only as I thought about the life of Mrs. Harris's lover that I realized how astute he had been to move to Westchester when he did and then to set up the Scarsdale Medical Center. As far back as the mid-fifties he'd had the foresight not merely to parallel the burgeoning suburban shopping center with a medical center but, what this includes, to recognize the existence of a new well-off population that was neither so grand nor advanced in age as to insist on receiving its day-to-day medical services at home. Youthful, energetic, self-determined Scarsdale was willing to be active even in caring for itself in illness: it made the perfect site for Dr. Tarnower's Clinic. First located in an apartment house, in 1959 the Scarsdale Medical Center built its present quarters in easy access of the new suburban branches of the large metropolitan department stores. In the long run, perhaps even the ill of Purchase came to see Dr. Tarnower at the Scarsdale Clinic, but when he'd begun the social climb that led to his obtaining his desirable residential frontage on Purchase Street, a Scarsdale medical prac-

32

tice wasn't necessarily a social recommendation. More useful was Dr. Tarnower's blessed bachelorhood and his willingness to make a fourth at bridge after medical visits at the homes of elderly wealthy German-Jewish widows. As the son of one of these early patients half-apologetically explained to me: "My mother expected that of her doctor!"

The distinction that Jews have themselves always made between Jews of German origin and Jews of East European origin is as stringent as that between Boston Brahmin and Boston lace-curtain Irish, though much finer. While the division is now less marked than it was before Hitler's rule of Germany, even today Jews of German ancestry don't casually write off their advantage of birth. The German "first families" of American Jewry are the subject of an interesting book by Stephen Birmingham, *Our Crowd*. Birmingham reminds us that in the matter of the artistic and philanthropic contributions made to this country by their grandparents and great-grandparents, a present generation of German-American Jews is overly reticent—perhaps some are even ignorant of this historical cause for pride—and he tells us, too, of a time when with rarest exception the great German-Jewish families refused all invitation to become a part of high Gentile society. It wasn't because they treasured their tradition as Jews that they withstood assimilation into the non-Jewish world but simply because one didn't go where one couldn't be certain of one's welcome. These old rich German Jews married other rich German Jews. Dynasty interlocked with dynasty.

I don't know at what point Dr. Tarnower, son of East European immigrants, fixed his eye on the German-Jewish social peaks. An impressive number of his early patients in Westchester and the acquaintances he made outside his practice belonged to the Century Country Club, the most elite of the Jewish sporting preserves, or were members of the same social set. Birmingham writes: "For years the Century was an almost exclusively German Club with an unwritten rule against 'Orientals.' . . . Only recently has the social cast of the Century begun to change, but a distinction is still drawn between the Jews of the Century and those of the Sunningdale Golf Club in Scarsdale, which is considered by many German Jews to be somewhat *arriviste*." If, when he was making his way alone in

Purchase, Dr. Tarnower could be thought neither too "Oriental" nor too *"arriviste"* for election to the Century Country Club, with a charming Gentile like Mrs. Harris at his side his continued social advance must have been assured. There is a sense in which these two, Tarnower and Jean Harris, were beneficiaries of Nazism. Had it not been for the new American awareness, after the rise of Hitler, of where a nation can be led by anti-Semitism, it's doubtful if Westchester would have democratized itself as it did—the East European Tarnower might never have attained to the German-Jewish Country Club nor made his public connection with a non-Jewish woman; or, the other way around, it might not have been possible for Jean Harris to have attached herself as she did to a Jewish man—the choice wasn't this available before the forties. We think of Edith Wharton's Rosedale in *The House of Mirth,* published in 1905, and how much more money and power he had than Herman Tarnower without being any more able to give Lily Bart the social anchorage that she required than she was able to give him what he needed to secure his foothold in upper-case Society. Something of great importance in the relation of Jew and Gentile in this country happened in the wake of Nazism. With humor and yet with deep intention, American Jews managed to transfer to Gentiles the sense of inferiority that they'd once been made to feel in relation to the Gentile world. Did not Gentiles have less energy, less color, less brains, less sex, less life itself than Jews had? Where Jews had once apologized for themselves to Gentiles, Gentiles now learned to apologize for themselves to Jews—even today this rich vein of advantage hasn't been mined out. By historical accident, Mrs. Harris was able to be of great social usefulness to Tarnower even while she was made to feel what was entirely so, that it was Tarnower who opened the social doors for her.

There's been question as to who inspired Dr. Tarnower to put his diet into book form. For close to twenty years he'd been distributing a two-page reducing guide to his patients who in turn copied it for their friends; it was passed from hand to hand like the baton in a marathon to health and beauty. On the acknowledgment page of *The Complete Scarsdale Medical Diet,* credit for the proposal is given to a friend, Oscar Dystel; Samm Sinclair Baker, who collaborated with Dr. Tarnower on the book, confirms the fact that this is a correct attribution. The plan to produce his diet book was a decision of some magnitude for Tarnower, for Mr. Baker, for the book trade—in its first ten months in hard-cover, there were twenty-one printings in addition to two serializations, and it was the choice of four book clubs. In paperback, it was in its tenth printing at Tarnower's death in March 1980, and sales increased dramatically after the shooting. Only Mrs. Harris was displeased, or forced into ambivalence. On the stand she was torn between contempt for Dr. Tarnower's literary production and the wish to be fully recognized for her contribution to its success. As for Aurnou, he couldn't have approached it with more respect if it were a marriage of *Paradise Lost* and *King Lear*. He stressed Mrs. Harris's valuable addition to its style, as if literary style were injectable into a work as from a syringe. Literary style doesn't of course figure in the Scarsdale diet book: it's a guide to weight loss and no more than that. I've seen a letter written by Mrs. Harris in late 1979 to *The Wall Street Journal* in protest of a book review that made slighting mention of Madeira. The letter is no doubt excessive for its occasion but it's not to be missed that it's written by a skilled hand—you either have this prose or you haven't. If Mrs. Harris tried to inject "style" into the Scarsdale diet book, the book refused it. And nothing she did altered her scorn for it; to write a diet book is to be a "diet doc," and it was an offense to her pride to have been so intimately connected with someone whose celebrity had been gained this cheaply; she is said to have spoken critically of Hi's project even in its earliest stages and to have belittled it among his well-placed friends when it became a best seller. In the trial it emerged that she wanted Tarnower honored not as the author of the Scarsdale diet book but as a cardiologist. In April he was to be given a testimonial dinner by the Westchester Heart Association; Mrs. Harris had two telling reasons for wishing to attend: she wanted to join in this attestation to his serious medical accomplishment and she wanted to claim her place, of which Lynne Tryforos was robbing her, in the society in which she and Tarnower had lived together.

Among the many sources of my early partisanship with Mrs. Harris, I'm sure that dislike of Tarnower played a decisive part; it was the other side of the coin of my sympathy for the Madeira

35

headmistress. Without having met him, I first "took against" him because of his looks; then that had been followed by my dislike of his book. I'd never seen the word "vulpine" in print until it suddenly sprang into existence in stories about the dead Scarsdale doctor. The dictionary defines "vulpine" as "Resembling or characteristic of the fox: clever, devious, cunning." For me Tarnower's face in his photographs is more reptilian than foxy. I see it as the face of a man who is cold to the touch and slithery. This is also a man who is cruelly self-engrossed. Long before the trial, my revulsion from Dr. Tarnower was reinforced by the extraordinary social pretensions of his book. There is reason to suppose that although the volume always had Tarnower's close supervision, it was Samm Baker, an experienced commercial writer who had published many books on nutrition, who conceived the various devices by which the book was expanded from its original two pages, but this doesn't exempt Tarnower from responsibility for its disagreeable social impulse and for the constrictions of the diet he had invented and made famous. For nineteen years Dr. Tarnower had put his patients on a regime that now turned out to be far more difficult than was necessary. And in making it less restrictive, he revealed the same mean taste for class advantage that is reported of him in all departments of his life.

As I say, the diet had been launched as an office handout. After Tarnower was dead, in the May 1980 issue of a journal called *Behavioral Medicine,* there appeared what was probably the last interview he gave. In it he's quoted as follows:

If you don't have a routine written out that you can give to patients with common disorders, it will destroy you. You try to go over all the instructions with each patient, but no physician has that much patience. I have a handout on labyrinthitis for example, and plenty of other conditions. If patients want to know more about certain procedures let them read about them. Then, if they have additional questions, they will ask you about them.

The Scarsdale diet was among these delicately described aids to a doctor's capacity to endure. Not alone in my opinion but that of most people I know who, well before the appearance of Dr. Tarnower's best seller, had put themselves to the Scarsdale routine, surely the grimmest day of the dieting week was Thursday. Here, from my old copy, is the diet for that day:

Breakfast (the same each day)
  ½ grapefruit
  1 slice protein toast, no spread
  Coffee or tea, no sugar or milk
Lunch
  Cold chicken
  Raw or cooked spinach
  Coffee or tea
Dinner
  2 eggs, any style but prepared without butter or milk
  Cottage cheese
  Cooked cabbage
  1 slice protein toast, no spread
  Coffee or tea

In the two weeks one was supposed to stay on the diet—two weeks on, two weeks off—the weight loss on Thursdays had to have been the most notable. Confronted at lunch with a mound of unviolated spinach, I know that I lost appetite for the cold chicken and, at dinner, after I'd swallowed two hard-boiled eggs and a blob of cottage cheese, I was ready to forgo my boiled cabbage and slice of dry protein toast.

A recognizable feature of almost all specific diets is that they prohibit substitutions. Dr. Tarnower's program was no exception: his book reprints a letter from a dieter who said that she preferred radishes and raw cauliflower to the celery and carrots which are the only between-meals snacks permitted in the Scarsdale diet. "Stick to the diet as listed!" was the doctor's unyielding reply. Dr. Tarnower does nevertheless allude to new insights that came to him from patients: he cites a patient who had recently asked him whether in summer, when grapefruit wasn't in season, a fruit that was in season mightn't be used instead. Oh yes, replied the diet doctor to whom it seemed never before to have occurred that from a nutritional point of view berries or melons were quite as satisfactory as grapefruit. *In every two-week period of the Scarsdale diet that Dr. Tarnower had been prescribing for close to two decades there were fourteen breakfast servings and four dessert servings of grape-*

fruit! Other than as an active lack of concern for his patients, how can one explain that Dr. Tarnower never in all those years thought of melon or berries as an alternative to grapefruit?

In *The Complete Scarsdale Medical Diet* the original two-page guide that Dr. Tarnower had always given his patients is called the Basic Diet and to this he adds four new programs: how else fill up a book? They're called the Scarsdale Gourmet Diet for Epicurean Tastes (!), the Scarsdale International Diet, the Scarsdale Vegetarian Diet, and the Scarsdale Money-Saver Diet, all of which are promised to produce the same good results. Even the Basic Diet indicates that it wasn't until Dr. Tarnower went public that he stopped to re-examine the diet that he'd for so long been giving his patients to see if it could be made more palatable—or at least more varied. The only change he now makes in the breakfast menu is the suggestion that fruits in season be substituted for grapefruit. But here are the new Basic Thursday lunch and dinner menus:

Lunch
  Two eggs, any style (no fat used in cooking)
  Low-fat cottage cheese
  Zucchini, or string beans, or sliced or stewed tomatoes
  1 slice of protein bread, toasted
  Coffee/tea
Dinner
  Roast, broiled, or barbecued chicken, all you want—
    (skin and visible fat removed before eating)
  Plenty of spinach, green peppers, string beans
  Coffee/tea

To be sure, the improvement isn't staggering. But it's visible. If broiled or roasted or barbecued chicken was as acceptable as cold chicken, why hadn't his patients been told so? And why this late introduction of zucchini, string beans, tomatoes and green peppers, where previously there had been only cabbage? Why, even, this belated sensible switch of the lunch and dinner menus?

But we have to turn from the Basic Diet to the other diets in the volume before we fully recognize not only the lack of thought for his patients that kept this regime unaltered for so long but also in what social grooves his thoughts travelled when Tarnower did at last expand the diet. On Thursday's Gourmet Diet for Epicurean Tastes, breakfast is basically unchanged; but Tarnower names the fruits with which grapefruit may now be replaced: ½ cup diced fresh pineapple, ½ mango, ½ papaya, ½ cantaloupe "or a generous slice of honeydew, casaba, or other available melon." Here are Thursday's other menus:

Lunch
  Eggs and Chicken Livers, farm style
  Tomatoes, lettuce, celery, olives, Brussels sprouts or cucumbers
  1 slice of protein bread, toasted
  Coffee/tea/demitasse
Dinner
  Consommé Madrilène
  Baked Chicken Breasts Herman
  Spinach Delight à la Lynne
  Peach with raspberries
  Coffee/tea/demitasse

And here are Thursday's lunch and dinner on the International Diet:

Lunch
  Pickled Eggplant and Cheese Sticks
  Salad greens, all you want, with vinegar and lemon dressing
  Peach with Raspberry Sauce
  Coffee/tea/espresso
Dinner
  Baked Stuffed Mushrooms
  Veal Napolitane
  ¼ cup boiled white rice
  Zucchini Stew
  Coffee/tea/espresso

On the Money-Saver Diet, however, the breakfast fruit is always "½ grapefruit or cantaloupe or [unspecified] fruit in season" and here are the other meals on Thursday:

Lunch
  2 eggs, any style (no fat used in preparing)
  Low-fat pot cheese or cottage cheese
  Zucchini
  1 slice protein bread, toasted
  Coffee/tea

Dinner
    Boiled, broiled, roasted, or barbecued chicken, all you want; skin and
      all visible fat removed before eating
      Or
    Broiled Chicken Hawaiian
    Plenty of spinach
    Coffee/tea

Having ascended the social-economic-gastronomical ladder, we now again descend and, as down we go, away go the chicken breasts, the spinach delights, the chicken livers, even the boiled rice of the better life—not to mention the melons, the papaya, the zucchini stews, the choice between "plenty of spinach" and other vegetables such as green beans and peppers which generally cost neither more nor less than spinach. Gone even is one's recourse to espresso, and the freedom to drink one's coffee from a small cup. Back to the unprivileged kitchen mug!

And I've touched on only a single day, Thursday, in Dr. Tarnower's recommendations. There are six other days in the week, for each of which the doctor had now found a miraculous means of introducing new items into a diet that, in the days when it was only a handout, distributed by other doctors as well as by Tarnower himself, hadn't allowed even the substitution of raw cauliflower for raw carrots. Dare we think of ourselves as epicurean gourmets? If so, we are permitted not only rice and veal, chicken livers and eggplant, consommé madrilène and stuffed mushrooms and cheese sticks and peaches with raspberries, but also shellfish, thin sliced ham, broths, artichoke hearts, bamboo shoots, bean sprouts, even candied kumquat peel, even wine to cook with, even rum, even the invitation to three ounces of dry wine each evening at dinner. But where were the screams of outrage from the parched throats of Tarnower's earlier public? When the Scarsdale doctor was shot, a listless joke made the rounds: Mrs. Harris had shot him because she didn't lose weight on his diet. The Madeira headmistress doesn't have to diet; that's not her problem. No, she had other problems. One was that she could so easily join her life with someone as small-mindedly class-involved as the author of the Scarsdale diet and so thoroughly give herself over to his style of life. We like to persuade ourselves that in any sense worth our notice, style is only of the arts. The artist isn't alone, however, in constantly delivering

a covert statement along with his explicit statement. In the style
of life that any of us chooses there's contained a psychological,
social, and moral message. No patient of Dr. Tarnower with whom
I've talked had missed his message. While none spoke in disparage-
ment of his medical skills, criticism of the man was all but universal:
he was vain, inflated, self-important; he condescended to people he
regarded as his social inferiors. One patient told me, with obvious
point, that the magazines to which Tarnower subscribed for his
waiting room were chiefly British publications. I had myself
sampled his esthetic pretentiousness. Suddenly I was filled with
rage at our present-day unwillingness to connect esthetic and
moral judgment. The bad esthetics of a society *matter* and so do
the bad esthetics of the individual within the society; Tarnower's
house matters, the pretensions of his diet book matter—style is a
moral mode, a mode in morality. In her testimony, Mrs. Harris
was scornful—saddened, would no doubt be closer to the way she
would put it—because Tarnower had become known as a mere
diet doctor. She could overlook the rather more significant fact
of what a tiny step it is, indeed no step at all, from the false values
of the Gourmet Diet for Epicurean Tastes to the false values of
the "Oriental" home which she was so glad to share with him, so
unwilling to give up. The question pressed itself upon one: had
the Tarnower style been the style of Mrs. Harris when the two
first met in 1966 or had she come to it only through their association? It was my guess that she was a ready disciple. And yet it
was in 1975, when she'd been with the Scarsdale doctor almost
ten years, that she bought her house in Mahopac. Seeing it as I
had after I'd visited the Tarnower estate, I'd been unable to connect
the two modes of life that these two different places represented.
How did the same woman who could buy this house for herself
accommodate Tarnower's brand of cultural pretension? I of course
didn't know then that she'd never lived in it. After the shooting,
people argued about whether it had been right for a school headmistress to live with a man to whom she wasn't married. It seemed
to me that what had been more worth discussing was whether it
was right for someone who could accept, as Mrs. Harris did,
Tarnower's social ostentation to be guiding the lives of the young. In
the week before the shooting of Dr. Tarnower, Mrs. Harris had

expelled four seniors because remains of marijuana were found in their dormitory rooms. The Madeira community had been sharply divided on the expulsion, and the fracas had taken its toll of the headmistress. Mrs. Harris is a person of strong conscience as Dr. Tarnower apparently was too in his own way: no one writes a will such as his, carefully meeting all obvious obligations, who hasn't a keen sense at least of the family proprieties. But conscientiousness doesn't finally determine moral character. There's the matter of the values to which Mrs. Harris made reference in the discharge of her duties: in terms of values, how did her expelled students measure up against herself and her lover? At the news of the shooting of Dr. Tarnower, everyone who'd ever questioned the wisdom of a school decision or tried to rescue a child from the authority of a school "expert" might well have pondered the process by which school teachers and administrators came to their positions of moral ascendency over mere parents.

For many people who came to the White Plains courthouse with much sympathy for Mrs. Harris, it was bound to have been a shock to discover the degree to which she had conspired in Tarnower's hard treatment of her—it's one thing to be masochistic, that's an old female trademark, but Mrs. Harris's cooperation in her mistreatment appeared to be more than mere capitulation to the humors of a lover. The picture that emerged in the courtroom didn't at all conform to the popular image of the headmistress as someone who in her own small person represented the suffering of all women through the centuries, a kind of secular *mater dolorosa*. The distinction between suffering endured and suffering invited and perhaps even unrecognized was not to be ignored. Much of the support that Mrs. Harris had won from the public rested of course on a harsh prejudgment, on the unspoken assumption, that is, that she had murdered Dr. Tarnower but that it was warranted—she was not to be thought a criminal since she had acted rightly and on behalf of all women. But if, as was being

42

made apparent in the trial, Mrs. Harris not only accepted Tarn-ower's abuse of her love but would have been happy to continue the relationship, prejudice in her favor had to find new grounds. And it wasn't only Mrs. Harris's willingness to protract her un-happiness that came as a surprise to some of her earlier sympathizers. It was a shock to discover her competitiveness with Tarnower and the part that money would seem to have played in the life she shared with her lover. Mrs. Harris turned out to have thought far too much of "who had sacrificed what for whom" in her years with the doctor. There had been too much talk of money, far too much. "April is the cruelest month"—Aurnou had quoted Eliot to me as Mrs. Harris had quoted him to Tarnower, but neither of them had completed the line: the cruelty of April was that it bred lilacs out of the dead land, mixing memory with desire. As one listened to Mrs. Harris tell the story of their love, *her* love which was so un-changing and could admit no anger, but also her love which was so conditioned by material interest, one had to ask what deceptive beauty could possibly have been bred out of Tarnower's death and what memory the headmistress could now mix with desire.

But I get ahead of myself: it was still spring and the trial was still in the future. I had gone to Washington to talk with people at Madeira about Mrs. Harris as headmistress. Although the campus had been open to visitors for some weeks after the shooting, by the time of my arrival this was no longer so. I nevertheless got to speak to past and present Madeira parents and even to some present students. The report I had of the headmistress was confusing. There was respect and even mild affection. Certainly there was compassion for her in her present misfortune. But no one was as utterly bewildered by this tragic happening in the headmistress's life as I'd have expected. I don't mean to imply that there had been premonitions of a disaster of this magnitude, but I'd put it that there was some quality in either Mrs. Harris's personality or her conduct which had somehow prepared the com-munity for the possibly untoward in her behavior, an extremity or potential for extremity with which they had become familiar. This consciousness had largely stemmed from her disciplinary actions. It was all very well that when the girls dropped orange peels on the campus, Mrs. Harris stopped having them supplied with fruit and in punishment ordered a day of short rations—Miss Keyser, her predecessor as headmistress, had inflicted such military penalties for even longer periods of time. But as it was explained to me, not only by Madeira people but by educational colleagues elsewhere, no disciplinary action taken by Miss Keyser provoked as much protest: Miss Keyser was so much "jollier" and "warmer," a woman who suggested so much less of "ideal" conduct, that her lash carried far less sting than that of Mrs. Harris. It was of Mrs. Harris, not of Miss Keyser, that the community emphasized the degree to which she was a "law and order" person. When Miss Keyser went by the book, her discipline was at least current. Mrs. Harris was not only on current but on retroactive guard against infractions of rules. For instance, in February of 1980, so short a time before the events of March 10, she'd learned that at a birthday party six months earlier, in September 1979, a group of Madeira girls had celebrated by drinking beer. This belatedly, she made them report themselves and they were briefly suspended.

From my Madeira conversations I had the impression that Mrs. Harris had lived in a friendly community—friendly, that is, to her, as she was friendly to it—but that she had lived in it alone. I was directed to no one as her intimate; no one was said to have been her confidante.

But there is an ultimate isolateness in Mrs. Harris's pre-Madeira history as well. "Even in Grosse Pointe she was tired and had a kind of desperation about her," someone had said of her. In paradoxical fashion she had always been a woman who easily made friends and yet was friendless.

There's a great deal that eludes one in Jean Harris's early life, more so than in Tarnower's; or perhaps, because hers is a Middle Western story and I'm less familiar with the circumstances, it's more elusive of my understanding. She was born in Chicago in 1923, the second of the four children of Mr. and Mrs. Albert Struven. Mary Margaret had been the first; Jean was followed by a brother Robert, and then by a sister Virginia. It was in 1934, when the economic depression had begun a bit to ease off even in the West, that the Struvens had moved from Detroit to Cleveland and settled in a pleasant though modest home on a pleasant modest street. Here Jean, an unusually bright child, attended the Roxboro

Elementary School. Then she entered the well-known Laurel School in Shaker Heights, one of two distinguished private schools for girls in that area—the other was the Hathaway Brown School, which was considered the more socially oriented of the two institutions, a deb's school. The Laurel School was thought to be more serious. It nevertheless represented something of a social "reach" for a child of the Struvens: most of the children of their neighborhood attended public schools. In fact, the choice of Laurel for Jean perhaps hints at the existence in her parents of the same kind of social ambitiousness that was to characterize their daughter's life. But this is only a possible interpretation of the decision: it could also have been a response to Jean's unusual mental gifts.

Early stories about Jean Harris after Tarnower's death said that her father had retained his title of captain from his Army service in the First World War, but actually Mr. Struven was a successful engineer with a high post in the R. G. McKee Company, a large engineering company in Cleveland, and I've been able to find no confirmation that he clung to his military past, though, to be sure, there's a family taste for careers in the armed services—Jean Harris's brother Robert is a captain in the Navy and James Harris, her son, is a Marine officer.

At the Laurel School Jean was a distinguished student and leader. Although non-denominational, Laurel had always had a strong religious emphasis or at least something close to it: in Jean's day, the girls attended chapel each morning and chapel consisted of prayers, discussion of moral issues, and talks on morality by the headmistress and other respected members of the community. Jean's best friend at Laurel was the daughter of the minister of the conservative Presbyterian Church of the Covenant, the Reverend Bird. Some years later, when Jean Struven married James Harris, the Reverend Bird officiated at the ceremony and his daughter, Jean's old friend, performed on the harp throughout the service and reception. The minister's widow remembers Jean as a "fine and exceptionally brilliant" girl, serious, studious, with impeccable manners and conservative values; she recalls no trace of rebelliousness. When Jean Struven went to Smith from the Laurel School the two friends were still close, but after Jean's marriage they drifted apart. Years later, after the Harrises were divorced and when both young women were living in Philadelphia, they tried to pick up the old companionship, but a single meeting was all they managed. The friend of her childhood and earlier young womanhood felt that Jean Harris's personality had changed so drastically that she could no longer be comfortable with her.

The Struvens were Episcopalian: at fourteen Jean was confirmed at St. Paul's Episcopal Church in Cleveland Heights. The year Jean graduated from Laurel and left for Smith, the family moved to a new and better address in Shaker Heights, and in her college vacations she joined the family at a place they had on Lake Erie—indeed, it was at the Lake that she is said to have met James Harris. At college she'd majored in economics. She graduated in 1945 *magna cum laude* and returned to the Middle West to teach in the Detroit University School which, already incorporated with the Grosse Pointe Country Day School, would in 1954 physically merge with it and become known as the Grosse Pointe University School; in 1969 this entity merged with the Liggett School and the combined institutions have since been called the University-Liggett School. In May 1946 she was married to James Harris in a home ceremony that seems to have had much of the formality of a large church wedding: not only Jean but also her sisters—they were her brides-maids—wore traditional gowns; Jean's was of point d'esprit finished with a wide ruffle and a short train, her gloves of the same fabric; she wore a cap embroidered with seed pearls and a short veil. As reported in the papers, even their bouquets and the floral decora-tions of the house would have been suited to a church occasion. Why the wedding wasn't held in church, we don't know. The war was over and even in wartime Cleveland, home weddings had been uncommon in Jean's social group unless the groom happened to be home on only a short leave. The wife of the minister who officiated at Jean's marriage dimly recalls the rumor that James Harris was Catholic but in Grosse Pointe, where James Harris grew up, no church of any denomination records that his family were members, and the best friend of his early married life in Grosse Pointe has definitely said that he was not a Catholic. That a question of James Harris's religion should have been raised by the widow of the minister who officiated at Jean Struven's wedding points, I think, to some unexplained fact in the Harris marriage or perhaps to some

46

social uncertainty about Jean Struven even prior to the wedding. To be Catholic in Shaker Heights was a considerable liability; marriage between a well-placed WASP and a Catholic would have been frowned upon. Something would appear to have been frowned upon in Jean Harris's life at that time for which a troubling religious difference between her and her husband would conveniently if mistakenly account.

Two contradictory impressions are created by what we know of Jean Struven's social situation up to the time of her marriage. While the two houses that the Struvens occupied in Cleveland speak of good middle-class solidity rather than social distinction or affluence, the second of them clearly represents a notable rise in the world though even the second had only a half-acre of ground. Both houses were in anonymous good taste. Yet Jean's associations in Cleveland would appear to have been upper middle class—she seems, that is, to have lived among wealthier people than her own parents, substantial as they were; people whose daughters "came out," though she herself did not, and who, when they married, had large church weddings. Perhaps at Smith Jean Struven had got beyond coming-out parties and fashionable church weddings. But if this is so, there would seem to be an inconsistency of principle in the elaborateness with which the home wedding was mounted. It's striking, too, that except for her friend at the harp, none of her earlier close friends was present.

The social picture focuses more clearly when the young Harrises begin their life in Grosse Pointe. There's now no question about the modesty of Jean Harris's house and the reason for it: it's the decent house of a couple just starting out in the world with little money. James Harris's parents lived on what is described as the edge of one of the more desirable areas of Grosse Pointe and their house must also have failed to hold its own in the crassly competitive society of this Detroit suburb—even today, as one hears of the social divisions of Grosse Pointe, there's the sense of a life controlled by the extent and location of one's real estate. The first home of the young Harrises was "all right," but like all the houses they would occupy in Grosse Pointe, it would have been better suited to Nantucket—this is how it was described to me. To supplement their income, Jean Harris taught history and social studies to the children of her wealthier neighbors. But with the birth of her sons, David in 1950, James two years later, she stopped teaching. Her friends in this period, chiefly friends of her husband, apparently also had none of the required Grosse Pointe claims to social status. For their small children and her own she started a neighborhood nursery school in what seems to have been the third of her Grosse Pointe homes, a small clapboard house on a dead-end street; at the end of the street was the site of a junior high school—today it's the location of a recreational facility. There would be only one more move before the marriage broke up: when the children were roughly six and eight, Jean and James Harris moved to a house only slightly larger than the previous one but with a two-car garage; the street on which this house was located ended at the parking lot for a large supermarket and a Sears, Roebuck. (In a recent sale a house not unlike that of the Harrises was sold for $50,000.) By this time Jean Harris had accepted an invitation to teach first grade at the Grosse Pointe University School. The couple no doubt needed the money: James Harris, an executive at Holley Carburetor in East Detroit, was not highly paid. But there was an added incentive: as a member of the staff, Mrs. Harris could have her own children attend the school without cost. The school had always been patronized by the socially prominent and wealthy of Grosse Pointe and Bloomfield Hills and it continues to be; but attendance doesn't automatically confer status. As one acquaintance of Jean Harris, also the son of a University-Liggett teacher and a Grosse Pointe resident, has said, Grosse Pointe and Liggett did wonders for his status outside the Detroit area but the elite of Grosse Pointe would have immediately recognized his humble situation from his address and from the fact that his mother was a teacher. Jean Harris, too, would seem to have suffered this kind of condescension in Grosse Pointe and for much the same reason, but reports I've had indicate that the distance at which she was kept by the mothers of her first-grade students had other cause as well. She was said to have "straddled the line": without being an "intellectual" in any recognized public sense, she was too intellectual in manner. She was alert, efficient, slim, attractive, well-groomed, and she did her job well, but she didn't "cut it." In Grosse Pointe, mind wasn't respected even in a man, let alone in a woman, and she unmistakably communicated the insecurity of living with people who had more money than she had in a society in which to be inferior in economic standing was to be inferior in being. I have the sense that this adverse judgment of Jean Harris, though masked by good manners, was cruelly far-reaching—it included even her dress. Yes—it was told me—she was well groomed but her clothes were wrong: the Capezios, the McMullen shirts, the plaid skirts. It was the kind of judgment that would be directed to her again at Madeira where the students said she wore too many pastels. For those of us, the fortunate majority, who have never been put under this kind of inspection, both Grosse Pointe and Madeira, but Grosse Pointe even more than Madeira, sound like patrician zoos. One can understand the eagerness with which Mrs. Harris left the Detroit suburb for Philadelphia.

And one also understands how different the world to which Herman Tarnower beckoned her must have seemed to a fugitive from the snobbery of Grosse Pointe: Jean Harris must at last have felt free. "Freedom is only the rattling of chains, always was," said D. H. Lawrence. He was talking primarily of sexual freedom but he could have been describing the life that Jean Harris got in exchange for her life at Grosse Pointe. If she couldn't make her way among the WASPs of the Middle West, she made it beautifully among the Jews of Westchester and from this base she could move to Madeira and close the circle. Madeira drew some of its students, perhaps even most of them, from the eastern seaboard, but it drew students and even trustees from elsewhere, some from Grosse Pointe. Now it was as their daughters' headmistress rather than as a first-grade teacher that Mrs. Harris met women who would once have found her not quite what she should be. Now it was as a visiting speaker that she came back to Laurel.

In having reached her goal with the aid of a Jewish doctor, son of immigrants, Mrs. Harris had known how to move with the cultural times. She had outwitted traditional America, that unsaving remnant, and proved herself worthy of a full dominating place in it. Surely the temptation is great to think that in killing Dr. Tarnower, Mrs. Harris was killing something other than just the cruel lover who had rejected her. She was killing the poor object of her social gratitude.

THE TRIAL

We'd been told that the rulings in the pre-trial hearings would be handed down at 9:30 this morning. It's 11:00 by the time we're led into a smaller court on the same floor; they need our large room for seating the potential jurors—there must be a hundred or more, weeded out from the thousand people who were impaneled. The hearings had taken more time than was foreseen; they'd begun the 6th of October, it's now November 4, Election Day. The building is shut except for the Harris trial; a sheriff brought us up in the elevator—there's something perilous about an automatic elevator when it's operated manually and even the officer had seemed uneasy.

Although only four motions were to have been argued, Aurnou had introduced a fifth: to exclude the press. He hadn't meant, of course, from the trial itself, only from these preliminary sessions, but it didn't take long for the opposition to make itself heard: by the end of that first lunch recess lawyers had gathered from *The New York Times* and the Gannett papers. Holding up great stacks of clippings from the local, regional, and national periodicals, even from foreign publications, the defense counsel argued that the widespread publicity that had been given the case and the errors in reporting had hurt his client; now the mistakes would be compounded in the accounts of these proceedings. It's a bit wild: Aurnou's like the boy who kills his parents but begs for mercy on the ground that he's an orphan. Does he forget his own cooperation in the publicity, his virtually total command of it? The most damaging instances he seems able to adduce are a reference to Mrs. Harris's "confession" on the night of the shooting, and a filmed enactment of "Mrs. Harris" shooting at a man on the floor. The latter had been used as a TV teaser for a series about

Mrs. Harris that was soon to appear in a newspaper. The word "confession" had obviously been used in its non-legal sense of "admission." Ugly as the ad was, even the two together didn't, I thought, warrant the exclusion of the press from the hearings. To the relief of the news people, Judge Russell Leggett rules against Aurnou. His decision is perhaps influenced by the fact that a few years ago he was reversed in a case where he excluded the press from hearings involving a child rapist. Aurnou has lost support by his action against the press but that's something you have to smell out. The reporters are mannerly, impersonal, and speak very little about the attack on them.

But Jean Harris isn't winning their votes either, so far as I can make out. I wonder a great deal about how she'd appear to me if I'd come into court with my original sympathy for her: would I have found her as estranging as I do now? But she grows on one in impressiveness. My first day in court, before things had got started, she'd been seated at the defense table not ten feet away from me and I'd not recognized her. She didn't look at all the way she had in photographs. She's very pretty: her features are excellent and her skin is fine and luminous. She has a lovely high, rounded forehead; it's a "brow." But she's meager—I don't mean merely small-boned, but she lacks presence, or she does when you first see her. The presence begins to accrete to her from her size as a personality. It's strange for Aurnou to emphasize her frailty as he does. Wounded she surely is, but a wounded bird trying to fly? That's how he's described her. He shouldn't succumb to his own rhetoric—he's Jewish, not Irish. I look for what has drawn people who have spoken to me of Mrs. Harris's charm. Thus far, I've seen it only once, with her younger son, James. He's twenty-seven or eight and he's in the Marines. In a court break he came up front to talk to his mother; he pulled up a chair and leaned forward toward her and she turned to him full face, smiling. She was very attractive. In the first days of pre-trial, she must have frightened Aurnou, she moved so abruptly from what was only foolish intrusiveness to flashing anger, from acting the schoolgirl who raised her hand to be called on by the Judge to a bad-tempered, willful lady who shouted accusations against the police.

One particularly bad time Aurnou led her from the courtroom but she could be heard haranguing him in the hall: "Doesn't anyone want the truth?" He works at soothing her and replied (of all things), "The press wants the truth." At a recess that day she had virtually spat out at the reporters: "They're lying! They're lying! How can they let them lie? That son-of-a-bitch!" She'll have to do better than this when there's a jury in the room.

The villain seems to be George Bolen, the thirty-four-year-old Assistant District Attorney, who's the prosecuting lawyer. He looks Ivy League and that ought to please her, but she regards him—the Judge too, I guess—as the enemy. It's my impression, though, that it's not the abstract authority of the State that troubles her; it's the authority of the law—there are murmurings about lies against her, evidence altered or deliberately withheld. The issue that has so far set her off on her worst outbreak is the second, so-called Alfinito, hearing, which pertains to the use of letters or whatever else was seized in Virginia. The Virginia police had searched her Madeira house on false information supplied by the Harrison police: it suggested that premeditated murder had been established. Bolen is aware that the State did wrong and he's willing to concede that the Virginia findings shouldn't be used. They aren't important anyway.

On both sides the first, Sandoval, hearing, which deals with whether Mrs. Harris had a previous criminal record or record of immorality, was disposed of quickly enough. When Judge Leggett asked if Mrs. Harris had been guilty of previous criminal, vicious, or immoral acts, Aurnou replied: "In this day and age, no." Mrs. Harris looked amused but not entirely pleased. I think she'd like to debate the implications of the question and of her lawyer's answer. The prosecution promised not to use anything from the headmistress's past against her.

Since her angry scene Mrs. Harris has someone from Aurnou's staff always at her side. She's probably seen her psychiatrist too—that's the press rumor—and she's no doubt being more heavily tranquilized. At any rate, she's now decently subdued though it's plain that she'd prefer to be in charge instead of having to take direction from Aurnou: she's restive about him. Which, I wonder, has been the more threatening element in her character throughout her life: loss of control or too much control? She writes constantly, left-handed, but not as if making notes; more as if she were getting on with a book. When, to demonstrate the international attention the case has received, Aurnou displayed an Argentine journal, she studied it closely. There have been sixteen pre-trial witnesses, examined and cross-examined in enough detail to make this a trial, if there had been a jury. Eight were called by each side, all of them police officers except the van der Vrekens, Tarnower's servants, who were summoned by Aurnou, and the physician whom Jean Harris had talked with at the police station the night of the shooting—because Mrs. Harris wouldn't waive the privileged patient-doctor relationship he was exempt from testifying about his examination of her. These have been no negligible days in preparing Mrs. Harris's defense. Apart from offering his various motions, Aurnou has been accumulating information about the conduct of the police the night of the shooting and in the days that followed; it has been his first opportunity to hear the testimony of people he'd not previously been able to question. Henri van der Vreken couldn't be more insolent, lounging in the witness chair and grandly answering "I don't remember" to almost every significant question the defense puts to him, but the police make a generally good impression, surely not as models of efficiency but as upright men. Aurnou would wish to paint a picture of police chicanery, even of direct unkindness to Mrs. Harris. It's not convincing. I'd had no notion from the newspapers of how chaotic the scene at the Tarnower house must have been the night of the shooting. There was no small amount of traffic: patrolmen, detectives, a lieutenant and a chief of police, all of them running in and out of the place, some of them going upstairs to give the dying doctor oxygen or help get him down to an ambulance, others talking with the defendant—and what an unexpected defendant! Piecing together the recollections of each person present, it's impossible to establish a time sequence with the precision Aurnou demands—he wants to prove that Mrs. Harris incriminated herself before being properly advised of her rights but it seems obvious enough to me that the headmistress not only repeatedly admitted that she'd shot the doctor but also expressed her impatience at the redundancy of the legal protection being offered her: "I know my rights. . . . I've been given my rights three times." And she'd willingly led the police to the car where she'd left her gun on the front seat. The "inventory" of the car the next day at police headquarters was another matter. Thirteen hours had elapsed between the arrival of the police at Tarnower's house and the examination of Mrs. Harris's car, and it had been a search rather than an inventory. A warrant could easily have been obtained but wasn't, and the police rules for tagging objects found in an impounded car weren't followed. Most of us find Judge Leggett's decisions on Aurnou's motions eminently sensible. It takes half a minute for him to deliver them: all evidence will be permitted in the trial except the findings in the inspection of Mrs. Harris's car.

Aurnou's hope of ruling the gun out of evidence has been defeated. He had attempted to show that Mrs. Harris, in telling Detective Siciliano where the gun was and leading him to it, was conspiring in the violation of her own rights. And without her informed consent, Siciliano hadn't the right to search her car if any part of his body had entered the car before he saw the gun. But what Aurnou does manage to eliminate from the trial is what was found in the car that Tuesday afternoon under the front seat on the driver's side: the box in which Mrs. Harris had no doubt transported the revolver. In it was another, smaller box with thirty-four live bullets and two spent shells. The jury will know nothing of this. The sort of ammunition that Mrs. Harris bought for her Harrington and Richardson .32 is commonly sold in boxes of fifty. Five bullets having been placed in the revolver, there's a question to be answered: what happened to the remaining nine? Thirty-four plus two plus five add up to forty-one. Were the other nine used for target practice?

Mrs. Harris has received the Judge's decision without emotion; perhaps Aurnou prepared her for it or Leggett told the lawyers his ruling in her presence. Back in the courtroom, the first panel of twelve potential jurors is called to the box; Judge Leggett begins the painstaking pedagogy of jury service, quizzing them (and by implication the roomful of other jurors from whom replacements will be selected) on their ability to accept the presumption of a defendant's innocence, on the task of the State to prove *its* case, on the concept of reasonable doubt, on the difference between direct and circumstantial evidence—all this after putting the usual questions of personal history: is the juror married or single, what is the occupation of the husband or wife, the professional interests of grown children, has a family member been involved with the police? The process is impressive but enormously boring. Leggett is no Freud or Trotsky but he has his own small gift of homely reference. He draws on childhood memories to clarify difficult legal points; they chiefly have to do with mothers who bake chocolate cakes and are too poor to spare dimes for little boys to squander. He speaks as someone who rose to his present authority from modest beginnings. I find a touch of self-consciousness in his style; this includes the "ya" that he substitutes for "you." Aurnou and Bolen also try to be "family" with the jurors but neither of them is very good at it. Bolen is too uptight, Aurnou too transparent in his effort. The jurors are notably serious when not nervous. The lawyers are of course trying to ferret out prejudice, unless it serves their own ends. But let's understand that in this courtroom prejudice is unknown. No, the fact that the person under examination has a master's degree in educational psychology and that both he and his wife are in special teaching won't influence his judgment of psychiatric testimony. No, the fact that a juror has repeatedly been burglarized and never recovered any of her belongings won't interfere with her ability to listen to police evidence with an entirely open mind. It's staggering, Westchester's small-crime record: is there no one in this room whose home hasn't been broken into, maybe more than once, or whose car hasn't been stolen once, twice, three times? When Judge Leggett talks to the jurors about the need to take part in the process of deliberation without conceding too quickly on their own views or, on the other hand, being too resistant to persuasion, they can all of them boast this splendid double faculty. I'd have to disqualify myself on both counts: immovability *and* the belief that whoever spoke last spoke best; on the latter score I belong in a mob scene in *Julius Caesar*. Yet I suppose they're right to answer as they do. Each of the lawyers is really asking them only one question, "Will you listen to my witnesses and try not to be biased," and they mean to try. The news people, for all the praiseworthy objectivity with which they write, are under no such constraints, they're ankle-deep in prejudgment. Among the reporters—the book writers aren't talking—Mrs. Harris is already pretty much guilty as charged. But they think she'll get off; her kind of person doesn't go to jail. One young reporter shrugs her pretty shoulders and asks dryly, "What's murder between consenting adults?"

Mrs. Harris sits at the end of the defense table paying the closest possible attention, studying the jurors. She dresses appropriately for her occasion, wool or knit suits, simple good blouses or sweaters. She seems to have an extensive wardrobe, doesn't wear the same thing two days in succession. Her pale-blond hair—is it faded or dyed?—is enviably disciplined, held back with an old-fashioned circular barrette; it's very nice. As a well-bred victim, she's from Central Casting. I'm shaken to think of the passions that seethe in that little body. On two days during the preliminary hearings groups of high-school students were brought to court by their teachers: they're being educated—in what? Social process? I'm apparently alone in finding it unseemly that in order to be instructed in the workings of the law they've been brought to a sensational murder trial. Everyone else beams approval; the Judge halts proceedings to hold class in a nearby courtroom—we're in an orgy of progressivism. Mrs. Harris is responsive to the young too. She smiles at them pleasantly. Later, in the corridor, someone hears an oversized black girl say, "Gee, I'm glad she didn't come over to us. I ain't never been that close to a murderer before." It being Election Day, Mrs. Harris's older son David, who works in a Yonkers bank, has joined his younger brother Jimmy. The Marine son has been steadily in attendance; he talks with anyone he can, like his mother. Fearful yet confident, he awaits her total acquittal. A black juror who is being examined says his conscience would be troubled if he had to sentence Mrs. Harris for the rest of her life, and the defendant's face lights up. Judge Leggett hushes the candidate. He's the first juror to be dismissed. It turns out that the final selections will be made in chambers and that we're not to be told whether a juror is let go for cause or by peremptory challenge. This bothers me but perhaps no other procedure is feasible in the presence of the prospective jurors. I'm told, though, that this sort of thing is usually out in the open.

No one can tell me there's no progress in the world. A potential female juror, young, unarmored, is being questioned about her acceptance of psychiatric evidence. She tells the court she had *anorexia nervosa* at seventeen. Her weight fell to eighty-five pounds. No murmur, giggle, or questioning glance from anyone. The Judge also asks kindly if anyone has claustrophobia and would find it upsetting to spend many hours in a windowless jury room. Someone tells me this is because the ventilating system in one of the jury rooms in our courthouse had been installed with no outlet. That's a thought for the day.

Although there are few questions Aurnou puts to the jurors without slanting or weighting, he is seldom challenged. Judge Leggett has several times referred to the latitude he'd given the defense in the preliminary hearings, and it's true—everyone's being very cautious not to provide any ground for appeal. When Aurnou asks a juror if he'd have difficulty keeping the length of the mandated sentence out of his deliberations, he casually describes the term as "horrendously long." "Brother Bolen," as Aurnou likes to call him, doesn't object and neither does Leggett.

Toward the end of the day a bombshell, or so it strikes me; it seems quickly to fizzle for everyone else but I guess the news people have learned to deal with such seeming duds. Aurnou asks the jurors if they have open minds on evidence that might involve the improper dispensation of drugs. The juror with the master's in psychology tells Aurnou the question is ambiguous: what does he mean by "drugs"? Aurnou replies that he means "controlled substances." Is he suggesting that Tarnower improperly prescribed controlled drugs to Jean Harris? Amphetamines? Antidepressants? What relevance does this have to the shooting? Is Aurnou going to argue that she came to Purchase that night under the influence of drugs, or even that she was addicted or dependent and that was why she couldn't free herself from the doctor's hold? That would be sensational—why isn't everyone as fired by the possibilities as I am?

This morning I've read several papers looking for the story about Aurnou's drug question but it's mentioned only in passing: I'm disappointed. Yet in court, with his first question, Aurnou returns to "controlled substances." Before the juror can reply, Judge Leggett asks both lawyers to his chambers. When they get back Aurnou puts the question once more. He frames it cautiously: "There may be—or might be—evidence in this trial to the effect that the use or non-use of controlled substances played a role in the events of March 10. . . ." It's plain he's not to pursue the subject further at this point. I suppose it's antidepressants he's talking about: the defendant was befuddled because she'd taken them or depressed because she needed them. More likely she was depressed plain and simple; drugs will be relevant only as a way of confusing the jury. I'm too eager for convenient handles and solutions to this case. There aren't going to be any: I have to remember to warn myself of that.

Out of hearing of the spectators, eleven jurors have been reduced to two, both of them men. The first is a bus mechanic, the second the psychology-trained teacher. The process of instruction and questioning re-commences. It must be gone through again and yet again; the lawyers and even Leggett can't disguise the dreariness of the duty. Almost always when Aurnou speaks to the jurors, Mrs. Harris looks disapproving; I can't think there's much love lost between them. I suspect she'd like to be her own lawyer— she'd indeed have a fool for a client!

"Phil." This is the name to which the young man who's just been added to the defense team responds when Aurnou addresses him. But who is he, other of course than an expert in jury selection? Several of us ask but we're not filled in. I've heard they're infallible, these new social psychologists who break the jury bank, but I've also heard they're terrible in murder trials, choose very badly. Phil listens and takes notes. Bolen ignores him—would he like to have a computer brain on his side too? He'd probably consider it a form of cheating. The lawyer for the prosecution is tall, rangy. He wears steel-rimmed glasses and is well dressed, much better than Aurnou with his inevitable brown suit that looks as if it'd been sprinkled with those shiny little grains that the TV commercials tell us give decaffeinated coffee its flavor. (Or am I mixing up two brown suits, one decaffeinated and one real, with milk in it?) Morality is in every line of Bolen's appearance. Yet I find him impressive in his young righteousness. Something about him takes me back to the paper dolls of my childhood, the kind that cost more because they're made of cardboard, not of thin paper. I see him mostly from the back and that's when his clothes and his hair, particularly his hair, look attached by tabs. Maybe he's athletic: good athletes often have a kind of physical rigidity when not engaged in their sport. He radiates contempt for Aurnou: never overt, of course. Aurnou acts the old pro having to suffer a novice in the ring with him, any minute the knockout. But I think he's not all that confident; they're both scared. Aurnou, though, has more to lose.

I read a local news story about Bolen that suggests he's no less firm and determined than he appears to be but that he gets very emotionally upset, sulks, and has even been known to cry when he feels he's been treated unfairly. I hope he doesn't cry in Aurnou's presence. Aurnou often plays for laughs but he never takes his eye off the target. From the questions he puts to the jurors he seems unerringly to be setting one stone after another in place, laying the foundation for a compassionate defense. And of course one of the ways to win sympathy for his client is to break down barriers between the jury and himself. He speaks, for example, of the deceptiveness of appearances and offers a hypothetical instance: One sees a middle-aged woman and she looks very trim, very attractive—a nice-looking lady but that doesn't necessarily mean that she feels that way about herself. This is Mrs. Harris. Then shamelessly he adds: "Or a little man, five foot six, chubby, balding—he might be an aggressive nasty lawyer." Or repeating the three-count indictment against Mrs. Harris, he speculates that the jurors might not be convinced on counts one and two; that might leave them with only the third count, possession of a weapon in the third degree. It's early in the game to be giving the jury a way out should it feel it needs to convict the accused of *something*, but preparedness is Aurnou's occupation—or perhaps I don't mean preparedness so much as I mean foresightedness, wily planning. His finale today is typical.

Aurnou: We don't want special sympathy because she is a woman, because of her age, because she is frail. . . .

Bolen: Objection.

Leggett: Sustained.

Does her lawyer really think of Mrs. Harris as this much gone in maturity? She's on the verge, he suggests, of irredeemable old age. This startles me: displaced by Lynne Tryforos she may have been but far from out of the race—she looks to me like a woman who, full as she may be of self-pity, has a quite sufficient sexual confidence, or surely has reason to have. It's possible that Aurnou thinks that she's reached an age where the best that can be said for her is that she's not too badly off for someone of her years, she's still slim and attractive, but he's shelving her. Maybe he needs to be told that not all depression is post-menopausal; young women have their problems too. I wish I could sorrow over Mrs. Harris: this is harder for me each day since I learned the facts that hadn't come out until the preliminary hearings. They'll never be able to talk at this trial about the box of ammunition found in her car, but I can't get it out of my head. Or I keep thinking of her having asked Henri who had been at the doctor's house for dinner that night—imagine a question like that when your lover of fourteen years has just been carried out dying! Whatever her intent, whether in the legal sense she had intent or not, it was her revolver that caused his death. She'd also stopped to look at her mouth in the mirror after phoning her lawyer in the van der Vrekens' bedroom, and she'd said to her lawyer, in those circum-

63

stances, when she'd just finished telling him that she'd probably killed Hi, "Henri is looking at me as if he'd like to kill me." Surely this is none of it the conduct of a sane person. The defense is challenging the very idea of an acceptable norm of human feeling by not offering a psychiatric plea in the case. Are we all of us to join Mrs. Harris in her denial of reality?

Eventually, acceptable jurors do seem to materialize: none of us in this courtroom can say from where or why; we've not been let in on the last step of the selection process. So far, the most interesting of the people who've been chosen is a small intense black woman, Juror 3, married and separated. Sharply outspoken, she alone of the jurors, when asked by Judge Leggett if Mrs. Harris's standing mute would create a problem, answers that it would. Bolen says he appreciates her candor; Aurnou puts it to prompt use. "You just want to have all the facts, right?" he flatters her. Then daringly he brings up "the matter of class," describes Mrs. Harris's background: headmistress of a school . . . Grosse Pointe. "She isn't exactly the lady next door." Bolen objects and Leggett intervenes with the creative assurance that what Mr. Aurnou means to say is that the defendant has lived in different parts of the country and this is what makes her different from the lady next door. "Partially, your Honor," Aurnou corrects him gently. "But also a different social milieu . . . a different educational background." Would the juror be able to judge her impartially?

Juror: I might not be able to do that, knowing perhaps her social background.
Aurnou: As compared to what?
Juror: Well, as compared to the lady next door.

Everyone is impressed, not sure that Aurnou isn't asking for trouble in accepting her on the jury. But I decide that if he's so confident she'll not be intractable perhaps it's because he thinks that having chosen her despite her candor he has demonstrated his faith in her ability to rise above class bias. What could be more winning? Certainly it imputes to her an intelligence that lifts her above prejudice. Juror 3 works as an administrative assistant in a federal community services program. Juror 4, also a woman, seems a more neutral choice: she's a special-education teacher, married to the treasurer of a maintenance company. Another uncomplaining crime victim: one burglary, three cars stolen. It's a hazardous path one follows to this courthouse: one lady was robbed of her wedding gown.

There's a wonderful moment when Aurnou asks some prospective jurors if they or any of their friends or family members have had experience of "real depression, clinical depression." Mrs. Harris seems to have been in a bad way longer and worse than I'd supposed. At first one of the men answers no, but then he amends his reply: "My father died when I was young, and my mother had periods of severe depression. But she died at the age of eighty-five and three-quarters, a very happy, very active woman." Poor Aurnou, for once he's nonplused. He stares at the man, can't find a response, gives up.

The defense description of Jean Harris's long affair with Tarnower has now been codified: it's to be known as an "adult relationship." Such is the thunderous wholesomeness of the formulation that I'm taken aback when a potential juror, mother of eight, says that she's worried by the effect that her condoning such a relationship might have on her children. She and the Madeira Board? And what about the effect that a child relationship has on adults: would that be all right? Apparently crime can more readily be made to seem encompassable than sex; whenever Aurnou refers to a crime that has involved a potential juror he chuckles or sometimes even laughs aloud. And revolvers certainly require no circumnavigation: he would suggest that it's foolish to be uncomfortable around guns.

To a part-time letter carrier the defense lawyer says with a big smile, "My children haven't bothered you? Or my dog?" He refers to his children the way Judge Leggett refers to chocolate cake. Maybe they're right and one does have to build a bridge from the legal profession to the outer world.

So far, of twelve women questioned, eight have been on the Scarsdale diet.

The reporters are a bit wry about Mrs. Harris's remark to the NBC court artist—the defendant thinks there are too many circles around her eyes. Perhaps perversely I find this spontaneous expression of pride in her looks a good deal easier to accept than I do her day-after-day ability to sustain this situation in which she now finds herself. The former is a response of habit but the latter strikes me as evidence of a defective sense of fact. Where, oh where is the dead body of Dr. Tarnower? I keep looking for it all over the courtroom—certainly Mrs. Harris didn't die that March night but neither, apparently, did anyone else.

Slowly, miraculously, the jurors multiply. We seem to have seven: four males, three females. Two among them are black. As the days pass, it's dullness that scores. Could a less exciting collection of people have been brought together in Westchester than have filled this courtroom? To relieve the tedium the out-of-town reporters interview the book writers. Why, they ask me, am I interested in Mrs. Harris's case? Everyone begins with the same question; they're surprised that I'm doing something that's this much off my usual line. I try to explain that I've always been interested in cases: political cases like the Hiss and Oppenheimer cases, for instance, with direct bearing on our contemporary society, and also situations and persons—the LSD phenomenon, the campus uprisings of the sixties, the death of Marilyn Monroe—which bring into conjunction our private and our public dilemmas. To be sure, the shooting of the Scarsdale doctor was sensational, as those subjects hadn't been, but I'm fascinated by the kind of world that Dr. Tarnower and Mrs. Harris inhabited together and what happened between them for their relationship to ensue in such tragedy. It had once been the high function of literature to deal with just such material, to acquaint us with our social variousness and our human complexity, provide us with the surrogates of our known and unknown strengths, terrors, perils. Through the imaginative experience of the exaltation and pain, the triumph or downfall of the characters in books, we'd discovered our own capacity for exaltation and pain, learned the range of our humanity and the size of our world. But literature no longer gave us this instruction. It had become abstract, remote from the objects of our immediate personal and social curiosity. The world of the Harris-Tarnower drama was by and large the same as that of readers of books: it was the world of the educated middle class. If its two chief characters were more ambitious or successful than the rest of us, this merely gave them an advantage that had always been given to the protagonists of drama; the traditional hero or heroine always had more to lose in defeat than more commonplace people had. Their emotional histories nevertheless fed our natural curiosity about ourselves. Now the literature that we were told was most deserving of respect answered this need not at all, devoted as it was either to the distillation of mood or to games of the mind, empty of our social and human actuality. Playfulness had its important use in art; I wouldn't want literature to be robbed of it. But there were things about our life of feeling and also about the way in which our society operated, the means by which social advancement was achieved or sacrificed, about which we needed to be told but weren't—the contemporary novel didn't speak of them, not in seriousness. In fact, our imaginative writing had reached the point where it even weakened our ability to distinguish between the actual and the fanciful: not long ago a book reviewer of repute, writing about a novel in which there were gnomes who had escaped from the pages of Washington Irving— one of them had become a servant of the heroine—described the author as a master of reality! Love and sexual passion, honor, money, envy, jealousy, greed, death, greatness and meanness of spirit, the anguishing anatomy of class differences: all these which were once the major themes of the novel were disappearing from literature to find their home in television, whose falsifications steadily weakened our understanding of life even while we boasted our superiority to its influence. How were we not to be influenced by something we regularly used and enjoyed? It was from "Dallas" that we were supposed to learn our psychological insights; Archie Bunker was our guide through the subtle maze of social conflict. To instruct us in the life of the heart, the TV reporter thrust a microphone into the face of the newly bereaved mother: "Tell us, Mrs. Pasquale, what did you think when you saw your baby's squashed body lying in the gutter?" As for crime, we read about it constantly not alone in the newspapers but even in gifted books such as Truman Capote's *In Cold Blood* or Mailer's *The Executioner's Song* which safely sealed it off from the middle class in some dark corner of life where the best dream was to see the blood splash. The shooting of Dr. Tarnower couldn't be sealed off from the middle class, it had erupted in our respectable midst.

Yet as I talk something keeps nagging at me; I think that what I am saying is true and important but I hear a note of self-justification in my voice. I'm carried back to my unease the day last April when I first visited Dr. Tarnower's house in Purchase, or tried to. In part I'd felt then that I was trespassing on the preserve of the professional newspaper reporter but I'd also felt that I was appropriating other people's lives for my own purposes. Judge Leggett's remark on the first day of court, "Once the trial is over nobody's going to be interested in this case," had been addressed, I felt, to just this point on which I accused myself: to write a book about someone's murder was to make capital out of another person's tragedy.

Mrs. Harris has begun to worry the courtroom regulars: will she last out the trial? They speak of how much thinner she looks each day and how pale she is, especially when she wears a white or beige blouse; in brighter colors she doesn't seem so drained of life. I don't find myself sharing their concern. I've been hearing about her fragility ever since I first spoke with Aurnou in the spring; I remember that he wondered if she was going to be able to hold up through a trial. I agree she's lost weight but I have no sense of any weakening in her resolution or in her attention to what's going on around her. Her brother, Navy Captain Struven, is in court these days: he doesn't look as robust as one would expect of someone in his job and he's pale too, almost pasty. In fact, when one sees them walking together it would be hard to tell which is the less fit, they both seem so drained of color and sunk into their bodies. In profile he has the same upturn at the corners of the mouth, as if preparing an enigmatic smile. It's my impression that with Phil gone Mrs. Harris is fortified by the sense of authority regained. No one explained his appearance at the defense table, now no one explains his departure.

At last we have a full complement of jurors, also a first alternate. But she can't stay an alternate long. For several days we've known that Juror 2, the one with the master's in psychology, has had an accident and been hospitalized. Now we're told it won't be possible for him to serve, the first alternate must take his place. This means that four more alternates must be chosen, but the process is greatly speeded up and we've finally made our quota.

Will Mrs. Harris be judged by her peers? Hardly. No one among the twelve is her match in either professional accomplishment or social authority. But what about the moral authority which up to now has been her particular boast: these eight women and four men that make up the jury, four among them black, three of them teachers, can we not assume that they are her equal in that? From where we sit as observers we can't of course know, but to judge by what we've seen and heard, surely there's no shortage of self-respect in this jury—it's not to be missed as these men and women sit together in their two rows, gravely attentive, somber really. One can almost hear them thinking that a human life is at stake, they must meet this terrible responsibility. Mrs. Harris has only once indicated a clear preference for a juror; she wasn't allowed that choice but whether it was Aurnou or Bolen who intervened I have no way of knowing. The candidate was a physical-education teacher, young, with a small trimmed beard; he said he didn't like the police: they tended to respond as a clan, a guild; they stuck together, wanted to make their stories jibe. When asked where he formed this opinion, he answered that it was at college in the sixties. Mrs. Harris had leaned forward in her seat to speak to Aurnou; she said something that sounded like "We want that man." She could have been right; perhaps Aurnou even agreed. Bolen's only comment was rather stiff: he went to college in the sixties too.

The jury complete, the Assistant District Attorney puts a series of rhetorical questions to a prospective alternate. As if preparing an opening statement he points out that they've all been hearing from the defense that the testimony may deal with an "adult long-lasting relationship." But what kind of relationship was it in actuality? What he is of course suggesting is that in imputing this solidity to Mrs. Harris's long affair with Tarnower, Aurnou is being assumptive, presenting covert evidence on which there can be no cross-examination if Jean Harris doesn't take the stand. We have a sudden new glimpse of Bolen as a fighter. It helps us remember that although his opponent is hard to come up against, he has his own record of wins.

Fifty-six names have been read off by Judge Leggett as potential witnesses: it's scary. The most familiar of them hasn't yet been mentioned in court: it's Lynne Tryforos. A question at the center of the case: had Mrs. Harris shot Tarnower in a jealous rage because she had been replaced in his affections by the younger woman? Her affair with Tarnower was neither new nor a secret from Mrs. Harris. It need not have been a secret from any of us, however strange we were to the doctor's social circle—at the Christmas season of 1979 I'd read the advertisement of it that Lynne placed on the bottom of the front page of *The New York Times,* a message of greeting and love to her Hi. I'd never before noticed a paid greeting on the front page of the *Times,* and without knowing anything about the people it concerned, I'd wondered who would want to celebrate her affection in this public way. Aurnou told me this was the ad Mrs. Harris had confronted over her morning coffee in Palm Beach on her last Christmas holiday with the doctor. Too, when Tarnower and Mrs. Harris travelled together he would leave his itinerary with Mrs. Tryforos, and Mrs. Tryforos would make her presence felt from a distance. Tarnower's medical assistant was obviously no passing fancy—in his will, written in January 1980, the doctor left virtually the same amounts to both mistresses: $200,000 to Mrs. Tryforos and $220,000 to Mrs. Harris (the will contained conditional bequests of $20,000 to each of

Lynne's two daughters to pay for their college educations). But as late as the publication of *The Complete Scarsdale Medical Diet* Jean Harris had pride of place, for what that might be worth, among the acknowledgments. Lynne came even after Suzanne van der Vreken, among a group of women thanked "for their assistance with the diets, writing and manuscript preparation." One had heard that Mrs. Harris was less than impressed by her lover's literary accomplishment in producing a best-selling diet book. But although Tarnower enjoyed the money and celebrity the book brought him, it could be that secretly he too was uncomfortable because of the means by which he had attained to this newest success —he was that best-certified of snobs, a pretender to literary knowledge and taste. Just as, watching Mrs. Harris in the courtroom, it was easy to imagine the cool, utterly democratic distance Mrs. Harris would wish to maintain between herself and the van der Vrekens as compared to the tie that Lynne had apparently established between herself and the doctor's servants, just so it was easy to imagine the condescension that the headmistress would have felt toward her lover in areas where she considered herself to be his intellectual superior. Lynne Tryforos would have been awed by his accomplishment in having produced a best seller.

When I remark to one of the local reporters that it sounds as if the trial will go on forever, she laughs and says it will outlast the building we're in. The courthouse is only six years old, it cost $33 million to construct, but it's sinking into the marshlands on which it is built and leaks at every pore; the county's in the process of suing the contractors. Also, one of the deputy sheriffs—there couldn't be a more attractive and pleasant group of young men than these courtroom guards—says that if you stand outside the jury room you can hear the shouting, the walls are so thin. Sometimes you can even hear what the jurors say.

The court artist who gave Mrs. Harris too many circles around her eyes is about to have a show of her drawings; or maybe she's already had it. Anyway, she's pleased with herself and seems to have reported this to Mrs. Harris: "You've made a star of me," she told the defendant. To this Mrs. Harris replied, "I'm an expert at that." Puzzled, the artist repeats this: whatever could Mrs. Harris mean? I feel a stab of pain, it's so obvious to me that she means that it was what she'd done for Tarnower, made a star out of him—it wouldn't be the success of his diet book that she'd have in mind but all that lay in back of its appearance, their years together and the part she'd had in advancing his social fortunes and therefore in preparing him for celebrity. For a moment my mind, like hers, is emptied of his death and I'm back where I had started from with the headmistress; I want her not to have been rejected, not to be in this terrible trouble she's in. I want Tarnower's indebtedness to her to have been acknowledged, not in a crudely conceived line of thanks at the start of his book but by a kept pledge of enduring love. But this is only for a moment. I become distracted by the artist's further report that Mrs. Schwartz, Dr. Tarnower's sister to whom he bequeathed the largest part of his estate, would like to buy one of her courtroom drawings of Jean Harris. Can this be possible? Such a report is too bizarre for me to believe.

It's November 21, the start of the actual trial, with a full jury in the box, the courtroom crowded. There's a more than perceptible stir in the air. News photographers and TV crews, not permitted above the street floor, have stationed themselves in the courthouse lobby—there's a kind of pit in the center of the ground floor: I have the impression of a modern zoological garden with cameramen instead of polar bears. Upstairs in our courtroom the front row is occupied by Mrs. Harris's supportive family, all of them in full splendid view of the jury. Her son David apparently has the day off from the bank; he's accompanied by his quiet, modestly pretty young wife and by Captain Struven. A detective in Aurnou's employ is also present but sits a bit apart. Until now Mrs. Harris's brother has been in mufti; today he's in naval regalia, four stripes, complete. In mounting a trial by emotion, Aurnou misses very little. Tomorrow morning, one can be sure, Mrs. Harris will be in all those newspapers about which Aurnou is so dramatically bitter, arriving in court on her brother's arm—Aurnou's client has the confidence of the U.S. Navy!

If we're to judge by today's opening statements, God knows she'll need every trick in her lawyer's bag. Bolen speaks first: he is simple, lucid, carries no excess baggage. Listening to his brief outline of the case that the State means to prove, I'm once again staggered by what I, the public, didn't know about that March evening of the shooting. How was it managed that in the face of one erroneous news story after another, everyone on the side of the prosecution—the police, the staff in the D.A.'s office, Dr. Tarnower's relatives, friends, servants, Lynne Tryforos and the rest of the staff at the Scarsdale Clinic—all maintained silence and let Aurnou do the talking, waited their day in court?

The narrative begins with Tarnower's return to his home that evening from his usual workday at the Clinic and hospital. He has two guests to dinner, not three as we'd been told: Debbie Raizes has come with Lynne Tryforos. The dinner is cooked by Suzanne, served by Henri van der Vreken, and Lynne has brought a birthday cake as a surprise for Suzanne whose birthday is the following day. The doctor looks tired so his guests leave early, around 8:30; Tarnower goes to bed. Shortly afterward Henri retires as well to the guest room. Suzanne alone stayed up; she was painting a watercolor and watching TV in her bedroom at the extreme left end of the main floor, the opposite end from the garage above which the master bedroom is located. Not long after 9:00 the house was dark except in Suzanne's corner.

Meanwhile Jean Harris, in a blue Chrysler that belonged to the Madeira School but had been assigned to the headmistress, had left Virginia for the five-hour drive to New York, taking with her the .32-caliber Harrington and Richardson revolver she had bought approximately a year and a half earlier at a gun shop not far from the school. It was licensed in Virginia but only in Virginia, not in New York State. As she enters the house she has ten rounds of ammunition on her person, five already in the gun—the prosecutor is forbidden to mention the ammunition that has remained in the car. The revolver has six chambers and can be fired in two ways, single- or double-action; that is to say, either by cocking the

73

hammer for each shot and then pulling the trigger or by just pulling the trigger alone—it is heavier, it takes a great deal more pressure, to fire the gun by double- than by single-action. The house is dark. She lets herself in through the right-hand garage door which, as she knows, is always left open when people are at home, and then through an inner door, and climbs the narrow spiral staircase that connects the garage to the main level of the house and to the doctor's bedroom on the floor above. No one hears her come in; it is now close to 11:00 P.M. and the only person awake in the house is Suzanne, watching TV. The five rounds of ammunition in Mrs. Harris's gun are fired; the doctor receives four bullet wounds: one in his front right shoulder that severs a vein and causes much bleeding, one in his upper right arm that fractures the bone, one in his upper right back that goes downward, fracturing three ribs and puncturing the lung and kidneys, one in the right hand, entering the palm and exiting the back—three bullets have been recovered from the body. Through her television program Suzanne hears the buzzer from the doctor's bedroom; it sounds in the kitchen. The buzzer is between the twin beds in Tarnower's room and it functions as a primitive intercom system. The beds rest against a partition that serves as a headboard with bookshelves and, on the other side, has closets and drawers; it divides the bedroom from a dressing-room area. On a shelf in the headboard, between the beds, there's a telephone, one of four on the same line; it is possible to communicate between the kitchen and the master bedroom above the dial tone on this phone. The van der Vrekens have a phone of their own on a separate line in their room. Surprised that the buzzer should sound at such a late hour, Suzanne goes into the kitchen and answers the phone. "Doctor?" she says. "Doctor?" As she holds the receiver she hears banging, yelling and screaming, recognizes the voice of Jean Harris, and hears a shot. She runs to wake Henri and then calls the police. The call goes to the White Plains police who inform Harrison. While Suzanne is trying to get help, Jean Harris leaves the house—she knows the servants are home, she's seen their car in the garage, but she doesn't call them for assistance or to use their phone. As Harrison Police Officer McKenna is coming to the scene he sees her car making a U-turn on the road. Mrs. Harris comes back to the house with the police car following her. Suzanne has gone upstairs where she finds Dr. Tarnower slumped on his knees on the bedroom floor; he is in blood-drenched pajamas, his head against the headboard, the telephone receiver off the phone on the floor near his hand. He has a barely detectable pulse. Mc-Kenna has entered the house with Mrs. Harris, passed Suzanne in the foyer. He goes to the bedroom and looks at the doctor, returns to the car for his resuscitation equipment and to summon help, then goes upstairs to give what aid he can to Tarnower. The two women go upstairs with him: Suzanne kneels over the doctor; Jean Harris sits on a bed watching. The bedroom is in disarray, and there is blood around the bed and phone. "Personal items" belonging to Lynne Tryforos are scattered about the room, and on the floor there are five rounds of live ammunition. Detective Siciliano arrives, followed by other officers and an ambulance, actually a van; with great difficulty the doctor is carried down the narrow winding staircase on a stretcher and taken to St. Agnes Hospital in White Plains where at 11:58 he is pronounced dead. That is, 11:58 is the time of the pronouncement; it is not necessarily the moment of his death.

Throughout this grim story Mrs. Harris has watched Bolen with the same unchanging expression she's always worn in court except in her moments of flashing anger or her even rarer moments of charm. There's no sign of horror. From where I sit I see her only in side face: to me her expression is that of the classic *belle indifférence* of morbid hysteria, the corners of the mouth turned up in the fixed beginning of a smile; there is pleasure in it as well as detachment. Not as hard to fathom as the smile of the Mona Lisa, Mrs. Harris's smile is more likely to be missed by the court spectators. She looks to me to be more effectively cut off from the world than the mysterious woman in Leonardo's painting. But it confuses me that her expression should be so closely duplicated by that of her brother whom I also see in profile. Why should they seem to share a pathology just because they share, as they so obviously do, their belief in a version of the story that is very different from that which Bolen has given us?

Aurnou's opening statement takes up the remainder of the morning: after Bolen's wholly factual report of what happened the night of March 10, can the jury miss the larding of assertion and sentiment in Aurnou's narrative? The familiarity of the story as we're now given it in broad outline reminds us of the extent to which Aurnou has controlled the account of the shooting that has so far been made public. In December 1979 Jean Harris and Tarnower spent Christmas and New Year's together in Palm Beach as they had for the last dozen years. In February Tarnower had given a pre-marriage dinner for Mrs. Harris's son David and Mrs. Harris had spent four days in the doctor's house, after which she had once more taken up her arduous school duties, travelling across the country fund-raising—he is making the relationship sound warm, familial, ongoing. No "event," the defense counsel stresses, took place between Tarnower and Mrs. Harris from the date of the party for David until March 10. She had mailed Tarnower a letter that very morning, taking the trouble to send it special delivery. The shooting was "a tragic accident." Mrs. Harris had intended to kill herself. He says: "The evidence [will show] that a woman is capable of having her own life, her own career, her own feelings, her own emotions, independent of a man, and that in this case there were things in Jean Harris's life, answers that were in Virginia, not in New York, how she felt about herself, her fears about aging, her depression about work, the end of her role as an active mother . . . and a physical fatigue that was overwhelming, a state of depression. . . . These factors led Jean Harris [to want] to take her own life." Eighteen months earlier she had bought, and got police clearance for, a .38-caliber revolver but she hadn't picked it up; instead she had gone back for a .32 whose trigger was not so heavy to pull—but she had got incorrect ammunition for it, short not long. On March 10 there had been a "triggering event" at Madeira—he doesn't tell us what it was—and she'd gone back to her campus residence to put her affairs in order "never expecting to return," then driven in a storm to New York. The gun hadn't been aimed at Tarnower when the bullet that hit his hand was fired, and Bolen was "not quite right" about the four wounds. A bullet had hit the clavicle, puncturing a vein and causing massive bleeding. A bullet "in back" didn't travel back to front but downward—but the doctor was 5'10" and Mrs. Harris was 5'4". The hinge was broken when the gun was found; the bathtub had pieces

76

of enamel gouged out, with specks of blood around it. It was Type B blood on the gun, which is Tarnower's type—already wounded, the doctor had held the gun in his hand, not unloading it because he felt no threat. A towel with blood would be explained, as would blood on the floor and on the bed where Tarnower had sat after he had been shot in the hand. Jean Harris and the doctor had rung the buzzer together: no one had dusted the buzzer for prints. The events in the bedroom took a long time and occurred in the light. Mrs. Harris banged the tub with the gun to get out the bullets to refill the revolver so she could kill herself; she didn't know how to unload. Without trying to get rid of the gun, she had then left the house to try to phone for help. She had led the police back to aid the doctor. The defense had not pleaded insanity but it had evidence beyond doubt that she was suicidal. She had called to tell Tarnower she was coming to Purchase; she had wanted, Aurnou says, "To say goodbye to the human being who meant more than anything else in her life." In her purse she'd had a list of people to be notified in the event of her death and she had handed it to the police. "The sad truth that you will ultimately come to know is that there came a time that night when Jean and Dr. Tarnower struggled over the gun, when both Jean and Dr. Tarnower fought over her life and both of them lost. He lost his life in what was a tragic accident and she was left with a life she no longer wanted to live."

I'd been prepared for an appeal to emotion yet this scenario surprises me. I expected substantial new factual material—unless he is trying to hold back information from the prosecution until the last possible moment, this is indeed a defense of desperation that Aurnou is making, directed chiefly to contradicting or countering the new and damaging facts adduced by the State. As to his reference to Mrs. Harris's letter to Tarnower at the Clinic, he's speaking of the so-called Scarsdale letter that had been retrieved from the local postal authorities just moments before the District Attorney's office attempted to get it; its rightful disposition is still being argued in the superior courts. But I'm startled to hear it spoken of as a special delivery rather than a certified letter, which is how it had originally been described in the newspapers. Certified mail can be of two kinds, to be signed for by the person who receives it or only by the addressee, and last spring Aurnou had verified for me that Mrs. Harris had sent the kind that would have had to be signed for by Dr. Tarnower. It seemed to me to have some bearing on her intent, at least as of the time she left Virginia, if she expected the doctor to be alive the next day to receive it. It isn't my picture of Aurnou that he'd permit his tongue to slip in an opening statement to the jury.

The jury has listened stolidly to both attorneys, revealing nothing of its reactions. Mrs. Harris has again put on her dark glasses: they're the screen behind which she occasionally retreats and I welcome them as an indication that she has emotions to hide.

In the interstices of these important sessions I marvel at the good temper of the newspaper people: there's been an attempted end run around the press and they have cause for anger. There was a free day yesterday. Announcing the break, Judge Leggett had explained that both Bolen and Aurnou needed time to examine certain material in preparation for their opening statements. It hadn't occurred to me that this wasn't the whole of the situation, but a couple of the reporters had got wind that something was up, and to the astonishment of Leggett and the lawyers who were there with him had appeared in the courtroom—the three men had had no choice but to continue with what they'd planned to do out of view of the press: Aurnou had subpoenaed the film and tape from all the TV and radio stations that had been covering the case in order to establish once again for the record how much misleading publicity the story was getting. Leggett is said to have been impatient with the defense attorney's performance; he'd nevertheless permitted the session—it went on for three hours, terminating by no perceptible process of logic with Bolen's request that Aurnou comply with the decision of the State Appeals Court that the Scarsdale letter be turned over to the prosecution. On his side Aurnou demanded that Bolen turn over a copy of the card that Mrs. Harris had brought with a bouquet of flowers to the doctor's house the night of the shooting. According to the reporters who'd broken in on the scene, Judge Leggett had granted both requests: Mrs. Harris's letter to Tarnower was to be given to Bolen on December 1 and the card that accompanied her flowers was to be turned over "forthwith." Although the newspaper people tend to feel that all the rules are being bent, if not broken, from solicitousness for the defense, they file their quiet stories without editorializing.

Pearl Schwartz has been in the courtroom all day. It's hard for me to believe that this pleasant-faced woman could be as attached as she apparently was to a man of whom I've heard so little that's appealing. She looks to be in the young sixties, a good advertisement for her brother's diet: slim, light in her movements. If I'd seen Tarnower across a room as I see her, would I have thought better of him? It's a troubling possibility and I put it from me.

When Mrs. Harris had been arrested at Dr. Tarnower's house, she'd been taken to the police station in Harrison where she'd spent the night of March 10–11. Then she'd been removed to the Valhalla County Jail. The first witnesses called by the Assistant District Attorney are two correctional officers from the women's unit at Valhalla who testify about Mrs. Harris's clothing collected by them on March 11—in addition to a fur jacket it includes a pair of panties, a bra, and two pairs of pantyhose, which are placed in evidence. During a routine "pat search," one of the officers tells us—it scarcely strikes me as routine information, for all that it is received so quietly—she had seen a handkerchief in Mrs. Harris's hand and taken it from her. It was a man's handkerchief, and a live shell with three scratches on it had been knotted into one of the corners. Nothing more is made of this. Aurnou points out that although only one bra has been offered in evidence, two had been listed among the defendant's possessions: the one that had been put in evidence had had a blood spot or "what appeared to be a blood spot" on it and had been cut into for blood-testing. Both officers testify that the defendant's upper lip and the underside of her upper left arm had been bruised and discolored when she'd got to the Valhalla jail.

The next witnesses for the prosecution are men experienced with guns, having worked at Irving's Sports Shop at Tyson's Corner Center not far from the Madeira School where Mrs. Harris bought her gun. They testify about revolvers in general and Mrs. Harris's purchase in particular. In October 1978 Mrs. Harris had come to the store to buy a gun for "self-defense," saying she lived back in the woods. It was obvious to the clerk who had served her that she knew nothing about firearms; she'd looked at the revolver he'd offered her "as if it were a strange object." Having chosen a model, she filed for a police permit and obtained it. The gun was laid away for her but she hadn't picked it up. But at a later date she'd returned, examined a lighter revolver than the one on which her clearance had now lapsed, and tested it by dry-firing it—she decided this one was better for her; it was more comfortable to her hand. The salesman instructed Mrs. Harris in how to open the cylinder and how to load that particular weapon. When she'd again got police clearance and after a new "cooling-off" period as required by Virginia law, she'd come to pick it up. The clerk had not sold her ammunition.

Lewis Andrew Baughman, Jr. takes the stand. He's the superintendent of buildings and grounds at Madeira where he's worked for seventeen years—his father had been the Madeira superintendent before him. Baughman lives on the campus with his wife and children; close to his house there's a five-hundred-gallon in-ground gas tank. Between 5:15 and 5:30 on the afternoon of March 10 the headmistress had driven up to his house in her blue Chrysler; explaining that she was late for a dinner party and that she didn't want to risk delay trying to get gas on the road, she'd asked if he could fill her car for her. To do this he had to use a hand pump; it took close to fifteen minutes. He noticed that during this wait Mrs. Harris seemed to be reading something behind the wheel; he also saw that there was a bouquet of flowers, daisies and something else, apparently in a bowl on the front seat near her. She left in haste as if she really were late for dinner. While this attractive young superintendent has been testifying, Mrs. Harris has once more put on her dark glasses.

Aurnou's cross-examination goes far afield from Mrs. Harris's need for gas on that March afternoon. He takes the superintendent through a crisis caused by the famous new solar-heating system of one of the Madeira buildings, through Mrs. Harris's remonstrance with him one summer because he hadn't sent his children to camp, through the re-covering of a set of chairs in one of the Madeira halls (apparently accomplished by Mrs. Harris's own competent hands) and the re-finishing of scarred tables in the school library. He elicits an account of Mrs. Harris's contributions to Madeira as a gardener, of the wreaths the headmistress helped make at Christmas, of her skill at flower arrangement, of her concern that the school grounds be tidy, even of her having hung a picture of Miss Lucy Madeira in the main public room of one of the school buildings. Designed as evidence that the headmistress's devotion to the school went well beyond the line of duty, the recital embarrasses me. Mrs. Harris has herself undoubtedly drawn up for her lawyer this impressive list of past services to which the school superintendent can attest, and obedient to her wishes the prosecution's witness becomes the defendant's character witness.

From the Madeira campus to the Harrison police station is a long day's journey into night. The trial has hardly begun but I already feel the kind of exhaustion that until now I've known only in hospitals waiting for the verdict on someone close to me. The two situations aren't connected as experiences of worry for a person I love, only as experiences of enforced inactivity in the face of danger. I don't love Mrs. Harris. In fact, each day I feel more alienated from her as I watch her fighting for her life with no apparent recollection that by her own account of what happened, it was her wish for death that caused the death of her lover.

The testimony of the matron of the Harrison police station, Mrs. Martino, who had transferred the defendant to the Valhalla jail on March 11 is brief but stupefying. When Mrs. Harris had arrived at the police station in Harrison, she'd been wearing a bloodstained white blouse. She asked the matron if she could wash it, and the permission was granted—the blouse had been washed, hung up to dry and then Mrs. Harris had put it back on again, clean. I look around the room: surely I can't be alone in finding this incredible. But I meet few answering glances—has everyone in this courtroom been so quickly sold on the privilege due a lady of Mrs. Harris's standing? What would have been the response if she'd been a black woman in Harlem who'd asked permission to wash away the blood of her dead lover? To which the answer is, of course, that if she were a black woman in Harlem we'd none of us be here—and this includes me. Without Mrs. Harris's class advantage the case wouldn't have had its public importance. In cross-examination Aurnou questions the matron about his client's behavior, even how she slept during her night in the Harrison police station after the shooting.

Aurnou: Was she in a particular position physically all night long?
Mrs. Martino: . . . A lot of the time she was flat with her legs pulled to her.
Aurnou: In sort of a foetal position?

Bolen objects. Mrs. Martino looks baffled.

Aurnou: Did Mrs. Harris ever ask you what might become of her?
Mrs. Martino: No.
Aurnou: How did she appear to you?
Mrs. Martino: Tired, weary, like in a daze; just stared.
Aurnou: Have you ever seen a person in shock?

Bolen objects and is sustained. But how could Aurnou have known to question Mrs. Martino along these lines unless he'd been briefed by the defendant? What a detailed chronicle of her life Mrs. Harris has given her lawyer! No; what a detailed observation Mrs. Harris made of herself in the aftermath of the shooting of the person who meant most to her in life.

November 25. Suzanne van der Vreken, Dr. Tarnower's housekeeper, or, as she now prefers to call herself, his house-manager, begins her testimony. Lynne Tryforos may turn out to be bigger box office but we know from Bolen's opening statement that Mrs. van der Vreken is crucial for the prosecution. She speaks with a

82

difficult accent: the Judge often repeats her replies for the court reporter. I'm not confounded by her speech but by her looks: can this be the same woman of whom I'd caught a glimpse behind Henri's shoulder the day I tried to see the Tarnower house? I recalled the housekeeper as a white-haired keeper-of-the-keys and keeper of her husband as well, and what I see here is someone trim, almost smart, almost youthful, her hair dyed an acceptable yellow and acceptably curled; in the contemporary manner even her eyeglasses have been made into an asset. I check my memory with some of the women reporters; I'm relieved to discover that there has indeed been a transformation: the witness has lost a great deal of weight—the Scarsdale diet?—and got herself a new hairdo to go with her new figure. The prosecution has its right to a bit of theatre too: Suzanne wears an eye-catching cross.

She and Henri had begun working for Tarnower in 1964 and had first met Mrs. Harris in 1967. In that year the doctor had added a new wing at the west end of his house; the addition had provided a servants' bedroom and bath and a guest room and bath, with lots of closet space in the little hallways into which the rooms opened. Much time is spent and much confusion generated by Bolen's attempt to establish the floor plan of the house. The Assistant District Attorney isn't what I would call glib. Mrs. van der Vreken had first met Lynne Tryforos in 1975, when the doctor brought her home to dinner; after Mrs. Harris went to Madeira in 1977 the visits of his new friend became more frequent. In this courtroom no one refers to the doctor's "sleeping with" his lady friends or "having an affair": Tarnower has "overnight guests," or there are occupants of the "guest bed" in his bedroom, or he "sees" a woman. In August 1978, when Mrs. Harris spent part of her summer vacation at the Tarnower house, she had on one occasion, but of course not in the doctor's hearing, talked with Suzanne about Lynne Tryforos. "She used some words—not very nice—about that lady," Suzanne recollects. "She said 'I will make their life miserable. I will ____ them.'" The verb has been lost; it sounded like "shoo"—is it shoot, sue, or show? The reporters have a story; they can't wait to crowd around Aurnou at the end of the day to find out what it was that Mrs. Harris had threatened. But Aurnou is as mystified as they.

Meanwhile Mrs. Harris watches with her customary little smile of superiority and disengagement, and Bolen continues with his witness. In the first week of February 1980 Dr. Tarnower had gone on a ten-day trip with Lynne and in his absence Mrs. Harris had phoned—Suzanne knew her voice. "Mrs. Harris asked me if I wouldn't mind to do a small dinner for David, and at that time she announced to me he was getting married. I didn't know about it, and she said, 'Would you mind?' and I said 'No, if Dr. Tarnower agreed with it.'" Then later in February, at the time of the wedding, Mrs. Harris had stayed at the doctor's house from Thursday to Sunday morning, when the doctor had left to go hunting.

For me, the news of the day is that the marriage dinner for David was not Tarnower's paternal gesture but only his deference to the wishes of David's mother—it somehow fits my picture of him better than the idea that he would propose such an occasion himself. As Suzanne leaves the court at the end of her day's testimony, the doctor's sister pats her kindly.

Tomorrow is Thanksgiving and we're edgy because Judge Leggett hasn't said what time we'll leave today or whether court will be in session on Friday. The first thing I hear when I come in is that after the close of court last night Aurnou, not for the first time, called for a mistrial and was again refused.

There's much significant testimony that bears directly on March 10. Suzanne starts, though, by setting the record straight on the missing verb. To everyone's disappointment Mrs. Harris hadn't said "shoot," she had only said "sue." Bolen even spells it: "s-u-e." Poor Mrs. Harris, maybe she still thinks one can sue for alienation of affections. On Saturday, March 8, and Sunday, March 9, Lynne Tryforos had stayed the night with Tarnower. She left before him on Monday morning—the two were planning a trip together. Twice on that Monday, March 10, Mrs. Harris had phoned the house, both times before 5:00 in the afternoon; the doctor had come home between 5:00 and 5:30, probably at

5:15 or 5:20. As a matter of fact, she had phoned several times over the weekend. In her first call on Monday she'd asked, "Is Hi there?" and when Suzanne said no, she'd hung up, sounding "very angry." The second time she'd asked if the doctor would be home for dinner. Although Suzanne knew that the doctor would be having dinner at home—she had already shopped and was preparing dinner for him and his guests, Debbie Raizes and Lynne Tryforos—she followed the instructions given her by her employer six or eight months earlier, that if the doctor had guests to dinner and Mrs. Harris called, she was to say he wasn't there. "Then she asked me, 'Is he going out?' I said 'Yes.' 'Is he going down to New York? . . . If he is going down to New York I could meet him there.'" When Suzanne replied that she didn't know, Mrs. Harris hung up. In this call she had seemed worried and annoyed. "When she hang up, it seemed to me that she was crying."

At 5:00 that afternoon the housekeeper went to Tarnower's bedroom to turn down his bed; the room was "in order." In the guest bathroom off the doctor's bedroom—the one with a tub, used by the doctor's women friends; his own bathroom, at the other end, had only a shower—were Lynne's nightgown, robe and slippers, and some jewelry on the washstand. Clothes that the doctor planned to take with him on his trip had been laid out on a ledge in the dressing area. The dinner served by Henri and topped by the surprise birthday cake that Lynne had brought for Suzanne was over by "8:00, 8:15," and the two women had left soon after, at approximately fifteen to nine, in very bad weather. The doctor had gone to the living room to pick up his nightly medicine, a small laxative mixed with applesauce—so the famous diet doctor took a daily laxative!—and then he'd turned off all the lights in that part of the house, including the light over the front door, and gone upstairs at about ten to nine; the front light would have been left on if he were expecting anyone. The doctor was approximately 5'11" tall and weighed about 175 pounds. He wore bifocals and his hearing had recently not been good. After sending Henri to fetch her painting materials from the garage, Suzanne had gone to her bedroom at 9:00 or 9:15 to paint and watch TV. Henri went to bed in the guest room at the front of the west wing.

The only lights that were on in the house were in Suzanne's room. Between 10:45 and 10:55, as the police film that she was watching on television was nearing its end, Suzanne had heard the buzzer in the kitchen. Surprised—"It was late at night and he never did that before"—she went to answer. On the way to the kitchen she heard the buzzer a second time. "Doctor? Doctor?" she said into the kitchen phone. There was no reply but through the phone she heard a lot of yelling. "I said, 'This is Mrs. Harris voice'"—it was not close to the phone—"and then I heard a shot, and I never heard Dr. Tarnower again." She'd wakened Henri, tried to call the police, but there was no dial tone on the kitchen phone so she dialed 911 in her bedroom. The police hadn't understood her so Henri called them. Then he half-circled the outside of the house, came in again through the front door. Suzanne went upstairs. "I saw Dr. Tarnower in between the two beds . . . he was like kneeling down and his body was against the shelf between the two beds, his head on the side, on the shelf, almost on the shelf. His left arm was under his body, against the shelf, and the right one was almost on the floor, close to the phone . . . close to the receiver of the phone which was on the floor. . . . He had blood on his back and I touched his wrist to see if his pulse was still working, and it was still okay. . . . So I rushed downstairs to call an ambulance." The call for an ambulance would await the arrival of Patrolman McKenna who came into the house a few minutes later, behind Mrs. Harris. The headmistress was carrying her fur jacket and wore a white blouse splattered with what looked like blood. McKenna supposed he was responding to a burglary but Suzanne and Henri explained that it was a shooting and that the doctor was upstairs badly hurt. Followed by the two women, Officer McKenna went upstairs. While Suzanne and the officer knelt by the doctor to put him on his back—it required that they push his bed toward the stairs—so that McKenna could give him resuscitation, Mrs. Harris sat on the doctor's bed and at one moment "bended down and she touch the tip of her hand to his face and she said, 'Oh Hi, why didn't you kill me?' I turned my head . . . I said, 'Come on, Mrs. Harris.'" Suzanne and Mrs. Harris go downstairs. The two of them, plus Henri, are in the foyer when Detective Siciliano arrives and asks what happened.

Jean Harris says, "The doctor has been shot." Siciliano asks who did it. Mrs. Harris replies, "I did." Siciliano asks where the gun is "and Mrs. Harris answered, 'It's in my car.'" More police arrive, also an ambulance, and the doctor is carried downstairs on a stretcher. Mrs. Harris asks, "Is that him?" and Siciliano answers that it is. Mrs. Harris appears to collapse; the detective holds her up and says there's need for another doctor, but Mrs. Harris just gets up "like if nothing happen." Later, as Suzanne stands in her bathroom, Mrs. Harris comes by on her way back from calling her lawyer on the van der Vreken phone and stops to examine her bruised lip in the bathroom mirror. She says, "Oh, he beat me. He used to beat me a lot." Suzanne has seen nothing on Mrs. Harris's face "not before she showed me."

Bolen: Did you ever see the doctor hit Mrs. Harris?
Suzanne: Never.
Bolen: How about beat?
Suzanne: Never.

After the doctor has been taken to the hospital Suzanne goes upstairs again. The bedroom is a "shamble"—clothes belonging to the doctor and Lynne Tryforos, jewelry, money, curlers from a set lent to Lynne by Suzanne are strewn about. Between the doctor's bed and his bathroom there's blood, and the buzzer is bloody. A window in the dressing area beyond the partition, facing the rear of the house, has been broken and there's a bullet hole in the glass door that leads to a balcony outside the doctor's room on the front of the house. One of Mrs. Tryforos's slippers is in the guest bathroom, the other in the dressing area. The doctor's bed and blankets are "really bloody." The bathtub is "chip on the edge" and several live bullets are close by on the floor.

All of this has been listened to by Mrs. Harris with the closest attention. As always, she consults papers and often whispers to her attorneys. Mrs. van der Vreken has avoided looking at her. In the housekeeper's testimony the headmistress is almost always Mrs. Harris; Mrs. Tryforos is often Lynne Tryforos.

In the afternoon Suzanne is interrupted for the appearance of Sergeant Batchie, the White Plains Police Communications officer. By stipulation of both attorneys the tapes of the relevant police communications are played for the jury instead of calling all the police and telephone people who handled whatever business related to the events that night at the Tarnower residence. On the witness stand Suzanne has been composed, and if she's not been understood it's because of her language difficulties. But in her calls to the police after the shooting she couldn't be understood because she was so overwrought that there was no language in which she could have talked intelligibly. As we listen to the recordings of her attempts to get help, there's a good deal of embarrassed giggling in the courtroom. Yet her hysteria in consequence of the awful occurrences in the house is thus far the most emotionally authentic moment of this trial, perhaps the only one. Eight and a half months have passed since the doctor's death but as the happenings of that March night are re-created in courtroom questions and answers constantly interrupted by objections and side bars, eight and a half centuries could have elapsed, the shooting and the subsequent events seem so remote from emotional actuality. I wonder how much this atmosphere of unreality is a reflection of Jean Harris's manifest disengagement from the story that's being told. I should suppose that Aurnou would instruct her to make some show of feeling rather than seem this impervious to the recital of the bloody details of her lover's death; but perhaps the jury interprets her detachment as evidence of her innocence and even of her "aristocracy"; or of course it may even be that they think innocence and aristocracy are in some mysterious way synonymous.

Nobody at the police station in White Plains recognized the doctor's name, nor could they get help from the telephone company. It had been transmitted to the Harrison station as "Tarno." So much for celebrity.

A recess. I'm grateful for the break; I think everyone else is too—we've been shaken by hearing the van der Vrekens' call for help. People go out to the corridors; the first two rows of my side of the court are empty. I've stayed in my seat in the third row. The other day, as we were waiting for court to resume after a break, Mrs. Harris had come forward from the defense table to try to speak to her son who was in front of us; but she'd no sooner risen from her chair than her constant attendant had risen as well and, defeated, she'd gone back and sat down. Now, momentarily unguarded, she approaches the first row and leans over it toward me, addressing me by name although we've never met. I dimly make out she's telling me of something I've written that she liked. I ask her what it is and she quotes a line: "Women have now been granted the status of an ethnic minority." I recognize the line but can't recall where I wrote it. Aurnou's assistants converge on her and she turns away as I thank her. The brief encounter makes me uncomfortable; personal contact with the defendant implies commitment. And she's chosen a bad moment, right after we've heard the tapes from the night of the shooting. But what am I supposed to do, shield myself from Mrs. Harris's approach: "Unclean, unclean"? The line of mine she has remembered of course has ideological force.

Suzanne comes back on the stand. Bolen puts in evidence twenty-three photographs of the inside and outside of the Tarnower house. Those on the inside were taken on March 12 and apparently corroborate Suzanne's description of the "shamble" in the doctor's bedroom: the blood and scattered clothes. One picture shows the shelf above Dr. Tarnower's bed with his eyeglasses on it. The pictures are passed among the jurors as becomes necessary but they're not shown to the press. At first we're told this is because Aurnou objects to our seeing the exhibits, and in violation of the code governing freedom of the press Leggett has acceded in his request. But later we're told it's Bolen, not Aurnou, who is withholding them. I sign a letter from all of us to the Judge asking him to reconsider. I inquire of the reporters who are experienced in covering criminal trials whether they're always this tiring; they say no. We're sent home early for Thanksgiving; there'll be no court on Friday.

Direct examination of Suzanne van der Vreken resumes after the holiday. She testifies that she'd gone upstairs to look at the bedroom after the doctor had been removed to the hospital and that among the things on the floor there'd been a black shawl in which clothes belonging to Mrs. Harris were wrapped, or half-wrapped; they had previously been in Mrs. Harris's drawer in the dressing area. These are now put in evidence: a black nightgown or slip, a bluish-green nightgown, a nightgown with the name "Bloomies," a brown tank-top shirt, a pair of tan slacks—with all this stuff spread over it to be marked, the prosecution table has the charm of a dry cleaner's counter. Isn't it humiliating to have one's underwear put on display like this? The headmistress watches unperturbed. Asked if the doctor had on his glasses when she'd first come upstairs after the shooting, Suzanne replies that he had not. Asked if she'd seen the eyeglasses that night, she says, "Yes, it was in the back of his bed, on the shelf." She points out the place on one of the photographs. She also identifies a picture of a bouquet of daisies and greenery wrapped in paper: it was lying on the shelf behind the guest bed after the shooting though not earlier in the day. She can't of her own knowledge say how the flowers got there but we already know: the bouquet had been put in Mrs. Harris's car by a Madeira colleague, and the head-mistress had taken it with her to Purchase and into the doctor's house together with her loaded revolver and the extra rounds of ammunition.

Cross-examination begins and we have our first demonstration of Aurnou's skill as a trial lawyer: he's precise, quiet, and death-dealing; even Mrs. Harris looks at him with new respect. There's a particularly bad stretch for Suzanne when she's questioned about the police officers or the people from the D.A.'s office with whom she'd talked on the night of the shooting and in the following days—Aurnou demands names, times, places. She testifies that she made only one written statement, two pages long, on the night of the 10th.

Aurnou: Are you sure it was only one?
Suzanne: I don't remember. I was very nervous at that moment.

She had gone to bed at 4:00 and got up at 6:00. She's hazy about interviews on the 11th and 12th and has particular trouble recalling who'd been present at a questioning on the second of those days: she mentions Mr. Facelle, Mr. Donnelly, Mr. Raab, all of them from the D.A.'s office, and "another gentleman." Aurnou prods her about the other gentleman's identity and finally supplies the lack.

Aurnou: Was he your attorney?
Suzanne: Yes.

This failure of recollection detonates dangerously in the courtroom. Suzanne looks like someone trapped.

Aurnou: Now do you remember his name?
Suzanne: Mr. Sirlin.
Aurnou: How long had Mr. Sirlin been your attorney at that time?

Bolen objects and asks for a side bar in which he successfully must have explained to the Judge that in addition to Suzanne's lawyer there had been yet another gentleman present, a Mr. Abinanti, whom she can't recall—it is unfair to make her reply sound untrustworthy. They return and Aurnou dutifully opens the way for her to amend her earlier statement as to who was present: "Mr. Facelle, Mr. Donnelly, Mr. Raab, another gentleman which I don't recall his name, Detective Siciliano arrived later on, and Mr. Sirlin." I'm not sure the jury has grasped what's happened but serious damage has been done to Suzanne's confidence; from here on, she pulls herself out of one pit only to fall into another. Aurnou makes even the fact that she dated one of her written statements 12/3/80 sound like evidence that her testimony is unreliable while Suzanne lamely tries to explain that it's the French way of writing March 12, 1980. On the 12th she had been served with a subpoena for a hearing. Aurnou asks what time of day she had been served.

Suzanne: I don't recall.
Aurnou: . . . How many times in your life have you been served with a subpoena?
Suzanne: Never.

The lawyer for the defense is of course doing no more than is required of him if he means to win his client's acquittal, but I find the process unbearable. It's clear that he's been briefed by Mrs. Harris on every possible detail that will rattle or undermine the prosecution's chief witness—he goes so far afield as to suggest that Suzanne, against the doctor's express orders, had permitted his two hunting dogs to sleep in the bathroom behind the kitchen. He goes back to the spring of 1967 when Mrs. Harris first came to the house with her children and asks whether Dr. Tarnower gave a diamond ring to Jean Harris. Suzanne doesn't recall. Aurnou continues: "At some point in time close to that, did you begin to consider working for someone else because you thought the doctor might have children around the house?" The day's chief triumph for the defense is Judge Leggett's order that Mrs. van der Vreken bring into court the next morning what she has described as her "Everyday Book." To the delight of all listeners, she seems to have kept household records throughout her employment by Dr. Tarnower. Under questioning, she says that she "was using it to write down all the guests at the dinner party of Dr. Tarnower."

Aurnou: Do these records have dates and people's names in them?
Suzanne: Yes.
Aurnou: And you kept them contemporaneously with the happening of the events?
Suzanne: Yes.
Aurnou: Have you showed those records to the police?
Suzanne: No.
Aurnou: . . . Did you see her [Mrs. Harris]* several times in April and in May of 1967?
Suzanne: Yes.
Aurnou: Is it correct for me to say that in April and May of 1967, when Mrs. Harris came to see the doctor at his home, she slept at the home of Mr. and Mrs. Schulte? Do you recall?
Suzanne: No, I don't.
Aurnou: Do you remember in 1967 whether or not Mrs. Harris spent the summer, that is, the month of July in particular, with Dr. Tarnower at his home?
Suzanne: I don't remember.
Aurnou: I want you to think about 1968 in particular and see if you can remember the patter of little feet. Was there a child

* In quoted testimony, material within brackets is either a summary of something said but not directly quoted or it is a comment by the author.

with her? [He is referring to the presence in the house of Jimmy Harris who was then fifteen!]

Suzanne: No, Jimmy never stayed very long. Not for a week—never.

Aurnou: [In 1969 and 1970] was the doctor seeing and dating other women? . . . Do you recall the name Charlene?

Suzanne: No.

Aurnou: Did you keep these [her records] in a separate book for each year?

Suzanne: Yes.

Aurnou: Will you bring them, please, tomorrow?

Suzanne (as if it were her choice)*: No.

Leggett tells Suzanne soothingly that she should bring the books to court but that she can hold them herself: they'll study them in chambers. Suzanne submits. The day ends with a catalogue of Jean Harris's travels with Tarnower outside the country in these earlier years of their love: a trip around the world in '72; Greece and Italy and the islands nearby in '74; Poland, Rumania, Hungary, Bulgaria, Paris in '76; the Caribbean by private jet as late as '79. It's plain that Dr. Tarnower's long-time companion had something to lose in ceding to a rival. But how is her lawyer to establish the degree of intimacy between Jean Harris and the doctor without at the same time suggesting how much ground there was for resentment when she lost her place as reigning mistress?

The *New York Post* carries the headline MAID KEPT LOVE DIARY OF SWINGING DIET DOC. Subhead: "He was seeing Jean Harris often but nearly every weekend he saw other women." Will Aurnou once more call for a mistrial?

I hear that Mrs. van der Vreken has brought not only her records to court this morning but also her lawyer. She's closeted for hours with the Judge and Aurnou in chambers; the word is that she's peeking into her books in reply to specific questions

* Any descriptive comment in parentheses after the name of a speaker has been supplied by the author.

from Aurnou. Meanwhile Bolen ostentatiously walks the corridors, feigning unconcern with the defense counsel's small-minded triumph. He's left his assistant, Mr. Lalla, to monitor the proceedings. The courtroom is jammed; for the first time spectators line up waiting for seats. In midmorning the Judge comes into the courtroom to ask our patience. On his next appearance he dismisses us for lunch.

With court once again in session Aurnou makes an immediate splash. Although Suzanne says she's been unable to find her diaries for '67 and '80, he refers to a day in late March in 1979 when Tarnower and Mrs. Harris had returned from their Caribbean trip and asks whether anything special had happened on that day and had Suzanne told him anything about it? She hadn't but now she must. It seems that Mrs. Harris kept clothes in the downstairs closet and when she returned from the Caribbean "she found her clothes ripped and slashed . . . one sleeve was ripping from the body . . . she had like a slash in her evening dress . . . in all of the dress and coat, they were slashed and ripped." It is brought out that the day before their return Mrs. Tryforos had been in the house—Suzanne had communicated this fact to Mrs. Harris and eventually to the doctor as well. (I daresay he found it exciting.) The diaries also refresh the housekeeper's memory of the number of nights that Mrs. Harris had stayed at Tarnower's house in 1977; as Suzanne reads off the dates I count at least forty-three. It wasn't until 1978 that Mrs. Tryforos began to appear more frequently. Asked about Mrs. Harris's share in the writing of *The Complete Scarsdale Medical Diet,* Suzanne would have us understand that it was somewhere between invisible and nonexistent. Of the new book that the doctor was engaged upon before his death she recalls only that Mrs. Harris was looking for a quotation from the Book of Genesis and that when it couldn't be found she'd consulted Will Durant's *History of Civilization,* a ten-volume gift she'd given Suzanne when Suzanne was proposing to become a United States citizen. In much the same way that Mrs. Harris's lawyer had led the Madeira superintendent to testify to the headmistress's concern for every detail of the school plant and even for the domestic welfare of its employees, he now leads Suzanne to recount Mrs. Harris's contributions to the decoration and management of the house in Purchase: she'd bought curtains for the living room, re-upholstered a chair, bought a telescope, watercolors, a bird print for the guest room, bought an iron, cheese plates, glassware, a dessert dish, towels for the various bathrooms, bath mats, plastic pillows for the outdoor chairs, a plastic bench, a pillow for the doctor's bed. . . . There was also a picture of "a man who was like a puppet" that Suzanne, herself a painter, didn't understand. (He was unattached: "No strings on me.") Obviously Aurnou has the gun charge against his client in mind and is trying to establish that the doctor's house was also her residence in New York State. He asks about Suzanne's title of house-manager and her husband's title of, as she put it, estate-manager and gardener. "He [Dr. Tarnower] described these positions when we had the interview with him," says Suzanne.

Aurnou: To your knowledge did Dr. Tarnower ever refer to your husband as the chauffeur?

Suzanne: No. We always used Henri. We would never use another word. We would use Henri or Suzanne.

Aurnou: Did he ever refer to you, to your knowledge, as the chauffeur's wife?

Suzanne: Not to my knowledge.

Abruptly Aurnou switches back to David's pre-wedding dinner, about fifteen guests, most of them young.

Aurnou: Did he enjoy having young people in the house?

Suzanne (smiling and pausing): Do I have to tell the truth? . . . He really didn't like to have young people in the house.

Suzanne describes the dinner as "a joyous occasion." Mrs. Harris had seemed very happy, but "she didn't seem so happy when she left." It was the last time Suzanne saw the headmistress until the night of the shooting. In August 1979 Tarnower had gone to Washington to the White House but Suzanne doesn't reply as to where he'd stayed.

The remainder of cross-examination is devoted to further attack on Suzanne's credibility. Did Lynne leave the house on the morning of the 10th at 6:30, as Suzanne had said on March 12, or at 6:45, as she had recently testified, or at 7:10, as she had told the Grand Jury; or had Suzanne in fact never seen her leave the house at all? Did Suzanne actually *know* what time the doctor had left that morning or only his *habit*? Since Mrs. Harris had been in the house only twice since the van der Vrekens got their own phone and never came to their bedroom, would she have known they had a phone? Most fully Aurnou probes Suzanne's testimony that Mrs. Harris had phoned twice from Virginia that afternoon before the doctor got home. Did Suzanne actually take two calls? At what exact times? Does she know exactly when the doctor got home, was it 5:30 or was it 5:00? On March 12 she'd given the time of his return as approximately 5:00, but she'd told the police that the time was 4:30 and on March 21 she'd told the Grand Jury it was 5:00. And she'd told Detective Siciliano on the night of the shooting that there'd been only one call, at 4:15, and to the Grand Jury she'd also said that she told Dr. Tarnower about "a call." That was the last call, Suzanne now tries to explain. "The first phone call was a very short phone call and it didn't occur to me that I had to talk about it. . . . I thought it was not important." Aurnou presses her on the importance of telling the truth— to Siciliano, to the Grand Jury, to everyone and anyone. Such is life on a witness stand: how all occasions do inform against us. All our carelessnesses about time and circumstance—they make the sum of our natural daily experience—suddenly present us in the guise of forked-tongued villains. "Somebody told you to lie and you lied?" Aurnou demands of Suzanne as she reports having obeyed the instructions of her employer and told Mrs. Harris that he would not be home later when in fact he would be. The supererogatory question of all time! Who in this courtroom, who of this jury hasn't told just such a lie time and time again at the behest of a husband, a wife, a friend, a boss? Or do jurors shed their familiar lives, and the commonsensical generalizations to be drawn from them, when they enter the jury box? Suzanne's testimony has left me with the clear sense that the doctor had regularly sandwiched trips with or visits from Mrs. Harris with visits from or travels with Lynne Tryforos. How much, I wonder, is this alternation a dictate of guilt and how much the enactment of a cherished phantasy.

Describing the stairs to the doctor's bedroom, Suzanne always says "speer-all" for "spiral." She also says "sever-all" for "several." Mimicking her accent, Aurnou repeats "sever-all" after her. He doesn't do it too broadly, nevertheless it's mocking. The only time I've seen the defendant really laugh, not just smile her disconcerting smile—that almost never ceases—is when Suzanne testifies that after Mrs. Harris bought the doctor a new pillow, he went out and bought another one.

Aurnou is wearing a new suit, very dark brown with a pin stripe: he looks citified and serious. Maybe it's his cross-examination-of-a-chief-witness suit. Mrs. Harris must have a hairdresser come to her house each evening or she is herself very gifted with curlers. Even in today's gale no hair is out of place; she's neat even when she pulls off her floppy mink-brimmed hat. Mink is her undoing: she has a mink neckpiece too.

There are women taking notes at this trial who are not writing books or pieces for periodicals; they're here to observe for women's groups. As one of them explains, her group spends all its time talking about the case "from a woman's point of view."

The other day the court was a dry cleaner's establishment; today it's a thrift shop. Aurnou has a large carton of Mrs. Harris's things—for some reason he delicately refers to them as "personal articles of a lady"—which, despite Bolen's request that they be marked as a group, he insists upon entering in evidence item by item. He means to show that Mrs. Harris wasn't attempting to flee with all her belongings. It's a motley display: a splashy flower-print house robe (or so it looks to me), a rain jacket, a hunting cap with an orange crown, a very large Christmas stocking, a pocketbook in a plastic bag, a pair of winter boots, a pair of black evening slippers, a pair of red evening slippers, a pair of painted kid or perhaps brocaded evening slippers, a pair of mules, a pair of sneakers, a blouse, a studded belt, a paperback copy of *A Woman of Independent Means* (not admitted in evidence), a nightgown, white gloves, a red dress belt, a plastic bag "filled with undergarments and some special hangers that she used," a receipt from Suzanne's lawyer for the box, a book, *The Case Against College*, belonging to the Madeira School, a bottle of perfume from which all the perfume has evaporated. "Fifteen apparitions have I seen. . . ." Throughout most of this exhibition Bolen sits bored, leafing through transcript: the jury is to see how little he makes of this evidence of Mrs. Harris's pervasive presence in the Tarnower house. How accusatory our clothes look when detached from our pleasure in them! It's like the ghostliness of our old shoes when we've taken them off in the store in order to buy new ones. Only the large red flannel Christmas stocking, made by Mrs. Harris for Dr. Tarnower some ten years earlier, is lingered over, described in detail, passed to the jury for closer inspection: across the top in green-and-red lettering is the name "Herman" and appliquéd upon it are a giraffe, a goose, a reindeer's head, five goldfish, a goofy little monster—the stocking is an infant at a horror movie. This is an unreadable jury: it studies the exhibit quietly, expressionless. Most of the objects, Suzanne testifies, came from a downstairs closet but some, such as Mrs. Harris's underwear and her mules, from the dressing-room closets or drawers upstairs. The stocking used to be upstairs but recently Mrs. Harris had brought it down and put it in a bag in the downstairs closet. The Madeira book was on the shelf behind the guest bed. The final exhibit is a plastic bag from the medicine cabinet in the guest bathroom; it contains a bottle of Femme de Rochas, Vaseline Intensive Care Hand Lotion, a deodorant, what Suzanne calls a "nail remover," a plastic box containing hairpins and a nail file, a toothbrush, lipstick, a bottle of Johnson's Baby Oil. Bolen asks if any of these items—like items belonging to Lynne?—had been found on the bathroom floor. Aurnou objects but is overruled. Suzanne answers, "No."

Aurnou: What happened, for example, when Mrs. Tryforos stayed over, but Mrs. Harris's things were in the bedroom? What if anything was done about that?
Suzanne: . . . Dr. Tarnower asked me to put them in the closet.
Aurnou: You mean, to hide them?

Bolen objects and is sustained.

Suzanne: The items in the medicine chest would stay. . . . If it was a robe or a nightgown, I would fold it and put it in the drawer of Mrs. Harris.

Aurnou: Tell me this. Let's reverse the situation. Let's suppose that Mrs. Tryforos had been there during the week and Mrs. Harris was coming for the weekend. What if any instructions did the doctor give you with regard to Mrs. Tryforos's belongings?

Suzanne: Oh, I had no instructions from Dr. Tarnower. Most of the time Mrs. Tryforos would take her things away herself.

Aurnou: Did you ever tell the Grand Jury on March 21 that the doctor hid the things belonging to each of the ladies?

Suzanne: Yes.

Aurnou: And if he didn't hide them he would ask you to hide them, isn't that correct?

Suzanne: I would follow his instructions, yes.

Aurnou searches out other discrepancies between her Grand Jury testimony or other statements and her trial statements. She told the Grand Jury that before March 10 Mrs. Harris had last phoned a week earlier but now she says that it was the day before March 10. She'd told the Grand Jury it was the doctor who'd put out his travelling clothes on the dressing-room ledge; now she says it was Lynne. She'd told the Grand Jury that Mrs. Harris made "about five" calls during the week of March 3 but she told investigators that she made no calls that week. "Yes, I made a mistake," says Suzanne. At a preliminary hearing she'd spoken of a time on the night of March 10 when she'd "got out of bed." Now she says she'd returned to her room but not got into bed. In a March 12 interview, she'd said she heard the buzzer again "after" she picked up the phone; now she says she heard it "before" she picked up the phone. "Maybe they didn't understand me. I was very upset that time," says Suzanne. At a pre-trial hearing she'd said that her husband had come upstairs with Officer McKenna, Mrs. Harris, and herself, but now she says she doesn't know if Henri came with them; and on March 12 she said she went upstairs with Mrs. Harris and two police officers. Eventually, as Aurnou tries to establish whether Mrs. Harris touched the dying doctor's face with just one finger or with several fingers, even the Judge protests the hair-splitting. An important language difference remains unexplained to the court as the defense lawyer presses the housekeeper on her varying versions of Mrs. Harris's remark to her about her bruised lip. She had earlier quoted Mrs. Harris as saying, "Oh, he beat me. He used to beat me a lot." Now it has become "Oh, he hit me. He used to hit me a lot." "Do you mean 'hit' or do you mean 'beat'?" Aurnou inquires and Suzanne asks, "Isn't it the same?" *Frapper* and *battre* aren't interchangeable in French—the latter involves the use of an object with which one does the hitting—but I suppose a French person might make them interchangeable in English. Still, the word "used"—"He used to hit me a lot"—introduces an accusation against the doctor by the headmistress. Suzanne has testified that she never knew the doctor to hit or beat Mrs. Harris. Is she imputing to Mrs. Harris a false charge against Tarnower?

At a recess Aurnou holds an impromptu courtroom press conference in which he acknowledges that his many questions about Mrs. Harris's presence in the Tarnower house—the household purchases she'd made and the belongings she'd kept there—were designed not merely to testify to her devotion and the frequency of her visits but also as a reply to the third of the charges for which she's on trial. In addition to being accused of murder and of possessing a gun with intent to do harm, Mrs. Harris is charged with gun possession outside her home or business; her gun was licensed only in Virginia. Aurnou wants to establish that Tarnower's home in Purchase was, at least in her view, Mrs. Harris's home too.

The defense lawyer also wants to tell the press of Mrs. Harris's large quantity of supportive mail, no hate mail at all. He offers to show the reporters some of it. Off the record he quotes from one letter: "The son-of-a-bitch got what he deserved." He also explains that the print of a puppet with no strings on him that Mrs. Harris had given Tarnower for Christmas was just one of the hundred ways Mrs. Harris told the doctor he was free. And he adds that Mrs. Harris had given him only two instructions when he'd become her counsel: he was not to criticize the Madeira School and not to criticize the doctor. Why? "Because she loved him."

At last I've been able to arrange to see the inside of Dr. Tarnower's house—the property has been sold by Mrs. Schwartz for a reported price of $490,000 and is now owned by people named Westheimer. Mr. Westheimer is a cotton broker; he and his wife live in New York—I'm told they use the house for weekends. I've called several times to try to ask permission for a visit but the phone is answered by a clouded male voice; I don't know whether he has at all understood me and I wonder how one leaves so celebrated (shall we call it?) a house in the charge of someone who can't seem even to take a message. (But then there's also the question: why buy a house whose previous owner has been murdered?) Now I finally penetrate the sound barrier and speak with Mrs. Westheimer in the city. What a world of talking ladies we live in—I'd never have had the courage to ask Mrs. Westheimer for the kind of interview she gives me by phone. She says that Henri worked for her alone, no Suzanne, for the first weeks after she got the property but he'd been unsatisfactory—the house and grounds were in an extreme state of neglect—and she'd had to terminate his employment. At any rate, this is the naked story; it's strung with garlands of brilliant details which I have to swear I'll never repeat. I forbear to ask why, if things were in such bad shape when she came into the place, she'd continued to employ one of the servants responsible for the neglect. Mrs. Westheimer generously grants permission for the visit and even says I can bring a court-mate with me. We make the excursion at lunch break.

This time I approach from an opposite direction to the one I took before. We drive past the much-spoken-of Century Country Club and I get a sense of the close-by countryside. And it's a clear winter day, the trees are bare, so I have a better view of the grounds. I realize that the charge I'd made that it was pretentious to call these houses estates was not wholly fair. Certainly Dr. Tarnower's place is minuscule compared to the property that had been given Miss Madeira for her school, but when I look out over the grounds from the balcony of the upstairs bedroom or even from the driveway at the front of the house it's more of an expanse than I'd thought: the land rolls in a pleasant way and it's at the edge of woods. But the house itself doesn't improve on second inspection. Although the façade hasn't as many terraces as I'd re-called, it's just as busy; and the inside is worse than I'd imagined. It's not the fact that the rooms are so few that amazes me—there's a living room, a kitchen, a dining room, and a sort of winglet with two bedrooms and two baths; at the rear of the dining room there's a patio beyond which there's a swimming pool and a tennis court. But all the rooms are of a size more appropriate to a modest garden flat than to a house on a half-million-dollar property. Still, a house could have rooms as small as these without being this . . . this non-existent. For instance, there's no breakfast room though wit-nesses have been testifying to events that took place in it. To be sure, there's a space one comes into from the outdoors. It accom-modates a table at which a person could eat breakfast. But it's neither a dining area nor a foyer; it's just an emptiness into which one enters when one comes through the front door. And as for the kitchen which opens into it, it could make even English housekeeping seem like luxurious modernity. If it was here that Suzanne prepared those gourmet meals of hers, she's indeed an undemanding cook—there's little counter or cabinet space. How did she prepare the food for a dinner party? Where did Henri set down the plates after he'd cleared away a course? And the dining room is an even more deficient area. Is this where the doctor served the meals for which the house was supposed to be noted? It doubled, I could now see, as a trophy room: a great kudu head frowned down upon the table from one end of the cheerless little room while at the other end a door was framed in other antelope antlers. On the side wall were stuffed fish on plaques. Apparently the Westheimers had bought the house from Mrs. Schwartz lock, stock and taxidermy.

The tour continues to the master bedroom; in fact, it concludes there. There's just that one room on the upper floor and, as the trial had made plain, it's not to be reached or departed except by the second flight of the spiral staircase that ascends from the ga-rage. The tortuousness with which this stairway winds was un-avoidable, I suppose, if space had to be rescued for the so-called breakfast room. But Dr. Tarnower built this house himself. He had six acres over which to spread his living quarters: why were they designed without enough room even for a normal flight of stairs and in such fashion that the master bedroom provided no closets and no place for dressers? These had to be improvised in a room divider which robbed the bedroom of desperately needed space. If the whole of the house is claustral—and claustral it is—the doctor's bedroom is a high-priced cell screaming for its walls to come down. I try to think what it would be like for a woman to be brought to this bedroom by a prosperous lover: if this is all the space he can buy with his money, what generosities of feeling should she count on? I also think what it must be like to occupy a room whose owner was murdered, to put one's own pair of beds where his had been and lie each night under the guardianship of his partition—the morbidity this proposes really doesn't need to be underscored by our coming upon a bullet hole in the side of the cabinet on the headboard, near the doctor's mean-sized bathroom. We peer at it in horrified amazement: it's not been mentioned in the trial. But we can be sure it will be: we examine the inside of the cabinet and see that the place where the bullet penetrated the rear wall has been circled in white chalk. We position ourselves where Dr. Tarnower's night visitor would have had to stand for the bullet to find this target—it would have had to be near the head of the staircase. Was this then a first shot in the dark? A last shot before leaving? And what could have splintered the window in the dressing area? I find I have small taste for playing detective on the scene; I prefer the clean fresh air of the courtroom. But before we leave I stop to glance at the tourist-trade ornaments on the shelves over the beds, African or perhaps Caribbean statuettes, and the books which I gather were also included in the Westheimer purchase: *The Ascent of Man, The Joys of Yiddish,* some Modern Library volumes: Milton, Kant, Aristotle, St. Augustine's *Confessions.* When we get back to the main floor—I loathe walking down that staircase: if the ship lurches I'll fall on my face!—we test the buzzer to see if it can be heard in Suzanne's room. With the doors open, perhaps. With the intervening doors closed, impossible. Suddenly the house rattles with the sound of a burglar alarm set off by an approaching repair truck—it's understandable that the Westheimers want warning of uninvited guests.

Outside I congratulate myself for having found the front door of the house in the rain that April day of my previous visit. I miss the forsythia. Today I can see that there's a rowboat on the little lake. The doctor could ferry himself out to that silly island with its misplaced Buddha.

It's Suzanne van der Vreken's sixth day on the stand. It begins with Aurnou angry at the press. Yet again? It seems that someone reprinted his off-the-record quotation from Mrs. Harris's fan letter; he says that now he'll not show anyone her mail. Boo! Once it's become clear to me that the defense counsel is in the business of seducing us writers in whatever fashion suits his purpose, I accept (or don't accept) this as the public-relations aspect of his job; it doesn't have to bother me. But it's different for the media people: they have a daily story to file and if no news is breaking they're eager for copy. I don't think they feel misused; I would in their place.

Cross-examination resumes with Aurnou asking Suzanne to mark where she remembers seeing blood in the bedroom—there's a large floor plan of the doctor's bedroom on a stand near the jury. When he gives her a red pen, the artist in Suzanne rises to the public opportunity—she starts to shade in big red bloodstains. Precipitously Aurnou insists that the red pen doesn't work; he substitutes a black one. According to Suzanne's too-vivid indication, there was blood at the foot of the doctor's bed, between the beds, and between the bed and the doctor's bathroom. She testifies that the back window in the dressing-room area has a screen but that the window was nevertheless broken. The screen was intact. As to Mrs. Harris's condition after the shooting on March 10, Suzanne says, "She seemed very—I don't know if this is the right word—she seemed very high." On March 12 she had said she'd never seen Mrs. Harris "direct anger" toward the doctor. Now she says that she had: "Sometimes. Two times."

Bolen's isn't a gift for probing or clarification, only for confident honesty. On redirect the prosecutor goes over Suzanne's confusion about the "other gentleman" who had been present at her March 12 interrogation. The situation isn't illuminated. He re-establishes that Suzanne and her husband hadn't slept at all the night of March 10; in fact, they'd been in bed only two hours. He has Suzanne recall "when I was talking sometimes with Mrs. Harris, my phone rang and I said, 'I have to go and pick up my phone, excuse me.'" He requests from the witness the number of days that Mrs. Harris spent at Tarnower's house in 1977, 1978, 1979. Suzanne consults her diaries.

1977—63 times
1978—49 times (Suzanne was herself away and has no count for the period between May 26 and June 19)
1979—26 times (Suzanne had been away October 1–13 and July 23–August 14)

Three further points: 1) Whatever the exact hour at which the doctor had come home on the afternoon of March 10, it was after the phone calls from Mrs. Harris. 2) The last time Suzanne had seen Mrs. Harris's clothes before they'd been slashed was two or three days earlier; a jacket that belonged to Mrs. Tryforos had also been torn and slashed.

Bolen: Do you know whether or not the day Mrs. Harris returned home, whether she went to that closet?
Suzanne: No, I don't know.

3) Mrs. Harris had done nothing to ask for help when the doctor was shot.

On re-cross Aurnou gets Suzanne to admit that when she'd responded to the buzzer on the intercom, she hadn't heard any words, so she'd not have known if Mrs. Harris was calling for help. Between 1977 and 1980 Mrs. Harris and the doctor had spent Thanksgiving, Christmas, and "time during the summer" together. Suzanne's diary doesn't indicate the number of days Mrs. Harris spent with the doctor in other parts of the world. He also successfully confuses the issue of whether or not Mrs. Harris knew that the van der Vrekens had a phone of their own by shaking Suzanne on the exact date of installation. He has started a question: "With regard to your ability to recall . . ." Suzanne interrupts self-mockingly: "Which is very poor." Aurnou stops and asks sharply, "Would you read that back, please?" He of course heard it perfectly but he wants the statement repeated for the jury. It's read back. "I'll leave it right there," he says quietly and sits down.

I learn that among the spectators there's a woman who's observing for the American Association of Retired Persons. She's a former psychiatric nurse and she files reports from the courtroom that are read by shut-ins. I don't know whether these are women only or whether she has a male audience too. Certainly the Harris-as-heroine faction is not to be ignored; it announces itself wherever the case is discussed. The other day at the hairdresser's I spoke about the trial with a woman in her late forties. She was very vehement; it was about time, she said, that someone stopped men from getting away with murder. "Do you think women should get away with it?" I ask. She looks at me oddly and I explain: "Aren't you in effect saying that Mrs. Harris killed the doctor but that she was justified? You're convicting her before you've heard the evidence." But I give her pause only for a moment. She shrugs her shoulders: "Yes." She is not a spokeswoman of any organized women's movement; the organized women's movement would be unlikely to choose her as its representative. But like so many women whom I've heard speak about the case she's a ripple from the agitation that has been stirred up in the female population by the movement of liberation—if there can be ripples on a stagnant pool.

I gear myself for long days of police testimony: these are Bolen's witnesses and most of them have appeared at the pre-trial hearings. There are no Kojaks or Starskys and Hutches among them. They're careless men, vulnerable to discreditation. There was much laxity in the handling of police routines. No notes were made in matters that required noting. Reports, when written at all, were incomplete, often self-contradictory. Important evidence—such as the bloody bedclothes from Tarnower's bed—was thrown unmarked into bags for deposit at police headquarters. The blood-spotted rug under the beds in the doctor's bedroom was left where it lay, then rolled up in the garage, then simply got rid of by the van der Vrekens with their lawyer's consent. Even Mrs. Harris's gun had been casually dropped by Detective Siciliano into his jacket pocket, extensively handled before being dusted for fingerprints. Police Chief Harris and Lieutenant Della Rocco of the Detective Squad made telephone calls that night on the bloodied phone in the doctor's bedroom without thought that the phone might be important evidence. Yet there was perhaps extenuation: unless you work by the book, how precise are you likely to be in a situation where it's been freely admitted, as it was by Mrs. Harris, that the gun in the car was hers and that she'd shot the doctor, even giving the police her reasons? Who could have foretold her present elaborate defense?

The first on the stand, as on the crime scene, is Patrolman McKenna; he is followed by Sergeant Carney and Patrolman Larkin. In this last summer McKenna has had a diving accident; he was expected to be permanently paralyzed but he appears to be recovering. He's nevertheless in obvious pain; everyone is solicitous of him. It was McKenna who, patrolling alone in his marked police car on the night of March 10, had received a radio call to go to the Tarnower residence where a possible burglary was reported to be in progress. Flashing his lights, he'd sped along Purchase Street where he'd encountered Mrs. Harris's car making a U-turn. He'd seen her Virginia plates and noted that the car was driven by a woman; he was behind her until she turned into the Tarnower driveway and parked before the house. While he was receiving another transmission on his radio, alerting him to a possible shooting, the woman had approached his car saying, "Hurry up, hurry up! He's been shot!" At the front door was the housekeeper who also told him to hurry. He'd gone upstairs where he'd found the doctor: there was "an awful lot of blood . . . pretty much all over." He'd returned to his car for emergency resuscitation equipment and radioed for an ambulance. Upstairs again, he'd administered oxygen. Later, having helped carry the doctor down the spiral staircase—no mean accomplishment, I could now testify—he'd driven in the ambulance with Police Surgeon Dr. Roth to St. Agnes Hospital in White Plains. There Dr. Tarnower had been pronounced dead. In the pre-trial hearings in October McKenna had testified that Suzanne had said, "Help the doctor, he's shot," and that he'd asked, "Who did the shooting?" Suzanne was then supposed to have looked at Mrs. Harris and replied, "His girlfriend." He had started to repeat this today but had been cut off. Bolen asks about the lighting in the doctor's bedroom. "It was dimly lit," the witness replies. Was the doctor wearing glasses? McKenna didn't see glasses on Dr. Tarnower. On cross-examination Aurnou concentrates upon refreshing the patrolman's earlier recollection that he and Dr. Roth had administered CPR, cardiopulmonary resuscitation, to Tarnower "all the way to the hospital." He asks McKenna to describe CPR and comments, "Of course, if the person had a chest wound, that would cause it to bleed faster." Bolen objects and is sustained.

Sergeant Carney is a law student in his free hours. He had been on desk duty at headquarters the night of the shooting. He is warier today than in October: in the pre-trial hearings it was he who was Mrs. Harris's "liar," the Harrison officer who'd told the Virginia police, "It seems that this apparently was premeditated." They'd used this communication to get a search warrant for the headmistress's house on the Madeira campus. Today when Aurnou asks on cross-examination if it was Carney who called the Virginia authorities, Bolen objects and after a side bar the matter is dropped. Quite so: Bolen had conceded in the preliminary hearings that he wouldn't use the material found in that search. We learn from Carney that at the Harrison police station after her arrest, Mrs. Harris was joined first by Mr. Riegelman and later by Mr. Leslie Jacobson, lawyer friends who said they represented her. Mrs.

Jacobson had accompanied her husband but Carney never saw any of the three give Mrs. Harris a bag of clothes. "There was a small disfigurement on her lip . . . a small bubble." The prisoner had said nothing about other injuries and her conduct had seemed to him to be rational. It was from Carney that Mrs. Harris had learned that the doctor had died. With Tarnower's death the charge of assault in the second degree was changed to murder in the second degree. How, Aurnou asks, did the defendant respond to this? "As I recall," says Carney, "she turned toward her attorney. . . . He put his arm around her. . . . I think if anything substantial happened, I would have remembered it." The examination of Sergeant Carney ends with questions about telephones near the Tarnower residence. Aurnou wants the jury to understand that Mrs. Harris was driving to the nearest outdoor telephone booth, at the Community Center, when McKenna met her.

Patrolman Larkin is so young that eggshell still clings to him. Little emerges from his testimony other than that it was he who drove the ambulance to St. Agnes Hospital—he'd kept his eyes on the road but when he had looked back Roth and McKenna were administering oxygen to Tarnower and also giving him CPR. He eagerly accepts the invitation to describe the Reade (collapsible) stretcher in which Tarnower was wrapped to get him down the difficult stairs and to demonstrate CPR to the jury—this is cruel: one of the women jurors is a cardiac nurse. He remembers the doctor's pajamas as brown and is baffled to discover now that they're blue. The patrolman's raw youth gives Mrs. Harris's lawyer an occasion for paternalism: I decide I'd rather, oh, much rather, be Aurnou's son in real life. Larkin's fingerprint was found on the telephone in Tarnower's bedroom and he's been informed of this by the prosecution; he's therefore not too rattled when Aurnou brings it out. The picture of Tarnower being carried, head first, down those spiral stairs, strapped into a flexible stretcher, is gruesome. Also Larkin reports having overheard Dr. Roth say in the ambulance, "I think we're losing him." Mrs. Harris listens unperturbed, not even putting on her dark glasses. She is reaching for papers on the defense table: there's work to do, the life she is saving is her own.

By now the relation of the two opposing lawyers is one of

overt hostility punctuated by formal courtesies; and I begin to see why Bolen is said to be given to flashes of petulant anger—fortunately they don't last long. But his retreat into righteous silence isn't a help either. Silent, he reminds me of the dissident in Nazi Germany who's handing out blank leaflets on a street corner: a passer-by takes one, looks at it and protests that there's nothing written on it, and the man says, "That's all right, they know what I mean." But I'm not at all sure the jury follows Bolen in some of the points he does pursue. I and most of the people around me certainly have trouble.

With each trying day Judge Leggett becomes more appropriate to his role; he manages to pay unswerving attention to every word that's said and yet at the same time to create an air of relaxation. In questioning Carney about McKenna's call for an ambulance Aurnou had said, "Did he do it by phone, by radio, or by calling out loudly?" Nobody found this funny, the Judge least of all—he looks even more disgusted than Bolen. I don't mind Aurnou's doing this as much as I do his correcting Carney when the sergeant refers to her attorney's "liberty" to speak to Mrs. Harris. Elaborately gentle, Aurnou tells Carney that he doesn't mean "liberty," he means "privilege." The young police officer is studying law: it's unkind to correct this unimportant error. The memory will torture him for a long time.

The woman with whom Mrs. Harris has been living, I think in Scarsdale, has been briefly visiting in court. The relationship is its own remarkable footnote to the life of the unconscious; I've learned about it by accident. The way it's been told me is that the headmistress, out on bail and confined to Westchester, had no place to stay and this woman offered her home as a refuge; it would be a help not alone to Mrs. Harris but also to herself since she lived in a very large house now occupied solely by her and her husband who is bedridden after a severe stroke. I look at this woman who reached out in this curious way to a public figure, the central figure in a murder trial, someone accused of killing the man who for years had been closest to her, and I'm struck by the physical resemblance between the two women: how easily her hostess could be taken to be the defendant's older sister! Aurnou explains to the press group that Mrs. Harris is being sustained by sympathy for this troubled companion: it is someone she can help. Can this complex man be this primitive in psychological understanding?

Day after day for four days Detective Siciliano has been on the stand. He starts bravely enough, even boldly: he all but barks, "Yes, sir," "Exactly, sir," during his first hours of testifying. But with neither youth nor a diving accident to shield him, he's wide open to Aurnou's pounding cross-examination. And even when Bolen is questioning him his mad ineptitude can't be concealed. He's the clone of a television interviewee.

Bolen: What did you do with respect to the door?
Siciliano: Entered through same.

"Where is the gun?" he'd asked Mrs. Harris when he'd come into the house on the 10th. "She said, 'In the car.' I said, 'Would you care to show me?' She said, 'Yes.' . . . Her and O'Sullivan started toward me." They'd gone out where Siciliano "retrieved" the gun which was in the car "centrally located" on what is "commonly known as a bench-type seat." He's shown a photograph of the car and says, "I recognize the car in question."

In the preliminary hearings the testimony of Detective Siciliano had been well at the center of Aurnou's failed attempt to prove that Mrs. Harris had incriminated herself before being given her rights. As the same road is now retraced, Siciliano is surer in his description of Mrs. Harris's resentment at having her rights forced upon her and in his account of the way in which the defendant had virtually forced her story upon *him*. "She told me she had driven up from Virginia to the Tarnower home with the hope of being killed by Dr. Tarnower. She then hesitated a second and said: 'He wanted to live, I wanted to die.' She hesitated. She says, 'I've been through so much hell with him, I loved him very much, he slept with every woman he could, and I had it.' And then she motioned in this fashion. [He makes a pushing-away gesture. When Bolen describes it for the court reporter as an outward motion, Aurnou insists that the words "and down" be added.] Shortly after, she handed me a piece of paper which contained some names she told me she recently prepared and were to be notified in the event her wishes were completed. . . . She also said she had no intentions of going back to Virginia alive. . . . I asked her if she cared to tell me what had happened upstairs. She says her and the doctor had a struggle, the gun went off several times, she asked the doctor to kill her, the doctor said, 'Get out of here, you're crazy!' They started to fight again, and the gun went off several times. I then asked her, 'Who had control of the gun?' She says, 'I don't know.' . . . I then asked her again, 'Who did the shooting? Do you recall holding the gun, or the doctor?' She hesitated and said, 'I remember holding the gun and shooting him in the hand.' Then tears came in her eyes. . . . She asked me if she could see the doctor . . . and I says I don't think it's a good time, or good idea, I don't recall. It just so happened that they were removing the doctor. He passed very close to us. His head was exposed. She put her arms around me and fainted, appeared to faint. . . . I yelled, 'Get a doctor!' . . . An officer sounded off. He says Dr. Roth has just arrived and he will be right in. She immediately got up off the floor and says, 'I don't need a doctor.' So I told her to please sit down again. So she sat at the table and I went back and sat with her."

Bolen asks if Mrs. Harris's conduct appeared rational or irrational. Siciliano replies, "Rational." During this important conversation, says Siciliano, he "took notes at random"—four yellow sheets are marked as evidence. Lieutenant Flick joined the defendant and himself at the foyer table, and Mrs. Harris told him, "'I don't want no medical aid, I had my rights three times.'" Before Siciliano goes upstairs to the bedroom he speaks with Officer Tamilio. "He presented to me a live bullet. . . . I placed it in my right pocket." The doctor has been taken from the house. According to Siciliano, Chief Harris, Captain Marsico, Lieutenant Della Rocco, and Detective Colaneri are in the bedroom. Everything is "disarranged: the sheets, the pillow cases, the mattress cover. . . . I noticed what appeared to be blood, reddish-brown spots between the beds." He sees the phone on the floor and blood spots leading to the doctor's bathroom. He sees a black shawl "neatly placed." He also sees a pair of men's glasses "neatly placed" on a shelf over the doctor's bed. On the shelf above the guest bed is a bouquet of daisies with a note next to it and he finds three live bullets together with some silver coins, a blue brooch, a lady's broken watch, and a pair of slippers on the floor of the guest bathroom. In the dressing area he notes fishing lures, some pieces of jewelry, lady's curlers. There's blood in the doctor's bathroom, on the floor, on the rug, even on the counter, and a trail of blood between the bathroom and the doctor's bed. He has also noticed a bullet hole on the left side of the sliding glass door that opens onto a deck at the front of the house. The hole was about thirteen inches above the floor. Bolen asks if the measurement was exact. "To my knowledge, sir, nothing's exact. . . . I was amazed. The furniture was all intact . . . nothing was overturned . . . the drawer was pulled completely right out . . . but not dislodged." There's a blood spot on an edge of the bedspread on the guest bed. The bedspread from the doctor's bed is on the floor five or six feet beyond the second bed. He identifies the doctor's bedclothes: an orange bedspread, a flat top sheet, a bloodied fitted bottom sheet and mattress cover, pillowcases. He had put them all in one of the pillowcases for Lieutenant Della Rocco to place in a safe at headquarters. He had himself taken the flowers and the "commercial" card signed "Ruth" that was next to it to the police station. Asked about the black shawl, he replies: "To my best recollection, it was left in its respective position." He remembers a glove "just laying below the shawl on top of the bundle." The glove was for the right hand; the glove for the left hand was never recovered. Mrs. Harris, we are reminded, is left-handed. The detective had given Mrs. Harris's gun with the five spent shells in it to Della Rocco for deposit in the police safe.

At about 12:30 that night Siciliano had begun to interview the van der Vrekens whom he characterizes as "extremely nervous." He had told them not to allow anyone upstairs under any circumstances and not themselves to go up "unless it was really necessary." At the police station it was the arresting officer, Siciliano, who had processed Mrs. Harris. The next day, after being up all night, he had accompanied Mrs. Harris with Mrs. Martino, the matron, to the women's unit at the Valhalla jail. There a corrections officer gave him a bullet—this would be the bullet found on Mrs. Harris, tied into the corner of a man's handkerchief—and then he'd returned to the Harrison police department and given the bullet to Lieutenant Della Rocco before going back to the Tarnower house where he'd taken the phone from the bedroom. He believes he obtained a statement then from Suzanne. It was on March 12 that he "confiscated the black shawl"; he names from memory seven items of clothes wrapped up in it: Suzanne had identified them for him as belonging to Mrs. Harris. On the 14th he located a bullet lodged in the left-hand cabinet at the doctor's end of the headboard, and on the 17th he had come back with Della Rocco and a ballistics expert, Joseph Reich. They'd taken pictures and retrieved this bullet. On March 19 Siciliano had taken the gun, the five spent casings, and three bullets removed from Dr. Tarnower's body in the autopsy to Reich.

In the corridor after Bolen's completion of direct examination of Detective Siciliano, Aurnou says that the Jean Harris Defense Fund is pretty much used up; forensic people cost a lot of money. Of Bolen he says, "He seems to think he's St. George fighting the dragon." He points to himself as the dragon.

Leggett has an announcement to make about the Scarsdale letter. On December 5 the Appellate Division of the State Supreme Court had ruled that Aurnou was to turn it over to Judge Leggett who was to read it and decide if, against the protests of the defense, the prosecution should be permitted to see it. Now we are informed that Judge Fuchsberg of the New York State Court of Appeals will hear arguments to determine if they should grant

Aurnou a stay pending further appeal. Aurnou is fighting hard to withhold the contents of the letter. He says that showing it to the prosecution would violate his client's protection against self-incrimination, also the privileged relation of client and lawyer.

By now I ought to be used to Aurnou's procedure in cross-examination. It's entirely correct but doesn't cease to upset me: I seem to have no temperament for watching people being deliberately tripped up or trapped. So far of course the prosecution has been presenting the salient facts in the case. The defense has been chiefly playing for the sympathy of the jury and trying to discredit the prosecution. Aurnou is a virtuoso in both enterprises. He's much more verbally adept than Bolen who often has trouble formulating his questions. We speculate among ourselves about how the jury reacts to this difference between the two attorneys: some of us believe the jury can ignore whether the questions are put well or clumsily and get to the evidential root of whatever is being discussed; others are sure Aurnou is not only knocking Bolen's facts into a cocked hat by his ability to reveal the contradictions in the testimony of the prosecution witnesses but also that he is able to suggest a kind of police undertaking, not a conspiracy, just a guild solidarity, to "get" Mrs. Harris. So far as I can see, the jury is not telling its secret but certainly Bolen's witnesses seem to crumble like graham crackers under Aurnou's questioning—and wouldn't we all! What kind of non-life would one have to live not to collapse under clever cross-examination?

Still, the Harrison police were designed for shredding. Poor brave Siciliano: where now has his initial boldness fled? He's been a policeman thirty years, a detective eleven: softly, Aurnou elicits these assassinating figures. And he is familiar with police procedures? Oh yes, Siciliano assures the court. But he took photographs at the crime scene without keeping note of where or when he took them; he removed evidence without photographing it ("Yes, sir, I just observed them very closely"); he put the doctor's bed linens into the pillowcase without indicating which end was at the head and which at the foot of the bed; he had no concern that one bloodied object might touch another; he didn't take any blankets with him; he doesn't recall if Tarnower's bed had one or two blankets on it; if there were blankets, he doesn't know what happened to them; he'd left the bloodstained rug from under the beds in the doctor's bedroom in the care of the van der Vrekens who had thrown it in the garbage. He'd signed and dated a report March 10 but he now testifies that it was prepared on March 11. In that report Siciliano stated that the bedspread from the doctor's bed had bloodstains on it; he now has a different recollection. In that report he'd stated that a bullet hole in the sliding glass door in the bedroom was fifteen inches above the ground; he now says that it was thirteen inches above the ground but it later turns out that he'd misread his own notes. Aurnou mentions four types of organized evidence searches: Siciliano did none of them. Did he make a metal test on Mrs. Harris's hands? The detective says no, it wasn't necessary. Did he make a memorandum when he moved the telephone? No. How did he secure the upstairs of the house: did he seal the staircase with a piece of string? "A heavy piece of string," says Siciliano. Had Suzanne called him on the 14th to tell him about the chips in the tub of the guest bathroom?

Siciliano: I asked her when she had time to enter the scene and anything unusual to let me know immediately.
Aurnou: And four days later she called you to talk to you about the chips in the bathroom?

At least three people, possibly more, had handled the gun before it was put in a plastic bag for safekeeping. Was Siciliano aware that a plastic bag can obliterate fingerprints?

Siciliano: I would imagine so.
Aurnou: You used the word imagine. You have been a police officer thirty years and a detective eleven. Correct?
Siciliano: Yes, sir.
Aurnou: May I suggest that you know that for a fact?
Siciliano: O.K., sir. Thank you. I appreciate it.

Had he checked the gun for bloodstains and made note of his findings? Did he mark the empty chamber position? On the night of the 12th were pictures taken of the gun, the shells, the inside or outside of Mrs. Harris's car? Were the dimmer and buzzer in the doctor's bedroom dusted for fingerprints? To all these questions, the answer is the same: no. Eventually, when we decide that Aurnou must surely have exhausted his fire, he opens yet another line of attack. He asks Siciliano whether he's ever been obscene in relation to the defense. It develops that at a time when Siciliano was at the Tarnower house several of Aurnou's investigators had appeared to serve Suzanne and Henri with subpoenas. How, Aurnou inquires, had Siciliano responded to them? Siciliano would have us think that he'd casually waved them away, but Aurnou has a photograph—taken from where? Did he have yet another investigator perched in a tree?—to prove that Siciliano had given them "the finger." The court laughs in relief after the build-up of tension, Mrs. Harris joining heartily, as the detective tries to recall whether it was his index or his middle finger that he'd employed in the gesture.

Aurnou: This gesture that you made, that was not you showing them your badge, was it?
Siciliano: No, sir, in no shape, form, or manner!

Has the defense scored with this brief interlude of fun? I can suppose so; even more than it discredits Siciliano, it indicates Aurnou's abiding confidence. Bolen intervenes: he'd like to get back to "something relevant in this trial." All laughter at once disappears from Mrs. Harris's face. Furious, she rises slightly in her seat to hiss something in Bolen's direction. Her venomous intention can't be missed, though even in the press rows in the front of the court, only a few yards from her table, we can't hear her words. The nice young man assigned by Aurnou to stay at her side pats her shoulder to soothe her, also to give her warning: a woman accused of murdering her lover in a fit of rage can't afford this show of temper. But I also think she can't afford the kind of attention she gives to her defense. She acts as if she were Aurnou's prize legal assistant. She not only takes notes but also reaches into the defense files on their table for papers or photographs as she thinks her counsel should have them.

There's a detail in Siciliano's cross-examination that bothers me. The bottom sheet of Dr. Tarnower's bed was fitted. We've been told that the room and the bed were "disarranged" but a fitted sheet doesn't slip off easily, of itself. Was there an explanation of how the bed came to be this disarranged, and have I missed it? Aurnou asked, "At that time did you observe whether or not the bloodstain that you saw on the fitted sheet was also on the mattress cover?" and Siciliano replied, "I would say they were different locations." Nothing has been made of this.

I make a note to myself. However egregious they may be, the errors of the Harrison police prove only their ineptitude; they are not proof of Mrs. Harris's innocence. But a view such as this requires that we hold two negative judgments in mind at the same time and nothing in our culture prepares us for so difficult a feat. Wherever there's wrongdoing on one side, we're accustomed to take it as proof that the opposite side is virtue incarnate.

Jean Harris's sister, Mrs. Virginia McLaughlin, is in court—how supportive this family is being. The sister is markedly different in style from Mrs. Harris. Where the defendant is all small-framed, small-featured prettiness, Mrs. McLaughlin has a kind of pleasant-faced sturdiness—she might be in the Peace Corps. Her hair has been allowed to go a mottled gray and is cut for freedom from care. I very much like the way she looks: no Gucci bags for her; she wears a lumpy pullover sweater lettered "M." Someone tells me it's for Michigan. Michigan what? At recess today Mrs. Harris introduces her visitors to each other like a cocktail-party hostess.

D etective Siciliano's last morning on the stand is largely taken up with questions from Aurnou about the emotional state of the defendant on the night of the shooting. Her lawyer wants to know, Was she crying, was she upset? Siciliano testifies that when he spoke with her, Mrs. Harris appeared to be upset "to an extent" and had probably been crying.

Judge Leggett had ruled that Aurnou was not to ask the witness if Mrs. Harris appeared to be sincere the night of the 10th but now in re-cross he says he has reversed himself so Aurnou asks Siciliano, "Did she appear to you on that evening to be answering you sincerely?" Siciliano replies, "I assumed she did." This leads to another lengthy side bar, after which Aurnou puts a different question: "When you asked her who did the shooting . . . did she appear to you to be very sincere?" Whether or not Siciliano sees the trap doesn't matter; there's no way out. "Appeared, sir. Yes, sir," he replies. Bolen has the last question: had the defendant at any time on the night of the 10th seemed to be acting? "Yes, sir," says Siciliano. Leggett announces the usual morning recess and the jury leaves the room. Mrs. Harris turns on Aurnou, gesticulating in anger. We can't hear what she says but we can see her hands shaking; she storms out the rear door to the Judge's chambers, returns to pick up her coat, stalks out again with Aurnou at her heels. The Judge and the other defense lawyers also leave. After about ten minutes, during which it's reported that she's striding up and down the rear corridor, Mrs. Harris comes back to the courtroom, still in her coat, and sits down in the front row of the press section. She addresses the reporters: "We have a sworn statement in the Grand Jury that we weren't permitted to make public, but I'm going to make it public later on." The youngest member of the defense team, the one whom we've taken to calling her baby-sitter, tries to speak to her. "Shut up," she snaps. "If you say that again, I'll . . ." The rest is lost or may not have been spoken. It's not yet noon but Judge Leggett quickly announces the lunch break. In the corridor Aurnou holds an impromptu press conference. Mrs. Harris is offended and hurt, he explains, because the Judge wouldn't allow him to read from pre-trial testimony in which Siciliano had said she was sincere. The reporters, or most of them, go off to lunch but the *Times* and UPI men are delayed. They're standing outside the courtroom door as Mrs. Harris returns to the hall followed mutely by Aurnou. She addresses Mr. Feron of the *Times* by name, tells him to come over to her. Aurnou and the UPI man follow. "This was the place for the truth to come out," says Mrs. Harris, "but I discovered it's not going to come out so I'm going to start talking to the press." She has the pre-trial transcript in her hand and reads Siciliano's statement of October 9—"She was very sincere"—and of October 14 —"She had answered me sincerely." "That was not permitted to be

119

read for the jury," says Mrs. Harris. "When that happens again and the jury is not allowed to hear the truth, I'm going to come out here and read from the script." She uses the word "script" instead of "transcript" with no apparent awareness that she's just been accused of playacting. As to the seemingly opposed statements —Siciliano's that Mrs. Harris was acting and Mrs. Harris's that the detective had previously described her as sincere and must therefore now be lying—they of course needn't contradict each other at all. The officer had distrusted Mrs. Harris's fainting spell when Tarnower's body was being brought downstairs; as soon as he'd called for a doctor, she'd sprung back to her feet. He no doubt regarded this as "acting." But when she'd told him that she'd shot the doctor and her reasons for doing it, he'd thought her sincere. Now it's to the advantage of neither side to make this distinction: the prosecution wants the jury to think of Mrs. Harris as playacting; Aurnou wants the jury to think that Siciliano is lying.

After a morning that has been climaxed by this much drama—unseen by the jury—the afternoon is unexciting. Mrs. Harris is again composed. Rumor has it that during the extended lunch hour her psychiatrist was called in to see her.

With convincing simplicity and directness, Debbie Raizes, Dr. Tarnower's niece and friend of Lynne Tryforos, answers questions about dinner at her uncle's house on the night of the 10th: no, there had been no phone calls while she'd been there. And she testifies that Uncle Hi always wore glasses. She resolutely avoids looking in Mrs. Harris's direction. Aurnou has no questions to ask her.

Detective Colaneri, next on the stand, is so boring, his voice trailing off into inaudibility, that one reporter falls asleep. Colaneri took general pictures in connection with the shooting but doesn't recall how many: he made no notes, he doesn't know what happened to his pictures. He took blood scrapings from between the two beds, from the floor at the doctor's end of the headboard, from the floor of the doctor's bathroom, and on the morning of the 11th he'd turned over the blood samples and bed linens to the forensic lab. Except he hadn't. He didn't turn over the blood samples—virtually everything he says he seems to unsay a few minutes later. Asked by Bolen whether he saw anyone touch the phone in Tarnower's bedroom, he says no. Asked the same question by Aurnou, he names Chief Harris, Captain Marsico, Lieutenant Della Rocco.

Aurnou: He [Della Rocco] just picked up the bloodstained telephone and he held it to his ear?
Colaneri: Yes.
Aurnou: And he is the chief of detectives?
Colaneri: Yes.

Aurnou inquires whether he took pictures between the twin beds, in the area of the doctor's bathroom, in the area outside the bathroom. To each of these questions Colaneri replies, "Yes."

Aurnou: Where are those photographs?
Colaneri: I don't know.

There's a potentially awkward moment when Aurnou, chiding the detective, asks him how much time he has spent as a police officer, except that Colaneri seems undisturbed. He glances toward the jury but coyly, not in embarrassment. "In front of all these people?" He then replies: "Thirty-three years."

Judge Leggett once more reverses himself; it has to do with Siciliano's testimony about "acting." The Judge has opened court today with an instruction to the jury that it is to disregard the question put to Siciliano about acting and Siciliano's reply to it because "the way it was framed invited speculation." Aurnou tells a member of the press that the reversal is Leggett's own; it was not asked for by the defense.

A new series of prosecution witnesses is led by Detective Areson testifying to the chain of certain physical evidence. It was Areson who had taken Mrs. Harris's clothes, her fur coat, a white bra, two pantyhose, from Sergeant Brown at the Valhalla jail and transported these and other items to the forensic lab. He'd also transported the gun, five spent shells, and three autopsy bullets to the Harrison police headquarters from the ballistics lab.

Patrolman Daniel O'Sullivan, next on the stand, looks strangely changed since October: gaunt, haunted. What's happened to him? He tells of his arrival at the Tarnower residence with Patrolman Tamilio, just ahead of Siciliano. In the foyer he'd seen Jean Harris and Suzanne and he'd gone to her car with Mrs. Harris and with Detective Siciliano; while Siciliano opened the door on the driver's side, he had opened the one on the passenger's side—he saw the gun on the front seat and he saw Siciliano pick it up. Back at the table in the foyer he'd been behind Mrs. Harris while she and Siciliano spoke. Then he'd helped bring Dr. Tarnower down on the stretcher and later he'd heard Mrs. Harris ask a male servant [Henri], " 'Who was at dinner tonight? Who did he have here?' "

Bolen: The tone of voice?
O'Sullivan: Normal.
Bolen: Softly?
O'Sullivan: No, loud.

Returning to an earlier moment on the evening of the 10th, Bolen asks what Mrs. Harris had said in O'Sullivan's hearing.

O'Sullivan: Mrs. Harris stated that the doctor was upstairs and that he had been shot. . . . She volunteered that. . . . Detective Siciliano asked her who shot him. . . . She stated that she did. . . . Detective Siciliano then advised her of her rights.

Aurnou objects that the word "rights" is "conclusory" and Leggett sustains the objection. This strikes me as ridiculous: in the context it's a neutral noun; it's been used repeatedly. Bolen sits down in a sulk. Morning recess is called and when it ends Bolen says he's finished direct examination of the witness. Personal offense is written all over him. If the newspaper people, used and misused as they have been, were as personal as the lawyers, this would be the most unreported case in history. The defense has little to add in cross-examination, several things to re-affirm.

Aurnou: You were able to see the revolver [on the car seat]?
O'Sullivan: Yes.
Aurnou: Was it hidden any way, or tucked behind anything, or was it out in perfectly plain view, right in the middle of the front seat?
O'Sullivan: Perfectly plain view, in the middle of the front seat.

Aurnou: Would you describe for us how [Detective Siciliano took the gun]?

O'Sullivan: I believe he grabbed it by the handle. [In pre-trial, Siciliano had said he'd taken it "by the barrel."]

Aurnou: Are you sure, or are you saying it's my best recollection?

O'Sullivan: It would be my best recollection.

Aurnou: At any point that evening while you were near or in the presence of my client, did you hear her say the words "Why didn't you kill me, Hi?"

O'Sullivan: I believe I did, yes.

Aurnou: Did you also at one point in that evening observe my client faint?

O'Sullivan: Yes.

Aurnou: Did you also have occasion to observe the area of her mouth at some time during the evening?

O'Sullivan: It was bruised and there was swelling.

Aurnou: At any time during the entire evening when you heard her speaking, did she say anything about wanting to kill or harm Dr. Tarnower?

Objection sustained.

Aurnou: Did you hear her say that she had come up from Virginia and that she wanted herself to die?

Objection sustained.

Aurnou: Did you hear her indicate that it was her intention that she never return to Virginia alive?

O'Sullivan: Yes.

Aurnou: Did she ever use the word "intent" in connection with Dr. Tarnower?

Objection sustained. There's now a protracted wrangle as to whether O'Sullivan heard her use the word "struggle" or the word "fight." On October 17 hadn't he testified that the gun "went off during a struggle"? O'Sullivan recollects using the word "fight." Aurnou reads from the pre-trial transcript: the word he used was "struggle."

Aurnou: Did you hear her answer that she did not know [who had control of the gun]?

O'Sullivan: Yes.

Can he describe her manner when she said that?

O'Sullivan: I would describe it as being quiet and reserved.

Aurnou: That evening did you also hear Mrs. Harris say, "Why should *he* die, I wanted to die"?

O'Sullivan doesn't recall. Aurnou refreshes his recollection. He asks did she say "while she was struggling with the doctor several shots were fired"? O'Sullivan doesn't recall. Aurnou refreshes his recollection.

Aurnou: And at the same time did you hear Detective Siciliano ask her who pulled the trigger? . . . did you hear Mrs. Harris say that she did not know?
O'Sullivan: That's correct.
Aurnou: Did you also hear my client say, sir, that she asked the doctor to kill her because she wanted to die?
O'Sullivan: Yes.

So here we are again. It was from Officer O'Sullivan's testimony back in March that the early widely distributed version of Mrs. Harris's motive in coming to Tarnower's house that night—her wish to have her lover kill her—had come. Still, it *was* possible that O'Sullivan had only heard Mrs. Harris say what he was now confirming, that she had asked the doctor to kill her because she wanted to die, and then it had been given a wider context than she intended, therefore also a mistaken interpretation.

In redirect, Bolen reads from O'Sullivan's testimony at a preliminary hearing on March 14: "She stated that Dr. Tarnower and herself had an argument and a fight. . . . Dr. Tarnower had pushed her away and told her, 'Get out of here, you're crazy!' " It turns out, in fact, that the word "fight" occurred in O'Sullivan's original report, but in re-cross Aurnou paraphrases O'Sullivan's earlier statements—he wishes to drive home to the jury the use, his own use, of the word "struggle."

How is the prosecution served by calling another and yet another of these Harrison police officers? They get up on the witness stand and reply to Bolen's direct questioning with convincing simplicity, then along comes Aurnou and down go the bowling pins. Of course the chain of events has to be established and each of these witnesses has his contribution to offer. And two of them, Lieutenant Flick and Patrolman Tamilio, manage to hold up if only by virtue of their self-possession and ability to pit their own personal integrity against the force of Aurnou's discreditation of them. Flick is particularly attractive: he has the frown of intelligence—he seems, that is, to have the kind of knowledge that's bred in thoughtful self-doubt. Tamilio has a pug-faced charm. It was Tamilio who'd brought a backup oxygen unit from his car for McKenna to use on Tarnower. Looking for a means of getting the doctor out without having to negotiate the spiral staircase, he'd found the live bullet in the dressing-room area and given it to Siciliano. And downstairs he'd accompanied Mrs. Harris when she'd gone to call her lawyer on the van der Vrekens' phone—he'd heard her say to Mr. Jacobson, "Oh my God, I think I've killed Hi!" Mr. Jacobson had then briefly spoken to Lieutenant Flick. Tamilio saw Mrs. Harris stop at the bathroom mirror near Suzanne and put her hand to her face, and he'd heard her say, "He hit me, he hit me a lot." Although he reports Henri's presence in the room while Mrs. Harris was on the phone, he doesn't mention her telling her lawyer that Henri was looking at her as if he'd like to kill her.

On cross-examination Aurnou makes as much as he can of Tamilio's ability to find the .32-caliber bullet in a room that was supposedly so dimly lit. But he moves on.

Aurnou: When you saw the bullet, was there any urgency about picking it up at that time?

Tamilio: No, sir.

Aurnou: Did you do anything to mark the precise location in which the bullet was at the time that you moved it?

Tamilio: No, sir.

Aurnou: You just picked it up and put it in your pocket?

Tamilio: Yes, sir.

Aurnou: . . . Did you make any notation anywhere before going down that spiral staircase for anything?

Tamilio: No.

Questioned by Bolen about Mrs. Harris's condition he agrees that the defendant had appeared faint: he'd assisted her into and out of her chair when she'd gone to phone. Under cross-examination he testifies that no, he had never heard Mrs. Harris say "he beat me" or "he used to beat me a lot" although he did hear her say "he hit me a lot." When she'd commented on her appearance in the mirror she'd been "very soft-spoken . . . like she was talking to herself." As she talked on the telephone to her lawyer, however, her voice had been "higher than what I heard her talking in the kitchen to the lieutenant. Excited."

We learn that the matter of the Scarsdale letter is before the New York State Court of Appeals and that at the beginning of next week they'll hear Aurnou's plea for a stay on complying with the determination that its contents must be shown to Judge Leggett so that he can decide if the prosecution should read it. Aurnou has made so many moves to protect its contents that by now most of us begin to think that we're being built up for a giant letdown.

An investigator from the D.A.'s office, Donald Raab, takes the stand to give further details of the routes that were travelled by clothes, bedding, bullet fragments—it was Raab who had removed the doctor's eyeglasses from the shelf behind the bed and taken them to Dr. Forrest, a White Plains ophthalmologist. It's a boring narrative; our interest isn't roused until Aurnou asks what other items besides the glasses the investigator had taken from Tarnower's bedroom and Raab mentions phone and address books which are now in the D.A.'s evidence room. Aurnou demands to see them. In fact, he proposes that there may very well be all sorts of evidence that was gathered at the Tarnower house that he hasn't seen—it sounds very conspiratorial. Leggett directs Bolen to produce whatever he has; the Judge will himself inspect it and decide what is or isn't relevant. This requires a long break that overlaps the lunch hour: Bolen has gone to his office nine floors below. But finally Aurnou retrieves his "goodies," among them personal notepaper belonging to Mrs. Harris and various forms and documents from the Madeira School. Aurnou pounces upon them speedily: they'll help establish Jean Harris's residential status in the Tarnower house. He's also pleased to discover photographs of the doctor without glasses; he circulates these among the jury.

After the Harrison police force and the D.A.'s investigator, medical testimony promises lurid relief. It seems that Dr. Marrero, next on the stand, was at St. Agnes Hospital when Tarnower had been brought in on the night of the shooting. Medical personnel had been alerted and preparation made in the emergency room but it was too late: there was no respiration, no heartbeat, no blood pressure—Tarnower arrived wearing an oxygen mask and being given external cardiac massage. In emergency they'd given him blood intravenously but had had to use the left arm because the right arm was at a ninety-degree angle—it was flailing about. Cardiac shock couldn't start the heart again. Fifteen hundred cc.'s of blood had been drawn from Tarnower's chest cavity. The doctors had worked for twenty minutes before they'd given up. Tarnower's pupils were fixed and dilated; just before midnight the doctor had been pronounced dead.

We are all of us unnerved by the vividness of the testimony—Mrs. Schwartz has left the room crying—but Mrs. Harris hasn't even put on her dark glasses, up to this moment the only sign she's given that she's present except as someone actively, often angrily, engaged in her own defense. For instance, Aurnou has inquired in cross-examination about the doctor's pajama jacket. It is badly torn; how had it been got off his body? With her usual speed of response the defendant reaches for her ubiquitous yellow note pad and quickly draws a picture of her lover's sleeping garment which she passes to the lawyer—the doctor's pajama jacket was the two-button variety; it would have had to be ripped down the middle below the buttons to be removed. I glance toward the jury: do they see what I see, do they think what I think? Good God, if she truly came only for her own death, how can she endure this description of what actually resulted from her intended suicide? How can she bear to draw a picture of the pajama top that, because of her, was soaked in the doctor's blood? Unless one is in the courtroom constantly observing Mrs. Harris, one has no means of knowing about her impenetrable self-absorption, her unmediated dedication to her own freedom, vindication, whatever it is she's fighting for. The attention with which the news reporters who are regularly assigned to Mrs. Harris's case have followed this trial, the care they take to make their stories as accurate as they can under the trying circumstances of the courtroom, inquiring of one another about any interpretation of the evidence that is elusive, has earned my deepest respect. But it's not the job of a news reporter to be concerned with the character of the defendant in a murder trial or in the psychological disposition of anyone in the courtroom, not the defendant's, not the Judge's, the lawyers', the witnesses', the spectators'. It's not part of the "story" to which the journalists have been assigned, unless of course it should erupt into action, something that constitutes an incident. If Mrs. Harris were to cry, this would be a reportable fact, but if Mrs. Harris fails to cry when she *should* cry, when she might normally cry, the imagination of what this failure portends belongs to a different kind of writing. When Stephen Crane was trying to make a journalistic career and was sent to report a fire, he wrote about the sparks struck by the fire horses' hoofs racing through the cobbled streets and lost his job—no doubt rightly. That wasn't what a reporter is paid to report. Still, several times the news people have reported that Mrs. Harris cried when I hadn't seen a tear. It's as if they have the moral need to find expectable emotions even where they don't exist.

Detective Della Rocco is next on the stand: he arrived at the Tarnower house after the doctor was removed. He describes what he saw in the bedroom and bathrooms: jewelry on the dressing-room floor, three live shells on the floor of the guest bathroom, yet another live shell on the floor of the bedroom near the guest bed, a shoe on the floor, a box of hair curlers on the floor, bloodstains between the beds and at the foot of the doctor's bed, blood on the washstand in the doctor's bathroom, blood on the shelf between the beds. He'd used the bedroom phone just after Chief Harris had used it, bloodstains notwithstanding—Aurnou is shocked. The phone, back on its cradle, was on the floor; the detective had kneeled to dial. He recalls blood on both beds; that is to say, there was blood on the bedspread of the guest bed. On March 11, Della Rocco accompanied Colaneri and another officer to the house to look for a bullet that had gone through the glass door. They hadn't found it but did find "a marking on the balcony." There's a moment during the detective's testimony when there's dissension between Aurnou and Bolen about how Della Rocco should mark a floor plan and Judge Leggett makes a decision displeasing to Mrs. Harris. She cries out: it isn't loud but it's audible. Why had she not cried out, softly but audibly, as she heard of the doctor's failed vital signs, of his eyes fixed in death, the pupils dilated?

Dr. Harold Roth is a thoracic surgeon and a volunteer police surgeon for Harrison. He has also been a police surgeon for New York City—one knows of fire buffs, it's the first I hear of a police medical buff. He'd arrived at the Tarnower house as Tarnower was being put in the ambulance and had accompanied him to the hospital. At first he'd been able to feel a weak pulse and had administered cardiac massage but by the time they'd got to St. Agnes there was neither heartbeat nor respiration: he thinks that Tarnower died—"expired"—in the ambulance. The right arm had been wholly disarticulated; on the trip to the hospital it had had to be restrained.

On cross-examination Aurnou undertakes to establish that in a case of chest wounds with severe bleeding, nothing is more important than to get the patient to a hospital as fast as one can. He should go in a car at once, without waiting for an ambulance.

Aurnou: If you had had seven or ten minutes more . . . would that have made a difference in his ability to survive?
Roth: It might very well, yes. . . . Any minutes would have made a difference.
Aurnou: You would have . . . met him [at the hospital], correct?
Roth: Yes, sir.

Aurnou asks if all those wounds could have been caused in a struggle between a 5′10″ 175 lb. man and a 5′4″ 115 lb. woman. "There is nothing in medical science that makes that impossible, correct?"

Roth: Anything is possible, sir. Yes, sir.

Interrupted by lengthy side bars, Roth manages to testify that he'd examined Mrs. Harris at the police station later that evening and seen a small abrasion, about a half-inch in diameter, below her right knee as well as the bruise on her lip. On redirect, Bolen establishes that the physician has no personal knowledge of the sequence of shots that struck Tarnower or of who handled the gun; also that he knows nothing about how the police responded in the situation. What nevertheless remains most firmly in mind from his testimony is the statement elicited by Aurnou that the doctor's life might have been saved had he been got to a hospital more promptly. On redirect, however, Bolen introduces the possibility that the bullet that entered Dr. Tarnower's palm and exited through the rear of his hand could have been what is known as the classic "defensive wound," produced when a person under attack tries to grab or ward off a weapon. Mrs. Harris laughs aloud at this suggestion and looks at Bolen in scorn.

Dr. Roth is followed on the stand by Tarnower's ophthalmologist, Dr. Arnold Forrest, who testifies that Dr. Tarnower had 20/200 farsighted vision. This means that "without his glasses he could only see the top letter on the chart." Forrest prescribed the bifocals found on the shelf behind the bed. Asked how Tarnower would have managed without glasses, he says, "He would not see details." Cross-examining, Aurnou demonstrates that even people like himself, who customarily wear glasses, don't require them under all circumstances. He removes his glasses and circumnavigates his section of the courtroom without accident; in the process he describes several articles of clothing worn by the jurors. It's good show biz but of course the condition of Aurnou's eyes hasn't been established. I don't understand why Bolen doesn't object. His silences bewilder me. Although Dr. Forrest testifies that Tarnower's vision wasn't "a very big problem," the fact that he hadn't put on his eyeglasses adds, I feel, to the atmosphere of unnaturalness surrounding Mrs. Harris's visit. It's of a piece with her entering the house through the garage.

Anthony Califana, Bolen's next witness, is a fingerprint man from the Westchester Department of Public Safety. There were no fingerprints on the gun, he tells us, but yes, there'd been several on the telephone including one, clearly visible in blood, from the little finger of Patrolman Larkin's left hand. This we already know.

It's been a dreary day but eventually, all unexpectedly, we're given our due of grim drama. Frederick Drummond is a forensic serologist. He'd tested Tarnower's autopsy blood and examined the bloody bedclothes on Tarnower's bed. On the fitted sheet he'd found "a large variety of red-brown spots from the top of the sheet to the bottom of the sheet . . . a large area toward the central part of the sheet which had a copious amount of blood. Further out, towards the head and foot end of the sheet, there were lesser amounts of droplet-type of blood." There were stains on both sides of the bedspread. Judge Leggett gives the jury a brief recess so that the defense can have time to examine the bed linens. Usually when there's a recess most of the press people go out in the corridor but today the exodus is arrested by the sight of what Mrs. Harris is doing—it's a scene none of us will ever forget. Oblivious of our presence just a few yards away, not only Aurnou and Victor Grossman, the chief defense assistant, but Mrs. Harris herself are looking at the sheets. Mrs. Harris is tracing with her fingers the extent and the distribution of the doctor's blood; she might be describing the design in an abstract painting. There's not a glimmer of pain in her expression, no reluctance or distaste in her examination of the evidence. The bloodied sheets are but another datum in her self-defense. Mrs. Harris's "baby-sitter" looks at us shyly, murmurs, "I never could stand blood," and removes himself from what's happening before our eyes. But instinct has deserted Aurnou— are we not supposed to think that Tarnower was shot in a "tragic accident" when the headmistress had come to say good-bye to him, the person she loved most in the world? Later I look back on this scene and crazily remember how dully unattractive the flower pattern of the sheets was in contrast to the pattern of the doctor's blood. Dr. Tarnower seems to have dominated the women close to him even in their taste in home furnishings. There's nothing, not even the bed linens, on which Suzanne or Mrs. Harris or Lynne Tryforos, any of them who was in a position to shop for him, spent his money to good effect.

Returned to the stand, Drummond tells of the gun brought to him by Reich. There were small bloodstains "on the cylinder, on the hammer, and inside the frame area where the cylinder usually sits"; no stains on the trigger, the barrel, the grip, the ejector rod. All the spots were small but "possibly the hammer was a little bit more extensive than the cylinder." The blood tested Type B, that of the doctor. Later, a defense witness will say, but no use will be made of the information, that Jean Harris is Type B too. Now it is accepted that Mrs. Harris's blood was nowhere—remarkable in a struggle between a man and a woman, he so much the taller and heavier of the two. Only he was wounded, repeatedly and fatally, while she suffered no worse injury than an abrasion of the lip. On March 12 the serologist had gone to the house and taken blood scrapings "on the rugging of the bedroom and also on the wooden floor and the tile floor of the bathroom." Together with Califana's testimony that there were no Harris fingerprints on the gun, Drummond's testimony that blood was found only in hidden parts of the gun suggests that Mrs. Harris wiped it clean of both prints and blood but failed to get into the recesses. When, though, and where could she have done this: in the bathroom before she banged the weapon on the bathtub in order to empty it for re-loading, or as she went to the car? And with what? So far no one has explained the source of the blood on the telephone shelf or on Mrs. Harris's blouse. We still haven't been told how the puddle of blood got into the middle of the doctor's sheet. But the word "puddle" is less accurate than it might be. The bloodstain that Mrs. Harris was studying so attentively looked to me to be roughly circu-lar in shape, more or less (I couldn't of course be sure) in the center of the fitted sheet, a bit larger in diameter than a bread-and-butter plate. It confuses me that it's this centered: we've had no evi-dence that, once shot, the doctor went back to bed. When Bolen returns to his direct examination of Drummond and asks his wit-ness to describe where he saw blood, Drummond says that it was on the left-hand side of the doctor's bed, then in a trail between the bedroom and the dressing area into the doctor's bathroom. There had been stains on the floor of the bathroom near the base of the vanity or sink area, none in the sink itself. Another trail led from the bathroom almost to the foot of the bed where it ceased, picking up again in the area between the two beds. There was a good deal of blood on the shelf, smearing of the stain, and a series of small finely divided spots about a foot above the clock-radio. The second bed, which Suzanne had called the guest bed, was devoid of bloodstains except on its left-hand side—that is, the side toward the other bed—and the witness had seen no stains at all in the dressing area. Bolen wants to probe further into the "finely divided" pinpoint stains on the partition shelf but strenuously and successfully Aur-nou circumvents him on the ground that Drummond is not an ex-pert on splattering—if the nature of these stains is as crucial to the prosecution's case as both lawyers now make it seem, it could be because Bolen wishes to establish that they came from Tarnower's painfully splintered right arm which had caused him to fall to the floor taking the phone with him; this would then be either the last shot, because it was the only one that Suzanne heard, or the next to the last, one of the several she didn't hear. Not permitted this line of inquiry, Bolen moves on to the piece of metal found in the post on the deck in front of the glass door in Tarnower's bedroom. No blood was found on this fragment. Therefore, in Drummond's view, the bullet that penetrated the door hadn't first gone through Tarnower's hand as Aurnou would have us believe. There was also no blood on Mrs. Harris's fur coat or on her skirt, but it had apparently penetrated to her bra under the left arm. Direct examination of Drummond ends, as does so much of Bolen's questioning of his witnesses, with nothing tied up, nothing for the jury to hold on to. The witness has been asked, for instance, about the chips in the enamel of the guest bathtub: what had particles in this area turned out to be? "Human blood," Drummond replies, and nothing further is made of this information. But if the gun was as clean as reported when it was taken from Mrs. Harris's car, how could it have been sufficiently bloody to have left blood on the bathtub—unless Mrs. Harris cleaned it before leaving, or in the car? Bolen has also inquired of various witnesses about the condition of Mrs. Harris's hands. Is he proposing that with the doctor bleeding to death on the floor, Mrs. Harris had washed the gun *and* her hands before she went—as she says—for help? And if so, why doesn't he pin it down? Cross-examination gives Aurnou the opportunity for a show of scientific erudition which, if it does nothing else, at least diverts the jurors from thinking about Drummond's testimony.

After Drummond comes Dr. Samarenda Basu, a Calcutta Ph.D who works at the New York State Police lab. Basu speaks in a liltingly accented English, pronouncing many words, especially technical ones, in such a way that the court reporter is hard put to follow him. One hears the jurors trying to help—until they come up against such twisters as "energy-dispersive" or "electron microscopy." And finally the witness undoes even the bravest of his well-wishers with his attempt to explain what is meant by an element. "Those of us who have taken physics would be familiar with what you are saying," Bolen whistles into the dark. Aurnou objects. Leggett sustains the objection: "Yeah, you're assuming something that's definitely not in evidence." He's eased the strain in the courtroom. Basu manages at last to make his point for the prosecution—a metal fragment taken from the post on the bedroom deck contains the same metals as a live bullet found at Tarnower's house that March evening—except that Aurnou pursues his customary diversionary tactic and in cross-examination goes into a disquisition on neutron-activation analysis, describing it as a different (no doubt better?) type of metal analysis from that used by the witness. From this he slides without a bump into a series of irrelevant, by now familiar questions about metal-tracing that might have been done on the hands of both Mrs. Harris and Dr. Tarnower. Although this in no logical way undermines Basu's testimony, it reinforces the case that Aurnou has been making against the Harrison police, or appears to.

A strange point of his own that Aurnou seems to be making throughout his questioning of Bolen's witnesses is that the doctor had had a bit too much to drink earlier on the evening of the 10th: sherry before dinner, wine at dinner, champagne after dinner in celebration of Suzanne's birthday. If everything was as open and amiable between Mrs. Harris and her lover upon her arrival that evening as he would have us believe, why does Aurnou want to plant the idea that Tarnower went to bed befuddled? Anyway, now the question would appear to be settled. Basu's successor as prosecution witness is Joan Vogel, a Vassar graduate. She is a toxicologist in the Westchester Department of Laboratories and Research, testing blood, urine, and tissues for drugs, and had tested Tarnower's blood and bile for some twenty to twenty-five drugs. All had proved negative. Was alcohol one of the substances she looked for? Bolen asks. "We did a screening test for alcohol on the blood," the witness replies, "and it was negative." Aurnou forgoes cross-examination.

"Oh, murder most foul . . ." But I doubt that Henri van der Vreken has been reading *Hamlet*. "Such an immoral murder" is how he speaks of the death of his employer. His voice is fierce and Aurnou seems stunned. The defense lawyer has been giving Tarnower's houseman no quarter, either in his difficulty with the language or in recognition of the strain that he and Suzanne had been under on the evening of the shooting. While the police had been questioning Mrs. Harris that evening she'd inquired of Henri who had been at the house for dinner and Henri's reply had been to ask the police to remove her.

Aurnou: You asked could she be removed from the house?
Henri: That's correct.
Aurnou: So you have strong feelings?
Henri: It's not a question of feeling, Mr. Aurnou, at that time. . . . You just don't have any feeling at all when you find yourself in such I will call immoral murder.
Aurnou: Do you know that? Were you in the room?
Henri: I was in the house.
Aurnou: Did you see what happened?
Henri: No.
Aurnou: So you made up your mind already before you found out what happened?
Henri: No, Mr. Aurnou. I will tell you something—
Aurnou: Just tell me whether you made up your mind at that point.
Henri: I was in the house.
Aurnou (shouts): Were you in the *room?*
Henri: No, Mr. Aurnou, I will tell you something—
Aurnou: Did you make up your mind at that point?
Henri: No.
Aurnou: You wanted to throw her out of the house but you didn't make up your mind?
Henri: I—

The Judge tells Henri not to go beyond the questions.

Aurnou: Did you make up your mind at that point?
Henri: No.
Aurnou: So you just asked that she be thrown out of the house, without having made up your mind?
Henri: I didn't say—

Bolen objects and is sustained.

Aurnou: Did you ask that she be removed from the house without having made up your mind?

Henri: I said—
Aurnou: Just yes or no.
Henri   (defeated): Yes.

I long for him to say, "Of course I'd made up my mind. Shouldn't I have believed Mrs. Harris when she said she shot him?" Not that this would uncomplicate the complicated matter of her intent but at least for the moment it would release us from the depersonalized world of law. Yet it's coming to be one of the new wonders of life for me that the eventual effect of these questions, which in their very literalness and insistence on precision seem as if designed to evade the issue of Mrs. Harris's guilt or innocence, is to produce such straight parallel columns: indictment, defense. With all its restrictiveness the system of legal interrogation somehow does its job.

Henri—he has said he pronounces it "Henry"—looks different from the way he did at the preliminary hearings two months ago. He's thinner, older, less easeful. His hair is grayer. Where, on his previous appearance, he'd been all lounging insolence, today he sports an air of gallantry—he's trying grandness on for size. I think he embarrassed Mrs. Schwartz when he stopped to kiss her hand as he came down the aisle of the courtroom—he must have planned this in advance. And he's dressed up: dark pants, brown blazer, black-and-white-striped shirt, wide brown tie striped with a single diagonal bar of red and yellow. This pair, Suzanne and Henri, think they have a tale to tell and no doubt they do, they do. At this moment they may even be holed up with a ghost-writer telling it: Suzanne thumbing the pages of her "Everyday Book," searching out yet another excitement in the calendar of the dead man's meals, his guests, his schedule of domestic pleasures; Henri . . . Henri doing what? He has a lazy memory. Still, he too had been in the employ of the famous man now dead by a mistress's hand. I don't understand why Henri went to work for Mrs. Westheimer or why, pursuing domestic employment until Mrs. Westheimer had let him go, he had taken a job without his wife. With Tarnower no longer around to bless their union, were Suzanne and Henri no longer a professional couple? It's interesting that Aurnou hasn't referred to Dr. Tarnower's bequest to the van der Vrekens, $64,000 if they pooled their bounty. Henri adds nothing substantive to the proesecution's case beyond a reiteration of the hour at which the doctor was supposed to have come home on the evening of the 10th. He says that he'd seen Tarnower "around 5:30, quarter to six maybe." After the doctor retired he and Suzanne had turned off the lights throughout the house, then at around 9:15 or 9:20 he'd gone to the garage to fetch some belongings of Suzanne's from her car, returning as he had gone, turning off the lights behind him. "[I] . . . go through the kitchen, closed the door, through the trophy room, closed the door, to Suzanne's room." Bolen: "And then you went to your room. Is that right?" "That's right. . . . The next thing that happened was when Suzanne came to wake me up, very much hysterical."

Although Aurnou spends much time probing the discrepancies between the statements made by Henri at the time of the shooting or in the days immediately afterward and in subsequent hearings, these attest only to the normal erosions of memory with the passage of time.

Then, near the end of his interrogation, Aurnou has been asking him how often he saw the doctor in the regular course of their lives. "Every day," says Henri. But, says Aurnou, presumably there were some days when the doctor was away and some days when Henri was away? "Suzanne and I, we did share the same house with Dr. Tarnower for sixteen years," Henri replies.

Aurnou: Did you come to hate him?

Objection sustained.

Aurnou: Did you ever make the statement that you hated the doctor and you remained there only because Suzanne forced you to?

The prosecution objects and the objection is sustained. There's a side bar. While it lasts Henri turns uncomfortably in his chair, occupies himself studying the diagram of the doctor's bedroom. He has reddened, shaken his head in pained disbelief at Aurnou's last questions. He seems unable to look in the direction of "the family." When finally he's dismissed, he glances at Mrs. Schwartz as he passes her on the aisle but she doesn't look at him, she looks straight ahead.

Having established the expertise of his next technical witness, Vincent Crispino, senior toxicologist at the Westchester Forensic Science Laboratory, Bolen begins his questioning by inquiring whether Crispino had been able to observe if the window in the dressing area of Tarnower's room had been broken from the inside or the outside. The witness says no, he had not. But he had observed a bullet hole in the glass door of the bedroom and inspected fragments of glass on the deck outside this double-glass door and found what could have been a ricochet mark, also a fragment of bullet in a stanchion. Appropriate photographs had been taken, he tells us, by the police photographer, Mr. Lindsay. So far, so good—but only so far. The chief purpose of Crispino's presence is to testify on the Walker test by which one can determine the distance at which a bullet has been fired. Although I listen closely, I'm lost: several times the Judge phrases the prosecutor's questions for him. This degree of verbal awkwardness in someone as manifestly intelligent as the District Attorney speaks to me of a cultural-generational defect. Has Bolen too suffered this endemic blight of present-day education, a deficient instruction in English speech and composition, or is his ineptness at least in some part the result of being the prosecuting lawyer, hedged around with restrictions? Bit by painful bit, important information is nevertheless got on the record. Crispino testifies that he chemically tested the three bullet holes in the doctor's pajama top for gunshot residue. This is the Walker test—if there are any nitrite particles on a garment and the garment is pressed between a chemically saturated cotton cloth and a piece of specially treated photographic paper, a bright red-orange spot will be produced. Spots such as these had been got from Tarnower's pajama top. The specific results of the tests are: 1) No nitrite particles were found around the front shoulder bullet hole. 2) Around the rear shoulder bullet hole there were a number of clearly discernible nitrite ion particles. 3) In the right pajama sleeve there were several nitrite particles around the hole. Bolen refers to the hole on the front shoulder, and Crispino testifies of this as of the other holes that "threads were pushed in" but there was no tearing effect, no singed or burned threads such as one would find if a gun had been pressed against the cloth. He's asked if he has an opinion as to why there was no residue. Obviously he has, if Bolen could find a way to put the question in permissible form. At long last Crispino testifies that, among other possibilities, there might be no residue because of "some type of filter interfering."

Bolen: Assume, sir, insofar as this case is concerned, that a bullet entered the palmar inside surface of Dr. Tarnower's hand and exited through the outer surface of the hand, and assume further that that particular bullet reentered the right front anterior chest of the doctor. O.K.?

Crispino: Yes.

Bolen: Assuming that state of facts, do you have a reasonable degree of medical certainty whether the results you observed, the Walker test you observed with respect to the cloth surrounding the wound to the right front anterior chest, would be consistent with that state of facts?

Aurnou objects. But to what: what was asked? It would have been fun if the witness had asked that the prosecutor repeat his question. One thing at any rate is plain: the prosecution believes that the bullet which entered the front of the doctor's right shoulder had first passed through his right hand held up to defend himself against an approaching revolver.

On cross-examination Crispino acknowledges that he'd not measured the thickness of the panes of glass on the sliding door of Tarnower's bedroom.

Aurnou: You know, do you not, that the thickness of glass has an effect on any projectile that travels through it?

Crispino: Yes, sir.

He also hadn't preserved the glass fragments he'd examined, nor had he or anyone separately measured the height of the holes in each of the double panes of glass.

Aurnou: Am I correct in suggesting also, Mr. Crispino, that as a result of all that experience you are familiar with a way of determining whether or not a particular mark was made by the impression of a bullet?

Crispino: That's correct.

Aurnou: Did you utilize that method at that time?

Crispino: No, sir, I did not.

Aurnou: Was the [bullet] fragment ever photographed in place?
Crispino: I don't believe so, no. . . .

But, Aurnou explains, a white triangle had been put at the place where the bullet had penetrated the stanchion "to make its location more visible."

Aurnou: . . . Did you make any computations, measurements, or anything, of bullet angles?
Crispino: No, sir, I did not.
Aurnou: But it is scientifically possible, is it not, when you have . . . two points, like the ricochet point and a hole in a window, to follow the path of the bullet right back into the room?

Objection sustained.

Aurnou: . . . As you sit here now, do you know with a reasonable degree of scientific certainty that that ricochet point is in fact a ricochet point?
Crispino: No, sir, I do not.
Aurnou: . . . But there was a test you could have conducted at the scene to confirm it?
Crispino: Taking a rod and placing it from that alleged ricochet point through the glass straight into the room would not, in my opinion, give an accurate representation of a trajectory from within the room, because the bullet would be deflected somewhat as it would be going through these two panes of glass. . . . It is not reasonable to assume that the bullet is going to go through that glass undeflected at any point. So while you can take a point and measure it to the bullet hole itself, taking a long rod or a string and placing it through . . . may not give you an accurate representation. . . .
Aurnou: You could have told that if you had taken the photograph of the stick through the two panes of glass, could you not?
Crispino: But on the 13th, we did go back to take additional photographs, which included some photographs involving string through the window.

This seemingly inoffensive statement has an electric effect on Mrs. Harris's lawyer. If there are pictures, why hasn't he been shown them? A recess is called so the subject can be pursued in chambers.

Today before the start of the session Judge Leggett appeared in the corridor and informed the press that on his instruction the attorneys would no longer discuss the trial with the press. What lies behind this gag order, as he allows it to be called, is sensational enough. In cross-examination of Califana earlier in the week there'd been mention of a pair of scissors found in a cemetery and presumably brought to him for fingerprint examination. Although nothing much had been made of this at the time, in the intervening day or two various elaborations on the scissors story had been leaked to reporters. From Aurnou's staff had come word that the scissors were left in the cemetery by Mrs. Harris when she went to put flowers on Tarnower's grave. And later Aurnou had added to the tale: he'd come to the press room to say that Mrs. Tryforos had found the scissors on the grave and rushed them to the Harrison police. Then, with the passage of a bit more time, several stories had appeared in the papers about an encounter between Mrs. Harris and Mrs. Tryforos at the grave site, and Bolen was said to have told the press, off the record, that the scissors had been found stuck, blade down, in the grave itself. It was at this ghoulish point that the *Times* had decided to run a story it had got from "a friend of Lynne Tryforos" but had been sitting on, that Lynne in fact had had two accidental meetings with Mrs. Harris at the cemetery and between the two meetings "found the blades of the scissors stuck into the grave." Aurnou of course hates the story, but Bolen hates it as well because it further discourages Mrs. Tryforos, already reluctant to appear in court, from wishing to help in the case.

Now, while the lawyers are in chambers, Mrs. Harris takes over with the press on her own—no gag order for her. She approaches one of the reporters and taps her on the knee. She's being a schoolmistress. "Do you realize how many times we've had to stop this trial to get evidence we should have had? I wish the press would tell the public what's going on."

"What did you think of Henri this morning?" a reporter asks Mrs. Harris. "What did *you* think?" Mrs. Harris asks. "I thought he was a bit hostile," says the reporter. Harris (sharply): "That's not the word." She begins to move away but turns back to say, "Do you know how many times they've cropped pictures so we couldn't make them out?" No one replies. "Isn't he bright?" she says of Aurnou to a reporter. And to another she remarks, "He's a genius. He may get me off."

And well he may. When the session resumes Aurnou has a field day of effective obfuscation: how can the jury not give Mrs. Harris the benefit of the many doubts her counsel sows in its mind? With Crispino he's especially strong on crime-scene procedure, a field of this witness's expertise. "Some of the primary rules in crime scene investigation revolve," says Crispino, "around maintaining the security and integrity of the crime scene . . . minimum personnel . . . only investigating officers . . . medical personnel. . . . After the victim is removed, the scene should be secured, limited access to only those personnel who are going to have a role in . . . collecting and recovering physical evidence. . . ." Aurnou easily establishes that none of these rules was adhered to. As we know, even the prime suspect, Mrs. Harris, had been allowed in the room. The bloodstained telephone had been used by the police. Evidence had been contaminated when being removed. The carpeting had been rolled up without the entire pattern of the trail of blood having been photographed.

Aurnou inquires whether Crispino's answers about nitrites had been "predicated upon [a] gun pressed firmly" to the material, and Crispino replies, "Yes, in contact."

Aurnou: But would the answers be the same if there was an inch, an inch and a half, or two inches separating the gun and the material?

Crispino: No, the answer would not be the same.

Finally the defense counsel lists his assumptions of what might have happened to the doctor's pajamas before Crispino tested them: they could have been crumpled, thrown on the floor with wet blood on them, stored in an unknown place. Would such handling not have an effect on subsequent testing? Wouldn't particles be dislodged when the doctor was put on a stretcher, given CPR? To all these questions Crispino answers in the affirmative.

When the day ends I'm unusually exhausted—it's been maddening. Sentence by sentence, the testimony could be readily followed even by someone as untrained as myself. But the purpose for which the witness was called has kept eluding me: I'm no sooner on track than I begin again to fall into space. I spend long hours putting these notes into working shape, giving them point. The self-limiting factual business of daily newspaper reporting suddenly reveals itself to be something of a small miracle, almost as much beyond ordinary human capacity as leaving the jury box each night with the sense of having come one day closer to truth—except, of course, the press people are allowed to consult each other and put some order into the day's complexities, which these poor jurors are not.

We've been delivered our headline: the Deputy Medical Examiner of Westchester County says that in his opinion the wounds sustained by Dr. Tarnower aren't consistent with a struggle. Dr. Louis Roh is Korean, a 1967 graduate of the Seoul National University Medical School. He's performed approximately twenty-seven hundred autopsies, participated in another twenty thousand. He's testified close to two hundred times. What does he do in his spare time?

In performing the autopsy on Dr. Tarnower, the witness had observed the "in-and-out gunshot wound" on the doctor's right hand. The perforation was round on the palm's surface with a large amount of blackening discoloration and gunshot stippling. The anterior chest wound, a bit large and elongated, had no blackening or powder stippling. The arm wound had a round perforation; the hole it made in the doctor's pajamas was surrounded by a large quantity of blackening but showed no tear or searing. The posterior shoulder hole was round, with a large amount of bloodstain and blackening, no tearing or singeing. The subject was "a moderately well-developed and nourished white male, measured 70 inches tall, weighed 175 pound." (Later, in the corridor, someone gleefully points out that this is fifteen pounds overweight by Tarnower's own chart. And to think that the doctor weighed himself twice a day!) The bullet to the anterior chest fractured the right clavicle, severed a major subclavian vein to the heart, travelled

143

through the lung lining and fell into the chest cavity from which it had been retrieved—venous blood, the doctor explains, doesn't shoot out like arterial blood. The bullet to the posterior chest fractured the fourth, fifth, and sixth ribs, tangentially entered the right chest and pleural cavities, striking and severing the middle and lower lobe of the lung and causing hemorrhage—in the autopsy there were still about fifteen hundred cc.'s of blood in the right cavity. It then penetrated the diaphragm and the front of the right kidney. This bullet had been recovered in front of the kidney; it had made a track of about fifteen to seventeen inches in length, virtually perpendicular to the ground with the patient erect. In the arm wound the bullet went through the triceps muscle and entered the right humerus; its track was slightly upward and right to left—the bullet was recovered near the armpit. The bullet to the right hand entered the palm at the base of the thumb and exited at the rear in "a through-and-through perforation."

Roh defines a defensive wound. It is one in which a person tries to grab a weapon or otherwise block it off. In the case of a gun, the muzzle would usually be close to the hand.

Bolen: Do you have an opinion, sir, as you sit here now, to a reasonable degree of medical certainty, as to whether or not that particular wound could be consistent with possibly being a defense wound?

Roh: It is my opinion it is consistent with a defense wound.

To counter Aurnou's claim that the police delay could have caused Tarnower's death, Bolen questions the pathologist as to how much blood the doctor would have had to lose to go into intractable shock. Roh believes that the doctor went into intractable shock within five to ten minutes after he sustained the injuries.

The witness is acquainted with the Walker test; it was he who had first made it known to Crispino. He now gives his opinion on the distance from which each of the shots had been fired. The hand wound was close range, the anterior chest wound was consistent with a distant shot, the posterior chest wound was close range, the wound to the right arm was close range. Would the wound to the anterior chest be consistent with a bullet passing through the hand into the chest? the doctor is asked. He replies that it is. Is it consistent with a head-on shot? "Then the person has to bend forward a little bit," he replies. Dr. Roh says that it is his opinion that "the one bullet that caused the wound to the hand is the one that caused the wound in the right anterior chest wall."

Here Bolen unveils a peculiarly revolting life-size brown plaster model of a man naked from the waist up. It's too much for Mrs. Schwartz who leaves the courtroom. I'd happily go with her—I find it unnecessarily graphic for Dr. Roh to illustrate on this life-like model what he's already told us so clearly.

Bolen (after Roh has marked the plaster torso to show where the bullets entered Tarnower's body and the model has been decently covered and put away): With respect to the wound to the back . . . [could] that particular wound have been sustained while Dr. Tarnower was standing upright?

Roh: [The muzzle would have to be] above his shoulder, pointing straight down.

Bolen: [Suppose he was in] a seated fashion, bent over at the waist?

Roh replies that yes, that would be possible if the person was sitting and bending forward, or lying down on the bed with someone stooping over and shooting, as long as the gun and the body were on the same plane. Several of the reporters later say that during this answer they heard Mrs. Harris moan softly. I too thought I heard a sound but couldn't have identified it.

And now Bolen asks whether in Dr. Roh's opinion and to a reasonable degree of medical certainty the wounds are consistent with a man of the doctor's height and weight and a female of the defendant's height and weight struggling for a gun.

Roh: It is not consistent with a struggle for the gun. . . . Number 1, the multiplicity, the person receiving three gunshot wounds and four wounds on the body . . . Secondly, the location of these wounds. If two persons are struggling over the gun and discharging during the struggle, I would expect to see the wounds mainly in the front part of the body. . . . I would expect to see the gunshot wound at very close range.

In cross-examination Aurnou presses on the changes in Roh's opinion since the original autopsy report. These seem to me to be sufficiently explained by the belated discovery of a bullet in the cabinet behind Tarnower's bed. Until this was recognized as a stray that never hit the doctor, the police had had five spent shells to account for but only four bullets: the one that had gone out the glass door of the bedroom and three retrieved from the doctor's body. Yet there had been four bullet entries in the body and Roh had very likely been thinking in terms of the entrance of four, one of which had gone through the doctor's hand and, although as yet unfound, might still turn up somewhere in the room. Roh must nevertheless admit that after his autopsy report had been testified to in the early hearings, he'd consulted with his chief and altered his earlier statements. On what *physical* evidence, Aurnou asks him, had he based these changes? Roh explains that he'd come to the Tarnower house, observed certain features, observed the bloodstains, the hole in the door. He'd also taken into consideration "the ability of the person's movement." Since there was nothing in the room that indicated the order in which the shots had been fired, nor had there been other support for any conclusions about the movements of the two persons in the room, and since no scientific procedure had been followed that could have aided Roh even in his examination of the glass door in the bedroom, Aurnou feels that the Medical Examiner has no basis for the new development in his thinking about the death of the doctor. And Aurnou reminds Roh that when Bolen had first questioned him about the hand wound he hadn't said it was a defensive wound. Roh now agrees that this was because there were a number of other possibilities with which the wound was consistent.

This agreement delights the defense counsel who now asks the court's permission to have Mrs. Harris join him in a demonstration. This is not to be believed, that she's willing to participate in the re-creation of the physical struggle, or any part of it, which is supposed to have led to her lover's death. Bolen objects and is sustained. I'm glad and yet, from the point of view of the prosecution's case, maybe he's wrong to protest. I should think the jury would be as shocked as I am at the defendant's readiness to reenact the scene. I find it confusing that Aurnou permits Mrs. Harris's remorseless behavior: shouldn't he tell her that she ought at least to *act* as though she's sorry Tarnower's dead? Chuckling about his own height which is so much less than that of Dr. Tarnower, Aurnou enlists the aid of Mrs. Cooke, the court clerk, to demonstrate the struggle. He has her point her finger at her left

146

temple as if to shoot herself. Then, coming up from behind, he swiftly brings down her left hand with his right hand. Presumably when they're both of them bent over the gun, as they now are, it accidentally goes off and the bullet goes through his hand and out the glass door. This performance completed, Mrs. Cooke is allowed to return to her place and the defense proceeds with its barrage of still other discrepancies between Roh's earlier report and his present statements. Aurnou offers variables—locations, people in the room after the shooting—which could have influenced the conclusions the Medical Examiner came to after viewing the scene. "I think we're getting perilously close to a mistrial," says the lawyer. No one seems much impressed by his threat. One of the women jurors is suddenly caught in an intense fit of coughing. The Judge becomes concerned, asks if she needs help, but Dr. Roh doesn't look in her direction. My neighbor whispers, "He's not interested in live patients."

During an intermission in Roh's testimony Mrs. Harris joined a friend in the front row and was heard saying, "I hope Roh is right. That would mean I only shot him three times."

We've been hearing about Joseph Reich, a prosecution expert, and now it's his day. Reich has been a ballistics authority with the New York City Police for twenty-one years before joining the Westchester Sheriff's office and then the Department of Public Safety. For the first time since the trial began Mrs. Harris shows signs of nervousness: through parts of the testimony she puts her fingers in her ears to stop out the witness's voice. She may be putting on a show but she may also be truly afraid of what he'll say. Her attorney is primed for the contest, never more so: he has the champion's gift of battling even harder where a lesser contestant would indulge fatigue or disappointment. Compared to the fight Aurnou puts up today, his cross-examinations even of Suzanne or Drummond or Roh were preparatory skirmishes. Today he's not satisfied to discredit the adversary expert; he means to put him out

147

of commission, render him incapable of speech—there's virtually nothing the defense counsel permits Reich to say. But how extraordinary it is that a contest as intense as this can be so wearisome to the spectator. I suppose it's because the objections lead to side bars or other long sessions in which the lawyers withdraw with Leggett. One of the Washington papers reprinted something I said in court the other day: how annoyed we are when arguments are presented in chambers out of our hearing, but how bored we are when we have to listen to them.

The few substantive facts that have emerged in Reich's testimony were elicited when he first took the stand. The double-action trigger-pull on a Harrington and Richardson .32 requires nearly three times the force of a single-action pull. When Reich examined Mrs. Harris's gun, he'd found a light amount of blood "generally in the rear portion"—i.e., at the hammer. Only five of the six chambers of the gun gave evidence of having recently been discharged; the sixth had never been used. Although the "swing arm" or cylinder hinge—what Aurnou's been calling the "crane"— of Mrs. Harris's revolver was broken, this wouldn't have interfered with its being fired; and although the ejector rod was bent, this wouldn't have been a factor in the release of the cylinder, only in the ejection of the shells to allow the gun to be reloaded. At the autopsy Reich had examined the location of wounds "with respect to any gunshot residue in and around them" and he'd also studied the doctor's pajamas. (Mrs. Harris plugs her ears.) The witness attempts to tell the court what he learned in these examinations but objections stop him. He also tries to describe the amount of gunshot residue that would result from shots fired at various distances—contact, close but not contact, distant—but is again so consistently interrupted that Bolen drops the line of questioning. The prosecution offers in evidence "representative photographs of some of the areas of those particular bullets" removed in the autopsy. Aurnou says, "We have a problem." There's a side bar and the prosecution withdraws the offer. When Bolen would have Reich explain the two parts of the Walker test, the Greiss chemical test and the powder distance test, he gets little more on the record than the fact that Reich did indeed perform the powder distance test in reference to Dr. Tarnower's wounds. In fact, there's no formulation of any question to which Aurnou doesn't object, usually successfully—things get so bad that at one point Bolen walks to the window and stares down over the city in long agonizing silence. Finally Reich is allowed what is essentially a repetition of Crispino's findings on the Greiss test: on the anterior chest wound the result was negative; on the right arm "there was a presence"; on the posterior chest wound "there was a presence." The lawyers retire with the Judge to his chambers and when Leggett returns he says he's dismissed the jury—the court will reconvene after the weekend. He adds that he has not yet received a copy of the Appeals Court refusal of Aurnou's request for a stay on the Scarsdale letter.

Reich's return to the stand after the weekend begins more promisingly: he's allowed to state his opinion on how far the muzzle of Mrs. Harris's gun was from the points of "impact"—Aurnou has objected to the word "target." In the posterior chest Reich approximates the distance as between twelve and fifteen inches; in the arm two to six inches; in the hand two inches "with a latitude of plus or minus one inch." He reiterates what we now know with some certainty, that there was no residue around the hole in the right front chest. He also testifies on the trigger-pull of Mrs. Harris's gun in both single- and double-action: the pressure is five and a half pounds for single-action, fourteen pounds for double-action. Bolen asks the witness if he knows the trigger-pull on a .38-caliber revolver such as most policemen—this includes the guards in our courtroom—use, and Reich begins, "Yes, the general ranges would be single action, three and a half to four and a half pounds pressure, and double action would be in the area of between nine and twelve pounds . . ." He is cut off. Aurnou objects vehemently to the implication that his client had to exert more pull on her gun than would be required of a police officer. He demands a mistrial. The objection is sustained, the request for a mistrial is denied. On March 17, Reich continues, he visited Tarnower's bedroom and extracted the bullet that had entered the cabinet at the head of the doctor's bed; the bullet had penetrated the wood at roughly a forty-five-degree downward angle, hit the door, and then imbedded itself to its entire length in the back panel of the cabinet. In his opinion this bullet was a direct hit, without the intervention of any object.

Then and at a later time Reich also studied the hole in the sliding glass door and came to a similar conclusion, that because of the force required for the bullet to pass through two panes of glass and imbed itself in the stanchion on the balcony, "it was fired directly from this particular revolver and with no encumbrance or object in between. A direct shot at the glass and through the glass." Did he have occasion, Bolen now inquires, to go into either bathroom? Reich replies that on his first visit to the doctor's bathroom he'd seen a trail of blood leading to the bathroom and on the vanity; in the guest bathroom there were chips on the side portion of the tub—Reich doesn't of his own knowledge know how the chips got there. Bolen ends direct examination by showing the jury photos of the tub and, for the first time, he passes Mrs. Harris's gun among them. The jurors don't seem frightened by it. Several of them, chiefly the women, pull the trigger—usually more than once. All but one of them scrutinize it closely, turn it from angle to angle: what are they looking for, the dark secret of its history? They are all of them careful to point the muzzle downward.

Cross-examination takes off with Aurnou's effort to prove that Reich would have had to live a hundred-hour day in order to examine fifteen thousand guns at the New York Police Department as he says he has.

Aurnou: May I assume, sir, that those were careful examinations?
Reich: I hope all my examinations are careful.
Aurnou: Well, examining a gun takes a lot of different aspects, does it not?
Reich: Yes, sir.
Aurnou: How long does the examination of a weapon in a significant case take?
Reich: Depending upon what processing that has to be done . . . The regular detailed examination of a gun could be done in a twenty- to thirty-minute period.

Aurnou enumerates some of the time-consuming tasks involved in gun investigation: matching the ammunition, recovering and marking the bullets, setting up tests, making up evidence tags, weighing the bullets.

Reich: Oh, including all the paperwork . . . anywhere from an hour to several hours.

150

Aurnou: At times you have to contact manufacturers, do you not, to get specifications?

Reich: Some of these are furnished on ballistics charts for each manufacturer.

Aurnou points out that there are also crime scenes to be visited. How much time would be spent on those?

Reich: It would vary. . . . I wouldn't even try [to approximate it].

Aurnou: And then there were times, of course, when you had to testify. . . . Testifying in New York City can be quite an ordeal, can it not, Mr. Reich?

Reich (stolid under the barrage of implicit ridicule): The same as it can be here, yes, sir.

Aurnou comes down to cases. Reich has testified that the empty chamber in Mrs. Harris's gun was in the two o'clock position. The defense lawyer forces from Reich the admission that if this is so, in the next to last trigger-pull the hammer would have had to fall on an empty chamber. The defense attorney moves on to ballistics mathematics: Reich had said that the pull on a double-action gun was three times as great as that of a single-action but he'd also said that the pull on a single-action was one-third less than that on a double-action. Didn't he mean two-thirds less? Reich finally grasps the error and admits it. Aurnou turns to texts in Reich's field: he quotes Sir Gerald Burrard's *The Identification of Firearms and Forensic Examination.* According to Burrard, says Aurnou, the normal trigger-pull of a single-action revolver is three to five pounds, of a double-action, sixteen to twenty pounds. "No," says Reich, "that's a little on the high side." Didn't he, asks Aurnou, get in touch with the manufacturers of Mrs. Harris's gun and didn't they tell him that the double-action trigger-pull was eighteen pounds? Reich says that he didn't inquire as to double-action. Aurnou quotes Burrard again: "Of course, if two persons are struggling for the possession of a loaded revolver, it can easily be fired by accident, because most modern revolvers have what is called a double-action as well as the ordinary single-action." Reich agrees that this is possible. Aurnou pursues the witness: studying the bullet hole in the glass door, had Reich noted the thickness of the pane? No. Did he take outside measurements? No. In plotting trajectories, had he determined a result to which he could testify with a reasonable degree of scientific certainty? No. Were Reich to have found a bullet nick on the floor of the balcony from which the bullet had ricocheted into the balcony post, would he not have been better able to establish a trajectory? Yes. But he hadn't established such a nick? No. Did anyone test the hands of Dr. Tarnower for the presence of nitrites? The hands of Jean Harris? Not that Reich was aware of. Did Reich have a camera mounted on his microscope to take pictures he could show the jury. No. Was there such equipment at Corning at the laboratory of Herbert MacDonell? (This is Aurnou's expert in criminalistics, no doubt soon to be heard from.) Yes. Had pictures been taken of Mrs. Harris's gun in Reich's presence before Drummond removed the stains? No. Where were the stains? In the hammer and breech areas, not on the cylinder. Aurnou picks up the revolver and for the next moments, while he continues to talk, his hands are occupied with taking the cylinder out and then fumblingly putting it back in again, taking it out and putting it back in again. He occasionally even stops talking to contemplate the difficulty he has in putting the cylinder back in the revolver. One is aware of Bolen's effort to restrain his growing fury at this dumb show.

Aurnou comes back to the distance between the gun muzzle and Dr. Tarnower's wounds. The posterior shoulder wound: had Reich not said the distance from the muzzle was twelve to fifteen inches? Yes. Did Reich know that Dr. Roh had said it was two to six inches? No. Would Reich now say that Dr. Roh was incorrect? Reich admits that he has to disagree—but only on this one figure, not on Roh's estimate of the distance from which the hand and arm wounds had been inflicted. Aurnou quotes Burrard on the necessity of testing trigger-pull not by spring gauge but by dead weight—Reich had used spring gauge, had he not? Yes. Burrard again: "It must be remembered that . . . the force required to pull a trigger is distributed throughout the prolonged movement, and consequently does not appear to be intense at any particular moment during that movement." Reich cannot dispute this. Does Reich know any unchallengeable test to determine a direct or indirect hit? Reich doesn't commit himself. But he did make tests of his own, he says, firing at a double pane of glass: he'd fired three shots. Aurnou absorbs this information. Did Reich know the thickness of the glass in Tarnower's door? No. The manufacturer? No. The tensile strength of the glass? No. The distance from which the gun had been fired? No. The angle? No. Aurnou moves to have all of Reich's testimony about the shot through the door stricken from the record on the ground of "No sufficient foundation." To Reich: "The opinions you gave us this morning are the opinions of Mr. Reich, but they are not the opinions which have been scientifically determined." Judge Leggett intervenes to ask the witness if he has done "prior tests with similar bullets, similar caliber and similar weapon against glass" before the present case and Reich replies that he has. But in this case were the tests done with the distance and angle of the shots and the tensile strength of the glass in the door unknown? Yes. Leggett orders that the jury should then disregard all testimony about direct hits on the cabinet and sliding door. No, no, says Aurnou. He wants the cabinet testimony left in, and just the testimony about the glass door stricken. After a side bar Leggett says that the "direct impact on the cabinet" has been stipulated; the witness's testimony as to whether or not it was a direct hit on the glass door is to be disregarded.

On redirect Bolen borrows Burrard's book from Aurnou and establishes the fact that it is outdated: it was published in 1934. At Corning, Bolen asks, did Reich see Herbert MacDonell? Yes. Did he see him test trigger-pull? Yes. Did either Reich or the Harrison police have a trace metal kit? No. What effect on the results of trace metal testing would wearing a glove have? It would make the test worthless. And if the glove were never recovered? Then it couldn't be tested. Would washing the hand affect the test? Yes. Fingerprinting? It might. Blood? It might.

"You don't really know, do you?" Aurnou asks the witness on re-cross. No, replies Reich.

The witness is dismissed; Bolen asks the court for a bit of time. There is now much suspense among the reporters because word has got about that before resting his case, Bolen has made one last attempt to persuade Lynne Tryforos to testify. Indeed the local reporters have phoned their papers to rush photographers to the courthouse. This courtroom is like what I've heard tell of Army camps: rumors travel thick and fast. Time passes, no one appears. The People rest. Out in the corridor Mrs. Schwartz is heard comforting Reich. "I've tried to be conscientious," he assures her. "That's the important thing," says Mrs. Schwartz kindly.

Back in court, before the room is cleared for the day, the press is allowed to study pictures that they were not previously permitted to see. These are in black and white, all of them except the autopsy photographs blurred as if slightly out of focus. The thirty-five of them have been laid out on the front benches of the room so that one has to bend over to examine them. By and large, it's a meaningless display.

Is the shoe now to be on the other foot, with Aurnou setting up the witnesses for Bolen to knock down? Dr. Schwartz, a Riverdale ophthalmologist, testifies that a person with 20/200 farsighted vision isn't dependent on eyeglasses. Without them he'd be able to walk around the house, eat, even be able to watch TV. There'd be difficulty only in distinguishing fine objects. Cross-examination: Bolen asks whether Dr. Schwartz had known Dr. Tarnower, had the dead doctor been his patient? No, but Schwartz had examined Tarnower's glasses that morning. It's quickly disclosed that the ophthalmologist is an acquaintance of Aurnou, treats his family. One witness struck out.

We're establishing a chain of evidence, how the personal documents in Virginia, not the ones taken by the Virginia police but those to be used by the defense, came to New York. An outside messenger for the law firm of Fried, Frank, Harris, Shriver & Jacobson in New York had been sent to La Guardia on the morning of March 11 to meet a messenger from Washington and to pick up an envelope and suitcase. ("I pick up and deliver. What's inside is none of my business," the messenger says belligerently and can't understand why he's provoked laughter.)

June Gertig, a young attorney in the Fried, Frank offices in Washington, had packaged the papers that were flown to New York. Early on the morning of March 11 she'd been called by Mr. Jacobson, a senior partner in the New York office, and told to drive to the home of people named Skallerup in McLean, Virginia, to pick up some articles that would be ready for her. At 7:30 or 7:45 A.M. she'd received a small suitcase and a number of letters and loose papers from Mrs. Skallerup. In her office she'd sealed the papers in an envelope addressed to Mr. Jacobson, and handed these to a messenger to fly to New York. The Skallerups had made up a receipt for the items but it can't be put in evidence because it hasn't been found.

It's the mild testimony of a mild young woman, but all at once it becomes the occasion of Leggett's only notable loss of temper since the start of the trial. Aurnou has tried to show the witness a "loose paper" which he wants her to identify. While the offer is being argued the paper is handed to the witness by the deputy sheriff. Bolen protests angrily. He objects to its being shown to her and asks that the deputy sheriff take it away from Mr. Aurnou. "May I have it back," he commands. Leggett jumps to his feet: "Look! I will run the court. I don't want you helping me and I don't need anybody helping me." He regrets the outburst and a moment later says genially but all too self-consciously, "Don't usurp my little job of running things and keeping them moving."

For me, but I'm sure for no one else in the court, the most interesting witness of the day is John Chandler, Jr. It would be my guess that he once had a significant place in Mrs. Harris's professional and social universe; even now she shows him more deference than anyone else with whom I've seen her. He's not Santayana's last puritan, there'll never be a last, but I suspect that he lives in a Boston that exists only in the imaginations of those who mean to wake up one day and find that the past half-century was just a bad dream. He's not Harvard but Yale; he was an assistant dean at Yale for three years after leaving the Navy. Now president of the National Association of Independent Schools, he was for fourteen years, from 1949 to 1963, headmaster of the Grosse Pointe University School where Jean Harris taught first grade; she'd taught at least two of the Chandler children. While at Grosse Pointe University School, had Chandler and Jean Harris been in the same professional community? Aurnou asks. Yes, very much. In school conversations had he ever heard anything adverse about her reputation "for truthfulness and veracity"? No, never. And outside

the school community of Grosse Pointe, in "the social structure"—
what Aurnou obviously means is Grosse Pointe society but he
doesn't want to make what would sound like too specific a de-
marcation—did the witness have "conversations on many occasions"
about Mrs. Harris's reputation and character? Now Chandler speaks
very carefully: "I would think not, except in relationship to her job
at the school and her work as a teacher." The quite simple point of
Aurnou's interrogation is of course to establish Mrs. Harris's high
standing for character both in and out of her professional group, but
unwittingly the defense lawyer has faced Chandler with a problem
of some delicacy for a man of honesty and caution. Aurnou thinks of
Mrs. Harris as so well situated socially that he seems not to understand that Chandler and the former first-grade teacher of the Grosse
Pointe University School had probably had only a professional connection, not a social one. Chandler's care in distinguishing between
the two spheres, that of the school and that of "the social structure,"
the first of them being where Mrs. Harris had to his knowledge been
accepted and respected but in the second of which she wouldn't
have been a subject of conversation, strikingly confirms the report
I'd been given of Mrs. Harris's life in Grosse Pointe. Ah,
classless America! As I read the story, Grosse Pointe and the
way Jean Harris had been treated there must have been crucial in
the development of her fierce determination to achieve a social
place from which she could never again be dislodged and in her
need to be sufficiently secure so that she'd never again have to
suffer condescension. At various times during the summer and
again while the trial was in progress I'd heard that after Lynne
Tryforos replaced Mrs. Harris as Tarnower's hostess, the Madeira
headmistress would drive to Purchase from Virginia while the
doctor was entertaining at dinner and stand at the window peering in at a scene over which she had once presided but of which
she was no longer a part. The relation between the indoors and
the outdoors of the Tarnower house, as I remembered it, didn't
make this a wholly feasible report. The story nevertheless had its
metaphoric truth: with Lynne at Tarnower's side in the affluent
society where previously she had been the doctor's partner, Jean
Harris was again someone on the outside looking in. In some remote way—also figurative, of course—I rather admired Chandler

for his refusal to yield his social advantage, even one that was now the worse for thirty years of wear, in order to play our easy contemporary game of social make-believe, this morally soothing game of supposing that we had only to raise high the banner of our egalitarianism to rub out the ranks and divisions and distinctions that so variously prevail in our self-conscious democracy.

What Aurnou wants for his client from this "education administrator," as Chandler describes himself, is a character reference on the score of her "truthfulness and veracity"—what does Aurnou think is the difference between the two?—and her "peaceability." There are seven hundred and fifty schools in the National Association of Independent Schools: Chandler knows many people who are acquainted with Mrs. Harris; he's never heard adverse comment on her truthfulness, veracity, or peaceability. And the president of the Association also knows her through work she's done on various committees of his organization. Apparently among these committees the most august body is the Commission on Educational Issues. He describes it as the Association's "think tank"—we are to understand that Mrs. Harris's membership in this committee qualifies her as an intellectual leader in her profession.

On cross-examination Bolen picks up on the defendant's "peaceability." How, he wants to know, would the subject have come up? Chandler allows that it probably hadn't. Bolen presses the witness: had he seen Mrs. Harris between January 1 and March 10, 1980? The witness thinks not. "Between the fall of 1978 and March 10, 1980, do you know whether or not Mrs. Harris had a revolver?" Chandler replies, "No." The prosecutor elicits the information that Chandler's advice had been sought by the trustees at Madeira in choosing Mrs. Harris as headmistress.

And now William Riegelman returns to the stand: he had earlier courteously given up his place to the out-of-town witnesses. A long-time Westchester resident, Riegelman is a partner in the law firm of Fried, Frank and tells us that he'd known Dr. Tarnower as a fellow member of the Century Country Club; they'd occasionally even golfed together but hadn't been good friends. He had met Mrs. Harris in Philadelphia in 1967 at a cocktail party given by his daughter when she'd been a student at the University of Pennsylvania. Since then he'd met her no more than twice. After Mrs. Harris had phoned Leslie Jacobson, a senior partner in his firm, on the night of March 10, Jacobson had called Riegelman and asked him to go to the Harrison police station and meet her there. He'd introduced himself to Sergeant Carney as her attorney and been allowed to speak with her privately. She'd appeared "somewhat disheveled. . . . She had a bad bruise on her lip, and another near her right eye, I believe. . . . She was wearing a blouse, slightly off-white blouse which was quite severely bloodstained. . . . She was sitting there, quietly crying." At first he'd been told the charge was aggravated assault and he'd wanted to take Mrs. Harris "out of there" on his own recognizance but with the news of the doctor's death the charge had been changed. He tells of her reaction when she heard of Tarnower's death. "She sobbed, very heavily," he says, "and I put my arm around her, and she leaned against me and just sobbed on my shoulder for a few minutes, and then she sat down quietly." Later Mr. and Mrs. Jacobson had arrived, and around 3:30 or 3:45 Riegelman had left; he'd come back at 7:45 A.M. Shortly after that, Aurnou's associate John Kelligrew had come to the police station. Riegelman had driven into New York to his office where Jacobson had given him some envelopes to deliver to Aurnou in Westchester. These were the documents brought to New York from Mrs. Harris's Madeira home.

Shown a photo of Mrs. Harris with a bruised lip, Riegelman attests to its accuracy. He also testifies that he'd seen Dr. Tarnower without eyeglasses. There are a few moments of cross-examination in which Bolen asks him to point out in a photograph of Mrs. Harris the bruise he says he had seen on her eye. Riegelman replies, "You are able to tell that as well as I can, Mr. Bolen."

Court has been dismissed and cross-examination resumes the next morning. Bolen is newly, understandably icy. During recesses in testimony, witnesses are not supposed to discuss any aspect of the case.

Bolen: Mr. Riegelman, when we broke yesterday afternoon, did you discuss the case with anybody?
Riegelman: No, sir.

Bolen: So you didn't talk it over with Mr. Aurnou or any of his
             associates?
Riegelman: I did have a brief conversation with Mr. Aurnou this
             morning.
Bolen: Relative to what had transpired yesterday in the courtroom?
Riegelman: Relative to one aspect of it.
Bolen: What aspect was that that you discussed with Mr. Aurnou
             after I commenced cross-examination of you?
Riegelman: The picture.
Bolen: How long have you been an attorney, sir?
Riegelman: Since 1938.
Bolen: And your particular field of expertise in the law is what?
Riegelman: I am a corporate lawyer.
Bolen: Have you ever done any corporate litigation?
Riegelman: No, sir.
Bolen: Would I be correct in saying that last evening after I
             started cross-examination your discussion with Mr. Aurnou
             pertained to the photograph I had shown you?
Riegelman: Yes.
Bolen: . . . Can you tell us about that conversation?
Riegelman: Yes. I told Mr. Aurnou when I looked at the picture very
             carefully that . . . the picture in my judgment was a very
             poor picture and it was very hard to see, and that the whole
             appearance of Mrs. Harris's lip on the night that I saw her
             was far more severe and the bruise was far severer than
             appeared in the picture, and that I thought that the same
             thing might be true of the bruise on the side of her eye.

Bolen asks the color of the bruise. Bluish. Was the skin puffed?
Slightly. Were any bruises other than those of the mouth and eye
mentioned that night in jail? Not at that time. Bolen once more
holds up the photo and asks, "Is that the vein we're talking about?
The blue vein?" Riegelman replies that the picture doesn't com-
port with what he himself remembers. Sitting among the press,
I'm not alone in wanting to cheer on the Assistant District Attorney against this adversary older man.

The witness remembers the blood on Mrs. Harris's blouse but
none on her hands. His wife had given him another blouse and
perhaps some underwear and stockings to give the defendant.

Bolen: Where was Mrs. Harris's pocketbook while you were there?
Riegelman: I haven't any recollection of her pocketbook.

159

Bolen: To your knowledge, to whom was Mr. Jacobson making all those telephone calls?

Objection sustained.

Bolen: . . . Do you remember whether at any time you were there you made any telephone calls to the state of Virginia?

Without eliciting anything substantive, Bolen questions the witness about prior discussions with Aurnou of Mrs. Harris's case and the contents of the envelope he delivered to the defense lawyer at his home. And had he been apprised of the testimony of Sergeant Carney and Dr. Roth? Bolen also questions Riegelman about how often he'd seen Dr. Tarnower without eyeglasses. "I can't recall any specific instance." He does remember Tarnower's occasionally wearing half-glasses and peering out over them. Across the aisle Mrs. Schwartz is heard commenting to a companion: "That was twenty or thirty years ago."

Riegelman has a curiously Dickensian look though I can't place the book or character. His face is long, pinched, tight-lipped. One feels that if we were in nineteenth-century London instead of twentieth-century Westchester, his clothes would be rusty. I wonder if Mrs. Riegelman, who sent a blouse and underwear to the jail for Mrs. Harris, has been among the defendant's visitors in court—several women in the row of Mrs. Harris's friends haven't been identified.

A second ophthalmologist is called: Dr. Matusow is Dartmouth '57, Downstate Medical School '62, "Ophthalmology consultant to the Eighth Army and United Nations command in Korea." (No friend of Hawkeye and BJ at M*A*S*H 4077.) He testifies that even without eyeglasses in ordinary light someone with 20/200 farsighted vision could see a revolver held in the palm of another person's hand. Cross-examination doesn't last very long.

Bolen: Your wife's name is Naomi?
Matusow: Correct.
Bolen: Is she involved in the legal profession?
Matusow: She is.
Bolen: Did she recently graduate from Pace University?
Matusow: She did.
Bolen: Upon graduation from Pace University, do you know

whether or not she became associated with Mr. Aurnou's office?

Matusow: She did.

Bolen thanks him and sits down.

And then there's Reid Lindsay, forensic photographer, who puts on record a long wearying account which he reads from his log of the subjects he photographed for the prosecution, together with the dates the pictures were taken and the number he'd developed and printed—he printed far from the large quantity he developed. His recital provides reason for a motion that the trial be recessed until January 5: Aurnou wants to study these pictures; Bolen will need time to put them together. But before that Aurnou demands a mistrial—yet again. He speaks indignantly of the obligation to give Mrs. Harris a proper defense and of the "prodigious number" of photographs of which he had no knowledge. Bolen counters that the defense has had only "work products" withheld from it; he himself never saw the unprinted pictures. Leggett sees no bad faith on the part of the prosecution and denies Aurnou a mistrial, but he orders that all the negatives now be given to the defense attorney. The jury is not present for this back and forth but at least we're in open court: the discussion is going on not in Leggett's chambers where so much of the infighting of this trial has taken place but in front of the press and other spectators. Far more slowly than I'd have expected, and much less noisily, resentment has been mounting among the press people at the insufficient regard for their professional due: whether it's first the responsibility of the lawyers or of the Judge, I can't make out, but the reporters assure me that it's unusual for so much that's important in a trial to be disposed of behind the scenes—it began, of course, with the picking of the jurors. Even I, who haven't their obligation to file regular stories, feel the handicap of not having full and easy access to all the exhibits. Most of all, I've minded not knowing how the lawyers went about the selection of the jurors—who challenged whom? "I've canceled my vacation plans," Judge Leggett now tells the lawyers as he announces the recess. "I'll be available to you." And he adds that it won't be a vacation for them either, which strikes me as supererogatory. Well, at least it gives the rest of us our much-desired Christmas break. I often think about Judge Leggett; he comes on as such a simple, decent, sincere, homespun man. (I'm told the court guards have nicknamed him "Fireside Russ.") I find him decent, sincere, homespun, but not simple. I have the impression that there are aspects of the criminal process that bother him, that his moral perception of life is somehow opposed to the activities of culture. I still strongly feel a sting from the statement he made at the start of the trial, that when it was over nobody would be interested in the case. A historian friend of mine had just shown me what Frederic Maitland, the nineteenth-century legal historian, had written: "If some fairy gave me the power of seeing a scene of one and the same kind in every age of history in every race, the kind of thing that I would choose would be a trial for murder, because I think it would give me so many hints as to a multitude of matters of the first importance." I ponder what Leggett would make of that. I doubt it would persuade him to alter the moral impulse that led him to want to encapsulate the trial, keep it as much as possible within the boundaries of the courtroom. Yet he welcomes our high-school visitors, which is anomalous. His attitude to them as distinct from book writers disturbs me: I feel an impulse to tell him that the young are only as virtuous as they'll grow up to be and that the educational process doesn't improve their future prospects by flattering their present moral capacities. He has said, I'm told, that he dislikes criminal law; he would prefer to be on civil cases. That would figure. But he governs his criminal court fairly and firmly, which often takes courage. And his quick wit has helped us over many bad moments. Taken in all, he's surely the best of middle America.

After Christmas recess, court reconvenes with Reigelman once more on the stand. Aurnou shows him a Manila envelope. "I had the label prepared by my secretary," says Riegelman, "and I hand-delivered it to you." And the envelope inside? "This," says Riegelman, "is an envelope sent to me by Mrs. Arthur Schulte." Aurnou removes a large red Christmas card from the inner envelope and the witness identifies it as having been recovered by him from Mrs. Schulte. I recognize it as the exhibit for which I've been waiting: the greeting from Mrs. Harris to Dr. Tarnower on the last Christmas the two of them had spent together in Palm Beach. The card is light verse written by the headmistress; it's the parody of *'Twas the Night Before Christmas,* a few lines of which Aurnou had shown me at his office in April.

Bolen requests a *voir dire* on the Christmas card. Can Riegelman with certainty attest to the fact that this is the original? Does he of his own personal knowledge know who wrote it and where the card has been since it was turned over to the defense lawyer? Inevitably the answer to these questions is "No" and Judge Leggett sustains Bolen's objection to entering the card in evidence "at this time." My disappointment runs deep—what Aurnou had let me see of the poem had stayed with me heavy with psychological implication. It was a list, I supposed, of other women in Dr. Tarnower's life, referred to only by their first names—I didn't know whether they were all or any of them actual figures from his past or whether, if real, they represented mild, intense, recent or remote involvements. But like Leporello singing of Don Giovanni's loves, Mrs. Harris hadn't been able to disguise her pride in the doctor's sexual attainments. Surely what I saw of the poem was as much a boast as a lament. But there was also a desperate cajolery in her teasing: Mrs. Harris was reminding her lover that she'd never interfered with his sexual freedom (remember the puppet with no strings attached?) so long as she'd been the indispensable woman to whom he'd returned. But now her ascendancy had been taken away from her. It was Lynne Tryforos who controlled the situation. Mrs. Harris had been able to live with triangles. She must even have taken a veiled pleasure in them—after all, no woman alternates her bed with other women out of a generous heart. However hidden from her, there had to have been satisfaction in the arrangement for her too: would we ever know its precise nature? And Tarnower, that unlikely apex of the triangle or series of triangles? What had been going on in him? To understand his obsessive need for sexual conquest together with the signs he gave of aversion to women, perhaps we had indeed to study

Don Giovanni as his model. A man can be unfaithful to a woman he loves, but that's not the same thing as dangling women as Tarnower seemed to have done at least with these two mistresses, openly playing them off against each other. It occurred to me that perhaps the more tender passions of this bachelor had never been meant for the opposite sex.

For the last week the courtroom has been overrun with significant female presences, teachers, school administrators, masked self-confident middle-aged women, shiny-haired self-confident young girls who will soon be as emotionally barricaded as their mothers. Madeira has come to Westchester. But not Madeira only: Mrs. Harris's memory of youthful friends, once students of hers, reaches back to the Thomas School in Rowayton where she'd been headmistress between 1971 and 1975. One of the reporters calls the stream of young people the parade of the preppies.

In mounting this week's procession the defense has a multiplicity of purposes. The jury is to be instructed in the arduous nature of Mrs. Harris's employment and learn of events that produced the special strain of the days immediately preceding March 10. It's to have a glimpse of the elevated society in which Jean Harris was a leading figure and of the splendid young ladies whose education was in her charge. Mrs. Skallerup and Mrs. Faulkner are of the Madeira Board: they're here to establish the earlier route of the Harris papers that we now know were flown to New York from Virginia on the morning of March 11 and, more important, put some of the contents on record. Finally, the impeccable purveyors of this information are character witnesses for the defendant. Suicide notes somehow lose their harsh self-reference and become sacred texts when they pass through such immaculate hands.

All educational institutions live by self-congratulation, and Madeira now has particular reason to show a proud front to the world: the school has a sizable scandal to overcome. But I've never been one for school babble and as I listen to these Madeira teachers and

Board members celebrate Madeira's achievement, I suddenly become the Donna Duck of my press row—quack, quack, quack, I rail at this wedding of class privilege to such grand assumptions of pedagogic and civic virtue. Tell us about the duties of the Madeira headmistress, Aurnou throws open the starting gates, and by the time his witnesses have hit their immodest stride they've made the board chairmen of *Fortune*'s 500 look like pensioners—the Madeira headmistress is responsible for dealing with the administrative staff, the faculty, the parents . . . she must travel to meet with the school alumnae, future students, for fund-raising . . . she supervises the physical plant, is at the ready day and night for students who need her . . . she must oversee and report to the Board on the state of health of the student body, the activities of the students, the budget . . . she must hire and "let go." (At Madeira they apparently don't fire.) It's a forty-eight-hour-a-day job—what was Aurnou doing when he mocked Reich's working day? Everything that's said about Mrs. Harris's responsibilities is accurate, I'm sure, but whose working life when broken down to its constituent elements can't be made to seem unduly taxing: Aurnou's, Bolen's, Judge Leggett's, mine? It's my experience that people either don't work at all or work too hard; such is our immoderate human condition. Although no one of course has said this, what makes the task of a Madeira headmistress so incomparably trying in the eyes of these witnesses is the unique quality that the members of the Madeira community, like all people associated with schools, would wish to impute to their particular educational enterprise.

In the account of life at Madeira what I find least appealing is the feature of which the school would seem to be most boastful: its co-curriculum program was almost the first thing told me about the school when I went to Washington last spring. All the students have a one-day-a-week occupation outside the school for which they get academic credit. Juniors spend their Wednesdays working for a senator or congressman on Capitol Hill. I look upon the whole program but especially this portion of it with a cold eye: it strikes me as being upper-class boondoggling. How can it benefit seventeen-year-olds to introduce them into the halls of power unless to confirm them in a sense of authority with which they've been already too richly endowed by birth? Surely without the social connections of Madeira parents these girls couldn't have got their Wednesday employment on Capitol Hill in the first place. Ultimately all such pedagogic gimmickry is an evasion of the dull work of imparting and absorbing basic knowledge. But of course Madeira has a parent body which still wants the best of traditional schooling for its children along with the moral glamour of progressivism, and it no doubt approved Mrs. Harris's introduction of Latin into the course of study, and perhaps even her emphasis on math, quite as much as it took satisfaction from such a pedagogic ornament as "decision-making."

Madeira had surely faced it: Mrs. Harris is not in the Social Register like Mrs. Skallerup or Mrs. Faulkner who will follow her on the stand—these two women are friends; they live next door to each other in McLean. Old family and old money are written all over them: in their bearing, in their lockjawed speech, in their clothes. (A courtroom visitor, male, identifies the small-figured gray-blue dress worn by Mrs. Skallerup as a Liberty print, which isn't necessarily correct but captures the style.) A member of the Board of Directors of the Madeira School, formerly its president, Mrs. Skallerup has two daughters who attended the school and she has taught there herself. She'd known Jean Harris many years ago back in Cleveland; she "followed her at Smith." We remember that in the early hours of March 11 it was someone of her unusual name who'd given papers and a suitcase of Jean Harris's clothes to June Gertig of the Washington office of Jacobson's law firm. Now we learn how Mrs. Skallerup had come into possession of these belongings of the headmistress. She'd been awakened at 6:45 the morning of the 11th by a call from Alice Faulkner, who brought them to her. Mrs. Skallerup's husband, a lawyer, had typed up an inventory of them which Mrs. Skallerup had later had her secretary Xerox. Had Mrs. Skallerup seen any of the items? Aurnou inquires. The witness replies that she had; she mentions "a small travelling bag with a few clothes," then gets to the papers. "The first of those was ostensibly in Mrs. Harris's writing, but not signed, and it was a letter to our president, Alice Faulkner. . . . Mrs. Faulkner had opened that envelope and I did see the contents of that letter. . . . I made a copy for Mrs. Faulkner and a copy for our files. . . . The next item I recall was one addressed by Mrs. Harris to her secretary, Carol Potts. . . ." There had been several other sealed letters, one of them addressed to Mrs. Harris's sister, "Mrs. Lynch dash Mary Margaret," and a note addressed jointly to Mrs. Lynch and David Harris. "There was a fairly sizable envelope full of a number of papers, none of which I saw." Aurnou chooses this moment to show Mrs. Skallerup the last Madeira yearbook, that of 1980. He refers her to page 98. Aurnou (unctuously, as whenever he approaches a family piety): "There's somebody very special on that page." Mrs. Skallerup (with commendable dryness): "There is a daughter of mine who graduated from the Madeira School last spring. . . . It's dedicated to Mrs. Harris." Mrs. Skallerup testifies that prior to March 10 she had last talked with Mrs. Harris around the 8th of March, and that she had not communicated with her since March 10 until this morning. On cross-examination Bolen asks: "[While Mrs. Harris was] headmistress, did you know of your personal knowledge whether she had in her possession a .32-caliber revolver?" Mrs. Skallerup: "I did not."

Alice Faulkner had previously been a member of the Madeira Board; since July 1978 she'd been its chairman. She was chairman of the Search Committee that chose Mrs. Harris as headmistress. Propelled by Aurnou, Mrs. Faulkner launches on a description of the Madeira co-curriculum in full celebrative detail: "The freshmen start off with . . . programs on decision-making, study skills . . . and by the time they are sophomores [they are working one day a week] in schools, hospitals, day-care centers, old-people's homes. . . . All juniors work on Capitol Hill." Some seniors go into career areas, and some work on Capitol Hill or for the Smithsonian, the National Zoo or such. "There are all kinds of wonderful places they often work." Mrs. Harris had been much involved in the co-curriculum program, we are assured. "She strengthened it." This is a character reference, naturally. How could anyone who furthered so sterling a program be guilty of murder? We get at last to the morning of March 11 when Mrs. Faulkner had received a phone call at approximately 1:30 A.M.

from a man who identified himself as Leslie Jacobson. As a result of this call she'd gone to Mrs. Harris's house on the campus at about 6:45 and been let in by young Baughman, the Madeira superintendent of buildings and grounds. Leaving Mrs. Harris's two dogs in his care, Mrs. Faulkner had put some personal papers of Mrs. Harris's in her car, also a bag she'd packed with a few of the headmistress's clothes. She'd left these items with her neighbor, Nancy Skallerup, while she herself returned to the school. Aurnou asks whether the witness opened any of the sealed documents and Mrs. Faulkner replies that she opened "a letter with my name on the front."

Court recesses for lunch and after lunch Bolen is routinely questioning the witness on whether she can say with certainty that the letter Aurnou wants to put in evidence is the letter she'd picked up on the morning of March 11 when Mrs. Harris notices that the prosecutor, holding the letter in his left hand, is abstractedly running the fingers of his other hand along its fold. Quickly she calls Aurnou's attention to this violation of the evidence and Aurnou protests to the Judge that "Mr. Bolen is changing the condition." Leggett says he doesn't think it is so but cautions Bolen not to keep rubbing the crease lest the paper come apart in two halves: "That's what happens in the nature of paper." The letter, we are told by the witness, is two paragraphs long with a final sentence below the second paragraph. Its first line, says Mrs. Faulkner, refers to March 6 and 7. The letter is put in evidence and circulated among the jurors who read it with their usual imperturbability except for Juror 1 who sits for a long time seemingly lost in gravest thought, his head bent forward. Aurnou asks Mrs. Faulkner if she remembers from the letter the words, "There are so many enemies and so few friends." Bolen objects and is sustained.

Aurnou: Do you recall the incident [to which the letter refers]?
Faulkner: Yes.
Aurnou: Mrs. Faulkner, did you have occasion to know what the event referred to was . . . ?
Faulkner: Yes . . . In my official capacity.
Aurnou: Did you also play a part [in it]?
Faulkner: No.
Aurnou: Had you discussed [it] with Mrs. Harris after it occurred?
Faulkner: In no detail.

Aurnou: With regard to the second paragraph, about "choosing a head the board wants and supports," did you know to what that referred?

Faulkner: That surprises me, in a way, but I know what she is referring to.

Aurnou: And the language about not being wanted in the first place, did you know to what that referred?

Faulkner: That is something that I don't understand.

Aurnou: And the statement "I was a person and nobody ever knew." Did that make any particular sense to you?

Faulkner: No.

Mrs. Faulkner had found this letter addressed to her on a chair near the front door of the headmistress's house on the campus. There had also been a note with the request to call Mrs. Harris's sister Mrs. Lynch and her son David; it contained their phone numbers. And clipped to a larger envelope there'd been a note with the signature of Mrs. Harris both printed and in script.

On cross-examination we learn that Mrs. Faulkner was contacted for her appearance in court by Riegelman; he'd met the two women at the airport that morning. Bolen inquires about Madeira policy: do school officials enter students' rooms in their absence? He means more than routine inspections for neatness. "We do occasionally search when there is good cause," says Mrs. Faulkner, "and there is a paragraph in our student handbook that says that if there seems to be a good reason, a search will take place." What the jury makes of these references to an as yet unidentified school incident I can't imagine. I'd heard the story in Washington. As it had then been told to me, Mrs. Harris had found the makings of marijuana cigarettes in a girl's dresser and had expelled four seniors. The disciplinary action, taking place so short a time before graduation, had excited much campus protest; it was thought too harsh. The District Attorney inquires whether Mrs. Faulkner has ever been in the headmistress's house on the campus. "Many times," says Mrs. Faulkner. Had she noticed any photographs? She doesn't remember any in the living-room area.

Bolen: What knowledge did you have as to Mrs. Harris's possession of a .32-caliber revolver?

Faulkner: I had no idea.

Mrs. Faulkner last saw the headmistress on Saturday the 8th of March, when Mrs. Harris had been invited to her home. That was the weekend before the shooting and at the start of the school's three-week spring recess.

Mrs. Skallerup and Mrs. Faulkner leave together as they came. They have reason to feel brave and selfless: Madeira is their life and cause and they have given much for it. Mrs. Harris put Madeira in jeopardy; unless they willingly testify for the defense they'll seem to have imputed guilt to the woman they chose to head the school. They have no public choice except to treat the shooting of Dr. Tarnower as the "tragic accident" that Aurnou calls it, a temporary block in the otherwise unimpeded onward and upward march of education. Certainly I see nothing personally supportive of Mrs. Harris in their behavior. Neither of them has come to Westchester to visit her since the shooting, neither has had a choked moment on the stand such as would attest to affection, even to past affection now hedged around with terror. Apart from a single public smile that Mrs. Faulkner has directed to the defendant, the witnesses haven't, so far as I could see, met her gaze. Their testimony is an act not of personal loyalty but of loyalty to the institution that is an extension of themselves. It has the same rationale as the dedication to Mrs. Harris of the 1980 yearbook: the good name of Madeira can't be tarnished by a wrongdoing that isn't recognized as such by those who most cherish the repute of the school. All at once, I get the full force of what could be meant by the sentence in Mrs. Harris's letter "I was a person and no one ever knew." If by this Mrs. Harris meant that she'd been a school *object,* an institutional appendage rather than a "person," I'd not dispute her. Yet why, with her experience of institutions, had she deceived herself that her Board members were her friends? Because she ate at their tables? She was in the same relation to them as a governess to the people who employ her—the governess always eats at family table. What gives the final turn to this screw is my sense that had the roles been reversed and it was Mrs. Harris who was the Board member, she'd have behaved to a scandalous headmistress precisely as these women behave toward her. It was in the world of official emotions, after all, that she'd chosen to make her professional name and place. These women spoke of her with the steady-voiced "understanding" that would seem to be the chief contribution that our century can make to the enlightened personal intelligence—it's the codified morality of television drama. It's bad enough as a public stance but as a sanctified personal attitude I find this kind of tolerance an annihilation. Understand and love us, Father, for we are aberrant.

At the end of the day, the press is made acquainted with the contents of Mrs. Harris's farewell notes. We're not allowed to handle the documents but when the spectators leave the courtroom the deputy sheriff reads them to us.

Unsigned and undated, one memorandum says: "Please call my sister, Mrs. Lynch [phone number]. My son, David [two phone numbers]."

Another, dated and carrying a double signature, print and script, reads: "I wish to be immediately cremated and thrown away."

The letter to Mrs. Faulkner reads:

> Alice,
> I'm sorry. Please for Christ sake don't open the place again until you have adults and policemen and keepers on every floor. God knows what they're doing.
> And next time choose a head the board wants and supports. Don't let some poor fool work like hell for two years before she knows she wasn't ever wanted in the first place. There are so many enemies and so few friends.
> I was a person and no one ever knew.

All are written in red ink. I ask the deputy sheriff to hold up the Faulkner letter so that we can see the handwriting. It slants but doesn't look disturbed.

In applying for the Madeira post, Mrs. Harris hadn't mentioned her relation with Tarnower—it was her private business, why should she? But it's not that simple: she no doubt knew that if she spoke of it, she'd probably not get the job. I've been told there were one or two members of the Board who knew of the affair but they didn't tell the others; either they thought it would disqualify Mrs. Harris or they thought it intruded an irrelevant consideration. In the early months after the shooting, before people became absorbed by the more lurid aspects of the triangle of which Mrs. Harris was a part, this facet of the case was much spoken of. I'd been astonished by the number of people, both men and women, even quite young people, worldly and tolerant in their sexual views, who took the position that it wasn't proper for the head of a girls' school to be having an affair outside of marriage. What was improper about it they couldn't readily say. Did it set a bad example for the students? Should the students also be forbidden sexual experience outside of marriage? But, it was protested, Mrs. Harris wasn't a girl, she was a woman of fifty-six. Oh, did the speaker mean that it wasn't the position, it was the headmistress's age that made the difference? At what age, then, did it become improper for a woman to have an affair with someone to whom she wasn't married, and would it be the same for a man as for a woman? To the question of whether it was better that girls be put in the charge of a woman with no sexual life rather than a woman with an unlicensed one, the reply was usually a stubborn affirmative bolstered by the lame reasoning that where there's no activity, there's at least no scandal. And it was even argued that, failing a married head for a girls' school (marriage being a guarantee against scandal!), perhaps a homosexual headmistress was preferable to someone in an illicit heterosexual relationship. Respectability is of course a public attitude: it has nothing to do with private conduct—this has always been so. It has only to do with witnessed behavior, nothing with what we do in private. Call it discretion, if you will; respectability is based in discretion and discretion has deception at its core. Hypocrisy is built into the respectable life. But denying the headmistress of a school, and precisely on the ground of her maturity, the sexual freedom that's given the students in her charge goes beyond hypocrisy to say with some firmness that sex is only for the young. In mature marriage, in the marriage, say, of a woman of Mrs. Harris's age, we can blind ourselves to the existence of sex if that's our preference, transmute it into affection, responsibility, devotion, all the solid emotions that comfortably attend the marital state. In the minds of their children parents don't make love. A headmistress is parent-surrogate to her students: in their minds she too doesn't make love. An unsanctified relation between a man and a woman spells nothing if not sex.

But in withholding the information that might have lost her the Madeira post, Mrs. Harris was surely playing a game with truth: in effect, subjectively as well as objectively, it's a lie not to put your cards on the table in a situation that involves your beliefs. Mrs. Harris strikes me, however, as a woman of assertions far more than of courageous principle. In the clinches she opts for safety. Even in her present dilemma, she's apparently found her safety hatch in the vagaries of memory. How much stronger her sense of herself and the Board's sense of her would have been if she'd dared risk the job for the sake of her right to pursue her private life. Economically, it wasn't all that dangerous. She had her well-paid job at Allied Maintenance to fall back on. She wanted the social prestige of the Madeira headship. She was made weak by her social ambition.

The parade of the preppies may not be the thing of beauty and glory that a beaming Aurnou obviously means it to be. I do my best to reserve judgment. Shortly after the shooting *The Washington Star* reported on Madeira's academic standing: "Madeira is sending few students to top schools. In 1979, when 73 graduated, 68 were accepted by 49 colleges, including 3 by Brown, 3 by Middlebury, 3 by Princeton, 3 by Tulane, 3 by Yale and 3 by the University of Virginia. This is not a scorecard comparable to the results of the best college prep-schools in the country." If one can judge the quality of a Madeira education—I suppose one can't, fairly—by the courtroom demeanor of our sample, this record isn't contradicted. These girls would get their best grades for poise. They're excessively self-possessed—in my experience, mind arrives on the public scene redeemed by a bit of awkwardness. I wonder how these girls were chosen to testify for the headmistress. Were they volunteers or did Mrs. Harris canvass the past for potential supporters? Did any one she proposed turn her down? In this last year of the headmistress's life, it would be a relatively insignificant detail. Still, it was something to think about: even among her Madeira students she'd had to test where she stood, whether she retained their respect. She had gathered new friends but could that heal the hurt of old friends lost? Aurnou speaks of her as frail. Thin she is, but frail? Each of the student witnesses represents several votes of confidence; that is if, as I like to imagine, the parents had to give approval for their daughters to testify. "Mummy, I'm going to New York to be a character witness for Mrs. Harris." I could hear the conversation. "Darling, I'm so proud of you. Yes I am, Howard: what are you frowning about? You think she killed him? But what has that to do with it? I think it's a great compliment for Carrie to be asked; not everyone's invited to do that—I'm sure they've been picked very carefully. You just wear your regular school clothes, dear. No, not slacks, Carrie, a skirt. Don't you think she ought to wear a skirt in court, Howard? Your father and I think you're doing absolutely right, honey."

When I had got to Washington two months after the shooting and found the campus closed to outsiders, I had been much disappointed. This wasn't because I was being deprived of interviews—there are always people to talk with—but because in the train of Dr. Tarnower's death one of the nicest things I'd heard about the school was the directive that had been given the students after they came back from their spring vacation to use their own judgment as to whether or not they'd talk with the press about Mrs. Harris: they were simply reminded to think before they spoke. This was good common sense and properly respected the students—of course a few of them had already been giving press and even TV interviews. When I was in high school the head counselor of the camp I'd been going to for several summers was involved in a much-publicized murder. She wasn't charged with a crime but she was implicated by her lover, a married man who had been slowly poisoning his sick wife. I remember how much I dreaded the thought of my parents talking about her. I wanted to be let alone to filter the scary event through my own feelings. Obviously Mrs. Harris's situation couldn't be ignored at Madeira; the student body had to be officially spoken to. But from everything I'd heard, this had been done with a minimal show of official righteousness. There had been a big "talk-out," and individual counseling had been provided for the students who wanted it. Religion and psychiatry joined to cushion a shock that the girls would no doubt have absorbed just as well, or just as poorly, on their human own. It was modern, kindly, and at the least it was occupational therapy for the staff. There must have been instances in which it was helpful—I still think of the girl of whom I was told that when she heard of the shooting she asked, "Is it our fault?" What she meant was, had the girls pushed the headmistress over the edge by their selfish disregard of her personal requirements and well-being. The students who had come to court at the behest of Mrs. Harris and her lawyers weren't, I suppose, likely to be this tender; with an exception or two, they didn't look to me as if they'd ever take blame on themselves for what happened to others. Like their elders, they were testifying for their school, and also, like their elders, they had information to put on the record.

Greer Emory, now a college freshman, was a vigorous type; by her own admission academics had not been her strong suit—she'd had a hard time when she first came to Madeira and because of her bad grades had got better acquainted with Mrs. Harris than she otherwise might have. From her we learn of the BH, the Brazen Hussies, a secret club of Madeira seniors who initiated new girls into the school. I'd heard in Washington of the unhappy incident whose recent repercussions were said to have contributed to Mrs. Harris's torments on the morning of the 10th. In one of these hazings, a caustic cleanser had been used by mistake instead of shampoo. It had been applied to a girl's face and she'd been badly burned. The witness is not allowed to answer questions about this occurrence; Bolen objects and is sustained. She's limited to testifying about the headmistress's reputation for honesty. "I knew her, I think, more as a person more than other people did. . . . We got to be friends." During a break Mrs. Harris joins her on the front bench of the courtroom and is heard to say, "Have you read Dickens? The line I mentioned? Well, it's true." Our in-house literary scholar suggests that this could be a reference to Beadle Bumble's remark: "The law is a ass, a idiot." But oh dear, the headmistress mustn't be this heedless. Just because Dickens said it wouldn't mean that she could say it to her young students, not in her present situation. But would she see that? In a class in decision-making, I was told, she'd asked the fourteen- and fifteen-year-olds how many of them planned to marry. She'd said that the worst experience of her life was to come home at night to an empty house. One of the girls said, "But you have Cider." It was the dog the students had given her. "Yes, I have Cider," she had answered sadly. Was she always this personal? I'd inquired when this story was told me, and was answered, "No, but she'd sometimes illustrate points with personal stories."

We move momentarily from Madeira to Yonkers. A storage man testifies that in November, shortly before Thanksgiving, Mrs. Harris had come with Grossman of Aurnou's staff and another man to the warehouse in Yonkers where he works and, after going through several of her boxes, had removed three ice picks. They are now in court and he identifies one of them by its bent tip. Patience: in due time we'll learn what this is about.

We are back in Virginia. Mrs. Kathleen Johnson, academic dean, now acting headmistress of Madeira, takes the stand. (On campus she's known as "Kiki": can one be surprised?) Against Mrs. Johnson I'm prejudiced. When I had arrived in Washington and found that all my Madeira appointments had been canceled, I'd phoned to ask the acting head if I could at least drive through the school grounds; I'd not get out of the car or talk to anyone, I just wanted to view the campus. "No. I don't like your manner or your timeliness [sic]." She was herself a Madeira graduate and has a child at the school. Before her present temporary appointment as acting head, she'd taught economics. In general the female heads of women's colleges, schools, summer camps, perhaps even personnel departments divide into two groups: the sweet and the hearty. Mrs. Harris was a sweet. Kiki is a hearty or, what is close enough to it, a downright-upright. Aurnou invites her to tell us—not again!—what it's like to be a headmistress. This time we get the routine in even greater splendid detail: it includes the thank-you notes that Jean wrote by hand, Jean's efforts to raise the teachers' salaries, Jean's appeal to the girls to plant daffodils on the Madeira lawns. Although Aurnou tries to elicit information about several extramural assessments that were made of the school, Bolen is successful in blocking these questions. We nevertheless gather that there had been a Browning report which was substantially negative, then a second assessment which was more favorable—the earlier of the two studies had been troubling in its references to the headmistress and apparently had mentioned a division of opinion among the members of the Board on her appointment. In the last week of February 1980 Mrs. Johnson had travelled west with Mrs. Harris on school business. On Thursday, March 6, there'd been a dormitory problem which involved four seniors and that night Mrs. Harris had called a meeting in her house which had been attended by the faculty and "major administrators" who lived on campus, also by the Judiciary Committee and the student presidents of the houses. This meeting had been followed by a disciplinary hearing. We learn no more about the situation. What were the BH? Aurnou now asks. A loose organization of girls, Mrs. Johnson explains, "who engaged in generally wholesome pranks." Had there been an event that required the headmistress's intervention? Yes. Had Mrs. Johnson seen Mrs. Harris on March 10? Yes, several times. Had she seen her in her office with Ruth Katz? Yes. Was there a letter Mrs. Johnson had read? Yes, Mrs. Harris had asked her to read it aloud. Was the writer involved in the BH incident? Yes. Had she noticed a "change in [Mrs. Harris's] affect"?

Johnson: I think it concerned her. I would even go so far as to say upset her. I told her, as did Ruth Katz, we did not think it was a letter she should get upset about. . . . I mean a calm upset, not an *agité* upset.

The court reporter interrupts: What?

Johnson: It's a French word. It was a calm upset. . . . [When we talked about the letter] it was as though if she had something pulled over in front of her eyes . . . that she was closed off. . . . [We told her] it's a child speaking like a child, don't let it get you down. Part of the letter was quite warm and affectionate.

The remainder of Mrs. Johnson's testimony is devoted to Mrs. Harris's untarnished reputation for honesty, veracity, peaceability. Funny, a member of the faculty at the Thomas School when Mrs. Harris had been headmistress there told me she'd been famous for her loss of control. Madeira people spoke of her outbursts too, but these weren't of course called as witnesses. Mrs. Johnson had seen Mrs. Harris six or eight times on March 10, the last time at 1:00 P.M.

Of the preppies, Ava Scott, the next witness, is the most effec-

177

tive. She's a senior, a very good-looking black girl who has been at Madeira for three years. She'd first met Mrs. Harris at orientation. "She seemed like a cordial person. . . . She told us that any time we felt homesick, all we had to do was come visit her, and so I felt comfortable, and I did." At Easter the headmistress had got in touch with her to dye Easter eggs but she'd had other plans and had gone up to her house to explain why she couldn't come. Mrs. Harris had said it was all right. Aurnou inquires about an occasion when she'd been ill. She'd had poison oak on her face, the witness replies, and she'd been in the infirmary but it wasn't getting any better. Mrs. Harris came to see her and took her home where she'd put something on her face. The next day she was cured. Did people at Madeira talk about Mrs. Harris's reputation? Aurnou asks. Ava: "Yes, everyone talked about Mrs. Harris . . . how strongly she supported integrity and how high her moral values were and her standards . . . how thoughtful she was when she was trying people when they had done something wrong in the school. Initially most people disagreed with the decision, but after they thought about it they realized it was the best thing to do. So she had support."

Bolen has no questions, the witness is dismissed. She leaves the stand and goes over to kiss Mrs. Harris who starts to cry. It's the first time I've seen her genuinely sob. I've grown accustomed to tearless tears but this is real: her shoulders shake. And Ava starts to cry too; as she goes down the aisle she covers her mouth with her handkerchief. The Judge quickly recesses the jury, calls the lawyers into chambers and says Mrs. Harris should join them if she wishes. He's trying to avoid an emotional display in front of the jurors or even before the court spectators.

What does and does not arouse emotional response in Mrs. Harris is now plain enough. Of remorse for the doctor's death she obviously has none. Whether it was an accidental or purposeful death, she's wholly detached from it: she can hear the details of the autopsy and even finger the sheets soaked with the doctor's blood without a perceptible quiver of feeling. What stirs visible emotion in her is self-pity and what is more rousing of self-pity than either the praise or pity of others? In the front row now her sister, Mrs. McLaughlin, quietly begins to cry along with her.

I too have a lump in my throat: how much of this is because the girl who so warmly gives her affection to the headmistress is black? Is it spurious to be more moved by the devotion of a black student than by her white schoolmates? I haven't the answer. There's awareness of color difference, the possibility of racial division, even in this courtroom. Where not? It suddenly surfaced the day that the wife of a black judge attended the trial with a white friend—before court, the two women had been greeted by Judge Leggett who had suggested they find seats in the front row. But this is where Mrs. Harris's family and other supporters sit and acc ing to the visitor it had been objected, behind the scenes of course, that the black jurors might be influenced by the presence of black visitors among the defendant's friends. Expectedly, at Madeira they work at erasing old social injustices; this goes on wherever privilege is linked with ideals of progress. I was told that in Mrs. Harris's last year the president of student government was black—maybe it's on the pious side but surely it doesn't qualify as counterdiscrimination. But unless these black students at Madeira are wealthy, what happens about the expensive extras that the school offers? Actually, what happens about these extras with white scholarship students? When the acting headmistress wouldn't allow me on the campus, I drove to the gates and peered in. I could see the outdoor riding ring. The grounds of Madeira— I've learned about them from photographs—are very lovely, more beautiful than any school campus I know. Before it was given to Miss Lucy Madeira the property had belonged to Eugene Meyer, publisher of *The Washington Post*. I'm not secure in the suggestion but I conjecture that Miss Lucy Madeira, she of the rousing slogans, commanded in her school what was in some wonderfully paradoxical way an outpost, albeit an imposingly elite one, of the settlement house culture of the metropolitan North which had done so much in the early years of this century—they were the years in which Tarnower's parents came to America—to bridge the old and new worlds, giving an immigrant population the sense of personal purpose and spiritual fulfillment in democracy that Miss Madeira would have wished to give the daughters of the wealthy newly responsible South. Behind Miss Madeira as behind all the great pre-suffrage and suffrage women of this century loomed the imposing figure of George Eliot, that pre-eminent Victorian instance of female independence and courage and rectitude. If I longed to read the novel that Scott Fitzgerald might have written about the Tarnower world, I longed as much to read the novel that George Eliot might have written about the roots and garlands of Jean Harris's struggle with respectability. More than most writers, it was George Eliot who from her own experience knew about that social imperative.

In the outdoor riding ring there were six or eight girls on horse-back. Young, straight-backed, they sat their horses well, moving with precision, the sun on their hair. It was a sweet May day, the light was as alive as in a Degas painting. In addition to instructing the girls in the matter of dress—"If a student is not wearing a brassiere, her clothing must be full enough to disguise that fact"—and pre-scribing that they be mannerly at all times, the Madeira catalogue informs the applicant to the school that there's an extra charge if she wants to board her own horse. Are there no horse-boarding scholarships?

A snowfall closed court for a day but otherwise it's been a week of continuing Madeira traffic, interspersed with doctors and other technical witnesses. The Madeira people are men as well as women, office staff, students and ex-students, teachers, develop-ment officers, a school psychologist, a minister. The girls are nice-looking in an homogenized way. Aurnou is so pleased with his student exhibition that he drops into the press room so the report-ers can tell him what a good impression his young ladies must be making on the "middle-class jury." Again the same question: what does Mrs. Harris's lawyer mean by "middle class" and how has it shaped the defense he's mounting? I don't want to overstate the situation by saying that it's a class defense that he's making, but surely he means it to be "classy"—it's not a word that's in use any more. He's out to impress the jury with how high class his client is. But this is a tricky game to play; his social perceptions aren't reliable, his idea of class was formed in another world than the one he's working in today. Right here in this courtroom, if we take the jurors, Bolen, Aurnou himself, Mrs. Harris, Judge Leggett, some of the witnesses who have so far appeared, we've run a full gamut from working class, as it was once called, to patrician. Our present-day middle class embraces them all. What criterion is there for membership in the middle class other than that one claims it? It's like being an intellectual: an intellectual is someone who calls himself an intellectual. But a keypunch operator or a bus mechanic or a hotel employee isn't to be thought of as a member of the same social-economic class as someone who spends $4,280 a year for a daughter's high-school tuition, $7,050 if she's a boarder. It's my guess that if they were intellectually qualified, the daughters of most of these jurors would be given scholarships at Madeira or any expensive private school in the country so that the more advantaged students could get to know a cross section of the American population.

In addition to being character witnesses, the Madeira girls report on the difficulties that Mrs. Harris had to meet in her last days in the school. Lynn Stein, now a freshman at Vanderbilt, had taken Jean Harris to dinner on March 7. No, it wasn't usual for girls to take the headmistress to dinner but "a good friend of mine felt sorry for her. She had a lot of troubles that week." Lynn was an editor of the Madeira yearbook for 1980. She's not allowed to tell of a meeting after Dr. Tarnower's death in which the yearbook staff discussed the dedication of the volume to Mrs. Harris but there's no objection to her speaking of a letter signed by various students and faculty and sent to the former headmistress along with the book. On cross-examination Bolen elicits the name of the faculty advisor to the yearbook: it's Kathleen Kavanagh. We've heard the name before; Miss Kavanagh had been out west with Mrs. Harris for the second half of the headmistress's tour in early March.

Tracy and Dana Schmidt are sisters; they come from York, Pennsylvania, and Tracy, the elder, is entering her junior year at Vassar; Dana is a freshman at Haverford. At Madeira Tracy had become well acquainted with the headmistress because in her senior year she'd been head of the student Judiciary. She begins to explain that "Jean and myself rewrote the rules" that had been in effect in the days when Miss Keyser had been in office. Bolen objects: a relationship of 1977–78 is remote. Judge Leggett rules that the account of "Jean and myself" be stricken—down with Tracy, up with Dana, whose Madeira memories are more recent. Dana was at a March 7 school meeting to discuss the expulsion of four seniors the previous day. The students had spoken in "open criticism against Mrs. Harris" and according to Dana the headmistress had been "obviously flustered"; she was "losing ground with the students, losing her position as headmistress."

If neither Tracy nor Dana has said what she hoped to say, at least each has put her small word on the record. But not so their mother who's scarcely permitted to open her pretty mouth. The very image of successful young matronhood, crisp, energetic, Mrs. Schmidt belongs in a which-is-the-mother, which-is-the-daughter commercial. She'd grown up in North Dakota and attended a one-room schoolhouse: she'd have us know that "Madeira is pretty far" from that. But the Madeira experience had obviously turned out better for her girls than she'd foreseen. Did she remember any events connected with Mrs. Harris and her daughters, Aurnou asks, and Mrs. Schmidt starts to tell about the time one of them ran in a school election and "was pretty bruised by this whole thing"; there had been a crisis in which the headmistress had invited Mrs. Schmidt to come to the school and stay at her house. This interesting event isn't enlarged upon which, so far as I'm concerned, is all to the good since with even this brief preface I hear it as an all too typical and irritating story of the emotional priorities in the private education of the privileged young. A student's been "bruised" by her failure to win a competition: the school's heart throbs with sympathy, the girl's mother is invited to join the team of healers and is even made a guest of the headmistress in this time of her parental travail. Such indeed are the wounds that bind!

But it's plain that Mrs. Schmidt has come to White Plains not only to talk of Mrs. Harris as tender protectress but to speak of the sterner duties of a headmistress—she's stopped at every turn. Did she know, asks Aurnou, of the effects of Mrs. Harris's attempts to exercise discipline? Objection sustained. Did she receive correspondence from the headmistress related to discipline? Objection sustained. What had she personally observed about discipline? Objection sustained. Had there come a time when she personally observed the reaction of wealthy and influential parents on Mrs. Harris's attempts to impose discipline? Objection sustained. Tracy and Dana's mother manages to say only that the Schmidt home "was one of discipline and rules and regulations" and that Mrs. Harris's disciplinary decisions had therefore created no problems for her daughters. She leaves the stand bitter; in fact, she looks as if she's on the verge of angry tears. She'd come to do brave battle for Mrs. Harris—as Tracy and Dana's mother had inevitably put it, the headmistress had been her daughters' "first role model"— and she's been defeated before she began. But Mrs. Schmidt is luckier than she thinks. She's been saved the embarrassment of having to say how she feels about a role model with a gun.

Mrs. Ruth Anderson Katz is head of the Madeira English Department. Among the teacher witnesses she's a "sweet," tremulously so. Patient in the face of one objection after another, Mrs. Katz manages to say that Mrs. Harris had been much upset— "numb," "glazed"—by a letter she'd received the morning of the 10th. It's the letter to which Mrs. Johnson also referred, no doubt from the girl whose face was scarred in the Brazen Hussies "prank." That unhappy child! She'd apparently written a letter critical of the headmistress and suddenly she's become a "triggering incident" in a suicide attempt and an alleged murder. The episode was widely reported outside court but thus far it's been only touched on in the testimony. According to Mrs. Katz, Mrs. Harris's weariness on the morning of the 10th was excessive even for end of term. A teacher can be exhausted when the term ends, she informs us gravely. The headmistress would be especially drained by her effort to consolidate the programs created before she came to Madeira, in particular the co-curriculum program which was designed, Mrs. Katz says, to show the students "the workaday world." Capitol Hill: our workaday world! The witness describes the high purpose of Madeira: "To encourage the young people to express independent thoughts and feelings in act and in word and at the same time to teach them the responsibility of restraining their thoughts and their feelings and their acts and their words. . . . The resistance . . . to this process can be great, and you have to have, it seems to me, an almost inexhaustible reservoir of energy and faith and hope to help this process of growth and sometimes of despair on the part of young people to take place." Did Mrs. Harris take an active role in that process, Aurnou asks solemnly, and without self-consciousness Mrs. Katz replies, "She did." But that afternoon of the 10th her weariness had been extreme. The witness took Mrs. Harris a bunch of daisies but not wishing to disturb her, she'd left the bouquet in the headmistress's car with a card. It was a way of showing her support.

Mrs. Dorothy Limbert, a Baltimore psychologist who has a master's degree in social work and forty years of experience in clinical work with the young, first met Mrs. Harris at a reception in 1977 at which the new headmistress was introduced to the Madeira community. Mrs. Limbert had volunteered her services to the school. When Mrs. Harris became aware that some of the scholarship girls were having problems—how not?—the headmistress followed up on this offer and, after that, Mrs. Limbert functioned in the dual roles of counselor to the students and consultant to the headmistress. It was in the latter capacity that she'd encountered dormitory difficulties: the dorms were previously supervised by the students themselves but Mrs. Limbert suggested adult supervision; the girls "needed more controls," and insofar as the budget permitted, Mrs. Harris had tried to implement the proposal. Asked about the character of the headmistress, Mrs. Limbert replies that everyone stressed her honesty, the directness, the interest, the caring, the wanting to help. On cross-examination Bolen asks if the witness had any professional connection with the school after October '79 and Mrs. Limbert answers, "I didn't because my son was taken hostage in Iran and I just couldn't go back. I couldn't function." She leaves the stand and the reporters rush after her in a body—it's been a dry day for stories.

And then we have Karl Wolf, the new public-relations officer at Madeira who must surely bring solace to that female sanctuary. He's a most personable young man and it's easy to see why Mrs. Harris engaged him as director of development. It's also easy to see that he's a loyal admirer of Madeira's former headmistress. In January and February of 1980 he'd started at Madeira part-time while still working at Yale. On March 1 he began full-time employment in charge of fund-raising, alumnae activities and publications, with Kathleen Kavanagh as his assistant. On March 10 he'd met with Mrs. Harris from approximately 10:00 to 11:30 A.M.—he'd been much impressed by her grasp of the professional matters they discussed and by her memory. Together with Kathleen Kavanagh he was to have seen her again after lunch but the appointment was broken. She'd passed him, though, outside her office and he'd been struck by the marked change in her demeanor since the morning—she was "exceptionally depressed and despondent . . . as if a veil had been put around [her] and as if she had aged ten years." He was supposed to have dinner with her that evening and go to the theatre (the witness seems not to know as we do that Mrs. Harris had also engaged herself elsewhere for dinner) but "we just weren't getting through in any meaningful way." In the midst of so much testimony from women, it's interesting to have this glimpse of the headmistress through the eyes of a young man. To judge by what I see in court when Mrs. Harris speaks with women visitors or with the young women of Aurnou's staff, she's not an enemy of her sex; she seems to have considerable impulse to "sisterhood." Still, she's not predominantly a woman's woman and if, in choosing more women than men for the jury, Aurnou was counting on the way in which she'd been made a female cause he should perhaps have also kept it in mind that women are often harsher with other women than men are. Indeed, professional associates have told me that she was very much a man's woman. She invites the protectiveness of men. The court guards call her "Miss Pretty," I don't know with how much irony. But certainly she's not a southern belle, which that name implies.

Miss Jean Gisriel ("Gis") is dean of students at Madeira, a voluminous laughter-prone woman. She had daily school contact with Mrs. Harris. In February '80 she'd heard the headmistress tell Baughman to bring together all her possessions that were scattered about the school. In August '79 Dr. Tarnower had been in Washington. We're led to suppose—as Miss Gisriel thought too—that this was for a visit with the President. I'm told it was not; the White House has many mansions. He'd stayed the night at Gis's house on the campus. But why? If it was unsuitable for him to stay with Mrs. Harris, I should think he'd have stayed in a hotel instead of hiding behind this woman's capacious skirts. In October '79 Mrs. Harris told Miss Gisriel that if anything happened to her there were three people to be notified. Also, her sons were to have an equal share of her belongings. Gis had seen Mrs. Harris twice on March 7, found her ill with stomach pain and very depressed. "No, Jean, don't go," said the headmistress. "Please don't leave me, I'm so very depressed." On March 10 she'd seen Mrs. Harris in her office between 2:30 and 3:30 to report on some inconsequential school affairs. "She wasn't with me," Miss Gisriel testifies. "There was a wall between us. . . . I was right in the middle of a sentence and she stood up and just said, 'I can't hear anything else, Jean, and I'm so desperately tired I'm going home.'" Although Karl Wolf and Kathleen Kavanagh had been waiting outside the office for an appointment, Mrs. Harris left without meeting with them.

"Gis" is followed on the stand by a minister. An Episcopal clergyman, co-adjutor Bishop of Pittsburgh, Alden Hathaway taught religion and ethics to Madeira seniors in '77, '78, and '79. On the afternoon of March 7 he talked with Mrs. Harris at some length; the headmistress was concerned that she might not be living up to the high expectations of her Board. It was very difficult, she said, to be both an example of gracious femininity and a firm school leader. She spoke with the minister of the frustrations of her job and the heaviness of her school burdens.

Yvonne Saffell is of the Madeira office staff. On the afternoon of March 10, shortly after two o'clock, Mrs. Harris came into her office and asked her to witness a document. Miss Saffell signed it and so did another person in the office. The document was three pages, written in red ink. Mrs. Harris had read the last paragraph out loud before signing and dating it; the witness understood that the papers were Mrs. Harris's will. Anne Green, also of the school office staff, similarly testifies about Mrs. Harris's will. On the afternoon of March 10 Mrs. Harris asked her to notarize the document. Although she'd been reluctant to do this because she didn't have her notary stamp with her, the headmistress had seemed so urgent about it and put so much pressure on her that she'd finally conceded. "She said it was totally uncontentious, a perfectly nothing document"; her son had for some time been wanting her to get it done but she'd been dilatory. The headmistress had looked "awful" and appeared to be very agitated.

The most attractive of these Madeira associates of Mrs. Harris is her youthful secretary, Carol Potts. She's the mother of four children. Mrs. Potts explains that she'd come to The Hill for dictation first thing each morning so that they'd be able to work without interruption. When she followed this routine on the morning of March 10 the headmistress had far less work for her than was usual on Mondays. Mrs. Harris's voice was normal but not her appearance; she'd looked as if she'd been crying. What about anonymous phone calls to Mrs. Harris? Aurnou asks. Objection mysteriously sustained. What about Mrs. Harris's reactions to the January meeting of the Board? Mrs. Potts replies that Mrs. Harris had been distressed. She'd cried and said she felt like packing her bags "and getting the hell out of here." The headmistress returned from her trip west, six cities in ten days, very tired. On March 7 she felt ill but she'd nevertheless met with several parents about the expulsion of their daughters. She'd gone home to rest at one point in the day. Mrs. Potts had gone to her house twice that afternoon and found Mrs. Harris lying under a blanket on one of the beds in the guest room as if trying to sleep. When she'd gone to the house on the 10th, instead of its being "neat as a pin," as it customarily was, it was disordered. For some time Mrs. Harris had been talking about the disposition of her belongings "if my plane ever goes down." Carol Potts (close to tears): "I said to her, 'You have one foot in the grave and the other one on a banana peel.'" It was in January and February that the headmistress had given the secretary letters that had to do with her insurance, and had had a piece of jewelry appraised. Between what the secretary has already told us and the brief testimony that follows we hear the passage of the remaining hours of March 10 like the tick of a distant clock—they are of course the hours in which Mrs. Harris drove to Purchase, shot Dr. Tarnower, was arrested and put in jail. Suddenly it's March 11, the headmistress of Madeira is no longer at her post. That day a box arrived in the mail for Mrs. Harris: Mrs. Potts put it in the school safe until the 14th when Jimmy Harris came to Madeira and opened it. Aurnou shows the secretary a box and two bottles of pills and she identifies them.

She remembers of one of the bottles that it was marked with a short unfamiliar name that began with a "D."

On cross-examination Bolen elicits the information that around 3:40 or 3:45 on the afternoon of March 10 Mrs. Harris had said to her secretary, "I'll see you in the morning." He inquires of Mrs. Potts about phone calls made by Mrs. Harris that morning and Mrs. Potts says that to her knowledge the headmistress had made one call, between 9:30 and 11:00. The secretary doesn't know to whom it was made, only that it wasn't very long.

At the end of Mrs. Potts's testimony, when the jury has been sent to lunch, Aurnou asks the court to put off reading Mrs. Harris's will to the press until the following Monday. Judge Leggett says he'll look at the will to decide if anything in it is prejudicial. I hear that information has already reached the press that it makes no mention of Dr. Tarnower.

The next court day, before lunch, with the jury and spectators out of the room, Judge Leggett reads it to the reporters. Though composed by Mrs. Harris, the will is a good simulacrum of a legal document; for all her upset, this competent lady had adequately managed the legal form and language. Distributing everything she owns, Mrs. Harris indeed leaves nothing to the person of whom she says that he meant more to her than anyone in the world.

At least for the time being we seem to be finished with Madeira. Except for Mrs. Margaret Stein, who knew Mrs. Harris as Dr. Tarnower's companion, the other character witnesses for the defendant date from her life in the Midwest; one of them even bridges the world of Jean Struven of Cleveland and Jean Harris of Westchester. That's Marjorie Jacobson, wife of Leslie Jacobson, the lawyer whom Mrs. Harris phoned on the night of the shooting. Jacobson is a partner of Riegelman; theirs was the firm that recommended Aurnou for defense counsel. A strikingly tall, strikingly white-haired, self-consciously modish woman, Mrs.

Jacobson is also a strikingly talkative witness. At one point the prosecutor tries to limit her to answering only the questions put to her. She nods docilely and says, "All right, I'll do it my way." Judge Leggett comments: "Perhaps you shouldn't. That's part of the problem. . . ." She'd known Dr. Tarnower for twenty-five years, they were members of the same golf club. And she'd known Jean Harris for over fifty years; their families had had houses near each other on the Canadian side of Lake Erie. Then at the end of 1966 she'd introduced Mrs. Harris and Herman Tarnower to each other. Aurnou asks what happened. Mrs. Jacobson couldn't be prouder. "Instant take. They really met each other, enjoyed each other. It was really the start of a very warm and wonderful friendship." Despite objections, we manage to learn that Mrs. Harris slept at Mrs. Jacobson's house, or that of other friends, throughout most of the first year of her acquaintance with Tarnower—ah, morality— and that he'd given her a "big emerald-cut diamond ring"—ah, property! Between 1966 and 1980 Mrs. Jacobson had never known Mrs. Harris to date anyone but the doctor. Yes, Mrs. Harris had been well aware in these last two years that the doctor was "seeing" other women—we're given this in the plural; we're not to think of Lynne as "the" rival. Mrs. Jacobson: "She stated many times she really never felt another woman was a decided threat in her life, and that she was aware that Hi saw other women, and she loved him very much and that this was something she was going to have to live with." Asked by Aurnou whether she and Mrs. Harris ever discussed travelling with Tarnower, Mrs. Jacobson replies, "Jean has stated she would rather travel with Hi in company than not at all. She would rather be with Hi no matter how they travelled. The one thing she did object to was wherever she went . . ." Wherever she went, what? We're not to know: Bolen successfully cuts her off.

Anne Kinzie takes the stand: she speaks to Mrs. Harris's old-established reputation for good character. At the time she met Jean Struven both of them were engaged to be married. At Christmas 1945 the two couples had gone on a skiing trip together. Between 1946 and 1966 they'd been part of a group of some fifty to sixty people who met several times each month at each other's homes. What a full social life this modest couple had! The Kinzies and the Harrises had children of the same age; the wives had played bridge during the day. Mrs. Kinzie is now a lay minister of Christ Church.

Charles Johnson had been a machinery salesman in Detroit, a very close friend of Jean Harris's divorced, now dead, husband. As part of a group "of hundreds," says Johnson, he and his wife saw Jean and Jim Harris once or twice every week—this was in the Grosse Pointe days; the young wife had indeed found a "social structure" of her own, and well populated it was too. Of Mrs. Harris, Johnson says, "She was probably the most highly regarded woman that I have ever known." I find the direct simplicity of the praise very moving. I've been thinking of the headmistress as the defendant in a sensational murder trial, reduced to dependence on scraps of loyalty thrown her by the more generous of her recent friends and associates. It takes someone as disinterested as this witness to remind me that once upon a time Jean Harris had been a person widely admired and respected, not a person to be pitied.

Mrs. Margaret Stein, a friend of both the defendant and Dr. Tarnower, recalls "a lovely walk in the woods" with Jean Harris. They were in Purchase, it was autumn 1979, and as they walked Mrs. Harris spoke of her concern about her future: she didn't know where her life was heading. She'd said she didn't think she could be a school principal forever. Mrs. Stein had suggested Washington: wouldn't that be a feasible place for her to make her life? But Mrs. Harris rejected the suggestion. She "couldn't conceive of life without Hi." The witness says she'd seemed depressed and worried. Bolen objects to the word "depressed" as conclusory and it's stricken.

I watch Mrs. Schwartz when people whom she thought of as friends of her brother come down the aisle from testifying for Mrs. Harris. She freezes as they pass her. With this shooting and trial there'll have to be a considerable re-shuffling of the social arrangements in Westchester. No doubt it's been going on since last spring.

Sometimes, before I leave for White Plains in the morning, I see my cleaning woman. She asks how the case is going—she follows it closely but, like everyone else with whom I speak, with little interest in the evidence. What she cares about is the outcome. She's long since decided that the headmistress is guilty. "If she wants

190

to commit, why doesn't she commit?" she demands of me. I say that I suppose she's changed her mind. This calls for a shift in tense: "If she wanted to commit, why didn't she commit?" She regularly repeats the question, it takes on her rhythm of insistence. I begin to hear it as the refrain of this trial.

By the time Mrs. Harris testifies I'm in bed with the flu. Except that it's not the flu, it's only a convincing masquerade of legitimate illness, as proved by the fact that as soon as I'm called on the telephone and told that Mrs. Harris is taking the stand, I leap from bed, dress in what I think is called a trice, rush to Westchester, and forget there'd ever been a thing wrong with me. It wasn't even normal exhaustion I was suffering; it was a collapse of the spirit, cowardly and total. I burned with the low fever of having to listen to difficult testimony in whose details I couldn't be interested. My aching head was no doubt a response to this unceasing talk about high-, medium-, and low-velocity blood impact, about bullet trajectories hypothecated upon the sine—yes, sine—of an angle of projection of an elliptical droplet—uh-huh—and about patterns produced by the gushings from minor arteries. The pain behind the eyes represented my refusal to visualize skin cells in basket-weave patterns, the pain behind the ears my refusal to hear another word about the inhuman stratifications of the tissue of the human hand: stratum corneum, stratum lucidum, stratum granulosum, stratum spinosum. (What, no stratum Kant, Hegel, or Marxum?) As in Poor Butterfly's wait for her Pinkerton, the minutes pass into hours, the hours pass into years—and I take to my bed. I may have been alone in finding so craven a way out, but I was far from alone in my suffering from this over-exposure to medical technology and criminalistics; the very word is an assault. The Judge and lawyers went full steam ahead under this battering but the jury was in a daze and the court spectators were plainly traumatized. There came a day when we were shown tissue slides on a screen, and the court, like the orchestra in Haydn's "Surprise"

Symphony, slowly emptied in the darkness; the lights went on to a roomful of deserted seats. In the press rows we tried to keep up our strength with candy and zany humor. Herbert MacDonell, the criminalists' criminalist, he of the Corning Crime Laboratory—"the only independent crime laboratory in New York State," Aurnou described it—and chief witness for the defense (it was rumored and later confirmed that, too late, Bolen had tried to get him for the prosecution) had been instructing us in the meaning of "transfer": bloodstains and other crucial evidence could be moved from one object to another and this could lead to mistaken conclusions by the crime investigators. The eye-catching TV reporter in the row ahead of me begins to pluck her golden hairs from her head, one at a time, and distribute them on the collars of the men within her reach. It's "transfer," she explains, and if it isn't enough of a lesson she has one even better: like an itchy dog, but rather more seductive, for the rest of the day she rubs her shoulder against any male shoulder in the vicinity. A friend of mine visiting me in court during one of the days when MacDonell was testifying was discomfited by so much giddiness among the press people—this was a murder trial, after all. But by its length and now by its nature, this trial was detaching us from reality: how did one assert sanity in such a Kafkaesque world? The press people, with a daily story to file, of course hadn't the escape I finally contrived for myself, of going to bed sick. In the elevator one afternoon a woman reporter had appealed to me: had I understood anything *any*body had said that day? I assured her gravely that the Harris case wasn't a case that women could understand. Women hadn't minds for science.

But our boredom apart, what in the way of evidence, hard evidence, had been produced in this long, taxing, expensive testimony of these many expert witnesses for the defense: James Chapman, Dr. Henry Ryan, Dr. Philip Bonanno, Dr. Jack Davies, Dr. Cyril Wecht, Dr. Albert Ackerman, Dr. Alfred Angrist, Dr. Michel Janis—all these in addition to Professor MacDonell? (MacDonell's claim to the honorific title which Aurnou lobs to the jury as often as he can turned out to be valid: he teaches at Elmira College. Aurnou had all but "professored" Chapman into the ground: Bolen meanly revealed that Chapman hadn't graduated from high school.)

Chapman's contribution hadn't been very extensive. All that he'd really told us was that most standard crime-scene procedures were violated by the Harrison police—it wasn't news. In cross-examination of the officers who'd been called by Bolen, Aurnou had abundantly impressed us with the fact that they were very careless in the handling of evidence. They'd broken most of the rules in the police manuals.

Dr. Ryan—he's Chief Medical Examiner for the state of Maine—fudges the question of whether Tarnower's first wound was a defensive wound: "While I would characterize it as what is described as typical defense wounds, my own opinion is that this cannot be said with any certainty." He believes that the case for it being a defensive wound would be stronger if there were other injuries in the same area. As to the doctor's front chest wound, it lines up with the hand wound; the same bullet that went through Tarnower's hand could therefore have entered his front shoulder. If this happened, Mrs. Harris's report of a struggle for possession of the gun would of course be untrue. But Dr. Ryan favors the possibility of a struggle because of the clustering of the wounds: they're all on the right side of the doctor's body and none of them suggests a mortal target. Dr. Roh, called back to the stand shortly before Ryan's appearance, had said that he'd just been reminded that tissue from one part of the body could be carried by a bullet to another part of the body. Roh had re-studied the three tissues in the cutting he'd taken from Tarnower's chest and discovered what he believed to be tissue indigenous to the hand. Dr. Ryan examined this slide but says he can't with confidence confirm Roh's opinion.

Dr. Bonanno, a Westchester plastic surgeon who specializes in reconstruction of the head and neck, the hands and arms, has really but one point to make: despite the wound to the hand, Dr. Tarnower would have been able to fire and unload a gun. Bonanno can have no answer to the question of how one could handle a gun with a hand as bloodied as Tarnower's without getting blood on the trigger, the grip, the cylinder—nobody had told him anything about whether there was or wasn't blood on Mrs. Harris's revolver.

Dr. Davies's demeanor (I've never used the word in my life, I've learned it from these lawyers) is more striking than his contribution as an expert. He looks like someone remembered from an old John Ford movie. He's British by birth and bows to the jury before taking his chair. He teaches at Albany Medical School. Dr. Davies says he doesn't know what Dr. Roh's bits of tissue are but he surmises that they are chest cartilage. He talks about Tarnower's four wounds as "fairly trivial"; had he been promptly treated, his life could have been saved. What's fresh in Dr. Davies's testimony is his suggestion that the multiple wounds suffered by Tarnower were involuntarily inflicted by the defendant. Dr. Davies says that Mrs. Harris's arm could have been "gripped in such a way that there are repeated convulsive movements."

Dr. Wecht, a Pittsburgh pathologist, says that in studying Dr. Roh's slides he'd found no tissue that wasn't readily found in the chest area. In his view, nothing about Tarnower's anterior chest wound warranted the conclusion that Tarnower's hand was an intermediate target between the gun and his chest. Although, unlike Davies, Wecht wouldn't characterize the doctor's wounds as trivial—the British are more dramatic than we are, he correctly remarks—he believes that the injuries could successfully have been treated if taken care of within, say, a half hour. The defense is becoming increasingly insistent on this point as if to prove that it's not Mrs. Harris who's responsible for the death of Tarnower but the Harrison police who failed to get him to a hospital. Dr. Wecht believes that a struggle between Tarnower and Mrs. Harris is "within the realm of possibility."

The build-up for Dr. Ackerman had been greater than perhaps even for MacDonell. "There's a witness coming tomorrow in a limousine," Aurnou teased the press, "and he's bringing five different colors of chalk." A graduate of Andover, Princeton, Columbia Medical School, Ackerman now teaches at New York University Medical School. He's Aurnou's first pathologist of Ivy League background and he'd been contacted only four days ago, I don't know at whose suggestion. Ackerman uses a blackboard inside a pair of folding doors set into the wall of the courtroom to explain the special configurations of skin tissue. He consulted with cartilage specialists and says with certainty that one of Dr. Roh's three pieces of tissue is cartilage, but it's his modest opinion that the other two are cartilage as well. He's sure that none of them is indigenous to the hand.

Dr. Alfred Angrist, from Albert Einstein Medical College, and Dr. Janis, who got his M.D. at the Sorbonne, are both skin pathologists. They, too, testify that they found no tissue unique to the palm in Roh's slides. In fact, Roh is thus far the only one who makes the claim.

MacDonell's expertise doesn't lie in the field of skin pathology but in point of significant testimony for the defense he's the most valuable of Aurnou's experts. Herbert MacDonell is a specialist in many fields of criminalistics—firearms identification, bloodstain, fingerprints—and he's testified in many notable cases: a Black Panther trial, the assassinations of Martin Luther King and Robert Kennedy, the Joan Little and Joanne Chesimard cases. He'd first met with Aurnou in August 1980 and early September, then with Aurnou and Mrs. Harris on September 25 and 26. It was in September that in Mrs. Harris's company he'd made a first visit to the Tarnower home. He'd returned on November 1, December 5 and 6, and on January 4, 1981 he'd made a last inspection of the crime scene.

MacDonell's confidence is no greater, I suppose, than Ackerman's and no doubt it's equally well based. It's also bolstered by a retinue that apparently came with the witness from Corning. I count five people, conspicuous among them a young, bouncy, full-blown streaked blonde who plants herself in the front row of the courtroom in the seats usually reserved for Mrs. Harris's visitors. I assume that this is the female "associate" to whom MacDonell several times refers in his testimony: Miss Bouncy delights in every victory for the defense and in every put-down of the prosecutor—such overt partisanship seems to me to be indiscreet. It doesn't support the supposed objectivity of MacDonell's findings. Mac-Donell is tall, thin, thin-featured, thin-bearded, balding, bespectacled; when he wants to study something closely, he takes off his glasses and peers at it myopically. He doesn't buy new date books, he tells us; he makes over his old ones. He's a character out of Chekhov. He has the vaguely dilapidated look of one of the bettersituated persons in a Chekhov story, a surveyor perhaps or a retired teacher, someone who brings the secret knowledge of defeat to his small successes. He's often sarcastic, as if turning outward a mockery he would like to direct to himself. He has to boast and shine. His obsessiveness isn't exemplary in the modern American or German literary fashion and it hasn't the dimensions it would have in Balzac—for all his tensions, MacDonell is too toneless for a French novel. Without question, he belongs in the classic literature of Russia. For the better part of four days he explains his diagrams, points out what is revealed by the bloodstains on the doctor's bed linens and pajamas. His testimony is central to the defense, crucial in its refutation of the prosecutor's belief that Mrs. Harris took the doctor by surprise and deliberately shot him. He substantiates Mrs. Harris's account of the struggle in which the doctor had his first injury.

We remember that a bullet had gone through the double glass door of the bedroom and that, according to the defense, it had hit the deck outside the door. It ricocheted and a fragment of it went into a stanchion on the deck. On the basis of the location of the bullet holes in the glass and in the stanchion, and accepting an indentation on the seventh plank of the deck as the ricochet point— this was never proved—MacDonell had traced a trajectory for the bullet. Then he'd found a tiny drop of blood on the aluminum frame of the glass door and traced *its* trajectory. The point of intersection of the two trajectories indicated where Tarnower and Mrs. Harris would have had to be standing when the doctor was shot in the hand. It's where Mrs. Harris had told him they were standing. MacDonell is sure that the bullet that went through Tarnower's hand didn't enter his shoulder but travelled out the glass door and that it was therefore fired in just such a struggle and from just such a location as Mrs. Harris described. It took a couple of harrowing days to make this essentially simple point that could win her case for her.

Mrs. Harris's reaction to MacDonell's testimony was remarkable. All the week before his appearance she'd looked notably brighter than she had during previous days. She surely had cause: his discovery of the blood spot on the door frame would be powerful confirmation of her story. Yet when MacDonell actually took the stand she began visibly to sag, and not, like the rest of us, from the weight of his pedantry or even from the stifling heat in the courtroom—sensibly she kicked off her boots and sat in her stocking feet—but for (as I figure it) a far more private reason. At the end of the first day of his testimony she looked at the reporters and said, "I wish somebody would let me tell the truth. I really want to tell them the things they want to know. That poor man will be up there a month the way this is going." In other words, she couldn't give up her control of the situation. Until MacDonell's appearance Mrs. Harris had been dominating the trial. It was *her* trial. She'd been busy every minute, taking notes, finding photographs for Aurnou to consult, whispering what seemed to be comments or suggestions to him and his associates. She'd been stage front. But now she's relegated to the wings; she's lost command of the show. Denied a place at the center of the proceedings, it's as if she'd been robbed of life. What did this tell us about her relation to people, about her relation to Tarnower? Was she in fact the passive creature that she was popularly made out to be?

And Bolen's behavior with MacDonell was almost as fascinating. By the end of day 3 of MacDonell's testimony it seemed plain to everyone in the courtroom, certainly everyone I spoke to, that a staggering blow had been dealt the prosecution. Worn down as we were by MacDonell's arcane language and tortuous analysis of evidence, we weren't so lost as not to appreciate his cogency.

In fact, by the third day of his testimony we left court sure that the case for the defense was in the bag: if Mrs. Harris was telling the truth about the struggle—and according to MacDonell's evidence, she must be—she was also telling the truth when she said that she'd come to kill herself and that Tarnower's death was accidental. If the case went to the jury at that moment, she'd be bound to be acquitted.

What happened? How did Bolen, in the face of such a fundamental impairment of his position, manage to reconstitute it? Trials are strange things, the temperaments of the contending attorneys are involved to a far greater degree than, in my inexperience, I'd realized. In advance of Mrs. Harris's trial we'd been told of Bolen that he was doggedly stubborn. To this there could now be added the fact that he obviously functions much better in adversity than when things are going well for him. We thought it was a defeated prosecutor who took up the cross-examination of MacDonell on the morning of day 4; we were wrong. Bolen didn't destroy Mac-Donell's credibility—this was never an issue—but he successfully attacked the authority of his conclusions. Everyone in the court-room remembered Aurnou's scornful attack on the Harrison police for violating the rules for crime-scene search and procedure. Bolen turned against MacDonell the same criteria that had been applied to the inept and careless Harrison officers, and MacDonell was found to have erred as they had and with no different excuse. When MacDonell found blood, as he did on the door frame, wouldn't it have been the proper first step, Bolen asks, for the spot to have been photographed? "Yes," says MacDonell, "if you have the equipment available." Didn't MacDonell tell his students that the correct way to collect blood spots was with tape lifts? "As a method," says MacDonell, "providing the surface is amenable to removal." MacDonell had tested the blood with benzidine: was benzidine specific for blood? Not under normal circumstances, Mac-Donell admits. And what about the samples MacDonell had used: where were they now? asks Bolen. "They were tested and they were discarded," says MacDonell. Had MacDonell used distilled water for his tests? No, he'd used tap water. And the material on which he had dissolved his samples: of what kind was that? Well, he had used Kleenex. And so it went. If one were looking, as Aurnou had been in the instance of the Harrison police, to chalk up black marks for laxity, surely MacDonell was open to similar criticism.

MacDonell's authority was so badly eroded under this examina-tion that it was impossible to suppose that he could ever restore it. And in fact he didn't thoroughly restore it though Bolen did his best to restore it for him or at the moment seemed to. Has MacDonell ever examined Tarnower's bed linens, Bolen inquires, and when MacDonell says he hasn't, Bolen asks if he'd like to examine them now. I don't believe it. It's like Samson asking Delilah if she'd like a pair of scissors. But later I learn that Bolen wasn't perhaps as egregiously self-defeating as had appeared: the prosecutor knew that in September MacDonell had been given a free opportunity to study the bed linens; since he hadn't made reference to them in his testimony, Bolen would seem to have assumed that this was because he hadn't found anything helpful to the defense. When we return from lunch MacDonell once more takes over the court. He has studied the doctor's linens and pajamas during the lunch break, examined the bloodstains, and on the basis of their patterns reconstructed the movements of Tarnower and Mrs. Harris *after* the shot to the hand. Everything that MacDonell deduces from the blood patterns conforms, he says, to the headmistress's recollections.

And there'd been a day when the reporters weren't bored, or at least when this wasn't the problem. They were restless and petulant: there was something lowering in being cooped up in a White Plains courthouse, concentrating our attention on Mrs. Harris as if she were a world-historical event, when historical events were taking place in the world. It was the day for the release of the hostages. From a press photographer with radio earphones we'd learned that two planes carrying back our hostages had left Iran; then somebody else said no, that was wrong, only one plane had left. Yet another reporter cautioned us that there'd been no official confirmation that any hostages had been flown out—and here we sat, waiting for this trial to re-commence. The Judge and the lawyers were in chambers, nothing seemed to be happening. The likelihood was that nothing would ever again happen in this court: should we leave and go to a bar or at least to the jurors' lounge where there was a TV set, or were we to wait here indefinitely? There was of course the inauguration too, as well as the hostages. Our decision was made for us: "Move it, kids! Out!" The deputy sheriff would notify us in the press room when court reconvened. The jurors' lounge was jammed. Everyone in the building was converging on it, drawn from private to public concerns. The TV set was so bad that all I could see was Mrs. Reagan's red hat—was I meant to see more?—and Carter's face fixed in its now-familiar lines of near-tearful bravery. Then all at once, when I'd stopped listening, there was a burst of applause and I took this to mean that the hostages were free so I clapped too. But the hostages hadn't budged;

Reagan had arrived to be sworn in. Reasonably enough, Mrs. Harris's trial chose this illuminating moment to reclaim us—we raced upstairs to retrieve our seats. My mind couldn't be held by the testimony: I had had more than my surfeit of skin pathology. These of course weren't prosecution witnesses who were piling it on us; they'd been called by Aurnou. But why did the prosecutor persist in making this much of the first shot? Why wouldn't he give up on the idea of a defensive wound and of tissue carried from the hand to the chest? Obviously if he yielded on the way Tarnower had received the hand and front chest injuries, he'd have to accept the premise that there'd been a struggle between Mrs. Harris and Tarnower. But why not accept it; why was he so fixed on the surprise element in Mrs. Harris's visit? With all the help of its experts the defense had been able to address itself, really, to only a single shot: the first of them. It couldn't do anything about shots 2, 3, and 4 except vaguely propose that they too were the consequence of Mrs. Harris's repeated suicide attempts. Suppose Dr. Tarnower *was* shot trying to get the gun away from Mrs. Harris. If suicide was all that she had on her mind, wouldn't she have been deflected from pursuit of this purpose by discovering that she'd repeatedly hit the wrong target? However skillfully MacDonell suggested the activity that produced the bloodstains on the doctor's sheets, he hadn't explained away the doctor's death or Mrs. Harris's share in it, and it seemed to me that the more Bolen battled with Aurnou's witnesses about the first of the shots, the easier he made it for the defense to by-pass the question of how the other three wounds had been inflicted. And surely the silliest mistake was to set the local Medical Examiner against all these other doctors and make it look as if he alone among pathologists recognized hand tissue when he saw it.

Well, at least now MacDonell and his entourage had disappeared and Mrs. Harris had begun to look better again, just very thin— she's losing too much weight. She's a chocoholic: she constantly eats Hershey bars brought her by the younger members of the defense staff. But who are we in the press rows to be counting her indulgences? We've been eating constantly too, anything that comes our way: chocolate bars, peanut bars, Tootsie Rolls, gumdrops, chocolate-covered peppermints; when we get desperate there are always Life Savers and Chiclets. It's even got to the Judge—from where he sits, poor man, Judge Leggett has had to watch us chomping and chewing and I think, I *think,* that today he secretly took to gum. It's become our favorite subject of conversation, how much weight we've gained. We ought to have had a pool about our collective weight gain; we have one about the date of the verdict. I guess Mrs. Harris eats no meals, she lives on junk; that's endearing in the mistress of a diet doctor. We hungry onlookers have no choice but to go from junk to junk here in White Plains, it's the world center for non-food. It's impossible to get a recognizable sandwich in the vicinity of this court or an unadorned piece of meat or fish. Order a tuna on rye and no doubt it'll be topped with melted cheese and a maraschino cherry. The food of White Plains is as creatively awful as its architecture.

Aurnou's red-headed wife has been in court with her red-headed twin sister: double your pleasure, double your fun! They sat in the front row with one of the TV artists who's also a redhead and who told me that she too was a twin. Something strange must be going on here.

There was a disturbing moment the other day when Mrs. Aurnou was visiting court. Aurnou had had a rather unpleasant hassle with Bolen, he'd been very angry, but then he'd turned away from the bench, caught his wife's eye and broadly winked—we weren't of course supposed to have seen that. Is everything, then, a show for the jury?

Before I collapsed there'd been a brief merciful respite from technical witnesses. Court had opened with the president of Allied Maintenance on the stand; this was the New York company for which Mrs. Harris worked from 1975 to 1977, between the closing of the Thomas School and going to Madeira. He'd testified to her good character and competence. And then a couple named Santy—

they live on the Madeira campus but Robert, the husband, is employed in the U.S. Senate; his wife Sandy runs the co-curriculum program and is in charge of chapel at Madeira—testified to Mrs. Harris's distress in the wake of the disciplinary incident of Thursday the 6th. Apparently the parents of the expelled girls as well as the students themselves were upset by the decision. It's unpleasantly instructive to learn that there had been reprisals: three people from staff had had the air let out of their tires. This is considerably more shocking to me than that a couple of seniors had smoked pot. Kathleen Kavanagh also testified for Mrs. Harris. We'd several times heard her mentioned in the trial; Miss Kavanagh was the one who'd joined the headmistress for the second half of her arduous western trip. Even before her appearance I'd got the sense, I don't know why, of a particular closeness between this member of the Madeira staff and Mrs. Harris: some special understanding or sympathy. Miss Kavanagh testified that she'd been present through all the campus upset following Mrs. Harris's return. She'd been at the meeting at the headmistress's house on the 6th and the "town meeting" that was called the next day to discuss the expulsions. She'd dropped by to see Mrs. Harris on Sunday afternoon: "She was in the living room. There were papers and things scattered around. She appeared to be working." An appointment she'd had with the headmistress for Monday afternoon had been broken but after lunch Miss Kavanagh had seen Mrs. Harris in the hall. "She looked quite ill. . . . She was white. Very white." Later in the day, approximately between 4:30 and 6:00, she'd seen her again, driving off the campus alone.

I could wish we'd been spared the rest of the day's testimony: there are things harder to take than boredom. I don't mean that I wish I'd been spared the appearance in court of David Harris's friends the Swartleys, and their account of Tarnower's party for David—long after I've forgotten more important details of Mrs. Harris's trial I'm sure I'll remember that Tarnower, with Mrs. Harris's apparent approval, had given his guests at David's pre-wedding dinner autographed copies of his diet book. Paperback. But I was unhappy that David's marriage, already referred to often enough, had again to be introduced into the court proceedings, and

I was more than unhappy that Mrs. Harris's sons were called as witnesses. Wasn't it sufficient that their mother was on trial for murder? Did they have to testify for her? Perhaps Jimmy had to appear because he was the one who'd cleaned out her house at Madeira and found the earlier version of her will. And it was to him that Mrs. Potts gave the pills that Tarnower had mailed to Mrs. Harris. But David had no such link to evidence. He'd been married only a few weeks when the shooting had occurred; his marriage had been launched in catastrophe.

Robert Swartley lives in Philadelphia. He describes himself as a banker—he looks much the same age as David, in his early thirties. There had been about twenty-five people at cocktails and dinner at Dr. Tarnower's house. "It was a festive occasion," he tells us. "Everybody was having a very festive time." It turns out that even a wedding party couldn't interfere with the doctor's bed hour: the party started at 6:00 and ended at 9:00 or 9:30. That night Robert and his wife Leslie had slept at David's house but the night after the wedding they'd stayed at Dr. Tarnower's. They had breakfast the next morning with the doctor and Mrs. Harris; the stay had been "very pleasant." What his wife Leslie seems to treasure from the evening is Tarnower's gift of his book "to remember that evening by." [The words are Aurnou's.] "He signed it for me. . . . The very first page before the acknowledgments." The page would be forever preserved: it was to be Xeroxed and placed in evidence.

Nothing could be more sweetly revealing of Judge Leggett than the moment early in James Harris's testimony, while the drug exhibits were being marked, when the Judge looked down from the bench at the defendant and smiled at her. He had not previously permitted himself any such show of personal feeling; I'm not sure it reached Mrs. Harris. The defendant's child was on the stand, the Judge was himself a father; his smile was meant to communicate that he understood her pride in her son and sympathized with Mrs. Harris in his being called as a witness. James identified himself as a first lieutenant and commanding officer of his Marine platoon. Shortly after the shooting he'd left flight school in Pensacola and gone to Madeira. He'd spent about twenty hours at The Hill. Mrs. Potts had given him the box with the two vials of pills from the school safe; he'd also found another vial in his mother's medicine cabinet. He'd gone through various drawers and found a handwritten copy of a will his mother had written. Aurnou offers the document in evidence. Did he recognize the handwriting? Aurnou asks. James Harris says firmly, "Most definitely . . . My mother's. Let there be no mistake about that." Why is he this emphatic, poor devil? The house in Mahopac owned by his mother was just a cabin, he testified, with a living room, one bedroom, a kitchen, a small bath. His mother had herself never lived in it though from time to time he and his brother used it—he remembered only one night she'd spent there, a Christmas Eve four years ago. "My brother and I had cleaned it to the best of our ability and had a Christmas tree out there and we all had Christmas there." Of the wedding dinner James tells us, "It was a good occasion. It was a good time." If he were twenty years older I'd say he'd been reading Hemingway. There had been about fourteen guests; Dr. Tarnower seemed to be having "a grand time." His mother was "also having a good time." Aurnou asks about his mother at the wedding. "Nervous as an expectant mother-in-law," says James, "and otherwise happy."

Bad enough. But must David now take the stand just to tell us that it was Tarnower who first brought up the subject of the wedding party and not, as Suzanne testified, his mother? Well, I suppose it's important for his mother's defense to discredit Suzanne at every opportunity. The doctor had proposed the party back in October, says David, and had wanted to hold it at his Club except that the Club closed at the end of November and the party couldn't have been put together in time. David estimates the number of guests at Dr. Tarnower's house in celebration of his marriage as twenty, "sort of a mixed bag of people . . . mostly my wife's friends," and agrees that it was a happy occasion. The doctor had been "very jovial. I hadn't seen him as talkative as he was for over those two days." David had lived in the Mahopac house for about four years, his brother for about four months.

Bolen had no questions to put to David. What questions were there? It was a day for tears though Mrs. Harris shed none. I left the court without stopping to talk with anyone.

I didn't feel good, I suspect I had a fever. It didn't help that when I got to court at 9:30 the next morning, our usual hour, nothing was going on and that nothing went on for the entire morning and most of the afternoon. The lawyers, I suppose, were at it again, battling behind the scenes. What now? Report had it that Mrs. Harris was in one of the smaller courtrooms on our floor, with her face buried in her arms on a table and that one of the young women from Aurnou's staff was stroking her back. We sent someone to peer in and spy out the situation. He returned to say that Mrs. Harris was indeed in the smaller courtroom, chatting happily. Then a short time later, with the appearance in the corridor of her psychiatrist, Dr. Abraham Halpern, another rumor got started, that the lawyers were conferring about psychiatric testimony. This time we dispatched one of the local reporters who knew Dr. Halpern to ask if he was about to take the stand. She returned with his assurance that he'd not been asked to testify. Dr. Halpern left the building; we remained. At 4:30 a witness at last took the stand; it hadn't been worth the wait. His name was Eisenberg, he'd been a pharmacist for fifteen years at a drugstore up the block from the courthouse. A few months ago an officer of the company that owned this pharmacy had pleaded guilty to having filled brand-name prescriptions with generic drugs but having charged the brand-name prices. Eisenberg testified that he'd got to know Mrs. Harris slightly; he'd not known Dr. Tarnower. Aurnou produced seventeen pieces of paper, prescriptions or copies of prescriptions supplied by the drugstore in response to his subpoena. Their numbers, dates, the name of the drug, the name of the patient, the name of the person who had picked up the filled order and of the doctor who'd signed the prescription: these were now tediously read into the court record. The first of the prescriptions, dated 7/15/79, was for Desoxyn and had been picked up, the witness believed, by Mrs. Harris. The list was not in chronological order.

> 9/1/79—Desoxyn
> 5/28/79—Desoxyn
> 10/18/78—Percobarb
> 10/28/78—Methamphetamine

9/4/78—Methamphetamine
6/26/78—Methamphetamine
8/21/77—Methamphetamine
12/4/77—Methamphetamine
8/12/78—Methamphetamine
3/28/79—Percodan
10/26/77—Methamphetamine
7/15/79—Plexonal
7/15/79—Valium
11/20/79—Valium
8/14/78—Nembutal

A last date was either October 19 or 29, 1978, but the name of the drug on that date wasn't mentioned. Percodan, we learned on cross-examination, was an opium derivative for pain, Nembutal a barbiturate, Valium a tranquilizer, a depressant, a muscle relaxer, Plexonal a combination barbiturate. I assume that methamphetamine is Desoxyn. The medicines had all of them been prescribed by Dr. Tarnower and, so far as the pharmacist knew, they had been picked up by Mrs. Harris. How many pills were ordered in each prescription or how often they were to have been taken, we'd not been told. By now I couldn't suppose it mattered.

It's the phone. I reach out from bed and answer dully. An excited voice says that Mrs. Harris has taken the stand, I must get to White Plains if it's at all possible. Of course I must, of course it's possible. I get up and dress; I feel fine. I get to court just after the lunch break: Mrs. Harris is still doing pre-1966 history. So it's been finally decided that she'll testify! How often we'd all of us discussed it, we'd worn the question to shreds. Who can doubt that Mrs. Harris has wanted to take the stand: she longs to speak in her own defense, lives for it. But there's so much risk to be weighed. Suppose she's cut off when she wants to talk, or she's asked a question that she prefers not to answer: she'll blow sky high. She hates Bolen, perhaps she even hates Judge Leggett. She can't think of them except as her personal antagonists. It's not only that the law is unjustly hounding her. They, these individuals, are unjust and inimical. Some of the reporters believe that Aurnou has no choice but to put her on the stand. They think that if she doesn't testify, he can't win the case. But I don't agree. I think it's the other way around, and that he's jeopardizing the case if she does testify. We recognize the dilemma. Yet as I drive to White Plains I'm suddenly struck by the implications of debating the question in these terms. For scores of women, for hundreds, thousands, Mrs. Harris has become a spokesperson. Her trial is their trial. In shooting the man who had misused her, she'd acted in their cause, made their statement, righted old wrongs done their sex. And yet this symbol of sexual justice is a woman whom we who have been watching her in court are afraid to have testify because she's so little steady, so unwell. Is the female cause this closely locked into emotional disorder? Is this the best we can do in the way of female champions, to represent our sex through someone who walks so close to the brink of breakdown? Surely what's wrong here is that we are confusing an irremediable and fatal collision between one man and one woman with a remediable attitude toward women in our society. We're careless about who it is that represents what.

When I get to court I learn that Mrs. Harris has asked that her son Jimmy stay in the corridor today, she doesn't want him present while she testifies. For whomsoever's sake the request is made, it's comforting to hear. But Jimmy's not in a good mood: I'm told he's angry at the press, he's angry at Aurnou. Perhaps Aurnou questioned the wisdom of having his mother testify. Jimmy says she *has* to testify. She'll tell the truth—it'll be a great day for her, for the country, no doubt for the Marines. I can't believe any of this: everybody's going mad.

It turns out to have been unnecessary for us to worry that Mrs. Harris would be too agitated to testify. Dear God, the role of witness on her own behalf suits her the way ecstasy suited St. Theresa. It's mind-boggling, her transcendence of reality. I've never seen aggression so thoroughly transformed into moral superiority: it combines an eagerness to speak, eagerness to shine, and contemptuous anger at the process which has ensnared her. She's so queenly in her scorn, you'd think the law was trampling on the royal preserves. Does it not enter this woman's mind that we are all of us here in this court because Dr. Tarnower is dead and that she's on trial for his murder? One of the reporters has told me that her sons respectfully and affectionately call Mrs. Harris "Big Woman." They know not whereof they speak, or maybe they do. What puzzles me is whether Aurnou can possibly be unaware of her over-weening moral confidence, or at least her stance of imperviousness, and the effect it has on a spectator. Who in decency wouldn't wish to give someone in Mrs. Harris's situation as much support as possible? But it's not compassionate gentleness that I sense in the way she's treated by her counsel and friends. Their manner is one of deference, almost of awe. To speak of religion, there's an odor of sanctity about this defendant. When she becomes bothersome she's patted and shushed because the jury mustn't see her lose her temper. But no one, not Aurnou or any of his staff, not any of her visitors, seems to make a connection between Mrs. Harris's courtroom capacity for threatening behavior and the "tragic accident" of Tarnower's death. Her world is a fan club.

I'm told that Aurnou took the witness smoothly through her biographical introduction. She'd been born Jean Struven in 1923 in Chicago, brought up in Cleveland where she'd attended the Roxboro Elementary School and then the Laurel School in Shaker Heights. In 1945 she'd graduated *magna cum laude* from Smith, majoring in economics. A year later she married James Harris and went to live with him in Grosse Pointe where he'd been raised. Her son David was born in 1950, James in 1952. Until David's birth she'd taught "history and social studies" at the school that would later be called the Grosse Pointe University School. Subsequently she'd started a nursery school for her own boys and a few of the neighborhood children. Then she'd been invited back to the University School to teach first grade. In 1965 she'd been divorced and she'd kept the children. A year later, for financial reasons, she'd given up teaching for school administration. She'd become director of the Middle School of the Springside School in Philadelphia.

All of this is familiar and so is the account of her meeting with Dr. Tarnower in December 1966 at a party given by the Leslie Jacobsons in New York. Tarnower had just visited Russia and Mrs. Harris had also been to Russia "so we sort of showed off to each other about how much we knew about Russia, I guess." The next week he'd sent her a book about Masada with a note, "It's time you learned more about the Jews." Then in March 1967, after his return from safari in Africa, they had met in New York for dinner and gone to the Pierre to dance; he was a wonderful dancer—Mrs. Harris is sentimental about the Pierre Bar. He'd taken her back to where she was staying and left as he always did "like Cinderella, at eleven o'clock when Henri came to pick him up." In the next five years they didn't meet very frequently because her children were young and she couldn't easily get away, but the doctor wrote regularly and soon began to phone every night, "and he sent lots of roses." Obviously there's something wrong here. At the start of her acquaintance with Tarnower her sons were already seventeen and fifteen; in the next five years they were moving toward twenty-two and twenty. It's rather an extreme of maternal responsibility to restrict one's social life because of children that age. These embellishments are slipped so quietly into the record that it's only on later reflection that they become troublesome. Testimony is interrupted for Bolen to *voir dire* a card, "Love, Hi," that accompanied one of Tarnower's gifts of roses. When he asks whether there's a date for it, Mrs. Harris replies cuttingly, "No. I think you've already discovered, Mr. Bolen, I don't put dates on things, and it doesn't need a date. It just says, 'Love, Hi,' and it doesn't need a date." In May 1967 Tarnower gave her a ring and asked her to marry him. "It was a diamond engagement ring, a very lovely one, a large one." (Indeed it must have been. I've been told that although its one-time appraisal value of $35,000 would have been too high in 1967 dollars, its value was well beyond that in present-day dollars.) Again I'm confused. I thought that because of the children they didn't often see each other in the five years after they'd first met. Yet it was only five months after they were introduced that the doctor proposed marriage.

Shortly after this, Mrs. Harris went west for several weeks so that her sons could visit their father, and on her return Hi had called her. She'd asked about setting a date for the marriage: the boys' school would soon be starting and she needed to know where she was going to live. " 'Jean,' he said, 'I can't go through with it.' " She'd felt neither particularly hurt nor surprised at this response. "I suppose he couldn't be married. I don't know what all the reasons were." She'd returned the ring with a note that said, "You really ought to give it to Suzanne. She's the only woman you'll ever need in your life." But Tarnower had brought back the ring and told her he wanted her to have it forever. "He was very sweet about it. . . . He did all the right things, and I was very much in love with him by then, and it was too late. Being married didn't matter that much to me. It was seeing Hi that mattered. So I wrote him a letter . . . and said you have to stop thinking it's so bad you're not married. I think Hi felt that was the final requirement for middle-class respectability." Later he would tell her he was married to his profession.

Bolen interrupts here to say to Leggett, "I don't know whether there is a question before the witness," and Mrs. Harris says, "I don't either, to tell you the truth. I am sorry for talking so much." The Judge admonishes her, as he already has several times, simply to answer the questions put to her. What a pair Mrs. Jacobson and she must make when they get together for a quiet cup of coffee. A letter is put in evidence—will we ever know what it's about?—and Bolen attempts a *voir dire*. He asks the date of the letter.

Harris (impatiently): Oh, Mr. Bolen, I have no idea. It was in 1967, and it seems to me he said it in August. . . . I don't think there are many documents I have to put in evidence that have a date on them. I didn't think they would ever be put in evidence.

Was the original document sent to Dr. Tarnower? Bolen inquires calmly. And is this it?

Harris: That's right.
Bolen: And you placed it in an envelope which you addressed yourself. Is that correct?
Harris: Yes.
Bolen: And then somehow you got this letter back again?
Harris: Right.

Bolen:	Did Dr. Tanower give you the letter?
Harris:	No. The answer to that is a long one, but I will be happy to give it to you if you will listen.
Bolen:	At some point you got the letter back. Is that correct?
Harris:	Yes.
Bolen:	Did you get the envelope back as well?
Harris:	Not if it isn't there. I guess I did. I don't know. I really don't know. [She calls over to Aurnou: this court is home.] Is the envelope there?
Aurnou:	We have one envelope in August of '67 which we cannot date to a particular letter.

Bolen objects to the introduction of the letter on the ground that it is self-serving, hearsay, and bolstering. Harris: "What was that? It sounded awful." The objecton is sustained.

Mrs. Harris testifies that while she continued to live in Philadelphia she and Tarnower didn't see each other very much. Laughingly she recalls his saying, "It would be lovely to go someplace with you without your children," and we're again given the heartwarming impression of the impatient lovers with a pair of demanding toddlers at their heels. But at last they manage a trip to Jamaica and "a wonderful trip out west." The Jamaican trip took place over the New Year of 1967–68 and was their first trip alone. Aurnou asks the witness if her parents, who were then still alive, knew about it. It's incredible but Harris answers, "Yes, indeed they did." She continues: "Somehow in a conversation with Hi that came up, he seemed surprised that I told them. . . ." Bolen breaks in to object and Leggett sustains it as irrelevant. "It really isn't," I hear Mrs. Harris say softly. She tells of leaving Springside to go to the Thomas School in Connecticut in 1971. She'd stayed there until 1975. Around March of 1971 she and Tarnower had made a world tour together: Kenya, Khartoum, Ceylon, Saudi Arabia, Vietnam, Hawaii. Then in the fall of 1971 he'd again spoken to her of marriage—but now he had another woman in mind. It's unimportant. These are the Rowayton years: she and Tarnower are "very close." David is at college, Jim is away, and she lives only twenty minutes from Purchase. Hi "had come to terms with the reality of the fact that he was never going to marry." They spend all their weekends together and travel a great deal: Nepal, Afghanistan, Bali, Singapore. Mrs. Harris is asked by Aurnou how she was feeling physically in 1975. "I was feeling the way I felt for a long time," Mrs. Harris replies. "I had one great fear and that was exhaustion."

Aurnou: At that time, just yes or no, were you taking any medication?
Harris: Yes.
Aurnou: Was it prescription medication?
Harris: Yes.
Aurnou: Who wrote the prescriptions?
Harris: Hi did. Dr. Tarnower.

While she'd worked at Allied Maintenance, where she supervised the getting out of bids, she had an apartment in New York and came to Purchase for weekends. Hi wanted to buy an apartment for her in the city, but she wouldn't let him. She kept many of her belongings at the house, bought or replaced necessary household furnishings for the doctor. Before she went to Virginia in 1977, she and Dr. Tarnower had travelled together through the Iron Curtain countries; then they'd gone to Paris. It was at the Ritz in Paris that they'd returned to their room one day to find a letter from another woman—"It looked more like a term paper than a letter"—on the floor. The doctor had fumbled it out of sight. But he'd put his cuff links, which she'd seen for several years and which he'd told her were a gift from a grateful patient, on the mantel. Their underside was up and she'd seen that they were inscribed with "all her love from Lynne, with the date February 1974 on it."

Aurnou: Did you continue to travel with the doctor on that occasion?
Harris (laughing): Ye . . . yes.

For several years they'd spent Thanksgiving in Nassau, Christmas with the Schultes in Palm Beach. In 1977 they still saw each other virtually every weekend. She moved to Madeira at the end of June 1977.

The witness reports on the condition of the Madeira School when she'd become its headmistress: the need for maintenance on the buildings, the haphazardness of the school organization, the insufficient number of administrative officers, perhaps a certain lack of concern and enterprise on the part of the Board, even the bad quarters for the school's servants. She'd been told she was the unanimous choice of the Board and she'd believed it until she eventually learned that this wasn't true. Preparatory to launching a Madeira fund-raising drive in early 1979, a consultant was hired to write what came to be known as the Browning report: it was a canvass of relevant opinion about the school. "The first comment about the head," Mrs. Harris tells us, "was that she was the most controversial head of a school in the country. I didn't feel at all controversial. (Slight pause) I couldn't make that statement now. . . . I knew that I was held in high respect." Once more I'm confounded by Mrs. Harris's view of her present plight: whatever public disagreement there may be about her guilt or innocence of murder, surely her situation isn't anything so simple as "controversial." To her surprise and distress the Browning report recommended that she be got rid of, and she'd begun to give thought to leaving. Then a few months later a second study had been commissioned and this one strongly supported her performance as head of the school. But individual responses even to these new findings had been negative. She knew it was only a matter of time before she'd have to go.

In the summer of 1978 Mrs. Harris had often visited with Tarnower in Purchase. The doctor had been persuaded to write a book; whenever they were together they spoke of it. "We wrote parts of it together." At the end of that summer, she'd spent her two-week vacation with him. "He was upset when I arrived, more than I had ever seen him before, actually, because Hi was wonderfully in control of his life." Mrs. Harris explains that the book had gotten too big for him. (How small is small?) "All during that summer we worked on it," Mrs. Harris testifies, "but during those two weeks we worked on it continuously, every day." Bolen interrupts to say, "I'm trying to [understand how this is] relevant to March 10" but Leggett lets Aurnou proceed and we're told how some of the pages on which Mrs. Harris worked were sent to a nearby typist, some given to a typist in the doctor's office. She identifies "a good deal" of her writing. She speaks of her "editorializing," her "cutting and pasting," her "constant day-by-day, evening-by-evening" contribution to what everyone in the court must by now recognize as the literary masterwork of the century. A few weeks later, back at

school, she'd received a letter from Dr. Tarnower enclosing a
check for $4,000.

Dear Jean,
   For reasons that I cannot explain, it is imperative that I make all book
disbursements at this time. I am enclosing a check for $4,000 that I
hope you will accept.

Love,
Hi

Mrs. Harris accepted it—at any rate, we're never told that she didn't.
She'd kept a copy of her eight-page reply and this is now offered
in evidence by Aurnou, but after a long break in which the Judge
and lawyers disappear into chambers Leggett says he's substantially
redacted it and Aurnou reads aloud this shortened version. "Working together with you for a few days, doing something that really
helped you for the first time in eleven years, ranks as high on the
list of good memories as all those very happy trips," writes Mrs.
Harris. "I actually felt quite at peace working on it Monday night
while you went out to a dinner party." [Pow!] Aurnou asks if she
wrote this and Mrs. Harris says she did. He continues to read: "I
don't want a pound of flesh, Hi. I was quite happy to settle for
thank you. I still am. If the book is successful, I hope you may decide on another trip somewhere, anywhere, together." Had she also
written that? Aurnou inquires. Mrs. Harris replies in a small tear-
ful voice, "Yes," and puts on her dark glasses.

Aurnou: Did you ever threaten Dr. Tarnower with suing him or any-
thing of that nature?
Harris: Never.
Aurnou: At some time, only a month or two after that letter, you
bought a gun. Is that correct?
Harris: Yes.
Aurnou: How were you feeling emotionally then?
Harris: It's hard to say. I was feeling frightened, I think, by the kind
of exhaustion I felt. I felt the possibility of not being able
to do my work any more.

Why had she bought the gun? Aurnou now asks. Harris: "I think
it was like a security blanket. I felt safer with it because I thought
if I couldn't function any more I could handle it and I didn't have
to worry so much about becoming helpless." As if a statement like

this is all in the day's work Aurnou recurs to the second Madeira report, the one more favorable than the Browning report, and to an October Board meeting at which it was discussed. Had something happened at that meeting in regard to her employment? Harris: "I was literally *told* I was on probation but not given a reason. . . . I was left with the impression that I was not ever in a school year to leave the campus on the weekend, and I was given no explanations for the things that were said." Had she asked? Aurnou asks and Mrs. Harris says she had. Aurnou: "Did you ever get an answer?" Harris: "No."

Of course we've already heard from Mrs. Skallerup and Mrs. Faulkner, both of them members of the Board, neither of whom alluded to any adverse judgment passed on Mrs. Harris by the Board. Now one can see that their position in coming to White Plains as defense witnesses had been even more delicate than one thought, and one also sees the fateful multiplication of Mrs. Harris's problems: she'd been rejected not only by her lover but also by her school. It must have looked as if soon there would be nothing solid in her life—it's the way disasters come, in such regimental closeness. Suddenly I have a great desire to talk to Mrs. Skallerup, Mrs. Faulkner, someone at the top level at Madeira. But of course they wouldn't be able to answer the questions I want to ask: was there a connection between the negative judgment of the Board and Mrs. Harris's alliance with Tarnower? Had there been a premonition of serious scandal, had the Board detected the emotional unreliability of the headmistress and attributed it to her off-campus problems? Were they trying to recall her to the primacy of her professional commitments? It certainly suggests a new view of the relation between the Board and Mrs. Harris.

And a new facet of Mrs. Harris's character has also been revealed to us in today's testimony: her attitude toward money. In extended love affairs as in marriage, money readily becomes the repository of exhausted or unrealized desire. Long-married couples balance their checkbooks as a substitute for love-making, or they refuse each other love by protesting one another's financial error or excess. Worries about the children, worry about jobs or health, translate into quarrels about the bills. Tarnower hoped, he said, that his old mistress would take the check he sent her for her work on his book. He was paying her off and she knew it, or should have. But I suppose she felt, naturally if not generously, that if she couldn't have Tarnower she could at least have his $4,000; she'd earned it not only by her editorial skills but also by long years of faithful services. About money, Mrs. Harris isn't masochistic, whatever she may tell us about refusing to let Tarnower buy her a house. But I'm repelled by the language of love in which she cloaks the wish to get something in return for what she's given. All the repayment she asks is another trip with her Hi.

Mrs. Harris had continued to function at Madeira, she testifies, and she'd seen Dr. Tarnower over a few weekends. They'd gone to Nassau for Thanksgiving and spent two weeks at Christmas with the Schultes in Palm Beach. It was in Palm Beach that she'd given the Schultes and Hi the parodic Christmas card—it's not yet put in evidence. Court closes for the day. When the spectators leave, Aurnou reads the various communications to Mrs. Harris that have been introduced in the day's testimony: Tarnower's card with the roses; the note of 1978 which accompanied the $4,000 check; a love letter of 1967. As a sample of Tarnower's art in verbal love-making, the 1967 letter doesn't cry for inclusion in a textbook, but as an indication of the world into which Mrs. Harris was being inducted by Dr. Tarnower it's not unimpressive. The schedule of activities for a forthcoming weekend includes cocktails on Sunday with the Smiths (no first name), "then dinner at the Seymour Toppings (foreign editor of *The New York Times*), with Knopf, Harrison Salisbury, and Mr. Ronning (Canadian Ambassador-at-Large, involved with various North Vietnam peace feelers). He is Mrs. Topping's father." And now Lynne Tryforos is replacing Jean Harris in this society! It couldn't be easy to take, not easy at all. Surprising to me, Aurnou doesn't appear to be familiar with the name of the publisher, Knopf. He pronounces it uncertainly and the reporters are lost too; they have to be helped by the book writers. Wryly I recall the Harrison police who tried to locate that best-selling author "Tarno." How soon will Aurnou become Ahnow, and as for Mrs. Harris—who's Mrs. 'Arris?

216

Day 2 of Mrs. Harris's testimony particularly concentrates on states of mind; this includes important facts about the changing relationship of Mrs. Harris and Dr. Tarnower.

Mrs. Harris maintains that it was Dr. Tarnower who proposed the pre-wedding party for her son David. She says it was discussed between them in the first week of January while they were in Florida, and it was only because of Hi's wish to give the dinner that she'd phoned Suzanne. The party had been very successful: "The catalyst was Hi, I think. He was warm and friendly to everybody, and in a little while everybody was having a good time. I think he got a kick out of having so many attractive young women around, for one thing, and they thought he was wonderful, and he made a fuss over them and they made a fuss over him, and he had written a special funny toast to David and Kathleen and . . . in a very short time everyone felt welcome and warm and forgot that they were strangers." Aurnou asks whether he did anything in particular for the young ladies there. Mrs. Harris replies that it wasn't just the young ladies. "He did it for everybody. I don't know whether he planned it ahead of time, but just at the right moment after dinner he went in and with a big smile on his face brought out his books and gave them to them. I guess it *was* the women he gave them to and of course they were all very tickled and pleased and thought it was very special and he wrote things to all of them." The doctor had also inscribed a copy of the diet book to Jean but that had been soon after it came out. "For Jean," he'd written, "whose great style added a much needed element to this book. Hi." Mrs. Harris had to have lived a rich life of illusion to cherish such an inscription: a woman who received a lover's book inscribed with this passionate sentiment should have recognized that she'd got her walking papers. But Aurnou abets her in this as in all her self-hallucination. Together they'd turn Tarnower's flagrant minimalism into the love motif from *Tristan and Isolde*. After the wedding weekend Mrs. Harris had taken back to school with her a chapter of the new book Tarnower was working on, on aging. She'd made revisions in it, apparently drastic—at one place she'd cut and pasted, she said, so that her secretary wouldn't think she'd "gone bananas." She'd returned the manuscript with

217

a note appended to it, but before we're made acquainted with its contents our attention is briefly diverted to Christmas of 1979. Was the witness aware at that time, Aurnou asks, that Tarnower was seeing other women? Mrs. Harris replies yes but that she hadn't firsthand knowledge of it.

Aurnou: Did you have any feelings at that time about his course of action in that regard?
Harris: It was something I didn't have a right to be judgmental about. It was his life and his business.
Aurnou: Did you convey to him at that time your feelings concerning his seeing other women?
Harris: I did, always in a very light vein.

Now at last Aurnou puts the Christmas card into evidence. It was written, Mrs. Harris had explained, as a Christmas present for Vivian and Arthur Schulte as well as for Hi. Other than Vivian's, none of the female names are those of real people. "The point of it was to be amusing and not to be annoying," says Mrs. Harris and she listens with an author's pride as Aurnou reads it aloud. Her lawyer chortles and chuckles, he is often unable to contain his mirth. The cover reads, "A Very Merry to Vivian and Arthur and Herman."

'Twas the night before Christmas,
When in part of the house
Arthur was snuggling
With Vivian, his spouse.
In the guest room lay Herman, who, trying to sleep,
Was counting the broads in his life—'stead of sheep!
On Hilda, on Sigrid, on Jinx, on Raquel,
Brunhilda, Veronica, Gretel, Michelle;
Now Tania, Rapunzel, Electra, Adele;
Now Susie, Anita—keep trucking Giselle.
There were ingenues, Dashers, Dancers and Vixens,
I believe there was even one Cupid—one Blitzen!
He lay there remembering, with a smile broad and deep
Till he ran out of names, and he fell asleep.
(Let me mention, my darling, if this muse were inclined
Toward unseemly thoughts, or an off-color mind,
It wouldn't be easy to keep this thing refined!)
But 'tis the time to be jolly—and very upbeat—

And for now that's not hard because Herman's asleep!
Beside him lay Jeannie, headmistress by Jiminy—
Who was waiting for Santa to come down the chimney.
A huge stocking they'd hung by the hearth, those four sinners!
In hopes St. Nick would forgive and they'd all end up winners.
Would he leave them a prize or a well-deserved switch?
And how would they know which switch went to which?
But for now they were snuggled all safe in their beds
While visions of dividends danced through their heads.
Then all of a sudden there arose such a clatter,
Herm woke from his sleep to see what was the matter.
And with Jeannie obediently three paces back,
They tip-toed to the living room to watch Nick unpack.
He smiled to himself as he looked at their list.
And thought to himself, 'What an ironic twist!
I know perfectly well they've been gambling and boozing
But they're likable sorts—so it's rather confusing.
I'll leave them some bauble to match their uniquenesses.
And cater a bit to their favorite weaknesses!'
Nick looked to the left and the right once or twice.
'That Vivian's a marvel—she sure keeps it nice!'
He said as he left her some sugar and spice.
Then he added a ten karat bauble or two
And a bunch of hard books that he knew she'd get through.
'Yes sir, she's a bright one—a real cerebellum,
The place is in good hands with Viv at the helm.
It's no problem leaving some goodies for her
But what can I give to that rascal Arthur?
He has lots of golf balls and ties and nice socks,
There's one thing he *could* use—complete with the locks,
But there just wasn't room in the sled for Fort Knox.
I'll start with this book—it'll cheer the poor feller—
Now he too shall have his very own best seller.
And one little thing more he can have while Viv snoozes,
A very small jug of his favorite boozes.
Now let's see—there's Herman—with Tarnower for a monicka
It seems to me he got his best stuff for Chanukah.
I see at the top of his long list of druthers
He wants a handicap one point higher than Arthur's.
But a handicap's something old Nick can't be cutting,
Herm'll just have to stop gambling on Arthur's great putting.
But here's one little thing that I *know* he will use,
If his evenings are lonely he'll have no excuse.

Here's some brand new phone numbers in a brand new black book
(I'm not quite the innocent gent that I look!)
This book holds the key, and the hope, and the promise,
Of a whole bunch of fun, with some new red-hot mamas.'
Then he put in a couple of more odds and ends
Of stuff that he wanted to leave for his friends,
Some of it useful, and some of it funny—
Remembering it's always the thought, not the money!
Then grabbing his sack up the chimney he rose,
Herman and Jean returned to their room on tiptoes.
If they'd been non-believers, now they really had proof,
You could still hear the fellow up there on the roof.
And the warmth that they felt, say the heart really melts,
This Santa Claus feeling is just—something else!

Most people in the court are entertained; Judge Leggett smiles. But Mrs. Schwartz is not amused, in mid-poem she quietly leaves the room. The jury reveals nothing of its feelings, whether it thinks the parody is innocent fun or sympathizes with Mrs. Schwartz in her familial outrage. Again what I chiefly hear in Mrs. Harris's light-veined communication is its masked anger. Under the guise of amused tolerance, Mrs. Harris is bitter at both men, not Hi alone but even Arthur. Only Viv is spared her barbs.

It was on New Year's Day during this visit to the Schultes that Mrs. Harris had seen the ad on the front page of *The New York Times*. "Happy New Year, Hi T. Love always, Lynne." Aurnou: "Did you bring it to the doctor's attention?" Mrs. Harris: "Yes . . . I said, 'Herm, why don't you suggest that she use the Goodyear blimp next year? I think it's available.'" Mrs. Harris is a sharp woman, there's no question of that; quick on the draw—it's an unfortunate image to evoke, almost as bad as that of my neighbor in court who calls her a pistol. I'm uncertain, though, that in the long run it's a good idea to make the courtroom laugh. Wit isn't a useful instrument of defense; it may make a short-run appeal but it creates a backlash—one saw this in the Hiss case and the Oppenheimer hearings; certainly one saw it in the trial of Oscar Wilde. I don't have the impression that with any of these people it was a calculated technique; they didn't set out to be seductive with their cleverness. But it's hard for witty people not to be witty, it's their habit of speech, and they forget that different worlds of discourse have different manners of address. Even when a jury responds with laughter it may not be comfortable with the humor of the educated; and it isn't the natural mode of law. Aurnou asks Mrs. Harris, "Did you also have the same feelings for Dr. Tarnower at that time that you had since 1966 and '67?" Mrs. Harris replies, "They never changed."

We return to the new Tarnower book that Mrs. Harris was working on and the note that she'd appended to it when she'd sent it back to him. Aurnou reads from a copy that Mrs. Harris kept of her letter. If you have Mrs. Harris for either an editor or a mistress you don't need a Hungarian! Apparently four women whom the doctor admired are named in the note. It's explained to the court that these are public figures, the doctor had no relation to them other than respect.

Dear Herman:

T. S. Eliot I ain't, but this may hang together a bit better. I don't know where you go in Chapter II. My secretary thinks I have gone bananas. I think a bit of cutting and pasting at the crocodile testicles bit. She's a loyal, unquestioning employee up to a point. Not to the point of your "loyal, unquestioning employee!" But then the "perks" aren't the same either.

You were wonderfully kind and generous to do all that you did for David and Kathleen—and me, my enigmatic friend. I wish—same old wish—there were many more ways I could do things for you. It just wasn't in the cards for me to fix the cottage cheese at noon and run errands—I wish you didn't feel socially obligated to those who do. If it's any help though, darling, I can find someone who would be thrilled to give the same 24-hour door-to-door services and take shorthand too!

I'm sure it has never occurred to you because you will never be able to think of men and women as equals, but the truth is, darling, if one of the few women you admire—say, Audrey or Ronnie Rothschild, or Elizabeth McCormick or Iphigene—were to adopt the male equivalent of Lynne as a lover and richly rewarded "boy Friday," you wouldn't ask them back to dinner a second time.

Not only are you the man I have loved for fourteen years, I think you're unconstitutional.

All my love and gratitude.

Expectably Aurnou picks out for further attention the sentence in the letter in which Mrs. Harris expresses the wish that there were more things she could do for the doctor—he isn't of course going to point to his client's literary lardings (T. S. Eliot, the rewrite man?) or her hyped-up jollity, and certainly he's not going to stop over Mrs. Harris's wish that the man who had introduced her to his wealthy and important friends wouldn't feel "socially obligated" to the woman who fixes his lunch.

Aurnou: When you said that you had loved him fourteen years, did you love him then as you always had?
Harris (sobbing): Yes. [She mouths, "I'm sorry," to Judge Leggett.]
Aurnou: How long had you known about Lynne?
Harris: About eight years, I think. Seven years. [Pause, then quietly] I don't know what you mean "know about her."
Aurnou (dropping his voice): In the biblical sense.
Harris: Six years, I guess. It was six years.

I'm afraid I'd be sceptical of the spontaneity of this delicate passage between Aurnou and his witness even without the syntactical confusion of who's supposed to be knowing whom in the biblical sense. Her lawyer elicits from Mrs. Harris a more detailed account of her fatigue following her school trip and the problems with which she'd been beset when she'd returned to Madeira: the discovery of the bongs and marijuana seeds in one of the dorms (they were in a clothes basket in a bathroom between two rooms); the meeting at the headmistress's house on Thursday evening to discuss disciplinary action; the response of students and parents to the expulsion of the four seniors; her worry whether she'd made the right decision. I happen to think that she did not, and that she over-reacted because of her own drug dependence; a week's suspension and firm warning should have been punishment enough. We learn—it's a timely moment—that from Thursday, March 6, Mrs. Harris had been without medication. Her supply had given out.

On Saturday Mrs. Harris began a new will but some students dropped by at her house and she'd had to hide it. Monday she couldn't find it and she'd started again. From the time of her return on the 5th she'd been regularly phoning Tarnower. She'd called him so often that she has to consult her old phone bills to refresh her memory of when she had or hadn't reached him. On the 6th they apparently spoke twice, once for three minutes, once for seven. Aurnou asks what they'd spoken about. Harris: "Just general things. About the trip. About how he was. About how his book was going." Did the doctor speak of anything else? Harris: "He was cross because two of his books were missing and he said he wondered if I had them, which upset me. . . . I asked him for some medicine . . . and he said he'd send it." Friday the 7th? Harris: "I recall calling Hi—it seemed to me that's what I spent the rest of the weekend doing. I don't believe I reached him on Friday. . . . Henri answered most of the time." And Saturday the 8th? Harris: "I think it was three different calls. . . . I got Henri." After a break Aurnou produces a letter that Mrs. Harris wrote to her sister Mary Margaret during the weekend and Bolen asks to look at it.

Bolen: I haven't seen this particular exhibit before.
Aurnou: What?! He hasn't seen that before?!
Leggett: Please, fellers, do me a favor. Just read it, Mr. Bolen. [To Aurnou] Leave him alone.

The rest of the afternoon is spent going through the various bits of business to which the headmistress attended in preparation for her impending death. I find it interesting in the day's testimony that Mrs. Harris has scarcely mentioned her depression and hasn't spoken at all of when, or in what shape and detail, the idea of suicide had come to her. Perhaps we'll be told tomorrow.

A third day of Mrs. Harris as witness and so far, so good: no collapse. Lots of tears, many of them dry—or so it seems to me—but neither breakdown nor explosion. Aurnou resumes the questioning. "Did you receive medications both in names which you knew were real people and names which you did not know at all?" Mrs. Harris answers, "Yes." We remember Aurnou's report to the press about the guidelines Mrs. Harris had given him: he wasn't to criticize the man she loved. He's obeying the rules: this isn't criticism, it's an indictment. We're told about a dinner to honor Tarnower at the Westchester Heart Association, scheduled for

April 19, 1980. It was absolutely necessary, Mrs. Harris felt, that she be present but Tarnower felt that Lynne too had a claim—Hi "was on the fence." Momentarily Aurnou drops the matter to touch once more upon Mrs. Harris's emotions during the weekend before the shooting. How had she felt on Saturday? Harris: "I've told you, Joel, I really don't have the words. . . . [Crying] I felt a growing panic because I have always felt inadequate but that weekend I was terrified by my inadequacy. I couldn't function. [Hi] was the one person who made me feel safe. . . . [Yes, some girls had let the air out of the tires of several staff members] which made me cross because I thought if the girls wanted to be mad, they should be mad at me. . . . I wrote more of a letter to Hi, sort of a wail, I guess, because I couldn't reach him on the phone." She had sent it by certified mail first thing Monday morning. Aurnou asks if she had called Dr. Tarnower Monday morning. Harris: "Yes, I called him at the office and we talked for a while. . . . I wanted . . . to be . . . good company and not to be a whiner, and it was a very whiney letter." She had told him that when it came he should throw it away without reading it. Aurnou asks what they'd talked about on the phone. Harris: "[He asked me] whom I would like, who we should ask for dinner when I came." That would be April 5, not the evening at the Heart Association. Aurnou returns to Madeira. Yes, the unhappy letter we'd already heard about that Mrs. Harris received at her office on Monday was from the student hurt in the Brazen Hussies incident. The injured girl had been back at school in a week's time and she would eventually be completely healed, but Mrs. Harris tells of the deep concern she'd had for the girl's well-being and how hurt she'd been by the girl's criticism. "It sort of put a box on my life. It finished it. . . . I thought that if she thinks I failed her too, I had really blown the whole thing." Aurnou: "Whom else did you think you had failed?" Harris: "I guess everyone. I guess I was doing the best I could do and it didn't seem to be enough, and I didn't have the strength to do any more." She recounts the preparations for her trip to Purchase: the writing of her will, having it notarized, writing letters to her sister Mary Margaret and to Alice Faulkner, putting together the papers that her family might need. Aurnou goes over the note to Mrs. Faulkner. What had Mrs. Harris meant by "so many enemies and so few friends"? It becomes very still in the court as if we're approaching revelation.

Harris: I guess that was just my general feeling about life. . . . I was always under fire. . . .

Aurnou (still quoting from the letter to the Board chairman): "I was a person and no one ever knew"?

Harris (crying): I felt that for many years.

Aurnou (softly, choked): Would you explain that please, Mrs. Harris?

Harris: It's hard.

Aurnou (now in tears): Would you please tell the jury what you meant on March 10 when you said "I was a person and no one ever knew."

There's a long pause while the witness sits with her head down. Aurnou (softly): "Jean, look at me." Mrs. Harris raises her head but looks at the ceiling. She speaks in a shaky voice: "I don't know. I think it had something to do with being a woman who had worked a long time and had done the things a man does to support a family, but still [been] a woman, and I always felt that when I was in Westchester I was a woman in a pretty dress and went to a dinner party with Dr. Tarnower, and in Washington I was a woman in a pretty dress and the headmistress, but I wasn't sure who I was, and it didn't seem to matter." Aurnou: "It mattered to you, didn't it?" Harris: "I was a person sitting in an empty chair, Joel. I can't describe it any more." She starts to sob, Aurnou takes out his handkerchief and dabs his eyes. Leggett orders a recess. I feel it as at once a most moving and hollow, even shabby, experience that we're being put through, an experience of emotion that may be valid in itself but is not anchored in reality. Surely it doesn't make sense. It plays shamelessly upon unexamined popular feeling about the mistreatment of women. What does it mean to sob that although she earned her living like a man, she was no more than a woman in a pretty dress? What's worse about being a woman in a pretty dress than about being a man in a good suit? Would Mrs. Harris have a firmer sense of her identity if she earned her living in an ugly dress? "A person sitting in an empty chair": it's a strangely haunting phrase. It too means nothing yet it suggests a great deal, like a phrase in music or perhaps a passage in an abstract painting. I doubt that there could be a better meta-

225

phor for female castration. Mrs. Harris can't be aware of what she's saying but when she describes herself as the occupant of an empty chair she's speaking about the female body, her body, and explicitly telling us that at bottom it is only unfilled space. Erik Erikson spoke of the "inner space" of women. He was talking about the womb, but Mrs. Harris is talking of an empty anteroom to the womb. Hers is the poetry of unconscious literalness.

When court resumes, Mrs. Harris identifies the notes she left at her Madeira house before taking off on the afternoon of March 10. For the first time the question of her intended suicide is put to her directly.

Aurnou: [When you wrote those notes] what did you intend to do?
Harris: I intended to kill myself.
Aurnou: Why?
Harris: Oh, come on. Because I couldn't function as a human—as a useful person anymore.

She'd chosen for the site of her death a place near Tarnower's pond "where there were a lot of daffodils in the spring." At around 5:15 she'd spoken with the doctor.

Harris: I said, "Hi, it's been a bad few weeks and I'd like to come talk to you for a few minutes." He said, "Debbie's coming for dinner," and I said, "That doesn't matter, she always leaves early and I couldn't get there before 10:30, anyway, and he said, "It would be more convenient if you came tomorrow," and I said, "I can't talk to you tomorrow, Hi, please just this once let me say when," and he said, "Suit yourself," and I said, "I'll be there, I'll leave right away."

Suzanne's testimony had of course contradicted Mrs. Harris's account of her attempts to reach Tarnower. But for me the words "Suit yourself" give a strong stamp of truthfulness to Mrs. Harris's report. After her conversation with the doctor Mrs. Harris had test-fired her gun on her Madeira terrace. "I shot a number of times," she says, "and it just clicked, and finally about the third or fourth time it got to the bullet in it and it exploded, which was a frightening idea to me." Unable to remove the shell with her fingers, she'd poked it out with an ice pick in her kitchen. Then she'd put a number of bullets in her coat pocket and filled up the gun. "I was concerned with getting the gun loaded so I wouldn't play Russian roulette with myself when I shot myself later." She hugged her dogs good-bye, put the papers that she'd prepared in the hall where they'd be quickly found, and went to Junior Baughman's for gas. (She doesn't mention—she doesn't have to—how she happened to take with her the box with all the rest of her ammunition: this has been ruled out of evidence.) She'd seen the bouquet of flowers in her car and while Baughman filled the tank she'd read the card that had been left with it. She "was going to see Hi one more time" and then shoot herself; she took no luggage. In the first hour of her five-hour drive she thought about calling the friends who were expecting her for dinner that evening "but I couldn't think of anything to say to them, I was afraid if I called them, I'd burst into tears." After that, when it was too late to do anything about this social delinquency, she'd "really had a very peaceful, mindless kind of a trip. . . . I finally had come to the end of the road and dying didn't frighten me. . . . Then just as I came across the George Washington Bridge, I thought if I stayed too long—what if Hi said something that spoiled my resolve to die, and I brushed that aside very quickly, thinking I won't stay that long, I just want to see him for a little while and I won't let him know what I am going to do."

Mrs. Harris had arrived at Dr. Tarnower's house to find that there were no lights on. It was still raining though not as heavily as it had been. She'd started up the front steps of the house but, remembering the flowers, she'd gone back to get them from the car; she picked up her pocketbook with them. Then she went up the front steps again but the door was locked so she went through the garage, through the door they usually had entered, and pushed the button to turn on the light. She called, "Hi? Hi?" from the stairs as she approached his room. "He was just beginning to stir. . . . I had the flowers and my pocketbook. . . . I walked over and sat on the edge of my bed and reached over and turned on the light and the light over his bed went on. . . . Hi was just waking up and rubbing his eyes and I said, 'Hi. I thought you would leave a lamp in the window' . . . and he was not enthralled to see me and he said, 'Jesus, it's the middle of the night' . . . and I said, 'It's not really that late and I'm not going to stay very long.' . . . And he said, 'Well, I'm not going to talk to anybody in the middle of the night,' and he turned toward me. He always had two pillows on his bed and he was lying on one and hugging the other one . . . and he closed his eyes. . . . I finally said, 'I brought you some flowers.' He didn't answer. And I said, after I waited a little while, 'Have you written any more on the book?' and he said, 'Jesus, Jean, shut up and go to bed,' and I said, 'I can't go to bed, dear, I'm not going to stay that long, I'm just going to be a little while. . . . Won't you really talk to me for just a little while?'" But finally she'd had to see that he wasn't going to talk, there was no way of cajoling him. There was a shawl she wanted for her daughter-in-law Kathleen in her drawer in the dressing area. She'd got it and a few other of her things and put them on the bed. (But she didn't mark them in any way. After she killed herself how would anyone have known what to do with them?) She'd left the flowers on her bed too. She'd never put the shawl near the sliding glass door where it was later found, nor anywhere on the floor: about this she's very positive. "I put it on the bed and I did not move it from the bed, nor did I move the flowers. . . . [I] looked at Hi and he still had his eyes closed, but I think by then he was wide awake." She went into her bathroom and turned on the light. "I saw a number of things in the bathroom, one of them a negligee, a greenish-blue satin negligee. . . . I took it off the hook . . . and I walked into Hi's room and threw it on the floor." Hi was still paying no attention to her. "By this time I felt hurt and frustrated because the script wasn't working out the way I expected it to. . . . I walked back into the bathroom and I picked up a box of curlers and threw them. . . . I heard the noise. They apparently broke a window. . . . And as I walked out of the bathroom Hi was standing at the door and his arm swung out and he hit me across the face." He'd never hit her before. "But then," says Mrs. Harris, "I'd never come to his house and thrown something before, either." And now at last Mrs. Harris is given the opportunity to say what she has long wanted to say: Aurnou asks her if she'd ever intended for Hi to kill her and she replies, "No, I certainly did not, and I am happy to finally be able to say it. It wouldn't have made any sense to get in a car and think I would drive there and hand a man like Hi a gun and ask him to kill me with it. He spent his life saving people's lives, besides which, I wouldn't have done that to him. I didn't want him to know . . . how desperate I was that night. I hoped it could be a quiet, pleasant, last few minutes." Aurnou asks what she'd done when he'd hit her. "My first reaction was to want to throw something else." She'd thrown a box at her cosmetic mirror and smashed it. Then, when she came out of the bathroom, he'd hit her again: "exactly the same way, exactly the same spot. I made him very angry," Mrs. Harris explained. (But could the doctor not have diagnosed her conduct as hysteria and been employing the only method he knew for dealing with it?) She says she now felt calm; she no longer had the desire to throw things. "I simply wanted to get dying over with. The pleasant talk was not to be. . . . I sat down on the edge of my bed facing away from his and I put my hair behind my ears [she demonstrates] and I raised my face to him and said, 'Hit me again, Hi. Make it hard enough to kill,' which I guess I told the policeman something about that and that's what started the stupid story that I had gone to Westchester to ask Hi to kill me. It was the furthest thing from my mind." The doctor had stopped in front of her while Mrs. Harris had sat waiting with her eyes closed "and wondered how much it would hurt if he did it but he didn't touch me again. He walked away and it probably took a great deal of self-control because I'm sure he was very mad by then." Mrs. Harris had got up. It was very quiet. "I picked up my pocketbook and I felt the gun and I unzipped the bag, and I took out the gun and I said, 'Never mind, I'll do it myself,' and I raised it to my head and pulled the trigger at the instant that Hi came at me and grabbed the gun and pushed my hand away from my head and pushed it down, and I heard the gun explode. . . . Hi jumped back and I jumped back and he held up his hand and it was bleeding and I could see the bullet hole in it and he said, 'Jesus Christ, look what you did.'" Aurnou asks whether that was the first shot, and Mrs. Harris replies, "I know it beyond a shadow of a doubt." There's a curious reminder of her son's emphatic "Let there be no mistake about that."

The doctor had gone to his bathroom but Mrs. Harris says that, contrary to how she'd normally reacted when he'd not been well, she hadn't concerned herself with his injury; for a while she'd just stood and stared. Then she'd followed him to the bathroom but when she was halfway around his bed she'd remembered the gun and thought to get it over with. But she couldn't see it, so she'd got down on her knees at the end of the bed and felt around for it. Just as she'd pulled it out, Hi came out of the bathroom, "flew over the bottom of the bed" and grabbed her left arm. "He held it very, very tightly, and it hurt, and it made me drop the gun." Then "he sat on the edge of his bed, next to the little ledge where the telephone was and the buzzer. . . . I was kneeling in front of him and he buzzed the buzzer. He buzzed it several times." The doctor had the gun in his right hand; he pressed the buzzer with his left. "He put it down on the bed and put his hand on the bed. . . . I was afraid Henri and Suzanne would come running up the steps any minute, and I said, 'Hi, please give me the gun, please give me the gun, or shoot me yourself, but for Christ sake let me die,' and he looked at me and said, 'Jesus, you're crazy, get out of here,' and he pushed me aside and he reached for the phone, because once you buzz the buzzer you have to pick up the phone and talk to someone on one of the other phones. . . . I pulled myself up on his knees, as a matter of fact, just holding on to them, and I was just about straight, and the gun was there. He wasn't holding it then. I think he put it on his lap by then. That's where I remember reaching for it, and as I got up, I grabbed for the gun and Hi dropped the phone and he grabbed my wrist and I pulled back and he let go and I went back on the other bed. I fell back the way you would in a tug of war and Hi lunged forward at me, as though he were going to tackle me, and his hands came out like that [she demonstrates] around my waist and there was an instant where I felt the muzzle of the gun in my stomach—I thought it was the muzzle of the gun—and I had the gun in my hand and I pulled the trigger and it exploded again, with such a loud sound, and my first thought was, 'My God, that didn't hurt at all. I should have done it a long time ago.'" Tarnower fell back. He was on his knees between the two beds. Mrs. Harris ran around the end of the bed—the doctor wasn't chasing her—and once more put the gun to her head and pulled the trigger. It clicked but didn't fire. "And I had gone to great pains to see that couldn't happen—and I tried to think of an adjective for that too." She thought there must be more bullets; she'd pulled the trigger and it had exploded. This was the shot that she later discovered went into the cupboard.

She put the gun back to her head "and I shot and I shot and I shot and I shot and I shot" but it just clicked. She was in a panic because Suzanne and Henri hadn't been heard from and she wanted to be dead before they got there. Her coat was on the floor next to the TV set; there were bullets in the pocket. She emptied these out on the bathroom floor but she didn't know how to empty the gun. She repeatedly banged it on the bathtub until the gun itself flew out of her hand into the tub. She took it out and saw it was broken. She returned to the room: the doctor had dropped the phone and was pulling himself up on the bed. Mrs. Harris picked up the phone and listened but heard nothing. "I said, 'Hi, it's broken,' and Hi said, 'You're probably right.' That was the only civil thing he said all night." She helped him onto his bed. "He looked exhausted but he didn't look dying. . . . I looked at his face and he looked at me and I guess we were both in a state of shock, wondering how something that ugly and sad could have happened between two people who didn't argue even, except over the use of the subjunctive." She ran down the stairs. The lights were on in the dining room and she heard Suzanne talking. She'd said, "Somebody turn on the goddamn lights! I'm going for help!" And she'd gone out leaving the front door wide open; she was going to a phone booth at the Community Center. She'd in fact turned in there but she saw the flashing lights of an approaching police car so she'd turned back onto Purchase Street and the car followed her into the doctor's driveway—Henri was standing at the front door screaming hysterically, "She's the one! She did it!" With Suzanne and Patrolman McKenna, she'd run upstairs. "Hi was on the floor then, lying on his back between the two beds." And this was what McKenna had put in his report, Mrs. Harris says, as opposed to what he'd testified in the trial. While the patrolman ran down to his car for his oxygen equipment, Suzanne held the doctor's hand and Mrs. Harris caressed his face. She'd said, "Oh, Hi, why didn't you kill *me*?" As she now tries to understand why he was on the floor instead of on the bed where she'd left him, she figures that he must have got up to try the phone again. Aurnou asks Mrs. Harris how many shots had been fired in addition to the three she mentioned. Harris: "I spent eleven months thinking about it, Joel. I know when the first shot was fired and I know when the last shot was fired. . . . I know the only time Hi and I were close together struggling for the gun was in that minute or so between the beds." She hadn't known he was shot any place but in the hand; she'd not seen blood coming from a back wound as Henri, having "changed his mind," and McKenna, having "changed his mind," were now testifying that they had.

The session ends with Aurnou asking the witness whether she had ever intended to cause the doctor harm. Mrs. Harris replies, "Never in fourteen years and certainly not that night." That's it for today: she leaves the stand and puts on her coat. The reporters stand around aimlessly. As Mrs. Harris catches the eye of my courtroom assistant, she gives him a friendly, tired, oddly happy little smile and mouths the words, "I want to go home."

D ay 4 of direct for Mrs. Harris—it's Aurnou's cleanup day. Had Mrs. Harris been aware of an independent phone line [that of the van der Vrekens] in the house? No, she had not. Had she ever fired the gun single-action? No, she hadn't known how it was done until MacDonell showed her. When the doctor was sitting on the bed near the buzzer, had he put on his glasses? No. Had all her belongings been returned in the box packed by Suzanne? No, some things had been missing: Mrs. Harris mentions a graphite fishing pole, a couple of bathing suits, a pair of long white gloves, a petit-point bag, toiletries from the bathroom, a sewing kit, papers and books she'd kept in the headboard. Why had Mrs. Harris not thought to go to a neighbor's house to telephone? Because the pay phone at the Center was just a half-mile down the road and she was familiar with it; she'd used it before this when the doctor's phone had been out of order.

On the night of the shooting had Mrs. Harris told Detective Siciliano that she'd shot the doctor? Yes, but she'd been speaking, of course, of the shot to Tarnower's hand which was the only wound she knew about. (But by the time she spoke with Siciliano she had seen the doctor dying!) Had she told Siciliano where the gun was? Yes, she'd said it was either upstairs or in the car and the two of them had gone out to the car together. Had she told Siciliano that there'd been a struggle and that she didn't know who'd had control of the gun? Yes, because she *didn't* know who had control; all she remembered was her finger on the trigger when she shot the doctor in the hand. But what about the other shots? Mrs. Harris remembers the next one: Hi was partly on top of her and she'd felt "something that felt like the muzzle of the gun sticking deep into my stomach or abdomen or whatever this spot right here is." (She indicates the spot. But is she not pointing to another side of her body than she did yesterday?) In addition to the three shots she has described, does she recall any other times the gun was fired? Harris: "I don't remember pulling the trigger, Joel. . . . I believe there was only one time it could have been, and that's when he grabbed my wrist and I fell back." Can she identify the black cotton glove that Suzanne had said was lying on top of her things in the shawl? Harris: "It's like identifying a pair of pantyhose. I mean there are millions of them." When she'd felt the weight of the gun in her purse, what did Mrs. Harris have in mind? Harris: "When I felt the gun, I just took it out to use it there. . . . I led a very quiet, private life and I wanted to die a quiet, private death. . . . It wasn't meant as a grandstand play, but it sort of sounds that way." Aurnou: "If you felt so strongly about dying then, why haven't you done anything to kill yourself since?" A good question, and Mrs. Harris mumbles, "I didn't think *you* would be the one to ask me that," as Bolen objects and is sustained. Aurnou asks whether she'd heard testimony in this trial about what she'd said at Suzanne's mirror the evening of the shooting. Harris (dismissively): "Yes, I heard. . . . I remember . . . saying, 'He hit me.' " With which hand had the doctor struck her? Harris: "With his left hand." Does she remember testimony about having said that it was ironic that Tarnower was dying and she was living since he wanted to live and she wanted to die? Harris: "Yes, indeed I do." Aurnou: "Was it the truth?" Bolen objects and is sustained. Mrs. Harris begins to murmur something and Judge Leggett says, "Mrs. Harris, there's no question before you."

Aurnou has his client recapitulate the account of her arrest and of being taken to the Harrison police station where she'd been seen by both Riegelman and Dr. Roth. Sergeant Carney had eventually told her of Tarnower's death. Mrs. Harris mimics the sergeant's offhandedness as he'd said, "Oh, he passed on." Although she's once more crying she interrupts to muse: "It's such a dumb expression, 'passing on.'"

There are a few random questions about where Mrs. Harris had had Dr. Tarnower's prescriptions filled when she was working in New York. Then we break for lunch. Soon after court reconvenes, Aurnou turns over his witness to the prosecution. The corridor gossip is apparently correct: Aurnou would stop in midafternoon because he wanted Mrs. Harris to have a taste of cross-examination before the weekend. If she knew what lay ahead of her—I guess that means that if she'd had the experience of handling Bolen— she'd be less worried.

Bolen is mild, tentative. At moments he phrases his questions so awkwardly that one becomes impatient. Mrs. Harris is arrogant. He begins his cross-examination with the meeting of Tarnower and Mrs. Harris at the Jacobsons' in 1966. "And from the time that you first met Dr. Tarnower at that party given in December '66, up until the events of March 10, 1980, during that intervening period of time there were numerous occasions when you had occasion to see Dr. Tarnower and were in his presence. Is that true?" Is language like this the occupational hazard of a prosecuting attorney? Mrs. Harris smiles as she answers yes. Bolen asks if the doctor had taken her on two trips around the world. "We accompanied one another," Mrs. Harris corrects him. Had she ever seen him with his glasses on? Harris: "Of course I did. . . . Yes, he often looked over the half-glasses." Did he wear glasses when he drove? Yes. For other things as well? Sometimes. For fishing? Harris: "He wore them then, I think, because of the way I cast. . . . It was for safety. . . ." Did Mrs. Harris remember that she'd said he didn't wear glasses for golf? Harris: "I never played golf with him, but I walked around with him a great many times." The prosecutor shows her three pictures.

Mrs. Harris studies them: "I see Hi at the Country Club with his glasses on three times. . . . He's just sitting in one, and he is standing in another, and he is swinging a golf club in another." But he's wearing glasses, is he not? Harris: "Yes. I don't know that they are prescription glasses, but he is wearing something." In the doctor's bedroom when she'd got there on the 10th, were his glasses in the headboard? Harris: "I wasn't examining things in the headboard, I was talking to Hi." Bolen gives the witness Tarnower's glasses to identify. Mrs. Harris looks at them without emotion: "Those look like fairly new ones." Can she identify them? asks Bolen. Harris: "If they were found on his headboard [I'll accept that]. . . . He lay there hugging his pillow and saying he wouldn't talk and he wanted to go to sleep." There was nothing, says the witness, to prevent him from putting his glasses on.

Bolen turns to Mrs. Harris's purchase of the gun. The headmistress had a Virginia driver's license, had she not, and paid Virginia state taxes? Yes. And she had various charge cards—Saks, for example—with her Virginia address? Harris: "All of them did: Saks, Lord & Taylor, the whole schmeer." When in 1978, asks Bolen, had she first gone to buy a gun? Harris: "I don't know, but here in this courtroom I've heard October. . . ." Had someone in the shop told her how to use it? Harris: "The only thing I did that was important to me . . . was to find out how to put bullets in it. . . . I know you had to pull something out and it was very hard to pull." Mrs. Harris explains that she didn't care about learning how to eject them because she would be dead. After she bought the gun where had she put it? Harris: "The top shelf of one of my closets in my bedroom." And the ammunition? Harris: "In the box with the gun." Had she ever fired it? Bolen inquires. Harris: "I did the day that I brought the ammunition back. . . . I went out on the terrace and I shot it, I think, two times." Bolen asks where those two spent shells are now. It's of course a trap question: two spent shells were in the box with the rest of the ammunition that had been found in her car. But Mrs. Harris is not to be trapped; she answers that she doesn't know. Bolen: "On March 10, 1980, when you left your house . . . you had with you, among other things, the weapon . . . and a number of live rounds of ammunition?" Again Mrs. Harris sidesteps the trap. She says, "I don't know how many. I thought I

235

had six in the gun and it turns out I had five." The prosecutor shows no frustration. How had the bullets got in her coat pocket? Harris: "I believe that I counted out either six or eight bullets out on the front terrace. . . . I wasn't sure how many holes in the thing there were." Holes indeed! This woman who has more technical mastery of anything that pertains to her case than anyone in this court. Bolen: "While you were in New York, you knew that you didn't have a license to be in possession of that gun. Isn't that true?" Harris: "It never entered my head, Mr. Bolen. I knew that I had bought it legally."

Bolen takes a different tack: he speaks of Mrs. Harris's health, refers to the fact that since June '75 she had had "a healthy fear of exhaustion." Harris: "I had it before that. [Muses] A healthy fear of exhaustion? . . . I had a very deep fear of exhaustion. I don't know that I would describe it as a healthy fear of exhaustion." When had it begun? asks Bolen. Harris: "I can't put a date on it, Mr. Bolen." But she took medicine because of her fear of exhaustion? asks Bolen. Harris: "I didn't take medicine because of the fear of it, I took medicine because of the reality of it. At least that's what I was told." Had she known this reality of exhaustion at Allied Maintenance? Harris: "Not to the same degree . . . my responsibility was pieces of paper and not people. . . . It was a different kind of pressure." Was she taking medicine during her time at Allied? Yes, she was. How frequently? asks Bolen. Harris: "As prescribed . . . I never took anything that wasn't prescribed. . . . I didn't take more than what was required. There were times when I took a little less, if I didn't feel the need for it." At Madeira, says Bolen, Mrs. Harris had "been instrumental in raising the salaries of various faculty members. . . ." Mrs. Harris interrupts: "Of all the faculty members. . . ." Had she herself got a raise in 1978? In 1979? In 1980? The answer in each case is "Yes."

About the letter that Mrs. Harris wrote to Dr. Tarnower on Saturday the 8th: does she recall how long it was, the color of the ink she'd used, how she'd signed her name, whether or not the pages were stapled together? Mrs. Harris remembers none of these things with certainty, nor even whether it was Purchase Street or the Clinic to which she'd addressed it. She believes "it was to his office because it would be easier for him to sign for it." Had she taken any steps on Monday to secure the return of that letter? Harris: "No, I didn't. I wasn't in a position to do anything about it. . . . The letter was at that moment no concern to me. All I was thinking about that night was Hi Tarnower." Bolen: "Did there ever come a point in time when you thought about the letter again?" Harris: "I probably said something about it to my lawyer." Had she ever seen it again? Harris: "Yes, I can't remember exactly when." Had she read it? Harris: "I may have had the opportunity. I didn't do it. I don't remember doing it." But she was aware that it existed? Harris: "I was aware that it existed." Bolen: "And at the present time do you know where that particular document is?" Harris: "In the possession of Mr. Aurnou, as far as I know." Bolen: "Do you recall when for the first time after March 11, 1980, you had occasion to see the letter again?" Harris: "It could have been a month or so, maybe. Maybe it was less than that." "Your Honor," says Bolen, "at this time I would like to have an opportunity to examine that particular document." With studied nonchalance Aurnou pulls the letter out of his inside coat pocket: "I just happen to have it with me, your Honor."

The afternoon is drawing to a close. Court adjourns. Bolen now has the opportunity to read the Scarsdale letter over the weekend. The Judge will perhaps read it too. Mrs. Harris has the weekend in which to think about what cross-examination holds for her, whether she's had a reliable sample of how the prosecuting attorney will conduct himself.

I was mistaken to have anticipated that the Scarsdale letter would be produced this morning: if Judge Leggett read it over the weekend and made up his mind about whatever it is that his mind had to be made up about, we're not yet informed. Mrs. Harris once more takes the stand. Bolen starts the day with a courteous, "How are you, Mrs. Harris?" Mrs. Harris looks sceptical: "Good morning." Bolen takes her through a morning of quiet polite no-news interesting chiefly for the defendant's unflagging snootiness.

While one understands that having to testify is inevitably an ordeal —haven't we heard this said even by the experts who testify professionally—for Mrs. Harris it seems not at all to be the ordeal of someone accused of murder and afraid of being pushed into self-betrayal, or even the appearance of self-betrayal. Of this kind of tension Mrs. Harris gives no sign. She's outraged in the way that an excellent student might be outraged when confronted with an unfair exam. If the questions are going to be this irrelevant, how can she do justice to her intelligence and get the good mark she deserves?

And it's indeed sometimes hard to see what the prosecutor is driving at with his interrogation. He asks Mrs. Harris about the Thomas School, about the balance she sought or achieved between teaching and school administration, about her pre-Madeira experience in student discipline, her relation with the members of the Thomas Board and her support of the school's merger, the moves she'd made to get her Madeira post, the administrative organization of Madeira, the circumstances in which the Browning report was arranged for and how it was received. Only when he speaks of the chain of command at Madeira do I perceive a possible direction in his questioning. The headmistress was frequently away from the school on weekends; he is suggesting that she failed in her responsibility to her job because there was no one who was officially second-in-command during her absences—each time she'd simply designate someone to be in charge while she was away and this created confusion and staff rivalry. A lengthy passage that deals with Mrs. Harris's use of drugs that were prescribed for her in names other than her own and that were sometimes sent to her in Virginia, where Dr. Tarnower wasn't licensed, is no doubt meant to show Mrs. Harris's much-vaunted character in a poor light. But it seems to me that this misconduct is more of a reflection upon Dr. Tarnower than upon Mrs. Harris. At most she was guilty of having tolerated, in extenuating circumstances, her lover's bending of the law. For a moment we get back to Thursday, March 6, when Mrs. Harris had been called by Miss Gisriel about finding pot in one of the Madeira dorms. Room-searching in a school dormitory is disagreeable even when required, and she had herself assumed, or shared, this "demeaning" task. A disciplinary meeting had been called at her house where, although "the buck stopped at her," she had given everyone a chance to speak. The rules against drug use at Madeira had been made explicit and the girls had accepted the school's regulations on this score. Though not wholeheartedly upheld by all the students present, the expulsion of the four seniors had been voted unanimously. Bolen: "Do you recall yourself making two telephone calls back to [Tarnower] before you received a call from Miss Gisriel?" Harris: "I know I talked to Hi that night." Had the calls been "somewhat unsettling"? Harris: "They weren't as settling as I hoped, but I was always calling Hi to make me calm down." Bolen asks whether in one of the calls to Dr. Tarnower the name of his close friend Dan Comfort had been mentioned? Harris: "His name was mentioned." Hadn't she been calling Dan Comfort? Bolen asks. Harris: "No, I hadn't been calling Dan Comfort." What about February 1980? Harris: "Yes, I did." December 1979? Harris: "I may have. . . . I don't know." What the significance of Dan Comfort is we're not told. In what seems to be a considerable jump, Bolen reverts to Mrs. Harris's early years with the doctor: when Tarnower broke their engagement in 1967 did Mrs. Harris know if he'd been upset? Harris: "Yes, he was." Had the doctor suggested that perhaps they shouldn't see each other? Harris: "That's right." After they broke the engagement was there ever a time when he told her he'd thought better of it? Harris: "[Yes,] we'd be driving along [and Hi would say], 'It was better that we didn't get married. I didn't want to worry about what retirement home your mother was in . . . and I didn't want to watch you die of cancer and I didn't want you to play nursemaid to me. . . .' I was always happy to be with him. I didn't sit around for fourteen years waiting for him to marry me, though, Mr. Bolen. I wasn't looking for the Good Housekeeping Seal of Approval."

Bolen speaks of the infrequency with which Mrs. Harris and Tarnower saw each other when Mrs. Harris lived in Philadelphia: was that because of the distance? Harris: "And children at home, which was the big thing." (Those high-school- or college-age babies of hers!) Referring to their subsequent travels, their trip around the world, the trip to Bulgaria, "the Grecian Islands and then Paris," Bolen speaks of the doctor having also taken her to the Caribbean. Harris: "I don't really like your constantly saying he 'took' me. We went together. I sound like a piece of his baggage." For the moment Bolen ignores this but a bit later he has his innings: when she and Tarnower travelled together who paid for the airline tickets? "He bought the tickets." And he took care of the hotel reservations? "Yes." Mrs. Harris would have it sound as if the doctor simply took care of the bookings. Did Dr. Tarnower contribute to the education of her sons? Bolen asks. Harris (indignant): "He most certainly did not. He didn't offer to and I wouldn't have permitted him to." Who did pay for their education? Harris: "[I did.] For thirty years I endorsed my checks and gave them to schools." During the time they'd travelled together, Bolen asks, would Mrs. Harris say the doctor had treated her well? Harris: "Of course he did. We treated one another very well. We were very fond of one another."

In 1969–70, Bolen has Mrs. Harris remind the court, she was forty-seven. Was she aware that at that time the doctor was seeing another woman whom he wanted to marry? Harris: "I never met her. . . . He told me she had four children, which made me know immediately he wasn't going to marry her." Did Mrs. Harris know that he had seen this woman a number of years before and that at the time she was a number of years older than herself? Harris: "I didn't know a thing about her, Mr. Bolen, except that Hi said he thought he was going to marry her." Bolen: "[While the doctor was seeing her] he had been seeing you as well, is that correct?" Harris: "From time to time." Had Mrs. Harris visited the doctor in his home during this period? Harris (sardonically): ". . . We know the expert in *that* department. I didn't have a record. . . . I think she had decided to marry somebody else by then, and did." Bolen: "Mrs. Harris, [would you tell us about] certain incidents that took place at Dr. Tarnower's home and particularly in the bedroom." Harris (laughs): "Could you be more specific?" Bolen begins a question about "a particular piece of embroidery destroyed with enamel nail polish." Judge Leggett halts him: he's making an assumption from a fact not in evidence. Harris: "You certainly are." Apparently rattled, Bolen inquires, "Did you have conversations with Dr. Tarnower?" Harris: "Yes, whenever we talked we had conversation." The questions aren't being properly framed, says Aurnou. Bolen presses on. Shortly after the doctor proposed marriage to this other woman, did something happen to a piece of embroidery she was working on and a rug that belonged to her? Harris: "I don't know anything about a piece of embroidery. . . . I know that practically everything in Hi's house was hemstitched, needlepointed, or engraved with some woman's name." She's not aware of the venom with which she speaks. "And I certainly didn't put any fingernail polish on any of it. It would have messed up the whole house." Bolen: "Did there come a time after you were told of this proposal by Dr. Tarnower that you learned that the doctor was not going to marry this woman?" Harris: "No. We did have a specific discussion then . . . and I said, 'Hi, you know perfectly well you're never going to marry anyone, so stop messing up so many different women's lives and just mess up mine.' And he liked that line. . . . Marriage was not what I required of life. I was in love with him and it didn't matter that much to me. . . . I think he was now very relaxed with me." Did the doctor ever have a conversation with her, Bolen asks, about "a rug that had been cut"? Harris: "No . . . it wouldn't have been discussed by Hi with me because he would know that I would have had nothing to do with it." Bolen paces away from his lectern and in the pause Mrs. Harris says quietly but vehemently, "It's getting dirtier and dirtier! It really is dreadful!"

Bolen at last gets to Lynne Tryforos. In 1975 had Mrs. Harris become aware that the doctor was seeing Lynne socially? Mrs. Harris replies that she knew that Henri and Suzanne saw her socially, not that Hi did. She'd seen the cuff links in 1974 and he'd had letters when they travelled but she'd not known from whom. She knew Mrs. Tryforos had two daughters. "They kept sending Father's Day cards to Dr. Tarnower, which I thought was rather sad." Yes, one of the daughters was named Electra. Bolen reminds her that the name Electra appears in her Christmas poem. Harris: "Well, Mr. Bolen, I was talking about Hi's women, not their children, for Heaven's sake. I think that's a little obvious." Against Mrs. Harris's warning that Bolen is eliciting something for which he'll be sorry, he inquires about a meeting between Mrs. Harris and Lynne Tryforos at the side of Dr. Tarnower's pool in the summer of 1976. Harris: "Yes, I can remember Mrs. Tryforos [and her two daughters] arriving one day with a gallon of paint and coming out and saying she was going to paint the doctor's furniture for him, and I said, 'Does it not seem bizarre to you that you are here painting his furniture while I am here?' And she didn't know what 'bizarre' meant so I said, 'Lynne, why in the hell are you here?' And she said, 'I'm here because I am allowed to be,' and I said, 'Not while *I'm* here, Lynne,' and she left." And what about the gold cuff links? Bolen inquires. Harris replies that yes, she and the doctor had had a conversation about them in Paris. "He wasn't heated. *I* was heated. . . . I was always a little bit sorry I hadn't tossed them out the window at the Ritz." But hadn't she in fact knocked them against something so that one of them broke? Bolen asks. Harris: "No, Mr. Bolen, I didn't, and really, this should not—I mean you can make up anything. . . . If one of them cracked it wasn't cracked by me, Mr. Bolen." As Bolen produces the cuff links to be put in evidence, Mrs. Harris comments: "I thought Suzanne had done all of this if it was going to be done. Am I going to look at some malachite?" Bolen: "[The crack] was not put there by you?" Harris: "It certainly wasn't. I don't play that game, Mr. Bolen." In Paris, when Mrs. Harris told Hi that it was "absolutely rotten" for him to have brought Lynne's cuff links on this trip with her, the doctor had agreed—and he'd added that she should "hurry up and get ready for dinner." She'd twice dried Suzanne's eyes when Suzanne came to her with stories about how Lynne was trying to seduce Henri. At first Mrs. Harris had herself thought of Lynne as "just one of a collection" of Hi's women, but she had come to know otherwise and it upset her because "it denigrated Hi." Had she ever said to Suzanne that she was going to make life miserable for the doctor and Mrs. Tryforos? Bolen asks. Harris: "No, Mr. Bolen, I wasn't there helping Hi with his book if I wanted to hurt him in any way. I hated having him write the book because I didn't want him to be called a 'diet doc.'" (But she has made much of her contribution to the diet doc's book.) Had she ever told Suzanne she'd sue the doctor and Mrs. Tryforos? "Never," says Mrs. Harris, but she'd thought of suing Mrs. Tryforos when a thousand dollars' worth of her clothes were destroyed. It develops that the Dan Comforts had given a birthday party for the doctor at which Lynne had been a guest. That had been on March 16, 1979. Mrs. Harris had spent his actual birthday, March 18, with the doctor in Nassau. The next week she'd returned to Purchase to find that all her clothes, except one dress, that she kept in the closet next to the van der Vrekens' bedroom had been ripped. Yes, a blue suede coat of Lynne's had been among these things; she'd not noticed its presence in that closet before. Suzanne had wanted to inform the doctor of this damage but Mrs. Harris had not permitted her to. Instead she'd herself left a note about it on the doctor's bed before she'd returned to Madeira.

At Thanksgiving 1979 Mrs. Harris and Tarnower had been guests of the John Loebs in Nassau.

Bolen: How did you treat Dr. Tarnower during that particular trip?

Harris: I don't understand why you asked it. . . . Lovingly and affectionately, and with the same kind of good humor that we both treated one another.

Bolen: Isn't it true, Mrs. Harris, that you were particularly antagonistic to the doctor and almost hostile to him during that particular trip?

Harris: No, it certainly is not true. . . . I made fun of [Hi's] book because I wanted everyone to know that he didn't take it too seriously, because he was a very good physician and I didn't want anyone to think of him as a diet doc. [She had read a report that Loeb had thought she was too hard on Hi about his book.] Being hard on Hi is something you didn't do. . . . Anything I ever said to Hi was affectionate and expressed great interest in his reputation.

Bolen: You were very concerned with the doctor's reputation?

Harris: I was indeed, and this thing is tearing me apart.

Mrs. Harris starts to sob but no matter how hard she cries, I see no tears—she weeps dry. Bolen asks for a short recess but Mrs. Harris says she doesn't need it, she's fine. "I'll wait a moment," says Bolen and sits down while she composes herself. When they resume, he asks whether it's not true that during the Christmas visit to the Schultes in 1979, the doctor had proposed a "cooling-off period" between them? Harris: "No, he didn't. It was a particularly happy two weeks, as a matter of fact." But there had been Lynne's New Year's greeting in the *Times:* hadn't she been upset by that? Harris: "Not upset, just appalled at how tasteless it was. It didn't seem like something that should touch his life in any way, or mine. . . . I tried to make fun of it as I did many things."

On her return from Florida she'd had the Madeira Board meeting to handle; that was exhausting. On February 8, following the doctor's suggestion, she'd called Suzanne to discuss David's pre-wedding party. She'd not been feeling out the possibility of a party; she'd been settling on the "menus and all sorts of things." And after the wedding weekend, says Bolen, she knew, didn't she, that the doctor was leaving for Georgia. "Yes," says Mrs. Harris. "Hi made love to me that morning and we had a lovely conversation about our relationship, and that was when I gave him the gold caduceus." If, as she says, it violates her sense of her independence for Bolen to talk about Tarnower "taking her" on their travels, why does she speak of his making love to her instead of the two of them making love? Funny, how Mrs. Harris's sexual frankness doesn't seem natural to me; there's something programmatic in her outspoken-ness. Her ladylikeness is her great stock-in-trade. It's important in the admiration of those who do admire her, especially the men who admire and want to help her, and yet she seems to have learned indelicacy. Of course this doesn't apply only in matters of sex: there's often a kind of studied violation of old manners in her idiom. For instance, her use of the word "schmeer" has this same kind of programmatic ring. She'd have us think that she's kicked over the traces of her upbringing but whatever goes on at a deeper level of her consciousness, I think there remains a level, deep enough, on which she's always the brave wide-eyed provincial in a metropolis that should never have been opened up to her. There are people who were born to stay home rather than follow the beckonings of their imaginations: the Emma Bovarys and Anna Kareninas of this world. If this is a counsel of their despair, it's also the counsel of their ultimate salvation.

The doctor had many friends in the community who would be attending the celebration of the Westchester County Heart Association in April and Mrs. Harris felt strongly about being there too. Was it important to Dr. Tarnower that she be present? Bolen inquires. It was very important to her, says Mrs. Harris. Referring to the fact that the doctor would be at the head table, Bolen asks would it be fair to say that Mrs. Harris wanted to be his guest? "No, it wouldn't," answers Mrs. Harris. "It would be fair to say that I wanted to be there, wherever I was, to honor Hi and see him be honored. I have no strong feelings about sitting at head tables, Mr. Bolen. I sit at a lot of them. It doesn't cut any ice with me at all." She had planned to be there with the doctor's close friends, the Dan Comforts, and hadn't considered where the doctor was himself going to sit; she assumed it would be at the head table. Yet, Bolen inquires, hadn't she on several occasions phoned Dan Comfort to discuss her presence at the dinner? Mrs. Harris remembers two such calls: she had made one of them, she knows, when she'd left Dr. Tarnower's house after the wedding weekend, using the pay phone at the Community Center—she had told Dan Comfort that she and Hi had "just had a gloriously happy weekend and Hi wants me to be there." Bolen: "So as you were driving down the driveway and this thought occurs to you, you don't turn around to go back to Dr. Tarnower's home to use the phone, but you proceed down the driveway . . ." Harris (interrupting): "I said when I was *out* of the driveway. There was nothing sinister about it, Mr. Bolen. I don't know why you want to pursue it." Bolen: "Had the subject of your attendance at that April 19 dinner come up during that weekend that you were at the doctor's home?" Harris: "Sitting on his bed that morning [presumably after their love-making] we talked about it." Bolen asks if she knew about a birthday party for the doctor that had been given by the Comforts; and what woman had celebrated with him? Harris: "No, I didn't. But I wouldn't be surprised if it were Lynne. Hi was a very private person. I didn't arrive at his house and he gave me a rundown on what he had done the night before."

Mrs. Harris admits that her relation with the doctor had somewhat attenuated in recent years. "Hi's feelings," she says, "were very different in the 1970's than they had been in 1967. . . . Hi was not in love with anyone. He was fond of me then. He had been deeply in love." Bolen asks whether in 1980 the doctor was deeply in love with Lynne Tryforos. Harris: "No. As a matter of fact, I knew quite the opposite, because I asked him, and I felt that if he were, I shouldn't see him. He said, 'Hell, I don't love anyone and I don't need anyone.' That was one of his favorite sayings. . . .

245

It doesn't warm my heart but it's true." In 1979 she'd asked him whether he'd meant to marry Lynne. " 'Jesus, you of all people ought to know better than that,' " Mrs. Harris reports that he had answered. " 'I don't love anyone, I don't need anyone.' . . . He was very, very positive about it." Had she asked him on that wedding weekend whether he planned on marrying anybody? Harris: "No, indeed I didn't. I wouldn't have been there and he wouldn't have been making love to me if he had been planning to marry someone else. . . . I think better of him than you do, Mr. Bolen." Clearly the rules are different for people engaged to marry than they are for people in a non-marital relationship.

Mrs. Harris remembers that she phoned the doctor at the Clinic on the morning of March 10. From her phone bills it is established that the call was made at 9:59 A.M. She can recollect two things of which they spoke: she'd asked the doctor to throw away the "complaining" letter she'd mailed earlier that morning and she'd told him something about "the trauma at school." They'd also talked about her impending visit on April 5 and the doctor had asked her whom she would like to have him invite to dinner. The conversation had had to be cut short because he had a patient waiting for him. Bolen asks her about the Scarsdale letter: would she consider it a love letter? Harris: "It had a lot to do with my very deep affection for him, yes." Didn't it have a lot to do with Mrs. Tryforos? asks Bolen. Harris: "Yes, but more with my own integrity by being touched by the other woman than by the other woman herself." Bolen asked whether the letter wasn't "replete with references to Lynne Tryforos." Harris: "Yes, shall we read it here? Is that what's going to be done?" Would she like it read aloud, Bolen asks, and Mrs. Harris replies, "No, indeed, I wouldn't, but I'm not afraid to have it read. I think it would be a terrible thing to read it." Why? asks Bolen. "Because," Mrs. Harris answers, "I think it would expose Hi in a way that I hoped he isn't exposed, and Lynne in a way I really don't feel that strongly about, and me, too. It's a very private letter, Mr. Bolen, as you very well know. But if you're going to play cat and mouse with it, I'd rather have the whole thing thrown right on the table."

Bolen recurs to the trip that the doctor and Mrs. Tryforos had taken a week before David's wedding party. He asks how Mrs.

Harris had felt about that. Harris: "George, it's so many years and you are really not going to get me that upset about it." Her chief concern was that the doctor was "denigrated by his book and by his choice of company."

Bolen: Tell us in what way you felt that Lynne Tryforos denigrated Dr. Tarnower. Please tell me that.

Harris: No, it's much too private, and it's based on very many ugly stories told me by the van der Vrekens and things that I experienced that I would not say publicly. . . . And having heard the van der Vrekens testify, I now accept the fact that perhaps some of the things they said weren't true.

Bolen: Some of the things that the van der Vrekens testified here were not true?

Harris: Indeed they were not. They perjured themselves repeatedly.

Bolen: . . . Would that also be true of Officer McKenna?

Harris: It certainly would. . . . I have a report sitting over here with chapter and verses of places where people have testified.

Bolen encourages the defendant to give examples of perjury. Mrs. Harris cites the difference between McKenna's first report of the position in which he'd found Tarnower lying and his testimony in the trial; also McKenna's early statement that they gave Tarnower CPR in the ambulance and his present sworn testimony that they did not, the latter a contradiction of Dr. Roth's sworn testimony that they did. "I think that's perjury," says Mrs. Harris. As to Suzanne: not only had Suzanne from occasion to occasion significantly altered her description of how she had found the doctor on entering his bedroom; she had also said that she and Henri hadn't heard Mrs. Harris call out that she was going for help for the doctor. "I believe they heard me," says Mrs. Harris.

About the Heart Association dinner, Mrs. Harris says what would surely seem to be an obvious truth: "I think Hi was in a bind. . . . He couldn't quite say 'yes' or 'no' to me. . . . We were two different women who filled two different needs in his life, and he couldn't quite get rid of either one of us." In the note to the doctor in which she'd spoken about how Dr. Tarnower would have responded had a woman he admired associated with the male equivalent of Lynne, she'd alluded to such a person as a "boy Friday" and said the doctor would not again have invited the woman to his house. What had she meant? Bolen inquires. She was trying to

247

make light of Lynne, Mrs. Harris explains. She was drawing a parallel between Tarnower's relation to Lynne and the relation that a woman the doctor admired might have with a thirty-five-year-old, uneducated, not overly bright man. He would not have countenanced it if such a woman chose the kind of companion that Tarnower had found in Lynne. Says Mrs. Harris of the doctor, "this was a man who read Herodotus for fun."

Bolen: You felt she did not have the education you had?
Harris: It wasn't a matter of education, Mr. Bolen.
Bolen: Breeding?
Harris: Perhaps just common sense and taste.
Bolen: Lynne Tryforos had no taste?
Harris: I didn't say that. You did.
Bolen: Well, did Lynne Tryforos have taste?
Harris: I think you have to judge people's taste by some of the things they do. I think writing to a man for eight years when he is travelling with another woman is rather tasteless.

Mrs. Harris seems able to ignore the fact that this tasteless woman was someone with whom she had been willing to share the doctor's bed throughout these years.

Bolen: You were upset about that letter which you referred to as a term paper, weren't you?
Harris: No, Mr. Bolen, that isn't precise. That isn't correct. I wasn't upset about the letter and I wasn't upset about the cuff links, because the person who did them was not of that concern to me. What upset me was that I was touched by it and Hi was touched by it, and I am a very idealistic person and I spent fourteen years thinking Hi was pretty close to perfect, which wasn't fair, because nobody is.

Bolen now asks whether her telephone conversation with Dr. Tarnower on March 6, after her return from her trip west, had been "upsetting" to her, and Mrs. Harris says that it was. "He said, 'I think you've got two books of mine. . . .'" Bolen reminds her that over the weekend she'd written the doctor, "How dare you accuse me of stealing two books and some money." Mrs. Harris says, ". . . By Saturday and Sunday, Mr. Bolen, I was very far gone, and I was in a very deeply, I realize now, seriously depressed state that I had been in for many years and it had been covered up. . . ." She'd always run to Hi "when the ice started to crack

248

and it was really cracking that weekend." Mrs. Harris starts to cry but goes on: ". . . From the time I was a young woman, the only prayer I ever prayed was 'Just give me the strength to get through this day, one day at a time,' and I always said I was fine and I always got through the day, but by that weekend I couldn't get through any more days." The witness is crying too hard to continue and a recess is called.

When Bolen resumes, he once again speaks of Thursday night at Madeira, the headmistress's talk at chapel the next morning, the various duties she'd discharged that Friday and the social engagements she'd kept. "I was on my feet," says the witness, "doing what I had to do." Bolen poses "an interesting question," as Mrs. Harris calls it. Mrs. Harris had said she had trouble in even hanging up a dress on the Saturday of that last weekend; had she had similar difficulty in writing a will? Harris (muses): "There was a lot of decision-making in that. No, I didn't have trouble writing it. . . . I concentrated on it very hard and it didn't take a long time to write." And the letter to Hi? That had been like the will, "a coming to a head of something I didn't understand." And what about the writing she did on Sunday? Harris: "I think suicide was on my mind." But she had said, had she not, that she had only resolved to take her life on the 10th? Harris: "No . . . At that point the decision was out of my hands. . . . I didn't specifically think of dying that Sunday but I knew I was beginning to get my house in order." Bolen: "Did you have these feelings of taking your life when you wrote the letter to the doctor?" Harris: "I had a feeling of deep depression and exhaustion, which culminated in that on Monday." At the moment the answers Mrs. Harris is making to these questions of Bolen's are convincing enough but later I'm told —can it be true?—that her letter to her sister Mary Margaret, after a request that there be no funeral expenses except for furnace fuel, had gone on to a detailed discussion of her property and its disposition: the school had a chair, some drapes, and other belongings of hers and was still indebted to her for an air conditioner; and her will, written on the 10th, noted forty-two items that were to be divided between her sons—they included andirons, a chair, a rack, a picture of a steamship, etc. Whenever it was that these decisions had been made, there could be no doubt of their range and specificity and of the tax they would have put on anyone's energies.

The prosecutor asks again about her attempts to reach Tarnower over the weekend. How many times had she called him on Sunday? Harris: "Maybe three or four. [She consults her phone bill.] No, I spoke to Henri twice and Suzanne once. . . . I asked if he was there and they said no." She describes a call in which Suzanne answered and wanted to know if she was all right. Bolen says wasn't this the call on the 10th? Harris: "I didn't speak to her on March 10, 1980. . . . Not on the phone. It was Henri who answered the phone in the afternoon when I called first." Bolen: "Didn't Suzanne answer the phone twice that afternoon?" Harris: "She didn't answer it once, Mr. Bolen. . . . She said she spoke to me on the phone on the 10th and she didn't. She couldn't quite make up her mind whether it was once or twice until in November she remembered the second call. But she never spoke to me on Monday. I don't know why Henri is written out of the case but he seems to have been." Bolen: "I don't know what you are talking about, Mrs. Harris." Aurnou: "I object and move to have this stricken, Mr. Bolen's comment, 'I don't know what you are talking about.' [He apes the prosecutor's statement.]" Leggett: "Don't get sidetracked and get involved." Bolen (to Mrs. Harris): "You were the one who entered the doctor's bedroom that night with a revolver and five rounds of ammunition. Is that true?" Harris: "That's right." Bolen: "In addition to that you had a number of rounds of ammunition in the fur coat. . . ." Harris: "That's true, I did."

Mrs. Harris acknowledges that Lynne Tryforos was "part of the letter that I wrote to Hi" and that she had referred to her in many very unattractive ways: dishonest, adulterous, a whore. Bolen's voice is now becoming loud and dramatic.

Bolen: Did you use the words "your psychotic whore"?
Harris: I might have. That's what Suzanne always referred to her as. . . . Suzanne always said she thought she was crazy. She didn't use the word "whore."
Bolen: What did Suzanne have to say about you?
Harris: I hate to think.
Bolen: Did you use the word "slut" to refer to Lynne Tryforos?

Harris (turns to Judge Leggett): How long do we go on this way, Mr. Leggett? This is not what I understood we were going to do. . . .

Leggett reminds the witness that she has a lawyer, he can make objections for her.

Harris: He's not saying a word.
Leggett: He will pose objections when he sees fit and I will rule on them.
Bolen: Did you use that word [slut] as well in the letter?
Harris: I might have. To me they are synonymous. A whore is a whore is a whore.
Bolen: And are these words you customarily used?
Harris: No, they are not words I customarily used. That is what was being so troublesome. It was being touched by something like this that made me struggle very deeply with my own integrity and I couldn't bring myself to walk away and I couldn't bring myself to come to terms with it.
Bolen: You were concerned with your own integrity?
Harris: You're darned right I was! . . . It's not like me to rub up against people like that.

Bolen wants to know if, by people like that, Mrs. Harris means people who hadn't her background and social breeding, people who, like Lynne Tryforos, "socialized with the doctor's servants."

Harris: Oh, come on, Mr. Bolen. You are throwing something into this that's silly. They had their friends and I had mine. I wasn't looking for that kind of friendship from them and they weren't looking for it from me. Lynne came looking for it. I didn't.

It appears that much of her knowledge of Lynne came from the van der Vrekens whom she has herself just characterized as perjurers. But Mrs. Harris says she had firsthand confirmation. "I knew by then it was Lynne who had been following him around the world with letters for eight years. I knew she had given him cuff links when she was married to another man. I knew a number of things first-hand." But she doesn't name them: she says they are not relevant. Asked if she ever "did anything to Lynne," Mrs. Harris speaks of little buttons Lynne used to make that said "Super Doctor": she'd thrown any of these that she found into the pond. And she'd thrown away Valentines that were left in the doctor's

251

car; it was inappropriate, she felt, for Lynne to have left things around when the doctor expected another visitor. But suppose, says Bolen, she came uninvited? Other than on March 10, she had never visited the doctor uninvited, Mrs. Harris replies, and even that night he had known she was coming. Bolen: ". . . Yet the lights were out, the front door was locked, no lights in his bedroom?" Mrs. Harris suggests that perhaps it was because he knew she was coming that Dr. Tarnower had sent Lynne home that evening and himself gone to sleep—Mrs. van der Vreken had testified at the Grand Jury hearing that it was Lynne's custom to stay at the house almost every night. Bolen: "You remember it from the Grand Jury?" Harris: "I read every bit of her testimony and I have been appalled by it. . . . By a lot of testimony." What other testimony had she been appalled by? Bolen inquires. Detective Siciliano's? Harris: "No, I wasn't. I think basically he was pretty honest. . . . I was appalled when he said he probably could have been there by two minutes after eleven. . . . I think he probably got there about ten after eleven." Bolen: "Nevertheless, Detective Siciliano in your opinion was fairly honest when he testified here. Is that correct?" Harris: "No. I didn't make that statement." She says there were several instances in which Siciliano had been mistaken. "I did not say anyone gave me bullets in the foyer. I said I wanted to give them to my lawyer. He misheard a number of things." Mrs. Harris says that she'd found two bullets in her coat pocket; she thinks they had been put there at the Harrison police station. Bolen: "Somebody put bullets in your pocket?" Harris: "I don't know. Somebody has to explain them. . . . My coat and my clothes were taken away from me and given to Lt. Della Rocco, and then they were handed back to me and I put my hands in my pocket and there were two more bullets in the pocket. . . . I took Joel Aurnou's handkerchief which he had given me and I wrapped them up in the handkerchief and meant to give them to him." Bolen asks how many bullets had been found in the handkerchief when she had got to the Valhalla jail and Mrs. Harris says one. She thinks the other might have fallen out in the police car. But weren't these two bullets already in her coat when she left Virginia? Bolen asks. Harris: "No, sir, they were not."

When, asks Bolen, had she washed her blouse? Harris: "It was when I asked if I could and they said yes. . . . I wish now I hadn't. It would have been one thing that wasn't destroyed that would help this case." And who, Bolen asks, was responsible for it being destroyed? Harris: "Not I. The police permitted me to do it."

What was the moment on Monday, Bolen asks, when she knew she had to commit suicide? Harris: "3:30 was the moment I knew I couldn't sit at that desk any more and be useful." How had her telephone call to the doctor that morning affected her? Harris: "I was somewhat heartened by it [because I would see him April 5]." Bolen: "So you had something to look forward to?" Harris: "That's right." And the afternoon call? Was it after that call that she felt a physical necessity to take her own life? Harris: "Yes, I did." But in the morning when the doctor had said she could see him on April 5, she hadn't felt that way? asks Bolen. Harris: "He didn't *say* I could see him. I wasn't given permission, Mr. Bolen. . . . No, I was *asked* to come on April 5."

Yet again Bolen returns to the defendant's relationship with Tarnower. Was her relationship with the doctor part of the reason Mrs. Harris wanted to commit suicide? Harris: "No. My loneliness certainly was, but it wasn't my relationship to Hi that made me want to die. Quite the contrary. He was the one person I wanted to touch bases with before I died." And Lynne Tryforos? Harris: "She made me uncomfortable with the relationship. She made me feel guilty about not ending the relationship. But she wasn't a threat. . . . I was troubled by my own integrity. . . . I rationalized [that she was filling some need for Hi]. . . . I didn't like being touched by what I was being touched by. I thought things were happening that were unsavory." Bolen takes the witness through a repetition of what happened the evening of March 10 after her arrival in Purchase: the removal of her shawl from the drawer in the dressing area; throwing Lynne's robe on the floor and hurling the curlers out of the bathroom; throwing a box at her cosmetic mirror; the unsuccessful attempt to shoot herself in the head. She's not shaken on any part of her story. The negligee she's shown by the prosecutor is not, she says, the one she threw out of the bathroom, and if the shawl and its contents were on the floor they'd been put there by somebody else—she'd placed them on the bed and never moved them. Finally Bolen asks whether in November 1977 something happened that involved Lynne and that was "a subject of discussion" with the doctor. Harris: "Not face to face, no. . . . It was something Hi told me about." In the Scarsdale letter, Bolen asks, had she alluded to a certain "grim day" in November? Yes, says Mrs. Harris. It referred to the situation when Lynne had told him that she had made phone calls to the office that bothered her. Had she? Bolen asks. Harris: "Never to harass her. I called her several times, since I have had three years of anonymous phone calls, and asked her to please leave me alone. I had strong reason to believe she was the one making them. . . . When she sent me her unlisted number and the taunting report and a taunting note with it, I called her, yes." Hadn't Mrs. Tryforos changed her unlisted number? Harris: "She also sent it to me, for reasons beyond my comprehension." Mrs. Harris testifies that from November 1977 to Christmas 1979, any time she went away with Hi on a trip, when she'd come back to Madeira there would be a memo from one of the secretaries saying that someone had phoned from a 914 number and that she was to call back; the caller had said she'd know who it was. Mrs. Harris had taken to calling Lynne, eventually late at night, because she'd failed to stop her in "every possible nice way." Mrs. Harris says that she'd been getting anonymous calls for eight or nine years. In the last seven years the van der Vrekens had assured her they were coming from Mrs. Tryforos.

Bolen: Mrs. Harris, aound this time did Dr. Tarnower ever refuse to let you see him because you were bothering Mrs. Tryforos?
Harris: That was the November that was so grim and that he called and apologized, yes.
Bolen: Let me repeat the question again. Did the doctor ever refuse to let you see him because you were bothering Lynne Tryforos?

If she's not permitted to give a complete answer she won't answer, says Mrs. Harris. But eventually she does reply: no.

Bolen: Mrs. Harris, did Dr. Tarnower ever threaten you with banishment?
Harris: I think if I had given him a hard time about things, yes. He wanted fun and games and happiness, and . . . if you talked about things that were troubling, he didn't want to hear about it.

254

Bolen: Mrs. Harris, did you ever consider yourself publicly humiliated by the fact that the doctor was seeing Lynne Tryforos?

Harris: I thought he was publicly humiliated much more than I, but he didn't feel so.

Bolen: . . . Did you ever consider yourself publicly humiliated by the fact that Dr. Tarnower was seeing Lynne Tryforos in public?

Harris: No.

Bolen: May I have that letter, please, Mr. Aurnou? Mrs. Harris, will you please take a look at this particular letter. [Hands Mrs. Harris the Scarsdale letter.] Mrs. Harris, is that the letter you wrote to Dr. Tarnower, parts of it on Saturday, March 8, 1980, and the rest of it on March 9, 1980?

Harris: I believe so, yes.

Bolen: And is that the letter that you mailed on the morning of March 10, 1980?

Harris: Yes.

Bolen: I offer that letter into evidence, your Honor.

But we'd not heard it. Court had adjourned and we'd had to wait overnight. And even this morning, the start of Mrs. Harris's seventh day on the stand, we've no assurance that we'll do more than hear *about* it. This letter that Mrs. Harris wrote the doctor: when she wrote it did she feel hostility to him? Harris: "No, I didn't." To Lynne? Harris: "If I have to give you a 'yes' or 'no' answer, I cannot. . . . I felt disgust and revulsion at her." Had the doctor ever been unkind to her? Harris: "Sometimes he could be very unkind. He was a difficult man at times." Bolen: "Were there ever times when you were unkind to the doctor?" Harris: "I tried not to be." Bolen (repeats): "Were there ever times when you were unkind to the doctor?" Harris: "Not consciously so. [There were things in the letter] and that's why I called him and said don't read it, because then he would learn what I had borne alone." So she was unkind in the letter? Harris: "I was simply shrieking with pain, Mr. Bolen." Bolen offers the letter in evidence as he had done at the close of court the day before. Aurnou: "Your Honor, we would not have read this letter in public, but despite the fact that it helps Mrs.

255

Harris . . ." Bolen breaks in: he has offered the letter in evidence, "we don't need any speeches." Aurnou: "I am consenting that you read it, Mr. Bolen. If that is what you want to do in a public court room, go ahead." And so at last Bolen stands at the lectern and reads the Scarsdale letter aloud, slowly, awkwardly. A decent man, he avoids histrionism. Aurnou has a copy on which he follows him, occasionally interrupting with a correction.

Hi

I will send this by registered mail only because so many of my letters seem not to reach you—or at least they are never acknowledged so I presume they didn't arrive.

I am distraught as I write this—your phone call to tell me you preferred the company of a vicious, adulterous psychotic was topped by a call from the Dean of Students ten minutes later and has kept me awake for almost thirty-one hours. [Aurnou: "Thirty-six hours."] I had to expel four seniors just two months from graduation and suspend others. What I say will ramble but it will be the truth—and I have to do something besides shriek with pain.

Let me say first that I will be with you on the 19th of April because it is right that I should be. To accuse me of calling Dan to beg for an invitation is all the more invidious since it is indeed what Lynne does all the time—I am told this repeatedly, "She keeps calling and fawning over us. It drives us crazy." I have and never would do this—you seem to be able to expiate Lynne's sins by dumping them on me. I knew of the honor being bestowed on you before I was being asked to speak [Aurnou: "Ever asked"] at Columbia on the 18th. Frankly I thought you were waiting for Dan's invitation to surprise me—false modesty or something. I called Dan to tell him I wanted to send a contribution to be part of those honoring you and I assured him I would be there. He said, "Lee and I want you at our table." I thanked him and assured him I would be there "even if the slut comes—indeed, I don't care if she pops naked out of a cake with her tits frosted with chocolate!" Dan laughed and said, "And you *should* be there and we want you with us." I haven't played slave for you—I would never have committed adultery for you—but I have added a dimension to your life and given you pleasure and dignity, as you have me. As Jackie says, "Hi was always a marvelous snob. What happened?" I suppose my check to Dan falls into the "signs of masochistic love" department, having just, not four weeks before, received a copy of your will, with my name vigorously scratched out, and Lynne's name in *your* handwriting written in three places, leaving her a quarter of a million dollars and her children $25,000 apiece—and the boys and me nothing. It is the sort of thing

256

I have grown almost accustomed to from Lynne—that you didn't respond to my note when I returned it leaves me wondering if you sent it together. It isn't your style—but then Lynne has changed your style. Is it the culmination of fourteen years of broken promises, Hi—I hope not. "I want to buy you a whole new wardrobe, darling." "I want to get your teeth fixed at my expense, darling." "My home is your home, darling." "Welcome home, darling." "The ring is yours forever, darling. If you don't leave it [Aurnou: "If you leave it"] with me now I will leave it to you in my will." "You have, of course, been well taken care of in my will, darling." "Let me buy an apartment with you in New York, darling."

It didn't matter all that much, really—all I ever asked for was to be with you—and when I left you to know when we would see each other again so there was something in life to look forward to. Now you are taking that away from me too and I am unable to cope—I can hear you saying, "Look, Jean, it's your problem—I don't want to hear about it."

I have watched you grow rich in the years we have been together, and I have watched me go through moments when I was almost destitute. I have twice borrowed fifty cents from Henri to make two of the payments on the Garden State Parkway during those five years you casually left me on my hands and knees in Philadelphia, and now—almost ten years later—now that a thieving slut has the run of your home, you accuse me of stealing money and books, and calling your friend to beg for an invitation. The many [Aurnou: "Very"] things your whore does openly and obviously (to your friends and your servants! sadly not to you) you now have the cruelty to accuse me of. My father-in-law left me a library of over five thousand books. I have given away in the past ten years more books than you own. I have thanked you most sincerely and gratefully for books you have given me. Ninety percent of them have been given to a school library and on at least four different occasions I have asked you if you wouldn't like a letter on school stationery that you could use as a tax deduction. Each time you have airily refused and *now*, for God's sake, you accuse me of *stealing* your books. It borders on libel. Any time you wish to examine my home or the school library, you are certainly welcome to do so—a surprise raid might be most convincing for you.

Twice I have taken money from your wallet—each time to pay for sick damage done to my property by your psychotic whore. I don't have the money to afford a sick playmate—you do. She took a brand new nightgown that I paid $40 for and covered it with bright orange stains. You paid to replace it—and since you had already made it clear you simply didn't care about the obscene phone calls she made, it was obviously pointless to tell you about the nightgown. The second thing you paid for (I never replaced it) was a yellow silk dress. I bought it to wear at Lyford Cay several years ago. Unfortunately I forgot to pack it because it was new and still in a box in the downstairs closet. When I returned it was still in the box rolled up, not folded now, and smeared and vile with feces. I told you once it was something "brown and sticky." It was, quite simply, Herman Tarnower, human shit! I decided, and rightly so, that this was your expense, not mine. As for stealing from you, the day I put my ring on your dresser my income *before taxes* was $12,000 per year. I had two children in private school. They had been on a fairly sizable scholarship until I told the school I wouldn't need it because we were moving to Scarsdale. It was two years before we got it back. *That* more than anything else is the reason David went to Penn State instead of the Univ. of Pennsylvania. He loathed every minute of it—and there is no question that it changed his life. That you should feel justified and comfortable suggesting that I steal from you is something I have no adjective to describe. I *desperately* needed money all those years. I *couldn't* have sold that ring. It was tangible proof of your love and it meant more to me than life itself. That you sold it the summer your adulterous slut finally got her divorce and needed money is a kind of sick, cynical act that left me old and bitter and sick. Your only comment when you told me you had sold it (and less than two months before you had assured me you would get it from the safe so I could wear it again!) was "Look, if you're going to make a fuss about it you can't come here any more. I don't need to have anyone spoil my weekend." Too bad Somerset Maugham didn't get hold of us before he died. He could have come up with something to top a *Magnificent Obsession*.

You have never once suggested that you would meet me in Virginia at *your* expense, so seeing you has been at my expense—and if you lived in California I would borrow money to come there, too, if you would let me. All our conversations are my nickels, not yours—and obviously rightly so because it is I, not you, who needs to hear your voice. I have indeed grown poor loving you, while a self-serving, ignorant slut has grown very rich—and yet you accuse me of stealing from you. How in the name of Christ does that make sense?

I have, and most proudly so—and with an occasional "right on" from Lee and others—ripped up or destroyed anything I saw that your slut had touched and written her cutesie name on—including several books that *I* gave you and she had the tasteless, unmitigated gall to write in. I have refrained from throwing away the cheap little book of epigrams lying on your bed one day so I would be *absolutely sure* [Aurnou: "Absolutely sure," double underlined] to see it, with a paper clip on the page about how an old man should have a young wife. It made me feel like a piece of old discarded garbage—but at least it solved for me what had been a mystery—what had suddenly possessed you to start your tasteless diatribes at dinner parties about how every man should have a wife half his age plus seven years. Since you never mentioned it to anyone under sixty-five, it made the wives at the table feel about as attractive and wanted as I did. Tasteless behavior is the only kind Lynne knows—though to her credit she *is* clever and devious enough to hide it at times. Unfortunately it seems to be catching.

The things I know or profess to know about Lynne—except for what I have experienced first hand—I have been told by your friends and your servants, mostly the latter. I was interested to hear from Vivian and Arthur's next door neighbor in Florida—I don't remember her name though I am sure Lynne does: "I took her to lunch, she seemed so pathetic"—that you sat at table while I was there and discussed Lynne and her "wonderful family—brother a Ph.D." I can't imagine going out to dinner with you and telling my dinner partner how grand another lover is. I told the woman to ask you something [Aurnou: "Sometime"] why if her family is so fine, Lynne decided to sell her kids to the highest bidder and make you and your family the guardian of her children if you should die [Aurnou: "If she should die"] before they do. It must go down as a "first" for a splendid family to do. My phone tells me this—that "mysterious" caller. I hope to God you don't know who it is! Who pays him?

When my clothes were ripped to shreds Suzanne said, "Madam, there is *only* one person who *could* have done it. You must tell him." In my masochistic way I tried to downplay it in my note to you, although in all honesty it was so obvious you would know who did it. Instead you ignored it and went happily off to Florida with the perpetrator. Suzanne told me—and I would think would say so in court.

1. The clothes were not torn when she went into the closet to find something of Henri's on "Wednesday or Thursday" while we were away.

2. On the Sunday morning before we came home Henri and Suzanne both saw Lynne drive hurriedly up to your house. They were outside and she did not see them. They saw her go in but not out.

3. Lynne knew you were coming home that evening and she would see you by 8:00 the next morning. What business did she have at your home that morning?

4. When I discovered the clothes destroyed Suzanne was sitting in the dining room at the wooden table right next to the door. I said, "My God—Suzanne, come look," and she was right there. When I called your slut to talk to her about it and see what she was going to do about it, she said "You cut them up yourself and blamed it on me." That was the first time it occurred to me they had been "cut," not ripped. Only someone with a thoroughly warped mind would decide that a woman with no money would ruin about one third of her wardrobe for kicks. Suzanne

still believes Lynne did it and I most certainly do, too. I think this is enough evidence to prove it in court!

The stealing of my jewelry I can't prove at all. I just know I left some things in the white ash tray on your dresser as I have for many years. When I thought of it later and called, Lynne answered the phone. When I called again and asked Suzanne to take them and put them away, they were gone. I only hope if she hocked them you got something nice as a "gift." Maybe I gave you some gold cuff links after all and didn't know it. I didn't for an instant think [Aurnou: "I don't for one instant think"] Henri or Suzanne took them. I had *never* [triple underlined] called Lynne at the office anonymously as you have accused me that grim November day in 1977. I had in fact called her at the office before I left and said, since I did not have your number [Aurnou: "Have her number"] and could not get it I would call her at the office every time I got an anonymous phone call if she did not immediately stop them. Within two weeks my "mysterious" caller told me her number. I have had it ever since then. Every single time she changes it I get it. And yet though I was the one being wronged [Aurnou: "I was the one being wronged, underlined"] you refused to let me come see you that month because a lying slut had told you *I* was calling her. The thought of it *had* [Aurnou: "Wrong. 'Had' is not underlined, your Honor"] never crossed my mind. Her voice is vomitous to me. The next month I called her virtually every single night *only* because of your rotten accusation while she sat [Aurnou: "Simperingly"] by, letting you mock it. [Aurnou: "Make it."] Not *once* [double underlined], not *once* did Lynne answer the phone. At one, two, three in the morning it was her children who answered, very quickly, TV playing. Where does mumsie spend her nights? That she "totally neglects her children" is something Henri and Suzanne have told me. That you admire her for it is sad. She uses them to write "super doctor" cute notes. With that kind of training Electra is going to be ready to earn her own color television any day now. I hope to God you're not the one who buys it for her. I don't think [Lynne?] would mind too much as long as you didn't change your will. "Stupid" is certainly not the word for Lynne. In that I was totally wrong. "Dishonest, ignorant and tasteless," but God knows not stupid. It would have been heartbreaking for me to have to see less and less of you even if it had been a decent woman who took my place. Going through the hell of the past few years has been bearable only because you were still there and I could be with you whenever I could get away from work, which seemed to be less and less. To be jeered at, and called "old and pathetic" made me seriously consider borrowing $5,000 just before I left New York and telling a doctor to make me young again—to do anything but make me not feel like discarded trash.

I lost my nerve because there was always the chance I'd end up uglier than before.

You have been what you very carefully set out to be, Hi—the most important thing in my life, the most important human being in my life, and that will never change. You keep me in control by threatening me with banishment—an easy threat which you know I couldn't live with—and so I stay home alone while you make love to someone who has almost totally destroyed me. I have been publicly humiliated again and again but not on the 19th of April. It is the apex of your career and I believe I have earned the right to watch it—if only from a dark corner near the kitchen. If you wish to insist that Lee and Dan invite Lynne, so be it—whatever they may tell you, they tell me and others that they dislike being with her. Dan whispers it to me each time we meet, "Why weren't you here? Lee hates it when it's Lynne." I always thought that taking me out of your will would be the final threat. On that I believed you would be completely honest. I have every intention of dying before you do, but sweet Jesus, darling, I didn't think you would ever be dishonest about that. The gulf between us seems wide on the phone but the moment I see you it's as though we had been together forever. You were so absolutely perfect over David's wedding and I will always be grateful. I wish fourteen years of making love to one another and sharing so much happiness had left enough of a mask [Aurnou: "Mark"] that you couldn't have casually scratched my name out of a will and written in Lynne's instead. But for God's sake don't translate that into begging for money. I would far rather be saved the trial of living without you than have the option of living with your money. Give her all the money she wants, Hi—but give me time with you and the privilege of sharing with you April 19. There were a lot of ways to have money—I very consciously picked working hard, supporting myself, and being with you. Please, darling, don't tell me now it was all for nothing. She has you every single moment in March. For Christ sake give me April. T. S. Eliot said it's the cruelest month—don't let it be, Hi. I want to spend every minute of it with you on weekends. In all these years you never spent my birthday with me. There aren't a lot left—it goes so quickly. I give you my word if you just aren't cruel I won't make you wretched. I never did until you were cruel—and then I just wasn't ready for it.

Bolen finishes the letter and returns it to its envelope. What can follow on this? For a moment it feels as if the trial is over: Mrs. Harris has convicted herself.

But so far as one can see, Mrs. Harris appears to be unaffected by what has just been read and Bolen resumes his interrogation. Prior to March 10 had Tarnower told her that she was included in his will? The doctor had given her an envelope to open in the event of his death, says Mrs. Harris, and told her that she was in his will. Bolen puts the question again: "Did you know on March 10, 1980 that the doctor provided for you in his will?" "I didn't know or care," says Mrs. Harris. She had been sent anonymously two pages from his will—apparently this is the will referred to in her letter, from which her name was scratched out and Lynne's inserted in the doctor's handwriting. Still, Mrs. Harris cannot believe the doctor did it. "I knew it wasn't something Hi would do, and as I said in the letter, I really didn't give a damn because I had always planned to die before he did, anyway. The only thing I asked of Hi was just to be with him, and that's all I asked of him for fourteen years."

Mrs. Harris's son David is in court when the letter is read.

At lunch several of the reporters comment on a new tone of harshness that they heard yesterday in the Judge. Had Leggett read the Scarsdale letter over the weekend? Well, now he's heard it, as have the rest of us. Before this he may or may not have thought Mrs. Harris guilty as accused, but I doubt that he thought her capable of writing as she does of Lynne. It has made him spare, firm, gray.

The letter has been a turning point for all of us but I'm not sure that we're all of us in this court revolving in the same direction. I'm not even sure I can say *what* direction I'm turning in: I know only that my head spins with the complexity of Mrs. Harris's character and the more so, I suspect, because her complexity is the sum of so many simplicities. I doubt there's an element in her personality that's in itself unfamiliar, it's the combination that defies—and the question of where to put one's emphasis.

I've said that Mrs. Harris is self-convicted. This hasn't directly to do with the charge on which she's standing trial: she's convicted of being something other than she was represented as being; she's guilty of not being what she seems and yet of insisting that we see her in the light of her own high opinion of herself. What makes the most immediate impact of the Scarsdale letter is of course the ugliness of the language, the almost gratuitous obscenity with which Mrs. Harris writes about Lynne, but the nastiness of her *feelings* about Lynne is much more alienating than the bad language. Guilty or innocent of the charge of murder, Mrs. Harris has been put forward as "every inch a lady." She was a lady strayed, a lost lady, a lady in anguish, in turmoil, even a lady perhaps capable of explosive emotion, but always a lady. This had been her distinction which made it difficult to think of her as a felon: ladylikeness had been her signature. But if there's one thing that the Scarsdale letter is not, it's the composition of a lady. The term may not mean the same to any two people in this courtroom but there's a common denominator of meaning: perhaps it's best called appropriateness. No matter what the circumstances in which she finds herself, a lady doesn't finally, not finally, transgress our expectations as Mrs. Harris has. Mrs. Harris had gutter feelings about her rival but the mud she threw at Lynne has splattered back on her like tell-tale splatterings of blood. The idea of the gentleman has to all purposes disappeared from our culture, but not the idea of the lady; the title has been largely discarded but the concept remains. It seems to withstand all our rebellions against these presumably outmoded categories. There's virtually no one, scarcely a man or woman in our society, for whom the idea of the lady, or the ladylike, doesn't have meaning, and there's no one in this court, however rebellious against traditional social assumptions, who hasn't been upset by the fact that Mrs. Harris isn't the lady we had thought her. After the Scarsdale letter the best we can do on behalf of the woman who writes about her rival as Mrs. Harris writes of Lynne Tryforos is to think of her as sick. The relation with Tarnower may have produced the sickness, or it could be that it was her sickness that had propelled her into the relation with a weak and selfish man like Tarnower. The causality doesn't matter. If we're ever again to think of Mrs. Harris as a lady, it's only as a sick lady, not wholly responsible.

Certainly she'd taken the reading of her letter in public as only a sick person would take it: she'd been unashamed, or appeared so.

By now we're acquainted with Mrs. Harris's saving capacity—in some sense it does save her—to detach herself from painful reality, from the doctor's physical suffering as he lay dying, from his bloodied pajamas and bed linens, even from the reality of being on trial for his murder. Is Mrs. Harris so superlative an actress that she simulated the calm with which she'd listened to Bolen read the Scarsdale letter this morning? One of the court artists who sits close to the witness stand and has her eyes on the defendant says that when Mrs. Harris drank some water while Bolen was reading, her hand never shook. I doubt that Mrs. Harris any longer sees what we see or hears what we hear. But surely she once did; this much imperviousness can't be native to her.

And in despair of love, how dismayingly Mrs. Harris turned to money. It's common, of course, for people to throw their most sacred emotions, the best of their defeated hopes, into the money bin; this we know. But the Scarsdale letter is flagrant in this regard, page after page that harps on the doctor's broken promises of payment, on Mrs. Harris's poverty and his wealth, her generosities as opposed to his meanness. Did Tarnower really make as much of the two missing volumes as Mrs. Harris says? It could be that in substitute for charging her with taking possession of *him*, the doctor charged her with taking his books—he was a book person, we remember, God help us: the man who read Herodotus for fun. The emphasis on money is disproportionate in Mrs. Harris's indictment of someone whose grudgingness went far beyond money. It may be that Mrs. Harris always liked money too much. Before I learned better I assumed that she'd been brought up in deprivation, that both she and Tarnower had lived as children in straitened circumstances, it meant so much to them to associate with the rich. But this wasn't so of Mrs. Harris's upbringing. She apparently needs money for a different kind of security, as power, and she needs power as a man needs power: the fact that her earnings were modest but that she lived as Tarnower's companion among people of great wealth would only have fed a peculiarly acute female sense of insecurity. Money is very *tangible* as power. But we also have to take into account the fear that Mrs. Harris may have had of jobless old age. Tarnower had not only rejected her, he'd made her feel of no more use in the world. And he delivered this pretty message at much the same time as she'd learned that at Madeira, too, she didn't satisfy. If no one wants you *or* your work, you had indeed better have money in the bank or try to collect on old debts. Having reached her Madeira pinnacle alone, without money or domestic armor, on a clear day Mrs. Harris could see forever: to teach girls tough male subjects didn't alter the worth of women relative to men in the common human market.

Facing her various kinds of bankruptcy, Mrs. Harris makes her least attractive, also least practical, not her most attractive or practical, move. She begs for reinstatement by Tarnower—the trial has prepared us for self-abasement but no one could be prepared for such an entire sacrifice of self-respect as she reveals in the Scarsdale letter. She calls herself masochistic but does she begin to understand what this means in her relation with the doctor? Her dependency on this undependable man is measureless. She can't be without him. She crawls at his knees—it's as she described herself on the floor between the beds the night of the shooting. This cruel doctor is what her nature orders; in fact, if he'd not been so cruel, she'd probably not be this much in thrall to him. Lynne is going to have him in March. Mrs. Harris begs, can she have him in April, she'll promise to be good. As a strategy of seduction nothing could be less useful. Mrs. Harris is intelligent enough to know that. But when did intelligence ever dictate a proper strategy with which to meet a need as profound and mysterious as Jean Harris's need of Tarnower?

But there's also something new that's been communicated in the Scarsdale letter, and despite the ugly emotions about Lynne and the self-pity and account-keeping in which it's embedded, it arouses in me a sympathy I've not had for Mrs. Harris since shortly after the shooting. I'm not talking about its shriek of pain, penetrating as that is: Mrs. Harris is wrong to characterize the letter as a whine; for all its complaint it is a tearing scream. When Mrs. Harris acknowledges that yes, she feels revulsion from Lynne but that what really troubles her is her integrity and Hi's; when, even stranger, she talks of the letter as an expression of love for the doctor, she isn't wholly deceiving herself and trying to deceive us. I think she's telling a truth that she can't articulate. She's possessed with the necessity of restoring her lover to the way in which she'd first thought of him;

she has to admire and look up to him. This can be said simply: if Lynne isn't worthy of Hi but Hi nevertheless loves Lynne, what does this say about Hi? It means he doesn't distinguish among the women with whom he involves himself, not reliably. He's guided by something other than the values by which Mrs. Harris would wish to be judged. What she feels is that if it doesn't matter to Tarnower whether he gives his love to a Jean Harris or a Lynne Tryforos, it's because a woman is a woman is a woman as a whore is a whore is a whore. Bolen is not being clever: it's not Lynne's inferior birth that troubles Mrs. Harris, not her breeding or lack of breeding, her education or lack of education or her association with servants. Lynne could have been raised in a slum and herself be a servant and this wouldn't bother Mrs. Harris, not per se. She's not a snob in that vulgar sense, or not here, not wholly. What she is trying to say and saying poorly is that Tarnower's feeling for Lynne and the place that he's giving her in his life is not supported by Lynne's *personal quality*. His blindness to the qualitative difference between Lynne and herself indicates that the two of them, Lynne and she, interchangeably serve his purpose. The sexual connotations of such a proposition are unbearable to a woman like Mrs. Harris, as they would be to any woman who has to spiritualize her sexuality before she can give it license, put it above "mere" desire. The requirement that she legitimate sex by love would explain what was reported of Mrs. Harris as headmistress, that she couldn't understand the light-minded sexuality of the young. Tarnower's lack of personal discrimination in choosing Lynne as his present partner reduces all his expressions of love to sexual appetite. She was herself only the object of his physical desire—so she would think of it, pejoratively. Not only is he lowered in her view but she is lowered along with him; they are both denigrated, that famous word of hers. Mrs. Harris's contempt for Lynne is extreme, it could scarcely be more so, but it is nothing compared to her contempt and anger at Tarnower for so grievously threatening her decent opinion of herself—her integrity—and making her feel so sexually exposed. Lynne is proof that the man to whom Mrs. Harris gave herself is not what she thought him. She begs for one more chance to recover him not only to herself but to himself.

We've had our high drama. Surely there's no way to go forward from it. Mrs. Harris is still on the stand and shows no reluctance to continue as a witness. She's not been at all daunted by the experience of hearing the Scarsdale letter read aloud to a roomful of strangers, indeed to the world. But one wants to put a period to the case: don't we already know whatever has to be known? Dryly, dutifully, Bolen retraces old ground. We talk about the evening of March 10. On first coming to Tarnower's house Mrs. Harris had sat on the guest bed in the bedroom and tried to get the doctor to talk. She'd then gone to the bathroom and thrown things. The first shot was fired when she was standing near the foot of her bed and the doctor "grabbed for the gun" she had put to her head to kill herself; this shot caused the wound to his hand. His hand bleeding, the doctor went to his bathroom while Mrs. Harris, kneeling on the floor, found the gun under the bed and, a second time, raised it to shoot herself, except that Hi came in and saw her and dove across the bed, seizing her arm hard to make her drop it. The doctor picked up the gun; he sat on his bed and buzzed for the van der Vrekens, put the gun down next to him and then in his lap. When Mrs. Harris again grabbed it, Tarnower dropped the phone and lunged at her; both his hands were at her waist and she felt what she thought was the muzzle of the gun in her stomach. She pulled the trigger and the doctor fell back. Mrs. Harris rose and ran around the foot of the doctor's bed. She saw he wasn't following her and for the third time she tried to shoot herself but the gun didn't fire. Baffled, Mrs. Harris lowered it and again pulled the trigger. This time the gun did go off. She supposed that the bullet had landed in the dressing area. Now in a panic to kill herself before Suzanne and Henri would come upstairs, Mrs. Harris took her coat to the bathroom, emptied the bullets from her coat pocket onto the bathroom floor—loose change fell out with them. She banged the gun on the tub to try to rid it of the old shells. The gun fell into the bathtub and broke. Mrs. Harris now gave up. She returned to the bedroom just as Hi dropped the phone. Pulling on her, he'd got back on the bed. Mrs. Harris tried to use the telephone but it didn't work. She went downstairs and left the house to seek help. As she passed the dining room she'd called to the van der Vrekens.

Mrs. Harris's story, as Bolen once more leads her through it, is met by the prosecutor with manifest disbelief. To me, not only the sequence of shots but also the manner in which they'd been fired is credible enough. The flaw I find in Mrs. Harris's story is one she seems not to recognize: the blatant contradiction between her continuing insistence that she was aware of only a single wound that Tarnower had received, the relatively insignificant injury to his hand, and her urgency after she left the bedroom, rushing down the stairs and out the door, pausing only to shout to Suzanne, "Turn on the goddamn lights," driving faster than the police car she guided back to Tarnower's driveway, pressing McKenna to "Hurry up! Hurry up!" when he stopped to listen to the radio transmitter in his car and herself "racing" upstairs to the bedroom. Although under examination by Bolen Mrs. Harris reiterates the earlier statement that when she got back to the house the condition of the doctor gave her no cause for ultimate alarm—after all, he "was able to move . . . trying to speak, still aware"—she reports that he was back on the floor, with McKenna administering oxygen and Suzanne holding his hand. Too, we recall previous testimony that she had herself touched his face and said, "Oh, Hi, why didn't you kill *me?*"

Mrs. Harris takes the recapitulation of the events surrounding Tarnower's death as another opportunity to be sharp and unpleasant with Bolen. "May I have a complete answer to that or do I have to say 'yes' or 'no' and do it the way you want it?" Or "I told you three times in the last minute." Perhaps these shows of arrogance are intended to compensate Mrs. Harris for the humiliation of the trial. But there's another brand of emotion, less acceptable, that's also revealed in the wake of the reading of the Scarsdale letter. Bolen is questioning her about why she drove to the pay phone at the Community Center instead of rousing a neighbor. Why hadn't she gone to the Knopfs'? Harris: "It's not a home you would run to to make a phone call." Had she ever been there with Dr. Tarnower, asks Bolen. Harris: "They lived on the other side of Purchase Street, Mr. Bolen. . . . It isn't the next door neighbor." Bolen: "Forgive me for my inarticulateness, Mrs. Harris. At any time before March 10, 1980, had you ever been at the Knopfs' residence with Dr. Tarnower?" Aurnou objects to the tone of the questioning but is overruled. Isn't it a fact, says Bolen, that the Knopfs lived on the other side of the street from the Tarnower driveway? Yes, says Mrs. Harris, "not right across the street but they lived on the other side of the street." Bolen: "So on March 10, 1980, you knew the Knopfs lived right across the street?" "They do not live right across the street, Mr. Bolen," says Mrs. Harris. "I have just said that. I would be happy to drive there with you and show you where they lived." Throughout this exchange, Mrs. Harris's manner has been one of all but overt hostility to the prosecuting attorney but of course the transcript of the trial will have the record only of the words, not of the way in which they are spoken. Documents don't always document.

Bolen has been letting Mrs. Harris have her say about the suicidal wish that brought her to Purchase on March 10. Now he winds up his cross-examination with one short fierce question after another. It's a devastation.

Bolen: Mrs. Harris, on March 10, did Dr. Tarnower tell you that he had proposed marriage to Lynne Tryforos?

Harris   (with a thin smile): No . . . Did he tell *you*, Mr. Bolen? I don't think that ever happened.

Bolen   (in a hard loud voice): Mrs. Harris, isn't it a fact that Dr. Tarnower had told you he preferred Lynne Tryforos over you?

Harris: No, he didn't.

Bolen: Mrs. Harris, isn't it a fact that during that March 10, 1980, morning telephone conversation with Dr. Tarnower he told you that you had lied?

Harris: No. He was angry . . . I think with himself. I think he was sort of boxed in at that moment and he was uncomfortable, but he did not say I had lied. About what, Mr. Bolen?

Bolen: Mrs. Harris, isn't it a fact that during that March 10, 1980, morning telephone conversation with the doctor he told you that you cheated? Yes or no.

Harris: No, indeed.

Aurnou objects, accuses Bolen of making it up. Overruled.

Bolen: Mrs. Harris, isn't it a fact that during that March 10, 1980, morning telephone conversation with Dr. Tarnower he told you that you were going to inherit $240,000?

Aurnou   (jumping to his feet): I move for a mistrial.

Motion denied.

Harris: No, he didn't, Mr. Bolen.

Bolen: Mrs. Harris, isn't it a fact that during that March 10, 1980, morning telephone conversation the doctor told you, and I quote . . .

Harris (breaks in): You do.

Bolen (continuing): "Goddammit, Jean, I want you to stop bothering me"?

Harris: No, Mr. Bolen, he didn't.

Bolen: And Mrs. Harris, isn't it a fact . . .

Aurnou: The same objection to that question, Judge.

Harris (to Leggett): How long can this go on? Forever?

Leggett: I am going to overrule the objection, Mr. Aurnou.

Bolen: . . . Is it a fact, Mrs. Harris, on March 10, 1980, you intended to kill Dr. Tarnower and then kill yourself because if you couldn't have Dr. Tarnower no one would? Yes or no, Mrs. Harris. [A gasp is heard among the spectators.]

Harris: No, Mr. Bolen.

Bolen (gathering his papers): I have no further questions.

Mrs. Harris shakes her head before the spectacle of injustice and says quietly to anyone who will hear her, "Unbelievable!"

In effect, the trial is at an end. I suppose it ended with the reading of the Scarsdale letter—except, of course, for the decision. Except indeed! We come back to court each day, we listen earnestly, we take our notes, we speak our public thoughts to one another, reserve our private thoughts. "What do you think?" "What do *you* think?" The reporters want a decisive voice to make itself heard. Those unfortunate jurors.

Aurnou has another witness from Madeira. Our fate now is either melodrama or anticlimax. Karla Cortelyou is anticlimax. She's head of the Madeira Mathematics Department. She'd seen Mrs. Harris at chapel on Friday morning the 7th, and again at dinner on Sunday evening. She'd also met with her on school business, the purchase of a computer, on the afternoon of Monday the 10th. The headmistress had been increasingly strung out as the weekend progressed; she'd talked obsessively of the school's disciplinary problem. Mrs. Cortelyou had suggested to Mrs. Harris that she could use a week in bed.

Mrs. Harris is recalled by her edgy attorney—where is Aurnou's easy charm of yesteryear?—to testify about the empty Desoxyn bottle that James Harris found in her house in Virginia after her arrest. It's brought out that Dr. Tarnower wrote prescriptions for Mrs. Harris in the name of Phyllis Rogers, who was in his employ; she has been left $20,000 in his will. Throughout the trial the drug issue has been delicate for both sides. Whenever Bolen approaches Mrs. Harris's use of a controlled medication, he wants two things: to get rid of the idea that drugs played a part in the shooting and to protect the good repute of Dr. Tarnower. But Aurnou wants to hold Tarnower responsible for Mrs. Harris's drug history while not letting his client say anything disparaging of the man she's supposed to love so uncritically. In this Aurnou can wholly count on her; Mrs. Harris is as alert as a lion-tamer. Never in this trial except when the subject of drugs is raised has she referred to the doctor other than as Hi. Talk of drugs and he at once becomes Dr. Tarnower. She remembers no dates of new prescriptions; she never says she was Dr. Tarnower's patient. Her formulation couldn't be more cautiously exact. She took medicines that she required as they were prescribed for her by a reputable physician, Dr. Tarnower. If a name not her own appeared on the labels, she didn't note it. Does she realize, Bolen asks, that it's against the law to transfer her medicine to anyone other than the person for whom it was prescribed? Harris: "Then I guess that means Phyllis Rogers and Dr. Tarnower broke the law, didn't they?" She adds in a pained voice: "Why would you do this to Hi?"

Still on the question of Mrs. Harris's medications, Aurnou calls two psychiatrists whose specialty is drugs. Taking into account Mrs. Harris's age, weight, and other individual characteristics, Dr. Lois Fishler calls the dosage most recently prescribed for her—ten mgs. a day—"high average." She testifies that its abrupt cessation

271

would probably cause "fatigue, lassitude, some anxiety, a feeling of being down-in-the-dumps, perhaps way-down-in-the-dumps, sadness, sense of melancholy, some agitation, or maybe slowing down, or maybe both, a sense of diminished self-worth, a negative self-image." Both environmental stress and individual variation are important factors, she adds, in determining a person's reactions to withdrawal. Whatever the reaction, it usually peaks in two to three days though it can last weeks or even months. The other drug expert, Dr. Burton Angrist, is the son of the pathologist who was an earlier witness. This Dr. Angrist describes much the same pattern of withdrawal symptoms as Dr. Fishler: "diminished drive, being somewhat lethargic . . . a tendency to feel rather pessimistic, easily overwhelmed . . . less able to cope with day-to-day stress, a sense of some helplessness." The effect, he thinks, would be at its worst in the first couple of days but it could remain at a plateau for a variable period of time before tailing off. With Dr. Angrist's testimony the defense rests.

But Bolen has a rebuttal witness. The rumor seems to have got about that it's to be Lynne Tryforos and the courtroom is over-flowing. Mrs. Juanita Edwards takes the stand. She identifies herself as a Westchester resident of forty years. She's a woman of middle age, modestly dressed, with gentle manners. Everything about her spells decency and trustworthiness; the trial has had no more credible witness. Dr. Tarnower, she tells us, had been her husband's doctor for more than twenty years and her physician too when her health warranted it. In her husband's long illness she'd often spoken with the doctor on the telephone; she was familiar with his voice. On the morning of March 10, consequent to a consultation with him the previous week, she'd had a ten o'clock appointment for which she'd apparently arrived at the Clinic a little early. There was no wait; she'd been at once taken to an examining room. It was a room she'd been in before, with an examining table on the right and, near it, a phone on the wall next to a little bracket. Dr. Tarnower had come in and just begun the examination when the phone rang. He went to the phone and said he'd take the call in his office. He put the receiver on the bracket but the connection wasn't broken. The doctor left the room, closing the door behind him. "Presently," says Mrs.

Edwards, "I was aware of the sound of muffled voices coming through the receiver." She recognized one of them as Dr. Tarnower's. "It was very loud and very angry." The other voice sounded like a woman's. " 'Goddammit, Jean, I want you to stop bothering me!' " she heard the man say in a loud voice. Then he said, " 'You've lied and you've cheated.' " And he'd also said, " 'Well, you're going to inherit $240,000.' " She didn't hear any more, Mrs. Edwards testifies, but presently there was a click and then Dr. Tarnower came back and hung up the phone, and he continued the examination. "He seemed more tense," says the witness. "And I thought he looked at me a little quizzically." She hadn't intentionally overheard the conversation, it had been unavoidable. She told the police about this phone call the next day, March 11.

So Bolen has been sitting on this for all these long months! It's a clincher. Aurnou is plainly fussed. It does him no good to take it out on Bolen—he and his client have already gone in for too much personal attack on their young opponent. While Mrs. Edwards is still on the stand and the Judge and lawyers are having a side bar, I see a fleeting interchange between the witness and the defendant. Or, rather, I see a fleeting response of Mrs. Edwards to Mrs. Harris. Mrs. Harris has her back to me, I can't see her side of the exchange, but I see Mrs. Edwards for an instant look at her in refusal of whatever it is that is being communicated. Mildly but firmly, she ever so slightly shakes her head. Of what is Mrs. Harris accusing her?

After this explosive testimony, what could be more fitting than a bomb scare? We're quietly moved from the twelfth to the eighth floor of the courthouse while the threat is investigated. The "bomb" is a football on the shelf of the coat closet at the rear of our court, a belated Christmas present for the son of one of the writers. We're all of us jittery these days, even our nice happy sheriffs.

W. Reid Lindsay, our old friend the photographer, is now for the first time called by the prosecution. He has a significant contribution to make to our understanding of the doctor's anterior chest wound. On Lindsay's infrared photograph of the hole in Tarnower's pajama top, Dr. Wecht had circled an area which he said was darkened by blackening due to gunpowder residue. Lindsay now testifies that he took the picture when the blood on the pajamas was dry and that these seemingly darkened areas were not caused by gunpowder but by dried blood. Infrared, he says, will usually filter out blood, but not when the blood is caked. This testimony is hurtful to the defense. Aurnou bases much of his claim that the front shoulder wound was a direct shot on the presence of gunpowder residue on the front of Tarnower's pajamas. Aurnou is indeed so upset by Lindsay's testimony that Judge Leggett has finally to tell him, "Cool off. We'll make faster time."

And after Lindsay Dr. Roh also returns. And Dr. Ackerman—except that Ackerman now adds a new occupation. He still arrives in the big black limousine, with or without his chalks, but now he's come not only to testify but also to act as the defense advisor in dermatopathology. He sits at the defense table taking notes and when Roh is being cross-examined he all but flies out of his seat with questions for Aurnou to put to the Medical Examiner—he starts by scrawling them on a pad and holding them up for Aurnou like cue cards, but then he shifts to peeling off the sheets and thrusting them into Aurnou's hand. Later, when Bolen protests the noise he's making, Ackerman lets Mrs. Harris more quietly supply him with sheets of paper. There's a bad bit, or what could have been a bad bit, in the corridor as Roh gets off the elevator and one of the women reporters says too loudly, "Oh, shit, another pathologist." "You call me shit?" says the Medical Examiner. But happily he adds a friendly grin and the air clears. Another of the young women reporters, catching sight of the recidivist Medical Examiner, says wonderfully, "Those who do not remember histology are condemned to repeat it."

Yet one time more Bolen takes Roh through the question of whether or not palmar tissue was found in the tissue from Dr. Tarnower's front chest wound. By now the matter seems negligible but I guess it's of consequence if the prosecution is going to stay with its position that there was no struggle and that Mrs. Harris took the doctor by surprise. I'm not convinced she took him by surprise. Nor is there particular reason for any of us to be convinced that the slides that Roh now projects for us on a screen support his contention that he found tissue indigenous to the palm of the hand in Dr. Tarnower's chest wound. Differences of judgment reappear. In essence Roh's opinions are confirmed by Dr. Martin Brownstein, a new prosecution pathologist. Then both men are heatedly and—so it seems to me—cogently contradicted by Dr. Ackerman who with unparalleled firmness announces that there is *no* specific palm tissue in the tissue that was taken from Tarnower's anterior chest wound. Our friend from N.Y.U. implies, "And that's that. It closes the argument." But for three days the debate has again been swirling about our heads and any kind of diversion is welcome. While we wait for at least another bomb scare, we satisfy ourselves with what the day can offer; it includes Aurnou's great stand on behalf of the American public. It happens that one whole wall of our courtroom is windows. On a bright day the room can't be properly darkened for Roh's skinflicks, so we're moved to a tiny inner courtroom across the hall where the few seats are at once taken by the press. Aurnou (angrily): "This is no longer a public trial. . . . Your Honor, I want this on the record. . . . I'm saying that half of the seats should be for the public." What? the indignant reporters demand. Aren't they members of the public? Leggett says soothingly that he'd always thought that the press covered for the majority of the people but, never mind, we'll go back to the old courtroom. We do, and wait in indecision until finally a large auditorium on the second floor is made available to us. Democracy has been vindicated. I also have my private diversion with Dr. Ackerman. Having watched him zip off question after question for Aurnou to put to the opposition, I approach him at the end of the first day of this return appearance with a question of my own. I've hastily written it out. "Dr. Ackerman, you've now made a public identification with the defense in this case. Are you aware of what this commits you to in terms that have nothing to do with your scientific expertise? Have you read the preceding testimony and taken it into account?" It's fair to assume, of course, that he hasn't. Dr. Ackerman ponders a bit and presently, pleasantly, replies that his sole commitment is to tell the truth within his own area of expert knowledge. Oh, then he's not being paid for his services? interposes a reporter at my side. The doctor says he won't comment. But the next morning he stops me before the start of court. It's obvious that he's troubled: he's been confronted with the ever-vexing question of having to choose between engagement and disinterestedness. Isn't there always, he asks, the necessity in life to come forward and tell the truth, however difficult? What about Nazi Germany and the failure of people to have attested to what was happening to the Jews there? I begin to blink—what Hitler is persecuting Mrs. Harris?—but the doctor goes on. Was I acquainted with Brecht's *Mother Courage*? Oh dear, I laugh, Dr. Ackerman mustn't cite Brecht to *me*—Brecht was the greatest moral opportunist of our intellectual century! Really? We must talk about this, says the doctor, but I move away from the discussion. Not too much later I see Ackerman comforting Mrs. Harris with a pat. He also puts a consoling arm around Aurnou's shoulder. It's clear that he's been drawn to Mrs. Harris and her lawyer as to a properly enlightened political cause and that he has moved from staying with scientific neutrality to taking, as so many other decent people have done, a stance of advocacy. But why? What in Mrs. Harris has such force of right that it solicits this identification with her defense? Perhaps her supporters fear the darker reaches of human feeling; they're lost in a dream of innocence. This would put them, of course, in the traditional line of American political enlightenment.

I want Mrs. Harris to have surrendered Tarnower with dignity, and just so I want Aurnou to conclude her defense with dignity. But it's not to be. For most of the way his summation is the expectable appeal to emotion. Mrs. Harris was tired, aging. Mrs. Harris was alone and lonely. Mrs. Harris had impossible decisions to make at school and had impossibly to make them without medication. Mrs. Harris had lost even the trust and friendship of a girl on whom she'd lavished much motherly affection. Mrs. Harris had had but one man in her life for fourteen years and selflessly gave him her love, selflessly labored on his books. By the testimony of good people, Mrs. Harris was "bone weary," both physically and emotionally ravaged by her western tour for the school and during her last weekend at Madeira. By Monday afternoon she was deaf to the world; she had nevertheless carried on her school duties and made the preparations to kill herself. Could anyone who heard her testimony have any question but that Mrs. Harris meant to end her life? It was suicide that she'd had in mind, not murder. To Aurnou they're mutually exclusive. Apparently if the jury believes that Mrs. Harris intended to shoot herself it must acquit her of murder.

Her life is at stake and Mrs. Harris wouldn't lie. Who, asks Aurnou, that made up a story to disguise a crime would say that she didn't recall how some of the shots were fired? But consistent with all the physical evidence, Aurnou can himself fill in the missing parts of the story. Quickly he completes the scenario. Shot 1 we know about. Soon Mrs. Harris is on the floor on her knees. She's found the gun, means to use it on herself. The doctor flies across the bed, tackles her, takes the gun from her. The doctor sits on his bed. "Remember what happens. In that space between the beds, kneeling in front of him, bringing herself up on his knees, Mrs. Harris reaches for the gun to get it and get away . . . and at that point he grabbed her wrist—try it in the jury room." [Aurnou doesn't say it but apparently this was when Mrs. Harris convulsively shot off the gun, producing the close-distance wound to the doctor's rear shoulder.] If somebody pulls your wrist and then lets go, as presumably the doctor would because he'd just been hit, and you fall back, what—asks Aurnou—do you do? You grab for something and try to pull yourself forward." Aurnou illustrates the action with his own body and seems to suggest that Mrs. Harris tried to pull herself up by the trigger of the gun that was in her own hand, much as one might clutch at air. Presumably this again fires the gun, causing the distant front shoulder wound. "So two shots probably happened exactly then." It's after this that the doctor lifts himself enough to lunge across Mrs. Harris's body, his hands at her waist, causing her to believe that the muzzle of the gun is sticking into her stomach. She consciously pulls the trigger. This is the fourth shot. It's the shot that hit the doctor's arm.

The story has taken no more than a minute or two, if that much, of Aurnou's three-hour summation. While this suggests a throw-away, I don't think that's Aurnou's purpose. I think it represents his effort, the whole of his effort—perhaps also the effort of Mac-Donell?—to solve the mystery that's haunted the trial, never dispelled and surely not now dispelled by this mechanical, possible but unlikely reconstruction. Yet if Aurnou was going into the question at all, why, one might ask, did he do it this cursorily, in a way that he might have known wouldn't win a jury?

But what does win a jury, or alienate it? I keep remembering Aurnou's wink to his wife when he turned back to the room after an angry scene with the prosecutor. He was pleased with the show he'd put on and he took it for granted that his wife understood that it was *only* a show and shared his enjoyment of the performance. This is the old-fashioned movie practice of criminal law: a trial is theatre; the lawyer appeals to his audience, the jury, to join him in his righteous wrath, merge its tears and sentiments of mercy with his own. But fashions change even in acting and the law. Old-time movies embarrass while they entertain, and so do old-time courtroom practices: at forty-seven Aurnou is too young to stay with this dated method. Movies are what make old movies look old-fashioned; they are in themselves the motion of time and they've had their part in dating courtroom histrionics. Listening to Mrs. Harris's lawyer, I put myself in the jury box. I'm repelled by his emotional defense. And there are occasions when I'm offended by his mockeries. Ours today is not a world in which one readily takes license to mimic the accents of the foreign-born as Aurnou mimics Suzanne—"Sometime in zee deestant past, I remember, I said to Mees Harris"—or as he ludicrously attributes a "cafone" accent to the Korean Dr. Roh, fabulating a conversation between Roh and "Vin," the Italian Vincent Crispino. And I'm outraged when he makes up a scene between Bolen and the Medical Examiner in which Bolen asks Roh to re-examine his slides: "Go back and look at the slides, dummy!"

Perhaps Aurnou isn't playing for effect when he demands that the jury not bring in a compromise verdict: his client is guilty or not guilty of murder and if she's not guilty of murder, she's to be acquitted. But it's a dangerous ploy. Mrs. Harris needs every break the law can give her and neither she nor her attorney should gamble with her life. The defense summation ends with the reading of a poem:

Time does not bring relief; you all have lied
Who told me time would ease me of my pain!
I miss him in the weeping of the rain;
I want him at the shrinking of the tide. . . .

Aurnou has said, "I'm going to inflict on you a poem." He just wants the words listened to. "I'm not going to tell you who wrote it." Is the jury to think it was written by Mrs. Harris? It's a sonnet of Edna St. Vincent Millay.

Bolen's is a different style. He speaks quietly, addresses the jury as "fact-finders," persons of whom he assumes that they are as plain and rigorous as himself, able commonsensically to assess Mrs. Harris's state of mind, the value of the defense testimony, the only-human failings of the Harrison police. He draws particular attention to Herbert MacDonell's reconstruction of the first shot and the many unsupported assumptions which, he says, went into his drawing of the bullet's probable trajectory. Can the jury indeed be satisfied that the indentation on the deck was the ricochet point of this first bullet? Would a bullet from a .32 have the power to penetrate the doctor's hand and two panes of glass, strike the deck, then lodge itself in a post? Why did Mrs. Harris's farewell visit to the doctor end, Bolen asks, with four wounds to him and none to herself?

But Bolen too has his venture in speculation and it carries him not only into unproved assertion but also—as Judge Leggett points out, to the laughter and applause of Mrs. Harris's supporters and of the defendant herself—far from the evidence we've heard in court. Mrs. Harris, Bolen maintains, arrived in Purchase unexpected; she took the sleeping doctor by surprise. He woke up angry; probably, says Bolen, this was the point at which he said, "Get out of here, you're crazy!" The defendant went to the dressing area and removed a shawl and other items which she wrapped in it. She set it down on the floor near the glass door. Then she went into the bathroom where, for the first time, she was confronted by the obvious signs of Lynne's possession of the place she herself had once had in the doctor's life. That she'd entertained thoughts of doing away with herself, Bolen doesn't question. But the "triggering event" wasn't the critical letter from the student who had been injured in the Brazen Hussies incident, it was Tarnower's having said to her on the phone that morning, "Goddammit, Jean, stop bothering me." Now she has a dual intent: before killing herself she'll kill the doctor. If she can't have him, neither shall Lynne. The doctor is seated on the bed. Mrs. Harris shoots the gun at him; the bullet goes through his hand and enters his chest. Tarnower lunges toward her and she fires again; this time the bullet hits the posterior shoulder. He falls back and in the process strikes the gun with his left hand, causing the gun to go off—the bullet goes into the cabinet. Bolen: "The defendant retreats . . . to the bathroom. All those things that were found strewn in the dressing area, all the things strewn on the floor [of the guest bathroom] she is throwing, she is tossing. . . . Unbeknownst to Jean Harris, Herman Tarnower recovers. . . . He gets up and he starts walking ever so slowly [to *his* bathroom]. . . . He now realizes, being a doctor, what a precarious state he's in. . . . [He comes out of his bathroom] and the defendant sees him, gets the gun. There are two rounds left in it. . . . They meet at the end of the beds. . . . The doctor, with his right hand bleeding, pushes Jean Harris on the bed. . . . She falls back. The gun is in her left hand. Her left hand is facing the glass door, and as she goes back the gun discharges through the glass window." But this is also when Leggett, in response to an objection from Aurnou, says, "I think we are getting fairly far away from the evidence now." Bolen concludes his scenario: the doctor reaches Suzanne on the buzzer. He's holding the phone, about to speak to Suzanne, when Mrs. Harris fires the shot to his right arm—it's the shot heard by Suzanne. The doctor collapses to his knees, the receiver falls to the floor. Mrs. Harris gets her coat, goes to the bathroom where she bangs the gun on the tub to open it, and taking the gun with her, rushes from the house.

So here we are, the slaves of our commitments, professional no less than emotional. Facts must bend to our needs, and a fact once bent has the consoling shape of permanence. Dubiety, the refusal to venture a firm conclusion, has little place in a court of law. It has little place anywhere. Asking the jury to weigh facts,

Bolen asks them to do what he himself has done only partially.

What is fact, of course, or almost fact is the prosecutor's statement that no one who saw Mrs. Harris the night of the shooting could report a tear for the dead doctor. We recall, though, that Riegelman testified that she sobbed on his shoulder. Shock can dam the flow of expressed feelings, and for me it is far more significant that there have been no tears for Tarnower at any time during the trial than that she did or didn't weep that evening. Throughout the trial her tears have been only for herself.

Worn, grave even when he tries to relax the tense atmosphere of the room—"We've all of us aged gracefully"—Judge Leggett stands to charge the jury.

The first count of the original indictment is murder in the second degree. To be guilty of murder the defendant must have had intent when one or more of the shots was fired, and the prosecution must have proved that it was her conscious objective to cause the victim's death.

In the charge of second-degree murder Leggett has included two lesser charges, manslaughter in the second degree and criminally negligent homicide. Before it can bring in a verdict of second-degree manslaughter the jury must find the defendant not guilty of murder in the second degree. If the death was caused by reckless conduct, as opposed to intentional conduct, or if the defendant was incapable of forming such an intent, the jury may consider the charge of second-degree manslaughter. The defendant is guilty of manslaughter in the second degree if she was aware of, and consciously disregarded, the risk of doing harm to another person and the conduct resulted in that person's death. The intention is without significance if the conduct is reckless. And the risk must be "a gross deviation from the standard of conduct [of] a reasonable person."

The charge of criminally negligent homicide can be considered only if the defendant is found not guilty of manslaughter in the second degree. For a jury to bring in a conviction of second-degree manslaughter, the defendant must be found to have acted in such a manner as to cause substantial and unjustifiable risk of harm to another person and to have failed to have perceived this risk. The failure to perceive the risk must constitute a gross deviation from the standard of conduct a reasonable person would employ, and the act must have been the cause of death.

The second count of the original indictment is possession of a weapon in the second degree. The count cannot be considered if the defendant has been found not guilty of murder in the second degree. The defendant is guilty on this count if she is found to have possessed a loaded firearm with the intent to use it in the doctor's murder.

The third count of the original indictment is weapons possession in the third degree. The defendant is guilty on this count if she possessed a firearm but not in her home or business, and was aware of its possession.

The lesser included charge is possession in the fourth degree: possession of a loaded or unloaded weapon in the defendant's home or place of business. This was the charge to which Aurnou was directing himself in trying to prove that Tarnower's home was also the home of Mrs. Harris.

The charges have been explained. The Judge goes back to the early days of the trial; he summarizes his recollection of the high points of the testimony that has been heard. He's notably fair-minded, accepts some minor corrections by both lawyers. He points out to the jury that its recollection of the testimony supersedes his.

It is of course not told the jury but later we learn that it was the prosecution that requested and was granted the down charge of manslaughter in the second degree, having first been refused its request for manslaughter in the first degree. Although Aurnou opposed the inclusion of any down charge, at this point, without waiving his opposition to down charges, he requested and was granted the down charge of criminally negligent homicide.

Murder in the second degree is a grave charge; it carries a minimum mandatory sentence of fifteen years to life. There can be no parole.

The press room, by which one means an anonymous space on the ground floor of the courthouse, isn't an attractive retreat. It's bare and dull, unpleasantly drafty. On an especially cold day, with the wind blowing in through the crevices around the windows, I'd heard the most experienced and gifted of the daily reporters explain to a friendly sheriff that it was hard, after all, to type wearing her mittens: could heaters be brought in? The furniture is so minimal as to be virtually non-existent. It consists of some half-dozen worktables and a scattering of wooden chairs; there are more telephones and typewriters than provision for their comfortable use. But much work has been done here in our months together: many thousands of words have been written and filed; the public has been given its news. The sketch artists and even the few television people originally assigned to the trial have worked in the press room too. The TV reporters use the room only to prepare their continuities. They videocast in the pit in the main lobby near the front doors of the building, close to the bank of elevators and the escalators to and from a vast subterranean garage. The pit is a sunken square that might be the new waiting room in a small-city railroad terminal. Early in the trial this was the stand of only one or two TV crews, but since Mrs. Harris's appearance as a witness—or is it since the reading of the Scarsdale letter?—not only has the press room become a jungle but the lobby chokes with traffic. The entire media world now converges on White Plains; even the BBC has sent a team. The sheriffs are maddened: our once well-regulated courthouse has gone off its trolley. Although friendly, even jolly, it rocks with competitive enterprise. The TV people, cumbersome with equipment, jockey for place in the overflowing pit. Still photographers have been positioning themselves wherever they can hope to shoot the woman who's accused of shooting her lover—language has a strange way of tripping us up. The woman in the case has been superb. She is what is unbelievable in this trial; justice or its failure are tales we've always heard. She has been arriving in the building by various secret routes and with a variety of escorts, members of her family or of Aurnou's staff. Sometimes she came up by escalator and, as if on signal, there was a stampede in her direction. The camera people walked backwards in front of her as she came up the moving escalator, shooting, shooting. She was undeterred, the little half-smile fixed. At her arraignment, long ago when Mrs. Harris was a novice in publicity, she'd been quoted as saying of the reporters in the Harrison courthouse, "Haven't they anything better to do with their time?" (Later her son Jimmy used the same words to my courtroom assistant.) That was like saying, "Sticks and stones can break my bones but words can never harm me." These mechanical statements of superiority are designed to help simple people meet vicissitude. If Jean Harris did indeed say this, the mediocrity of the remark was as unsuited to a person of her experience of the public life as her sick smile was unsuited to the situation that put her in the spotlight. Such self-falsification has nothing in common with innocence. Quite the opposite, it draws on some unfathomable awareness of one's own emotional lie. How times had changed for her and how well Mrs. Harris had adapted to her altered circumstances. This was a resilient lady—in a way. Not altogether, but in a way. She'd become a practiced performer: she'd not only come to understand the importance of the press in her defense, she'd even learned to offer herself, not too generously, just generously enough, to public inspection. As she faced this insistence of cameras did she have to battle hysteria? I think not. She no doubt had her moments of blackest panic, but I suspect they were hedged around with confidence, also with unreality. But it would be a mistake to underestimate Mrs. Harris's deep native power to contend and last: that's the mighty gift she has, her endowment of perdurability. The Madeira headmistress spoke, we recall, of having reached the point that March weekend where she felt she could no longer cope, yet of course she'd coped all the time she was getting ready no longer to cope—as her son would say, "Let there be no mistake about that!" Jean Harris coped beyond the capacity of most of us.

It's my first experience of waiting out a verdict. I want never to do it again. Under the persuasion that I'll be able to write, I take a room in a nearby hotel and arrange to be called by a friend in the press corps as soon as there's word of a decision. I'm assured there'll be no problem in reaching the court on time: we'll have a full ten minutes before the verdict is delivered. But by midafternoon each day, I'm inexorably drawn back to the press room. Until Mrs. Harris's case is disposed of (what an expression!) I belong with these people: we may each of us have gone through something different in Mrs. Harris's trial but we've gone through it together. I don't resent the newcomers who throng the courthouse. They're not my line of business, these big-name reporters who now arrive not in limousines but surely with many colors of chalk; but I need the society of my old companions in confusion and boredom. If they've graduated from chocolate bars and gumdrops to pizzas and congealing sweet-and-sour spareribs, I want to pig along with them. The press room couldn't be filthier: the world has no refuse container big enough to hold our empty cans and cartons. The floor is carpeted with paper wrappings and redundant newspapers—I'd not seen this particular kind of fresh daily mess since ten years ago when I'd visited in my old college dormitory. But each day, once I enter the press room in midafternoon, I'm unable to return to my hotel until I hear that the jury has retired for the night. Doesn't everyone know that the moment one turns one's back and interrupts the vigil is always the decisive moment?

And so it is that I'm present on February 24 to hear the decision in the case of Mrs. Harris. Had I disciplined my restlessness and stayed at the hotel, there'd have been no possibility of my being there on time—that's not how it happens.

Even in the din of the press room the phone can be heard. Incoming calls are infrequent; any one of them may be from upstairs, the summons we're waiting for, and therefore the moment the phone rings, a hush falls on the room. One of the phones rings. A woman reporter quietly answers; she's been waiting at her post. While the room listens, she says, "Yes, yes." She nods into the phone, raises her hand in message to the rest of us: this is it. Until she hangs up—it's but a second—no one moves. Then in a mass everyone surges to the elevators already blocked by the lobby people. The courthouse officers do what they can to marshal us into lines. No one is trampled or even badly jostled but everyone's on his own, willing to hold back for no one. It's inconceivable that I could have been phoned at the hotel by the most faithful of friends.

The crowds in the lobby hadn't needed to be called by phone, they'd had their own signal that the jury had reached a decision: the arrival of Mrs. Harris. She'd come alone. It was late afternoon on the eighth day of deliberation. On day 1 the jurors asked for all the exhibits. On day 2, which was actually the first whole day that the jury was out, they asked to have all the testimony that dealt with what had happened in Tarnower's bedroom the night of the shooting read back to them; this took six hours. And then again, a day or two later, they'd asked that all testimony be read back to them that dealt with Mrs. Harris's actions from 3:30 the afternoon of the 10th until her arrival in Purchase. Several requests had also come to Judge Leggett for further explanation of the legal meaning of intent. By day 5, or certainly by day 6, with no decision, it was the opinion of many of us that the best Mrs. Harris could now expect was a hung jury. By day 8, today, I had begun to suspect that Mrs. Harris would be found guilty of murder in the second degree. Perhaps Aurnou had reached the same conclusion. It seemed so to those who caught sight of him in the building—he'd probably prepared his client for this outcome. As Mrs. Harris told one of the reporters, bidding her a friendly good-bye when the trial was drawing to its end, she could take anything but sympathy: she received the verdict alone rather than in the company of her family and friends.

Judge Leggett asked that there be no demonstration in the courtroom. "I've tried to run a dignified court," he said. He instructed the courtroom guards to empty the room row by row so as to keep the reporters from rushing to the phones. Without putting a hand on Mrs. Harris a woman police officer stood by during the few minutes that it took for the foreman to deliver the decision and for the jury to be polled: the defendant had been found guilty of murder in the second degree, guilty of possession in the second degree, guilty of possession in the third degree. When the date of sentencing had been set—March 20—the woman officer gently guided Mrs. Harris from the room and, I suppose, to the police car awaiting her downstairs. They moved together quickly. In the lobby there was pandemonium. The media took over; the day could now be theirs.

Old court hands say that a jury that's bringing in an acquittal will look at the defendant but that a jury that brings in a verdict of guilty avoids looking at the convicted person. This seems to be true. No one in the jury looked at Mrs. Harris, I think that some of them were crying. I saw no sign of pleasure or satisfaction on the face of anyone in the jury or in the crowded courtroom.

On March 20, 1981, a little more than a year after the death of Herman Tarnower, Jean Harris was sentenced to jail for fifteen years to life for his murder. It was not in the discretion of the Judge to give a lesser penalty; it was mandatory to impose at least a fifteen-year sentence. It was in his discretion to order, as he did, that the two sentences on weapons possession be served concurrently with the sentence for murder. Before pronouncing sentence Judge Leggett inquired if Mrs. Harris wished to be heard. "Yes, I do," said Mrs. Harris. She rose to speak. I wasn't in my old place in the courtroom: the deputy sheriff had told me I could sit in the first row where Mrs. Harris's family and friends had sat during the trial, supporting and applauding her. None of them was in court today: for her sentencing as for the verdict, Mrs. Harris was alone with counsel. Close to a month had passed since I had last seen her; I was frightened by the way she'd changed. In her first days at the Valhalla jail where she'd awaited sentencing, Mrs. Harris had been reported to be refusing food and she'd been put on a twenty-four-hour suicide watch. But the assumption that she was trying to starve to death was apparently mistaken: word came that it was the prison food she rejected, or perhaps she wanted to avoid the prison dining hall. Officials at Valhalla said she was eating food brought to her by visitors, chiefly junk food. She drank milk. Then only a day or two ago, after a period of reassuring silence, there'd been report that Mrs. Harris had made a troubling scene when she'd been routinely handcuffed to be taken for a medical examination. There was no reason to expect her to look well. The nature of the deterioration rather than its degree was shocking. Thread by thread she was being unwoven; quite literally she was being wasted. Her hair had lost its lustre; her familiar clothes no longer had their prim crispness. Most difficult to account for was a drainage of color from her face. While most of her face was normal in color, there was a white parenthesis around her nose and mouth. It wasn't powder, it came from inside her; had it been powder it would have had to have been applied by someone mad. Seated so near her, I could almost feel the trembling of her body in my own body. Under her chair, one of her feet moved incessantly up and down, up and down. It was like an accelerated metronome.

I didn't think I should be seeing her in this condition in order to write about it. Several times in the course of the trial I'd been interviewed about the book I was doing about Mrs. Harris, and once I'd been asked, not too unkindly, whether it wasn't ghoulish, an exploitation, to make a book out of so terrible a personal tragedy? I don't recall how I replied but I remember thinking that there was ground for the question only if all reporting of human events was felt to be an exploitation and if all writing which had its source in the actual lives of people, whether the form was fiction, biography, or memoirs, was subject to the same accusation. There was a sense, indeed, in which even the re-creation of history was exploitation: to write about the Holocaust was to exploit six million human tragedies. To be immune to the charge and still be a writer, say, of fiction would require that one limit oneself to the writing of fantasy, one's subject werewolves or ape people; a fiction already grievously detached from experience would be left no human point of departure. And privacy, after all, was the most relative of privileges. It was granted us by society under ungenerous conditions, the most fundamental of them that whether for pain or profit, by design or accident, we not call public attention to ourselves.

Nonetheless, I wanted not to be a spectator upon a Mrs. Harris so much defeated. More even than I'd had a sense of intrusion when I'd driven to Purchase a year ago to view the Tarnower house, today I felt it to be an insult to my own emotions of privacy to be present, observing, while the curtain fell on Mrs. Harris's drama.

Mrs. Harris had risen to her feet to speak. She had accepted the opportunity offered by the court but for a moment it looked as if she might not manage it, she might lack the strength. But she found the strength. She remained upright and spoke in a voice sufficiently firm:

I want to say that I did not murder Dr. Herman Tarnower, that I loved him very much and I never wished him ill, and I am innocent as I stand here. For you or for Mr. Bolen to arrange my life so that I will be in a cage for the rest of it, and that every time I walk outside I will have iron around my wrists, is not justice; it is a travesty of justice. The people in that jury were told Mr. Bolen will prove to you beyond a reasonable doubt that Mrs. Harris intended to kill Dr. Tarnower. In their many statements, and a number of them decided to become public figures now, and they have written for the newspaper and they have been on television shows and they have been on radio shows—in every single statement they have said, in essence, Mrs. Harris took the stand and didn't prove to us she was innocent, and therefore we find her guilty. In the 10,000 pages of testimony that have been taken here, there isn't a page, there isn't a paragraph and there isn't a sentence in which anyone suggests, in which the prosecution suggests, how I was guilty of intentionally hurting Dr. Tarnower. And certainly for him to suggest [she's speaking now of the prosecutor and his comment, in calling for her sentence, that she's shown no regret or remorse for the death of so valuable a person as Dr. Tarnower] that he cannot adequately articulate how people feel the loss, that is really gratuitous, because he certainly doesn't have to explain it to me. No one in the world feels that loss more than I do. I am not guilty, your Honor.

There was a burst of applause from the audience and Judge Leggett reminded the spectators that they were not to express their feelings in this manner. Mrs. Harris resumed her seat and again her body seemed to buckle but she didn't collapse—we recall that when Detective Siciliano described Mrs. Harris's behavior on the night of the shooting, as the doctor's body was being carried from the house, he'd testified that she'd momentarily collapsed in his arms but then immediately straightened herself again; her recovery had been so quick that he'd taken this to be playacting. Well, before us now we had evidence of the speed with which Mrs. Harris could recover at least the appearance of composure: this was not playacting. She'd not only made it to her feet where a moment before we'd have thought it impossible, but on her feet she spoke with brevity, clarity, directly to the point. Then once more she'd threatened collapse and once more recovered herself.

Aurnou had nothing, he said, to add to his client's statement. With much emotion, Judge Leggett pronounced sentence: "Mrs. Harris, it becomes my obligation now to impose a sentence on you, and imposing a sentence is never an easy job for any judge, and it's particularly difficult for me in this case, and very particularly when I am involved with a woman who is charged with a crime, and the sentence that I impose is a sentence that is mandated by law. . . . Commenting on the jurors, I can only say they worked slavishly to try and evaluate the facts, and I am satisfied that they worked from the standpoint of the presumption of innocence. . . ." His voice breaks. "I wish personally, as you do, that the events of March 10 had never taken place and that you never left Virginia. . . . I now remand you to the care and custody of the Department of Corrections, to be confined at the Bedford Hills Correctional Facility forthwith. Before I do that, Mrs. Harris, I want to advise you of your right to appeal."

Aurnou said he would file notice of appeal. Bolen requested a side bar. After they had briefly conferred, Judge Leggett returned to the bench and spoke again: "Mrs. Harris, in regard to my observations of you, I found you to be a brilliant, brilliant woman, and I am going to ask this: in regard to Mrs. Harris in Bedford Hills, my feeling is that she can be a most useful person in that facility and help other people. Her brilliance can probably bring some light into some other women's lives because of any ignorance and lack of knowledge. Anything that can be done with respect to giving her the opportunity to help her fellow women that are in that prison I would like it to be done. I think that she has so much to offer the women that are there that not to afford her that opportunity would be to deprive society and the other inmates in there of a very great advantage and a blessing. It's unhappy that you have to be sentenced, Mrs. Harris, and the best I can say to you is, the best of luck to you." Mrs. Harris: "Thank you." It had to end. "As I say," said Judge Leggett, "I wish the events of March 10 hadn't occurred. I would stand in recess."

AFTER THE VERDICT

The jury in the trial of Jean Harris deliberated long and carefully and I'm sure with great conscientiousness but it reached a verdict in which I don't concur. I don't think that Mrs. Harris was properly found guilty of murder in the second degree. I offer this opinion with no confidence that I'm right and the jury wrong; the subject is infinitely debatable. A case that had begun a year earlier with Mrs. Harris's admission that she'd shot Dr. Tarnower —he'd slept with every woman he could, she told the arresting officer, and she'd "had it"—closed with Mrs. Harris battling to persuade the world of her innocence, and with its central question unanswered, or at least not answered to my legal satisfaction: had Dr. Tarnower died, as the defense claimed, in a "tragic accident" brought about by the attempt of Mrs. Harris to kill herself or had she purposely killed him? Or there was yet another possibility: Mrs. Harris could have come to Purchase only to commit suicide, as she said, but the conditions of the visit—the doctor's behavior or perhaps the sight of Lynne's belongings in the bathroom that she thought of as hers—had impelled her to take the doctor's life instead of her own; or she could still have meant to kill herself afterward.

This is surely a great deal of uncertainty to be left with after one of the longest murder trials in the history of the state—including the pre-trial hearings, the selection of a jury, and a brief holiday at Christmas, the trial had run from October 6, 1980 to February 24, 1981. One would be reluctant to compute the cost to the taxpayers. Yet I was still in doubt not merely as to whether the defendant had told the truth in reporting what transpired in Dr. Tarnower's bedroom the night of the shooting but also whether she'd told the truth in reporting what she'd forgotten. The events remembered by Mrs. Harris she recounted with a precision that was close to compulsive, but what she'd forgotten she'd forgotten just as absolutely.

Thus, Mrs. Harris told us in detail of her preparations for suicide, of her trip to Purchase and her arrival at the doctor's house, of Tarnower's resistance to waking and his refusal of conversation, of what she did when she saw Lynne Tryforos's bathrobe and curlers in the bathroom, of the doctor's reaction to her outburst of temper, and of her attempt to shoot herself in the head after the doctor struck her. It was in this initial attempt of Dr. Tarnower to restrain her from suicide, Mrs. Harris said, that he'd received his first injury, the bullet through his hand. But there were four bullet holes in the doctor's body, and of the other three Mrs. Harris could remember the source of only one, and this was a tentative recollection. Her memory was muzzy: there was a shot she'd thought she was firing into her own abdomen but it hadn't hit her; apparently it had hit the doctor though Mrs. Harris couldn't say where. For the other two wounds that Tarnower sustained she offered neither location nor explanation—Aurnou ventured these in his summation; MacDonell had helped clear the ground for his conjectures. As a matter of fact, Mrs. Harris wasn't even sure that the shot she'd meant to reach her own stomach was second in the sequence of shots. When she spoke of what happened after she left the bedroom, memory had been restored. She remembered that as she rushed from the house to go for help, she had called to the van der Vrekens in the dining room to turn on the lights and that on her way to the telephone booth at the nearby Community Center she'd met Patrolman McKenna's car and led it back to Dr. Tarnower's.

Many witnesses were called for the defense. Although some of them attested only to Mrs. Harris's good character or to her troubled state of mind in the week prior to the shooting, there was also expert if not undisputed substantiation of her report of the events in Tarnower's bedroom. In this expert testimony a large portion of Mrs. Harris's case was made to rest on whether or not one accepted her account of the initial struggle for the gun which, she said, had resulted in the doctor's hand wound. The jury was said to have had difficulty in reproducing her description of her physical encounters with the doctor but I incline to accept the defense version of the first shot. The prosecution, however, clung tenaciously to a different view of what happened. It was Bolen's contention that Mrs. Harris arrived in Purchase unannounced, taking the doctor by surprise in bed, and that after going to the dressing area to gather some clothes and to the bathroom where for the first time she'd confronted Lynne's full possession of territory that had formerly been hers, she'd deliberately and purposely shot Tarnower as he sat on the bed facing her. The wound to the doctor's hand was defensive, according to the prosecution: Tarnower had held up his hand to ward off Mrs. Harris's gun and the bullet had gone through it and entered his front shoulder. The further shots had been similarly purposeful. Maddened with jealousy and rage, unwilling for Lynne to have him if she herself couldn't, Mrs. Harris had murdered Tarnower.

By legal definition murder in the second degree involves the conscious intent to kill—fortunately we're not tried on our unconscious wishes or we should all be in jail. Intent is not the same thing as premeditation: it can appear at any time up to the last instant, just as the life is being taken. As the trial progressed, the prosecuting attorney apparently came to accept Mrs. Harris's statement that in coming to Purchase she had meant to kill herself. But the prosecution didn't of course believe that this remained the only idea in her mind. For the jury the determining question was whether, at the time the trigger was pulled, Mrs. Harris had the conscious intent to kill the man she in fact did kill. So far as the law is concerned, this has nothing to do with whether or not she also meant to do away with herself. It has nothing to do with whether Mrs. Harris is a good or bad person, or whether she was or wasn't jealous of her younger rival, or whether Dr. Tarnower was or wasn't heartless. Motive enters the case only as an adjunct to credibility. That Mrs. Harris had a motive to kill Tarnower may make it more plausible that she had conscious intent in his death. It doesn't prove that she consciously intended to kill him.

I'm afraid that on the basis of what I heard and observed in Mrs. Harris's trial, I find it entirely possible that Mrs. Harris murdered Dr. Tarnower. But "possible" is not enough on which to convict a person of so serious a charge or any charge. Had I been on Mrs. Harris's jury I could not have voted as it did. The burden of proof lies with the prosecution which has to prove its case beyond reasonable doubt—where there's reasonable doubt it must go to the defendant. Without questioning the seriousness that the jury brought to its decision, there seems to me to be justification for Mrs. Harris's protest of the verdict at her sentencing: I see no travesty of justice in the jury's decision, but I agree that the charge wasn't sufficiently proven. Much else was proven but not that, not sufficiently. Judge Leggett gave the jury alternatives to the original charge. It could have convicted Mrs. Harris of manslaughter or criminally negligent homicide; in neither of these charges is conscious intent a factor. But before it could move to these down charges, the jury had to acquit on the murder charge. Aurnou had gone for broke; even in his summation he insisted that there be no compromise verdict. The jury granted his flamboyant request.

And yet, though I question the verdict against Mrs. Harris, I have no doubt at all that deep in her mind and heart she wanted to kill Dr. Tarnower. I think her fury at him was murderous and that this was plainly and repeatedly revealed in the words she spoke and wrote. But if there'd ever been a time when the wish was conscious, this was no longer so. It had departed her conscious mind, gone far away where consciousness doesn't follow. And it's conscious action that is judged in a court of law.

It's my impression that many members of the press corps and others who regularly attended the trial were also of the opinion that Mrs. Harris shouldn't have been convicted on the murder charge. But I'm not sure that this was because they felt, as I do, that the prosecution failed to prove conscious intent—in or out of the courtroom the distinction between conscious and unconscious intent was never very much a subject of talk, not in my hearing. I've heard many people say that they seriously doubt that Mrs. Harris's account of the evening in Purchase was or could have been the whole truth but they draw no conclusions from this doubt. It's as if they're willing to question the veracity of Mrs. Harris—that word of Aurnou's—and even her innocence, but stop there. They're reluctant to address what it is of which she may be guilty. In part, this has to do with cultural pressure. It's come to be thought unfeeling, intolerant, moralistic, retrograde to pass judgment even in the domain of politics unless we reach our strong opinions through sympathy for those weaker than ourselves; in the circles of contemporary enlightenment we encourage sympathy only where there's an obvious oppressor. Mrs. Harris had of course two obvious oppressors, Tarnower and a social force called the law; and even as an individual she invites a response appropriate to an oppressed minority. She's a woman whom no one of generous feeling seems to want to put down, let alone bring to justice. It's not the components of her extraordinarily complex character but the tragedy of her life that most people prefer to think about: the humiliation of her recent years with Tarnower, her loss of personal and professional hope, the public scandal and ordeal of her trial. And surely these were punishing enough: with each week of the trial one saw Mrs. Harris wearing away. Physically she was a shadow of herself by the end of the trial, and always there had hovered over the courtroom the fear that she'd not survive to a verdict. In such cruel circumstances did one send a person to jail? In any circumstances did one send Mrs. Harris to jail? I think one of the reporters summed up the unspoken attitude of the courtroom when he said that what he'd like was to see Mrs. Harris pronounced guilty but given a suspended sentence (that's of course not legally possible but he wasn't being legal) and a job at the Botanical Gardens—we'd learned she was a good gardener. He was speaking lightly but he was basically serious. She was regarded as a special instance even by those who weren't convinced that she was innocent in Tarnower's death.

As in all psychological drama, the nature of Mrs. Harris's consciousness poses a challenge: it is impossible to speak of her consciousness without at once speaking of her unconsciousness. Freud made no claim to having discovered the unconscious life. He credited the great literary artists with having made the exploration long before him. All he had done, he said, was to systematize their insights and try to put them to therapeutic use. By literary artists he chiefly meant the great imaginative writers, the novelists and playwrights who deal with character, particularly with character in conflict; for it was in conflict that Freud found the essential truth of the human condition. No character in art or in life is wholly of a piece. While most of us manage to live in relative comfort despite our warring impulses, we never live in entire self-accord; even a fanatic strips down to contradiction. It's the means by which we resolve our conflicts at least enough to live our lives with some modicum of stability or, on the other hand, the kind of problems we create for ourselves by the failure to bring our inner contradictions into working agreement that finally make us more or less interesting as creatures of fear and desire. Conflict doesn't in itself guarantee largeness of spirit; it can as well make for pettiness. But it is a first source of the mystery of human character.

Early in the nineteenth century Hazlitt wrote with calm expository explicitness of the hidden universes of the mind and of the need to harmonize the harsher discordances of our natures. In his essay "On the Knowledge of Character," speaking of the way in which the unconscious can be used to make us easier in our conscious lives, he turns to a famous crime to illustrate the curious strategies that the mind can employ to protect a person from painful self-awareness. Hazlitt is writing about the case of Eugene Aram, the defendant in an English murder trial of the 1750's:

The defense made by Eugene Aram of himself against a charge of murder, some years earlier, shows that he in imagination completely flung from himself the *nominal* crime imputed to him: he might, indeed, have staggered an old man with a blow, and buried his body in a cave, and lived ever since upon the money he found upon him, but there was 'no malice in the case, none at all'. . . . The very coolness, subtlety, and circumspection of his defense (as masterly a legal document as there is upon record) prove that he was guilty of the act, as much as they prove that he was unconscious of the *crime*.

This sharp distinction of Hazlitt's between the awareness that Aram was able to bring to his act while unaware of his crime reinforces the understanding I've come to of Mrs. Harris's present psychological situation. I think that, like Aram, Jean Harris has wholly flung from herself the crime imputed to her. Coolly if not circumspectly or subtly, she has denied her jealousy of Lynne Tryforos and her anger against Tarnower. Although the Scarsdale letter trumpets these emotions, when it was read in court Mrs. Harris seemed to be deaf to this obvious communication. She was veiled off from the fierceness of her own feelings much as she was said to have been veiled from her friends at Madeira before she left the school on March 10 and as she was veiled from the distressing details of Tarnower's death when they were testified to in her trial. In fact, I think that the denial of her hatred of Tarnower has gone so far as to carry with it her memory of anything that happened the night of March 10 that isn't comfortable for her to remember. I believe it unlikely that this memory will be restored.

I use the word "denial" here in what is now its quite technical meaning in psychoanalysis: it is the mental process by which we bury unwelcome truth. The burial can be very deep, so deep that unconsciously the actual facts are more than forgotten; they cease to exist. We all of us engage in the conscious suppression of un-flattering or disagreeable experiences or thoughts. Aware of what we're doing, we put from our minds the unpleasing idea that our waists are thickening or that last month's bank balance was less than we'd counted on. We also engage in unconscious suppres-sions, some of which may lie close to consciousness and not contrib-ute to disorders of character or function, but others of which, harder to unearth, create symptoms which we may or may not recognize, according to how much trouble they make for us. Clini-cally speaking, denial is not thought to be a useful way to meet our problems. It nevertheless has its place in the happy working out of what we like to call civilized life—perhaps it should be more fully appreciated. While the "facing of facts" is usually presented to us as an unmitigated good, something we should encourage in ourselves and in others as the confirmation within our personal lives of the authority of external reality, there are many circum-stances in which love or loyalty or confidence would be badly un-dermined were we fully to confront facts. These are situations in which denial is a practical beneficence, helping us to maintain our affectional or comradely relations. To take an immediate example: refusal to face the facts may be the best guardian of marriage pro-vided us by nature.

But denial isn't always a happy strategy. Dangerous impulses can breed in its hidden recesses or take shelter there after being acted upon. And this buried life can become all but inaccessible.

Mrs. Harris is said to have written in the *Madeira Alumnae Magazine* of the "schizophrenic ring" of both her educational philosophy and her life as a woman. This appears to be one of the few occasions when she fell into the language of popular psychiatry. She's more a values lady than an insight lady, considerably less tempted by clinical talk than are most educators of her generation. To be in conflict between traditional and non-traditional ideas in education, which is what I suppose Mrs. Harris had in mind in speaking of the schizophrenia of her educational philosophy, is not sick but thoughtful. And to be torn, as a woman, between one's professional and non-professional needs or desires is far from pathological. It's simply, or not so simply, to be under pressure in the disposition of one's energies. Though disharmony of impulse may derive from pathology or conduce to it, it is not in itself a pathology. It is human; "only human," as we like to say.

Mrs. Harris has a strong sense of female victimization, unusually strong even for our time and even for someone who may have been building it up in the trial in order to excite the sympathy of the female public. But her conflicts as a woman had considerably less bearing on the events of March 10 than the conflicts she had come to feel between her attachment to Tarnower and the moral code by which she'd always shaped her conduct. We don't know anything about the physical relationship of Mrs. Harris and Dr. Tarnower and probably never shall. This is finally the untold story in almost all lives. But I think it's fair to guess that it had its sadomasochistic aspects. This not only fits the temperaments of both Mrs. Harris and Dr. Tarnower but might account for Mrs. Harris remembering to mention switches in her Christmas poem—I'm not sure that's entirely innocent, not any more so than the inclusion of the name Electra, the name of one of Lynne's daughters, in Mrs. Harris's list of the doctor's phantasy loves. We know that Dr. Tarnower wearied of her and turned to other women, not Lynne alone but others before Lynne and, presumably, since. Lynne was "the" rival in the crucial sense of now being her replacement in the doctor's social world but she didn't constitute his only infidelity to Mrs. Harris. He was moderate in all things except women, a long-time acquaintance of his had told me. Sexual variety was the pattern of Tarnower's life, its boast really, which he protected by bachelorhood. No one had to take his way of life who didn't want to. If Tarnower deceived Mrs. Harris or even himself that his usual sexual needs wouldn't appear in their affair, he didn't deceive her when his wish for variety did appear. She was well acquainted with his affairs with other women. It was obviously one of Tarnower's pleasures that his women should be aware of each other—he gave Lynne permission to paint the poolside furniture while Mrs. Harris was in residence; when he travelled with Mrs. Harris her rival had their itinerary. It may not have been the relation of Tarnower and Lynne that initiated Mrs. Harris's receipt of anonymous phone calls but these apparently increased in number and nuisance as Tarnower's relation with Lynne continued and as Mrs. Harris's jealousy grew; who supplied Mrs. Harris with Lynne's unlisted phone number each time Lynne changed it is a mystery one scarcely wants to pursue. All of this Mrs. Harris countenanced, and not only countenanced but responded to in a fashion that was profoundly at variance with what we can presume was her upbringing and the morality she still looked for in others, in the young and in married people—she was shocked by Lynne's adulterousness and by the suggestion that Tarnower would make love to her if he were planning to marry Lynne. She tells us that she'd dried Suzanne's tears over Lynne's alleged seduction attempts on Henri, but she hadn't walked away from the man whose new mistress was accused of trying to seduce his servant. And in revenge for the calls that came to her in the night she herself took to calling Lynne in the night, which gave her the added torture—or was it torturing satisfaction?—of discovering that Lynne wasn't sleeping at home. By her code Mrs. Harris had indeed, as she said, been touched by something "unsavory." But is "touched" the right word to describe it? Had she not been a full participant in the unsavory arrangements? She and Lynne were obviously in this unsuitable relation to each other only because of the relation of each of them to Tarnower, but it was of course impossible for Mrs. Harris to let herself see the extent to which Tarnower was responsible for her feelings of degradation without also recognizing that she'd given herself to someone unworthy.

There's both paradox and emotional logic in the fact that almost in the degree that Mrs. Harris came to despise Tarnower she also came to depend upon him for such self-respect as she could still scrape together. She had to find her moral support somewhere, and where was she to look for it if not to the man whose standards she had substituted for her own? Tarnower's presence became a requirement of her emotional stability, indeed of life itself. Without him she felt as if she'd lost her way. She'd become critically disconnected from her former self, with no definition for her new self since he was the only person who could give it to her. I've suggested that in speaking of herself as "a woman in an empty chair," Mrs. Harris was describing her sense of female deprivation, but I think she was saying something more than this: I think she was also describing an acute moral-emotional disorientation, virtually a depersonalization. Mrs. Harris's narcissism is very great. Her emotional world is self-bounded: this was unhappily visible in court where one observed her undeviating attention, hour after long hour, to every detail of the legal procedure but where one could perceive no concern at all for the misery she'd brought on her children and her loyal brother and sisters. One also saw her unflagging care with every detail of her dress—her clothes were, if anything, too well put together, too matched, for contemporary taste. Narcissism doesn't replenish the selfhood of a grown person, it empties it. Although it offers itself in the guise of emotional protection, it actually adds to one's vulnerability. With a failing career to reconstitute, surrounded by young lives under her supervision, Mrs. Harris had very little in herself with which to buttress her crumbling self-esteem. Without Tarnower at her side, her self was all she had to go on and this "all" was an empty shell that echoed with self-accusation.

Many disparate elements in Mrs. Harris's psychic situation contributed to the disaster of Dr. Tarnower's death, but it seems to me that central to any understanding of her tragedy is the recognition that it represented the defeat of a life of principle, of perhaps even excessive principle. In her connection with Tarnower she had let herself be led off her own moral path. This surely had to do with far more than merely the fact that their tie wasn't sanctified by marriage. It involved the doctor's flaunted infidelities and his dictatorial command of the terms of the relationship: not only when, where, and how they travelled, but even the times when she might or might not visit him. Though she was essentially self-supporting, Mrs. Harris's role resembled that of a kept woman more than an equal partner in the love affair. Persuade herself as she might that in her relationship with Tarnower she was freer than she'd ever been before, released from the need for "the Good House-keeping Seal of Approval" and yet thoroughly accepted, along with her lover, in the respectable Westchester community, Mrs. Harris must have been heavily burdened with unconscious guilt. At great emotional cost, she had buried the precepts of earlier years. In classical literature the tragic hero or heroine was always someone of high birth. The defeat was to be measured by the extent of the fall from glory. In significant part the wide public interest in Mrs. Harris's case may derive from her social position and Dr. Tarnower's, but her private tragedy derives from her fall from her own high moral standards. Even if the death of Tarnower was an accident, not murder, it could never have occurred if Mrs. Harris had stayed with the principles in which she'd been reared—that is, if she'd retained her famous "integrity." Was she a female victim, as she thinks? Yes, I guess she was, in the limited sense of having yielded her own standards in return for advantages that could be given her by a sex more privileged than her own. But, more personally, she was driven by her inner need for degradation and, more generally, she was a cultural victim. She'd been seduced by our present-day culture into believing that a free sexuality is anyone's for the taking, that one can throw over one's moral rearing without emotional consequences. Perhaps some people can but very many people, both men and women, cannot. The decision of how to live one's sexual life continues to be a dilemma for people who have a conflict between present desire or imagination and earlier moral training.

In Mrs. Harris I'm afraid that this conflict was a killing one. One wonders what had been her upbringing, what had been the parental authority that had saddled someone of her lively intelligence with such a devastating conscience. Surely it can be very perilous to be an imaginative puritan, someone as delicately rooted—I mean this in a moral and emotional sense—as I take Mrs. Harris to be and yet unable to keep the necessary check on impulse. It's harder to manage than the difficulties of being a woman in a society ungenerous to women.

I know little about the relation of Mrs. Harris with her parents, no more, in fact, than that when she was already in her forties and the mother of two, she had felt it necessary to inform them of her illicit association with Tarnower. In her testimony, when Leggett ruled that this information was irrelevant, she said that he was mistaken and that it was very relevant. (I've also heard that her father, still alive when Mrs. Harris was arrested, refused help with her bail.) Tarnower, so much older than herself, a solid citizen in a community of solid citizens, the kind of person who's given a testimonial dinner, made a feasible father figure, perhaps one who was an improvement on her actual father. He also had the authority we so magically vest in doctors. From the start he must have had this symbolical meaning for her, else how had she been able to accept his broken promise of marriage and his infidelities? If he said it was all right, it would have had to have been all right if only in the realm of consciousness. The way in which Tarnower combined an entire conformity to convention with the license he took in his private sexual life was a sanction for the way in which she herself combined conventional cautions with the longing for release from middle-class restraints. If everyone in our culture wants to be a writer, this is not only because of the promise of celebrity but also because of what the life of the artist promises of freedom to make one's own rules. Quite rightly, Mrs. Harris snubbed Tarnower's achievement as a writer, yet at the same time she treated the doctor as if he had a claim to literary standing. Even in retrospect she didn't find it ridiculous that he'd inscribed copies of his diet book for the guests at her son's wedding party. The sexual liberty that Tarnower took to himself while still retaining the esteem of his Westchester friends all but qualified him as a latter-day bohemian. By virtue of his sexual unreliability, he became the moral equivalent of an artist.

So long as Tarnower gave her the illusion of love, Mrs. Harris was more or less able to subdue her overbearing conscience. It was when he wanted to be rid of her that she came to hate this man who had taken her so far and was leaving her stranded. With some valiance she tried to direct her hatred of Tarnower to herself, and for some years she managed it. She quietly suffered her depression, took her medicines. Finally, depression climaxed in her decision to kill herself. She prepared for suicide, she set her house in order. But even this brave effort failed her: she couldn't successfully subsume her loathing of him in her self-loathing.

Mrs. Harris's failure to kill herself may of course have been only the practical failure of someone inexperienced with guns. Or I suppose one can think of it as an ultimate failure of generosity on the part of a woman who had been for too long too generous to her lover and too little generous to herself. But it was also a dictate of honesty. Consciously or unconsciously, Mrs. Harris killed the person she meant to kill. She didn't kill Lynne, whom she still accuses of having threatened her integrity. She killed Tarnower who had had her integrity in his keeping and destroyed it.

I speak of Mrs. Harris as a values lady. Honesty is a first principle in her system of values. She has remarkable intellectual capacities—the ability to absorb large quantities of new information, her retentive memory, her reasoning powers, her uncommon verbal sharpness and clarity, her wit—and she takes pride in them, is even arrogant about them. But it would be my guess that more than these she esteems her intellectual honesty.

As witness after witness took the stand for the defense, Aurnou would ask the same stilted question: what about the headmistress's reputation for "veracity"? The question became silly. It had to be plain to anyone that for Mrs. Harris veracity is a moral imperative. Aurnou's client reeks of truth. There's an important sense in which she's sick on truth—if she didn't over-estimate truth for its own sake and be pledged to stay true to her ideals, she wouldn't have to resort to denial as disastrously as I believe she did and does. Mrs. Harris tells the truth even when she lies. In a way this is what is meant by denial: the process of self-deception spares one

305

the need to lie just as it spares one the confrontation of truth. But I also mean this statement more literally. While I suppose that like the rest of us Mrs. Harris knows that lies are an occasional requirement, I think that especially where a lie would implicate her in an unfavorable self-judgment, she has to turn it into a truth before she can tell it. She avoids an untruth until it has reached her consciousness as truth. For example, she very likely knew at the time she was given them that her prescriptions for controlled medications were issued in another person's name but she would seem to have conveniently suppressed this knowledge and can now "truthfully" say that she didn't pay attention to the name in which the prescriptions were written. It's not an uncommon ability to transmute a lie into truth before one speaks it, but different people have different methods for achieving this result, some less hurtful than others. In Lincoln Steffens's *Autobiography* there's a beguiling account of the difficulty that Theodore Roosevelt had when it was necessary for him to be untruthful. As a politician he had to lie, but he wrote the lie down on paper and studied it at length until it had the force of truth for him—woe to the friend who had witnessed the process and dared to remind him of it. I doubt that Mrs. Harris has to go through this kind of ritual to convert a conscious into an unconscious lie. But she has her own alchemy, and by and large the product that she manufactures is an excellent imitation of the real thing. But not always. If, for example, Mrs. Harris thought she told the truth about her behavior after she left Tarnower's bedroom, I for one was not convinced by it. She'd been criticized for not calling the van der Vrekens or seeking other help for the injured doctor. Mrs. Harris countered the charge by saying that she'd alerted Tarnower's servants—"Turn on the goddamn lights!" —as she rushed from the house to the phone booth at the Community Center. But if she'd been this concerned to get assistance for Tarnower, I don't believe she'd simply have shouted to Suzanne to turn on the lights or, for that matter, that she'd have turned around at the Community Center to lead McKenna's car back to the doctor's driveway instead of honking for him to stop. She had no way of knowing that the police car was going to follow her.

In his summation Aurnou said that Mrs. Harris was fighting

for her life and wouldn't lie, and I took this to be saying, not that Mrs. Harris was fighting for her life and *therefore* wouldn't lie, but that even though she was fighting for her life she wouldn't lie. This is not how I would put it. I see Mrs. Harris as someone who might lie and probably did lie to try to save herself but who, when she lied, did her best to make it feel like truth. Her account of what transpired immediately after the shooting would constitute one effort that wasn't wholly proof against doubt.

Throughout her trial Mrs. Harris constantly asked that she be allowed to tell the truth to the court, to the press, to the world. Surely there was something undue in this reiteration and in the implication that the truth was hers alone to tell, indisputable. Often in her testimony Mrs. Harris spoke darkly and, I felt, with entire credibility of the sense she'd always had of her "inadequacy." She'd had little confidence in her sexual charms (she spoke of having thought of getting a face-lift but she was worried that she would be "even uglier"), in her powers of physical and emotional endurance, perhaps even in her professional capacities. But on the score of her honesty she had no such self-doubt. On the contrary, she seemed to feel that there was no one, not the best-trained criminalist or physician, who was more to be relied upon as a vehicle of truth. I think that most people, after so long a trial and under the pressure of cross-examination, would have got their stories a bit mixed up. Not Mrs. Harris. Under the stress of her trial Mrs. Harris frequently betrayed emotional instability but never a trace of confusion. Her mastery of the testimony was so firm that I found it disturbing. To be as beleaguered as Mrs. Harris and yet keep all this detail so well in mind wasn't necessarily a recommendation of psychic soundness. I felt that Mrs. Harris functioned *too* well in circumstances that would destroy people who looked as if they had ten times her stamina. I attributed this to her morbid unimpeachability.

Mrs. Harris's probity was handmaiden to her intellectual arrogance. Just as no one was kinder, more caring, more dutiful, more dedicated and hard-working than the headmistress, just so no one was clearer-minded or more intelligent. The claim of intellectual superiority was not an unwarranted one for Mrs. Harris to make;

no one in the case was reliably wise but she was more than the intellectual match of anyone on her legal team or opposed to her. Yet she had to have estranged the jury by her overbearing manner on the witness stand. It's much to the credit of Bolen that he was undaunted by her imperiousness and by her scorn of him in cross-examination. I guess he wore the armor of his own righteous dedication. Mrs. Harris treated the prosecuting attorney like a schoolboy whom she held in deserved contempt but with whom, by a concatenation of idiot circumstances, she had to have traffic. She was sharp, biting, mocking. She constantly addressed him as "Mr." Bolen to indicate the remove at which she would wish to keep him. She appealed to the Judge, vainly, to curb this young man who dared to question her so persistently. But of course it wasn't just Bolen, the individual, over whom Mrs. Harris wanted to assert her superiority. She was superior to the very idea of prosecution; she thought of it as persecution. On her own but not, one can guess, without the encouragement of her lawyer, she saw herself as a victim of the law—always another kind of victim. Throughout the trial Mrs. Harris personalized her legal situation. In her statement when sentence was being passed on her, she addressed the Judge: "I want to say that I did not murder Dr. Herman Tarnower, that I loved him very much and I never wished him ill, and I am innocent as I stand here. *For you or for Mr. Bolen to arrange my life so that I will be in a cage for the rest of it, and that every time I walk outside I will have iron around my wrists, is not justice; it is a travesty of justice.*" (Italics mine) It was not possible for Mrs. Harris to think of herself as, innocent or guilty, involved in a mandatory process of which the prosecuting attorney and the Judge were designated agents.

No one easily accepts the charge of denial. Even in unimportant circumstances there's something humiliating in the idea that one has been fooling oneself, and when we lay this charge against another person we feel that we're being unfair. Mrs. Harris would of course be particularly unwilling to have pressed upon her the realization that she manipulates truth in response to emotional need. She obviously didn't even see how differently she dealt with her hostile feelings toward Lynne and toward Tarnower. In speaking of her contempt for Lynne, she was stopped only at the point where she might be led to acknowledge anger at Tarnower. Otherwise she wasn't at all inhibited in expressing her dislike. She didn't have to be ashamed of it. She would have been ashamed to admit to rivalry and she couldn't permit herself rage, but her poor opinion of Lynne not only conformed to her own moral values, it was something of which she could speak openly and even harshly with her friends and Tarnower's—we remember that in the Scarsdale letter Mrs. Harris made a point of telling Tarnower that Dan Comfort had laughed along with her at her picture of Lynne rising, chocolate-frosted, from a cake. She had no such permission for an adverse judgment of Tarnower, not from herself or anyone in their shared social circle. Even if she knew what it was that she wanted to say about her lover, to whom could she have said it? There was only one thing Mrs. Harris could do with her hatred of Tarnower: exile it beyond recall.

It was not a unique moral-emotional dilemma into which Mrs. Harris was catapulted by her relation with Dr. Tarnower. Many people come to hate their lovers and, like Mrs. Harris, find it intolerable to admit that they've given their devotion unwisely, even catastrophically. But they don't usually come to feel as cornered as Mrs. Harris did, they allow themselves some space. Many people want to kill the people they've loved and may even still love. But they're better able than Mrs. Harris to confront destructive thought and therefore not let it lead to destructive act. They're luckier than she; they've been spared her absolutism. They can admit to human error in themselves, even to wickedness. They don't so thoroughly damn themselves that they finally drive themselves to do something that's really a damnation.

Mrs. Harris is still convinced, and I think she always will be, that when she drove to Purchase for a last moment of peace and security with her lover, suicide was the only purpose she had in mind. If one grants that this was so, one can't help but wonder what the outcome of the evening would have been had Dr. Tarnower, instead of refusing to open his eyes, instead of just lying there hugging a pillow—could Mrs. Harris have made *that* up?—had bestirred himself, talked to his night visitor and tried to comfort her, perhaps made love to her. At least for the time being it might have dispelled her distress, bought the doctor his life and bought Mrs. Harris her life. Was there not a note of hope at the end of the Scarsdale letter? At the last had Mrs. Harris not always reached out her hand in appeal to Tarnower for re-instatement in his affection? This eminent physician wasn't a very bright man; selfishness like his makes a person stupid. Mrs. Harris says that she spoke with Tarnower on the phone that Monday afternoon and told him she wanted to come to Purchase to talk to him that evening, and I believe her; I don't think she took the doctor by surprise. From just this one call Tarnower should have guessed she was in trouble. In fact, I think he *did* guess, not that she was in trouble, but that she meant to make trouble for him. When I first heard of the shooting of the Scarsdale diet doctor and mistakenly thought that Tarnower had had Lynne Tryforos and his sister Mrs. Schwartz and his niece Debbie to early dinner that night, I had decided it was a cabinet meeting to discuss what the doctor should do about this woman who was refusing to let herself be got rid of. From Debbie's testimony there's no reason to assume that the subject was discussed at dinner but I still believe that when the doctor shut up the house and turned off the front lights, it wasn't because he didn't expect Mrs. Harris but because he did. This would be his way of telling her that if it suited her to make the trip, she still wasn't welcome. It was horrible for a woman who needed to talk, who needed to be helped, to be cut off as he cut her off: "Jesus, it's the middle of the night. . . . I'm not going to talk to anybody in the middle of the night." And when she behaved as excitedly as she did in his bedroom, there was hardly a worse thing he could have done than to tell her, with her pride of mind, to get out, that she was crazy. What kind of pride was his that he couldn't for a moment yield to her desperate need for his compassion?

Tarnower's was a meagre soul, a spirit without generosity. He would seem to have had an insatiable appetite for small power. Whatever his seriousness as a physician, in his private life he was in the business of indulging some profoundly unserious notion of what constitutes manhood. There's something disturbed and disturbing in the sexuality of someone who plays women off against each other as he played these women of his. This is not altered by the fact that they obviously conspired in it. The world is full of masochistic people dedicated to their own worst interests but a developed person doesn't look for his proofs of strength by moving in upon other people's weaknesses. Socially Jean Harris and Tarnower made a fair partnership, they shared their worldly goals. But emotionally he had the upper hand and he knew it and he liked it, though eventually it became a bother. Mrs. Harris didn't come crawling to him for drugs but the way in which she crawled to him for love was like nothing so much as the behavior of an addict. She was totally shorn of self-respect. Out of respect for both of them, himself as well as her, Tarnower shouldn't have let her be this abject. What could he have done? I suppose been honest from the start, not repeated his incantation about how he didn't love anyone or need anyone, but told her he didn't love *her* and didn't want to see her again, ever. And decently stuck to it. On the witness stand Mrs. Harris had an excuse for him; one could be touched by it if it weren't so inappropriate. She made out that his inability to give up either Lynne or herself was the familiar lovable cowardice of a man too kind to hurt either of them. But Tarnower wasn't kind, not as I read him. He was a small-time emotional imperialist, a respectable middle-class bullyboy of sex. Little wonder he became famous as a diet doctor: he was a glutton for other people's vulnerabilities.

From the start of my interest in Mrs. Harris's case, I didn't like the Scarsdale diet doctor: I've already reported this. I didn't like his face, his house, his book; and in the course of the trial, as I learned about the musical chairs he played with women, I didn't like his games. What came to me as a surprise in Mrs. Harris's trial was the suggestion of sordidness in his respectable household. People unpleasantly intruded upon each other, informed on each other, shifted loyalties. They took money without saying they were taking it, cut up their own or each other's belongings, placed anonymous phone calls in the night, left disturbing messages and maliciously revealed unlisted phone numbers, smeared or could be accused of smearing one another's clothes. Dr. Tarnower was a prominent doctor in a good suburban community. He'd made a steady upward social climb to acceptance among the established old families of Westchester, the German Jews who got him his membership at the Century Country Club, the Gentile friends who got him his membership in the Mill Reef in Antigua where he was on terms of equality with such as the chairman of IBM or General Electric. A younger friend of the doctor who'd known him from childhood reports that he was a very charming man, a good listener, a man with a wide range of interests. He told me of the many times he'd been entertained in Tarnower's home at "carefully orchestrated luncheons," impeccably planned, prepared, and served. Tarnower, he says, would carefully select the guests for these occasions, arranging that each of them had an interesting and pertinent topic on which to talk. It doesn't perhaps come up to one's imagination of the joyous life, but then neither did the life of the Guermantes. We were in mid-trial before I saw the inside of the Purchase house in which these luncheons were given: the unshaped space through which one passed into Dr. Tarnower's small dreary dining room where one feasted so fastidiously under the eye of dead antelope and equally dead fish. In a house with so little of charm or comfort, what false distinction Tarnower bestowed upon himself and his friends! And behind the doctor and his gourmet food, his vintage wines, his orchestrated discourses, what was there that was not to be discoursed upon? The unseen life of middle-class respectability has always had its secrets, marvelous or squalid. Sometimes when the hidden is suddenly uncovered for us, we receive it with a pleasurable shock of recognition. Surely this was the case when we recently were given Edith Wharton's own detailed account of her long-secret love affair or when we learned of the boldly perverse activities of Vita Sackville-West. But these were stories of sexual adventure pursued with courage and flair. They weren't revelations of nasty little cheatings and snipings and revenges such as we have hint of in the Tarnower ménage. Tarnower would seem to have been as tasteless in his sexual excitements as in his preference in architecture.

It was shortly after the shooting, when the newspapers were filling us in on the background of the case, that I'd learned that Dr. Tarnower liked to hunt and had a room devoted to his trophies. Mistakenly I came to the conclusion that it was Tarnower who had persuaded Mrs. Harris, living alone as she did at Madeira, to buy a revolver for her protection, and I even remember thinking a bit later, when I drove to Mahopac and saw the isolation of Mrs. Harris's nice little house there, that it was sensible of him to have insisted that she have a weapon against intruders. Although my initial picture of the Madeira headmistress was of a sturdy and independent modern woman, I also thought of her as a person of some delicacy, not fragile as in the image of the "wounded bird" that Aurnou would evoke for us, but recessive in the traditional sense that would make it unlikely that she'd buy a revolver.

Certainly the use of a gun as her instrument of suicide wasn't consistent with the womanliness I attributed to Mrs. Harris. Women don't customarily kill themselves with a gun or any weapon of war. In Greek tragedy, female suicide is in most instances accomplished by hanging rather than the sword; a sword is the weapon of manliness—at most, without too great violation of sexual appropriateness, a Greek woman might thrust into her own body the sword by which her husband had died. Even in the modern world, shooting is more a man's than a woman's method of self-inflicted death. In or out of books, women jump from buildings or throw themselves before moving vehicles. They run the motor of a car in a sealed garage or, much the same thing, turn on the gas or put their heads in ovens. They swallow poison or walk into the maternal sea or, at an extreme, slit their wrists. Long before we became as programmatically concerned as we now are with what does or doesn't define female character, Stendhal wrote a story, "Mina de Vengel," about a strong-willed woman destroyed by reckless love. It was in accord with the character of Mina that she killed herself with a pistol-shot to the heart. The story ends: "Hers was a soul too ardent to be content with the reality of life." Stendhal meant, I think, that Mina's ardor was too strong for her sex and that hers was a masculine heroism.

Mina is barely discernible in the character of Mrs. Harris in whom ardor appears to be considerably outweighed by dependence, self-pity, emotions of female deprivation, and a terrible equipment of moral inhibitions. The way in which her passion is made to yield to peculiarly female timidities and insufficiencies becomes clear in her description of how she felt about possessing a gun. Mrs. Harris speaks of it as a "security blanket" and says it made her feel "safer." We recall that her purpose in going to Purchase to say good-bye to Tarnower was also to have one more moment of feeling "safe." Mrs. Harris explained that as the owner of a gun, if she could no longer function, she could "handle it." She didn't have to "worry about becoming helpless." This is strange language, strangely un-brave language, in which to speak of owning a gun, and what I think Mrs. Harris is saying is that her gun was something she could hold on to alone in bed at night—what else is a security blanket? If she wasn't able to function, she was no longer helpless; she could "handle it." She could take her gun in hand.

As a witness Mrs. Harris navigated her testimony with extraordinary skill. Although she accused herself of talking too much, and did talk too much, she was very much in control of what she said; it was from willfulness rather than lack of command that she failed to answer the questions put to her with a simple yes or no. Yet inevitably, without her awareness, important clues to her personality emerged in her replies as of course they did, too, from various documents put in evidence, most spectacularly from the Scarsdale letter. In particular, Mrs. Harris told us a great deal about how she feels as a woman: she feels very sorry for herself. She feels unfairly used, unappreciated, unrewarded, deprived, inferior. At the same time that she can be abjectly passive, as she essentially was with Tarnower, she's markedly competitive with men, perhaps more than we've come to expect even in a period like ours in which the comparative standing of men and women is at public issue. The treatment she received from Tarnower, whatever her share in stimulating it, was obviously not designed to diminish her sense of sexual grievance, but I suspect that she brought to her first meeting with him the kind of low opinion of herself that would tempt many men to take advantage of her even while they felt protective of her. Her insufficient recognition of her capacities was probably always closely associated with how she felt about being a woman. Her feeling that she was inferior *because* she was a woman must indeed have been central in the "inadequacy" that she tells us had always haunted her.

It's hard for me to imagine Jean Struven as a child or early adolescent. Was she an inhibited tomboy, an encouraged tomboy? Was she made jealous of privileges given a brother but withheld from a girl? When a girl is as mentally gifted as she was, the contradiction between ability recognized and ability hindered for no reason other than that of sex can be deeply painful; the idea of sexual injustice gets burnt into one's view of the world. When she gets to college I begin to see Jean Struven more clearly. It was the early forties, a particularly bad time in the history of American women, especially for someone as susceptible as I think she was. Mrs. Harris graduated from Smith in 1945, shortly before the end of the Second World War. The GI's would soon be coming home and want back the jobs that women had filled while they were away. During the war, although women often did the work that had been done by men and made the decisions that had previously been made by husbands and fathers, this change in status was understood to be only temporary. It wasn't allowed to challenge in any basic fashion the way that women had always thought about the distribution of power between the sexes. What women were doing was holding things together until men would reclaim their old place in the social order.

Still, for many women it was a heady experience to have been this independent of male authority. Well before the war ended, people began to worry about how men who had been in control of tanks or bombers would adjust to lives as clerks or salesmen—would they become fascists?—and now they also began to worry about whether women would again be willing to accept male social dominance. A major effort of public relations was mounted to prepare women for demobilization and the return to female submission. Psychoanalysis, which was now at the height of its influence in America, contributed to this impulse to emotional re-education and supplied some of its vocabulary along with its basic doctrine: Freud not only refused women cultural equality with men but also gave a strong charge of condescension to the analytical emphasis on female "passivity." So far as I know, this phenomenon of the forties hasn't been studied by cultural historians: I can't say how much of the program was planned and, if so, by whom, and how much was spontaneous, an expression of economic-social instinct. Although it contained a large element of economic necessity—it was the emotional concomitant of a return to a peacetime economy—it was presented to women only as a confirmation of their distinguishing biology.

Suddenly the distinctive psycho-biological nature of women was anatomized, glamorized, promoted throughout the society. A new phenomenon called "female-ism" was introduced into our sexual culture: this was the need, indeed the divine right, of women to fulfill their special psycho-physiological destiny. Although women, Jean Struven among them, were still educated for gainful employment, the emphasis was subtly but importantly shifted, from the ability of women to do virtually anything that men could do, to the primary difference between male-appropriate and female-appropriate occupations. Women must of course work outside their homes if they had livings to earn. And if their energies were sufficient, they might work in positions to which they were drawn by special talents. But true female fulfillment lay in women's pursuit of their destiny as wives, mothers, homemakers. It was the function of women to be nourishers and sustainers, not doers or achievers. This is when the concept of gracious living was introduced into American popular culture. It had the lasting benefit of making American women into better cooks than they'd been before and of making the design and equipment of kitchens a major American industry.

Throughout the postwar years, in popular fiction, in both hortatory and seductive writing for popular journals, in the schools and in the clinics, women were taught to think of themselves as a lovely sex, a useful sex, an indispensable sex, and a second sex. Women with first-rate minds were made to feel unfeminine, even vaguely unwholesome, if they asked for equal footing with men in the work-world or even in their leisure activities. In 1950 it was thought daring of Margaret Mead to write a book, *Male and Female,* in which she asked reasonably, even apologetically, for an end to sex stereotypes, and proposed the possibility that there were men in the world who might by nature be nurturers just as there were women who by native endowment had the right, denied them by Freud, to seek a life in culture.

As one thinks of Mrs. Harris one borrows—with obvious wryness —the Freudian concept of female castration anxiety. It no doubt exaggerates the influence of environmental factors to trace Mrs. Harris's marked sense of sexual inferiority solely to the culture of her college and post-college years. She was twenty-two when she finished college; in a fundamental sense her character was formed, her cast of mind determined. She already suffered, perhaps even more than most girls do, the unconscious fear that she was some-how biologically insufficient, incomplete. But the feelings she brought with her into young maturity were bound to have been greatly intensified by the female-ist emphasis of the forties. They could not have failed to be. It was a monstrous and all-pervasive influence that was abroad in the land, no doubt the more insidious because it gave no formal warning that it was not God-given law but man-made doctrine and therefore was to be applied to women with caution. No young woman, no woman even of an older generation than that of Mrs. Harris, could escape it.

Mrs. Harris took a teaching job after graduation and was married the following year. We see her at once settle into domesticity. She has her little house in Grosse Pointe; she and her husband have their social circle and presently she has her carefully spaced babies to the required number of two—and it must have been reassuring that they were boys. While tending her infants, the young mother plays bridge. Then she starts a neighborhood nursery school: could there be a better compromise between her proper function as a female and her modest yearnings for a career? There's not much money in the Harris household: she's offered a job teaching first grade at a good private school where she'd taught in the past and where her sons will be given free tuition if she's a staff mem-ber. Like a properly supportive and budget-minded wife and mother, she accepts the offer. The trouble is that there's no strong male in the domestic vicinity alongside of whom Jean Harris may

317

justifiably be considered an inferior. It may even be that her husband matches or outdistances her in emotions of inadequacy. In 1965 she decides on divorce: she won't do worse without him, she may do better. The imagination of her own possibilities, subdued by the forties, has been rekindled by the revolutionary sixties.

I think one has to be older than Mrs. Harris to understand that even in 1966 it took, not great courage, but some strength of intention for her to move east with two sons who were still in early adolescence and to launch a new life for herself. Even today this degree of female self-sufficiency isn't as easy to attain to as is popularly made out; in the mid-sixties Mrs. Harris could well have felt that if she wasn't exactly opening a new frontier, she was moving into a territory that was still thinly settled. Yet in the Scarsdale letter, as again on the witness stand when she speaks of this stage of her life, her attitude isn't one of satisfaction with what she'd managed for herself. Although she talks about having earned her living like a man, the context is one of bitterness and self-pity because she'd been under-appreciated. She looks back upon her years in Philadelphia with pleasure in the blossoming of her romance with Tarnower—she'd met him soon after she got there. They'd danced, he'd phoned. He sent her roses, she fell in love. But there's a full ledger of complaints. She'd had the children to take care of and not been free for dates and travel. She'd been so pressed for money that she'd had to borrow from Hi's houseman to pay her highway tolls. When the doctor left her house in Philadelphia, he left her on her hands and knees, a scrubwoman. The piteous self-dramatization is dismaying and often ridiculous, and frequently it's without foundation in historical reality. As I've already pointed out, by the time Mrs. Harris moved to Philadelphia, her sons were considerably too grown to require baby tending. It's unlikely that she'd been on her hands and knees scrubbing, or at any rate it had not been necessary—the cleaning woman of whose interest in Mrs. Harris's trial I've already spoken has cared for my house for twenty-seven years without once being on her hands and knees; long-handled floor mops are not a new invention. Mrs. Harris bitterly reminds her lover in the Scarsdale letter that when she left her diamond ring on his dresser—would this be 1968? 1969?—her salary before taxes was $12,000 a year, but she should herself be reminded that this supposed extreme of poverty was not too uncomfortably shared throughout the academic profession. Between 1966 and 1969 the basic salary of a full professor at Columbia College was $14,000 and it was only in 1969 that it was raised to $16,000. And those were days in which one climbed a long hill to reach this exalted rank.

To what extent is Mrs. Harris's complaint of economic disadvantage simply a displacement for sexual disadvantage? Certainly when Mrs. Harris writes of herself in the Scarsdale letter as if she were among the poor of this earth, it seems fairly obvious that at the root of her grievance is sexual grievance; her deprivations have as their model her deprivations as a woman. With great resentment she speaks of having watched Tarnower grow richer in the years they've known each other while she's grown poorer. Can she be talking only of money? To be sure, Tarnower's success had strikingly increased in recent years but Mrs. Harris's fortunes hadn't as notably declined, or certainly not her economic fortunes. She took a salary cut to go to Madeira from Allied Maintenance, but there were sizable perks in the school post: free house, free meals, free services, free car. And she'd had a salary raise each year at Madeira.

She'd been made poorer not by a diminution in her real earnings but emotionally, by the loss of her lover. And though this did indeed rob her of the expensive travel and other costly pleasures that came with being Tarnower's chief mistress, it was still more of a psychological and emotional than financial loss that she suffered.

And in fact Mrs. Harris responded to the loss in language of emotional insecurity: she needed something to hold on to, she wanted to feel safer. What she actually did was acquire a gun, than which few things are more tangible symbols of power. There are women for whom the ideas of masculinity and fierceness are not to be disentangled from one another. Just as they think of femaleness as a vulnerability, they think of manliness as conquest of a weaker by a stronger sex. There's much envy of this dominating man by this weak woman, just as there's substantial gratification in having someone this much more powerful than oneself with whom to identify. This is not unconnected with women's phantasies of sexual exoticism. White women secretly endow black males with

319

a malignly wonderful sexuality, and for a WASP woman as limited in experience as Jean Harris a Jewish male may have represented a similar meta-sexual fulfillment. In acquiring a gun she too, poor insufficient woman, became capable of assault. She was supplied with what she'd been deprived of by biology.

Yet if there's little justification for the lament of poverty that runs like a ground bass through the Scarsdale letter, there was of course reality enough in Mrs. Harris's perception of the difference between her economic situation and the economic situation of other women with whom she associated as Tarnower's mistress. With Hi, Mrs. Harris travelled with the very rich to very expensive places. In the company that Tarnower kept, Mrs. Harris was indeed poor— it would be hard for her to have retained her earlier sense of proportion about money. After Dr. Tarnower's death, in no way connected with that story, there was a lengthy illustrated article in the Home Section of *The New York Times* called "A Perfectionist's Approach to the Perfect Home." The "perfectionist" was Mrs. Arthur Schulte and the perfect home had just been built in Connecticut by the Schultes, the friends with whom Dr. Tarnower and Mrs. Harris had been accustomed to spend their Christmas holidays in Palm Beach: they're the Viv and Arthur for whom, together with Hi, Mrs. Harris's parody was written at their last shared Christmas. The home was designed for the Schultes' retirement and if there's such a concept as compulsive planning, this must be its monument—if I think of the diet doctor as a compulsive character (and who that is not himself compulsive urges compulsiveness upon others?), Mrs. Schulte must have been his object of worship. According to the *Times,* for three years before the building had begun Mrs. Schulte had kept a notebook in which she listed "both the luxuries and 53 'practicalities'" that were to be included in the design of her house. She had had twenty-three interviews with architects before choosing the firm that would best meet her needs. She had not only measured all her kitchen appliances and planned their storage; she had also provided a special area near the back door for the "unpacking of boxes, with a sink with a high faucet for washing flowers and filling tall vases . . . and an ingenious gift-wrapping counter, complete with brown and colored wrapping paper on rolls, adhesive tape, labels and ribbon."

The indoor pool in which she swam each morning before breakfast put her at eye level with her outdoor garden so that she could see if there were weeds. Mrs. Schulte and her husband each had a dressing room, the wallpaper of hers patterned with the name "Vivian," his with the name "Arthur." Vivian's clothes hung from high racks, those for winter separated from those for summer, seasonably stored. And in the center of her dressing room was a large counter for packing her suitcases for travel. She had found just the right place, she said, for her husband's hunting trophies and the right plastic plants to fill his favorite elephant foot. The heart of Arthur Schulte was delighted by his air-conditioned wine room. . . . Thus the description goes on. The article identifies Mrs. Schulte as a former food and home editor of the *Times* with a Ph.D. in foods and nutrition. It would have made for a professional bond with Tarnower. But what was the bond between a life of this kind of "perfectionism" and the life of a professional educator such as Mrs. Harris was supposed to be? Mrs. Schulte's "practicalities" not only cost astronomical sums of money to provide and make use of. They pointed toward a different social, economic, and eventually even moral universe than any to which Mrs. Harris had been directed by her professional commitments.

But associations such as Mrs. Harris's with Mrs. Schulte bore even more immediately on Mrs. Harris's emotional than on her social-professional dilemma. The article about Mrs. Schulte's house described a *female* enterprise, yet one that made Mrs. Harris's poor effort to replace Tarnower's plates and towels look like a *reductio ad absurdum* of domestic rule. All women dream of domestic empire, the clothes and setting that will best show them off. A large part of our advertising addresses this innocent dream. Mrs. Harris knew too many women whose actual domestic kingdoms were dreamlike.

The *Times* told us of Mrs. Schulte's Ph.D., and we remember, too, that in her Christmas poem Mrs. Harris had recommended "a bunch of hard books" as a gift for Viv and talked of her hostess as a "real cerebellum." This was gracious of the headmistress who herself may have been an even realer cerebellum in this world of wealth. Mrs. Harris had only her intellectual funds from which to repay the hospitality she received as Tarnower's companion.

But this is no insignificant funding in the present-day world of wealth: people who have everything can't now afford to be without their Herodotus. Among our most privileged classes, mind has become the next best thing to money as an emblem of power.

Mrs. Harris was in the wrong company. She should never have been in this society; it didn't fit her personal style or her moral style. Or, rather, it shouldn't have fit her style as well as it turned out to. So far as her best interests went as a professional person and as a woman, she should no more have allowed herself to be tempted into this expensive life than she should have allowed herself to be implicated in the petty squalors of the Tarnower household.

Everyone expected psychiatric testimony in Mrs. Harris's trial and was disappointed that there was none. The jury was said to have missed it very much. Its absence was blamed on Aurnou and in some sense it's fair, I suppose, to hold him to account for its omission. From the start there could never have been any question but that the safest line for Aurnou to pursue would be to plead some form of mental incompetency for Mrs. Harris. She would have been remanded to a mental institution for a year or two and then be free. But the situation wasn't that simple; what situation ever is? The shooting of the Scarsdale doctor quickly became a celebrated case; this was in no small part due to Aurnou's skill in public relations. For Aurnou acquittal would of course be a far more attractive outcome than sending his client to a hospital. But in addition he had reason to believe—he had told me this when we first spoke—that if Mrs. Harris were committed to a prison hospital from which she could be released only with the consent of the prison psychiatrist, it would be the equivalent of a death sentence. This was perhaps his exaggeration or perhaps it was hers; but it need have been neither. From an acquaintance of Mrs. Harris I've heard that well into the summer she was still saying that under no circumstances would she ever spend another night in jail. She spoke with horror of the night she'd spent at the Valhalla jail: she said she'd been among prostitutes who threw their bloody sanitary pads on the floor of the cell. Athough this may have been a cover memory for a suppressed recollection of the blood that had been spilled in Dr. Tarnower's bedroom, it didn't invalidate the reality of Mrs. Harris's revulsion from the thought of jail. Her unwillingness to contemplate imprisonment had to have had great force in the decision of the defense against pleading mental incompetence and in Aurnou's gambling on an acquittal. We must also suppose that a decision as basic as this would have had to be concurred in by the lawyers who recommended Aurnou as counsel for Mrs. Harris. But none of this would of course explain the absence of psychiatric evidence when she was on trial. Aurnou announced well in advance of the trial that the case hinged on Mrs. Harris's "state of mind." As might have been foreseen, he largely meant her state of mind as a woman caught in her particular personal and professional circumstances— he was speaking, as it were, subclinically. In the trial he touched on pathology only through pharmacology, when he dealt with Mrs. Harris's medications; indeed the two psychiatric witnesses he did use were called only to speak to the defendant's drug dependence. As for Mrs. Harris, she made herself clear on the subject of her mental condition. She told a favored member of the press group that she was tired of having it said that she was mentally ill. She wasn't sick and she was sick of being told that she was.

Mrs. Harris is a commanding woman and unusually competent. Except when she felt crossed, which didn't happen frequently, her manner with Aurnou's staff was friendly. With Aurnou himself it alternated between irritation or disappointment—this was early in the trial and it wasn't concealed as it should have been—and always-increasing approval which bordered on flattery, even flirtatiousness, and was very charming. How much, one wonders, was the decision to omit psychiatric testimony dictated by the defendant and how much was it due to other considerations that were weighed without her interference, more dispassionately?

When Mrs. Harris had been arrested she'd been put in the care of Dr. Halpern, a Westchester psychiatrist. She was in a hospital very briefly and after that saw the psychiatrist on a private basis. Several times Dr. Halpern was apparently called to the courthouse to help quiet Mrs. Harris. These were occasions when she was agitated or when there was a sudden flare-up of anger—as I say, they were more numerous early in the trial when MacDonell had not yet offered his account of the happenings on the night of Tarnower's death and when Mrs. Harris's relation to her lawyer seemed to be less secure than it later became. I have the impression that the psychiatrist was an important supportive figure for Mrs. Harris in the protracted ordeal of the trial.

After the verdict the Westchester press reported that Dr. Halpern strongly protested the absence of medical testimony in the trial of his patient. He was said to have been outraged that she'd not been given the kind of psychiatric defense that was warranted and was needed. He repeated his earlier public statement that Mrs. Harris suffered from severe suicidal depression and he seemed to be suggesting that testimony along this line should have been supplied.

It appears obvious enough that Mrs. Harris is emotionally ill. But this doesn't necessarily mean that Dr. Halpern's earlier diagnosis would have held up against opposing medical opinion. I suspect, in fact, that, against psychiatrists who had had the opportunity to study her present pattern of behavior, a defense doctor would have had a hard fight to convince the jury that Mrs. Harris still suffered from suicidal depression and that this diagnosis bore on the legal resolution of her case. I don't question that she *was* suicidally depressed and might become so again. But there was no sign that this was now her malady. Quickness to anger, agitation, suspiciousness, obsessive over-attention to detail: all of these were symptoms that manifested themselves during the trial. But the most perceptible and surely the gravest of the symptoms that made their appearance was something quite other: it was Mrs Harris's lack of affect, the dramatic absence of feelings appropriate to her situation. While it was no doubt gratuitous for Bolen to comment as he did at her sentencing that Mrs. Harris showed no remorse or regret at the doctor's death—I suppose even a victorious prosecutor has to have his comfort—no one who had observed the imperturbability with which Mrs. Harris heard the details of Dr. Tarnower's last moments or who saw the readiness with which she examined his bloody bed sheets could argue that Mrs. Harris showed any remorse for her share, however accidental, in his death. Mrs. Harris talked a great deal about her unchanging love for Tarnower, this man who of all people in the world meant most to her. But an outright enemy of the doctor might have been more upset than she was by the graphic account of his fatal injuries. And, as I've said, Mrs. Harris appeared to be wholly lacking in concern for what her sons, her brother, her sisters were suffering as a result of her actions. Emotionally she already lives in a high-walled prison, cut off from an external world.

Could Dr. Halpern have himself been a psychiatric witness for Mrs. Harris and yet dealt with this aspect of her emotional situation? I doubt it, not if he meant to remain her physician. Although he would have been released on the score of their privileged medical relationship, he wouldn't have been released from the continuing responsibilty to give her the kind of support she required and that would have been thoroughly undercut had he publicly gone into this aspect of her pathology. Too, our courtroom view of Mrs. Harris was bound to be different from the way Dr. Halpern had come to see her. The psychiatrist or analyst doesn't address his patient as a free-standing personality; that's not his undertaking. His job is to use what the ill person says in order to help her to better self-understanding, and the process makes for a close imaginative identification; there's even greater empathy between doctor and patient than between lawyer and client. There's little in the psychoanalytic or psychoanalytically derived methods of treatment that encourages a doctor to see a patient out of the context of treatment, as the patient actually appears and performs in the world rather than in her own report of external reality. In fact, this may be one of the chief unacknowledged hindrances to the psychotherapeutic cure of mental disorder: the treatment of a person in psychotherapy is like a trial in which only one witness testifies, the defendant.

And there would have been other problems for a defense psychiatrist: perhaps it was decided that they had best be avoided. What about the motive, not the overt but the hidden motive, of Mrs. Harris's wish for suicide? It is widely believed in the psychiatric profession, especially among Freudian analysts, that the hidden purpose of suicide is to inflict punishment on others by one's act of self-destruction. Obviously, the taking of a life, even one's own, is an aggressive act—let's be done with this life! I nonetheless have always found it difficult to believe that suicide necessarily incorporates the desire to do violence to another person. It does usually give pain to others, very great pain, and perhaps this can be one of its incentives. But it seems to me there are other motives even more compelling than the wish to cause grief and guilt in someone else: fear, despair, the inability to endure further suffering, even the imagination of rebirth and transfiguration. If I think, for instance, of the suicide of Marilyn Monroe, it's hard for me to be persuaded that she meant even to die, let alone give pain to others. I think she wanted to stop her torment; she wanted to sleep.

But what was the character of Mrs. Harris's suicidal depression? It's understandable, nothing could be more so, that Mrs. Harris didn't want to live in her circumstances: Lynne having usurped her place with Tarnower, her professional career threatened, not knowing what to make of her life. Yet her testimony seems to me to indicate that ancillary to the wish to end her life there was indeed the wish to punish the people who had caused her so much pain— what she actually accomplished, after all, was to kill Tarnower and forever take him away from Lynne! If she weren't trying to punish Tarnower, she wouldn't have had to drive five hours to do what she could just as well have done at home. And certainly she didn't have to plan to deposit her corpse in a spot sacred to the memory of their best years together. He couldn't have looked out of his bedroom window without being reminded of where she had taken her life.

I don't see how Dr. Halpern or any psychiatrist called by the defense could have escaped this area of questioning. The prosecution psychiatrists, unrestrained by personal relation to the defendant, would have been bound to dwell on the emotions about Tarnower and Lynne that lay behind Mrs. Harris's impulse to suicide. And they would undoubtedly have been led to point out that with Dr. Tarnower dead, Mrs. Harris had lost the wish to kill herself. While there may be disagreement among psychiatrists about some of the motivations of suicide, I think the profession is pretty much in accord that depression represents the turning inward of anger that one has forbidden oneself to express. Did Mrs.

Harris get rid of her anger at herself because she had now turned it against its real object, Tarnower?

Mrs. Harris was in psychiatric treatment for only a very brief period and it was belated. Tarnower wrote prescriptions for her but it apparently never occurred to him to recommend a different form of therapy. In her few sessions with Dr. Halpern what Mrs. Harris seemed chiefly to have learned was that the symptoms she'd always thought of as fatigue, or as the fear of being unable to meet the demands of her life, were symptoms of a clinical disorder. In her testimony she referred to this new insight: she spoke about her "depressed state" as if she were indeed seeing it in quotation marks. Even if her treatment had continued, we don't know how far it could have carried her in self-understanding.

In the realm of evidence where we have finally to sort out the actual truth from self-deception and outright lies, Mrs. Harris's trial left many uncertainties. Why, if it required a "triggering event" for her to decide on suicide, had Mrs. Harris bought a gun eighteen months earlier; in fact, ordered a first gun, failed to pick it up, and then ordered a second? There are other ways to kill oneself than with a weapon in whose use one is inexperienced—she had a medicine cabinet full of pills. Or if Mrs. Harris was about to end her life near Tarnower's pond, why had she first gone to the dressing area of the bedroom and gathered up some of her clothes and wrapped them in a shawl? She said the shawl was for her new daughter-in-law, but what did she intend to do with the other things? How did the shawl get to the floor from the bed where Mrs. Harris said she had left it, and what about the single glove (it was for the right hand and she is left-handed) that was found on top of the articles in the shawl—if it wasn't Mrs. Harris's glove, how had it got there? And if it did belong to her, why did she refuse to say so, and where was the other? And there was the bullet that the matron at Valhalla found in Mrs. Harris's hand wrapped in a man's handkerchief: was Mrs. Harris telling the truth when she said it was one of two bullets that she'd inexplicably found in her coat pocket, the other of which had perhaps been lost in a police car?

Or again, who actually cut up Mrs. Harris's clothes and Lynne's suede coat, and what had Bolen been heading toward with the suggestion, which he'd not been allowed to pursue, that long before Lynne's time some embroidery and a rug belonging to another of Tarnower's women friends had been mutilated? And what had happened to Aurnou's assertion, in his opening statement in the trial, that Mrs. Harris had also tried, along with the doctor, to summon the van der Vrekens on the buzzer system? Had Aurnou failed to come back to this because it didn't fit with MacDonell's reconstruction of what happened between Mrs. Harris and Dr. Tarnower after the firing of the first bullet? Or very puzzling: how could Mrs. Harris maintain that when she'd left the bedroom she'd thought that the doctor had suffered nothing worse than a hand injury, when both she and Aurnou had conceded that immediately on her return to the bedroom she'd said, "Oh, Hi, why didn't you kill *me?"* meaning that she knew she had killed *him?* How, in fact, could one reconcile Mrs. Harris's testimony that she wasn't aware of the extent of the doctor's injuries with her insistence that she was rushing to get help for him in the fastest way possible or with her statement to Detective Siciliano that she'd shot Tarnower because he slept with every woman he could and that she had "had it"?

Questions such as these of course neither prove nor disprove Mrs. Harris's guilt of second-degree murder. Still, they make a disquieting array especially when taken in conjunction with statements that seriously undermined her credibility: most notably her insistence that she was never angry at the doctor, but also such things as her repeated reference to the limitations put on her freedom of movement by her "children" in the Philadelphia years— when she came east David was already sixteen, Jimmy fourteen. In order not to be left with some suspiciousness of the case for the defense, one had very much to want Mrs. Harris to be beyond suspicion.

But questions of another kind were also raised by the trial and they linger in the mind quite as persistently as questions in evidential logic. They concern the strategies of Mrs. Harris's defense. There was no psychiatric defense but quite as interesting were the various kinds of defense that Aurnou did employ. It's possible to count four of them: an old-fashioned compassionate defense; a defense based on social deference; what might by a stretch of definition be called an ideological defense (it dealt with Mrs. Harris's dilemmas as a woman); and a defense based on physical evidence. I was myself considerably estranged by three of these; I respected only the last of them.

Mrs. Harris's lawyer was said to have come to professional note by his skill in the use of physical evidence, and he built an impressive case on a reading of the physical facts in the shooting of Dr. Tarnower. The observations, analyses, and determinations that Aurnou offered in this sphere were lengthy, boring almost beyond endurance, and difficult for a layman to understand. They nevertheless had to be taken with the greatest seriousness. I thought long and hard about the points that were made, and if at last I was not wholly convinced by Aurnou's experts that the injury to Tarnower's hand had been received in the struggle over the gun and that this was the same bullet that went through the glass door of the bedroom and embedded itself in a stanchion on the deck, certainly I thought there was more reason to accept this view than the prosecutor's theory that Tarnower had been taken by surprise in his bed and that the first wound had been sustained when he put up his hand to ward off Mrs. Harris's gun and that the same bullet that penetrated his hand also entered his front right shoulder. In the area of ballistics, MacDonell was a far more precise authority than the prosecution's Mr. Reich, and in the matter of skin pathology Dr. Ackerman was a considerably more persuasive authority than Dr. Roh. Not all of Aurnou's experts inspired equal confidence. But those that inspired least confidence were the ones least counted upon for fundamental testimony. Bolen's attempt to undermine MacDonell's reliability as a crime-scene investigator was effective for the moment—of that there's no doubt—but in the long run it couldn't destroy the force of his opinions. Where the specialists called by Aurnou, and especially his two most heralded experts, MacDonell and Ackerman, did the defense a disservice, it seems to me, was in their demonstrated partisanship with Mrs.

Harris. MacDonell's female associate was all too visibly unrestrained in her support of the defendant and MacDonell basked in the enthusiasm of his colleague. And as a consultant to Aurnou, Dr. Ackerman, correct as he no doubt was in his scientific judgment, was too markedly an advocate to reassure a jury that he was altogether objective.

From the start of the case, long before the trial, Aurnou had presented Mrs. Harris to the world as a victim, misused both professionally and emotionally. But Mrs. Harris apparently has as abundant a memory of her good deeds done in the line of duty, and beyond it, as for the wrongs that have been done her. These private account books she opened to her lawyer to guide him in his choice and interrogation of witnesses, and what needed adding or underscoring she supplied when she herself took the stand. There was a notable absence of moral modesty in this self-appraisal. By her own showing, and from the questions that she must have suggested that Aurnou put to various witnesses, Mrs. Harris is a woman of implacable virtue, singularly exempt from most of our human shortcomings. Probably no one should be presented to the world as at once this virtuous and this victimized. I'm not saying that the combination is impossible in nature, only that we don't comfortably accommodate it. The idea of virtue unrewarded is unlikable in itself; it's always better not to have complaint, even warranted complaint. If we're told that someone was done wrong who never did wrong, it makes us feel guilty—automatically we wish to divest him either of virtue or of grievance. This is so, at any rate, when we're dealing with an individual. It's when a person is thought to speak for a social group rather than as an individual that the response alters. As the representative of her sex Mrs. Harris had indeed to be superlatively virtuous in order to be considered sufficiently misused. Ideologically speaking, she was an exemplary figure exactly in the degree that she deserved better of life than she got. The common denominator of Aurnou's compassionate defense of Mrs. Harris and what I call his ideological defense, by which I mean his appeal to women whose consciousness of grievance has been properly heightened, was her female victimization. If it was as a woman that Mrs. Harris had been wronged by her lover, it was also as a woman that she lived with pain in the professional world. Although she earned her living like a man, she had been exploited as only a woman is exploited; referring to the fact that the new head of Madeira was a man, she pointed out that no man would do the work that *she* had done. In her profession, as in her personal relations, she'd been denied the respect that she'd have been automatically given had she been of the ruling sex. There was something shameless, far too tailored to our present moment in culture, in Aurnou's depiction of his client as so peculiarly a female martyr. Mrs. Harris may have been judged unfairly by the Madeira Board and the Browning commission. Although she had perhaps been away from the campus too often in term time and there would seem to have been a disturbing inconsistency in her personal behavior and especially in her disciplinary actions, from such information as I have been able to consult I have the impression that she did a good enough job with the curriculum and as a faculty administrator. But heading any school, college, university is eventually a no-win situation, and it is of course an insult to women to imply that the judgment directed to Mrs. Harris as head of Madeira was directed to her because she was a woman, or that because she was a woman she should have been exempt from rigorous assessment or even from unfair assessment—it's people, not women, who are unfairly judged. There was much to weep about in Mrs. Harris's life, but it was only the outcome of her Madeira experience and not her professional career in itself that was to be sorrowed over, and that was because when everything else collapsed in her life, her profession also was failing her.

For a person of Mrs. Harris's professional accomplishment, it was unseemly that her professional story was bathed in the same tears that washed around her story as a woman wronged in love. Aurnou plucked the heartstrings; Mrs. Harris cried. He choked and wiped his eyes; I'm told that members of the jury began to weep though I didn't see it from where I sat. In Westchester, said Mrs. Harris, she'd been a woman in a pretty dress. In Washington she'd been a woman in a pretty dress. The courtroom was drenched in the tears of her self-pity. It was an embarrassment for a presumably enlightened modern woman to play a role not readily distinguishable from that of the old-time defendant in a murder trial who weeps her way to acquittal. Except that Mrs. Harris wasn't acquitted. She was convicted by a jury two-thirds of which was her own sex. What went wrong?

The miscalculations were several and large, and they perhaps began with this appeal of Aurnou's to pity. This no longer may be as viable a method of defense as it once was, or perhaps it's not as useful in a courtroom as it is in the press. "We had no fear of its contents," Aurnou said of the Scarsdale letter in his summation. It was "a window into her soul." And with this he sobbed. But his sobs were wasted. The letter was on the record; it couldn't be cried out of existence, and his weeping for its author was in too marked contrast to the tone in which he spoke, in his summation, of Roh and other of the prosecution witnesses. Jurors are instructed to listen to evidence and I think they try—it's my sense that they perhaps take their duties more seriously than they once did. It's an insult to the intelligence of serious people to feel that their emotions are being played upon. Even if they cry on demand, this doesn't mean that in the end their sympathies will over-ride their thoughtfulness.

Another miscalculation, in my opinion, was the way in which the social defense of Mrs. Harris was conceived and executed. Ours is not a culture in which it's easy to make social judgments. We conspire in the myth of our monolithic—perhaps only monolithically faulty—democracy. If we even take note of a variation in class behavior, we're thought to be encouraging invidious distinctions of class. Bolen taxed Mrs. Harris with snobbery because she said she was sullied, and Tarnower denigrated, by the association with Lynne. He automatically assumed that she looked down on someone who hadn't her advantages of birth and schooling—as I've indicated, what I think Mrs. Harris was doing in relation to Lynne was no more than what everyone in the courtroom was doing in relation to *her*, drawing inferences of character from her conduct and style. Mrs. Harris may be a snob. She was certainly ambitious for the company of the rich and celebrated. But on the basis of how this trial was handled, it seems to me that it's Aurnou much more than Mrs. Harris who's the snob: a tone-deaf snob but a snob nonetheless. Perhaps the only thing endearing about the way in which he made his social assessments was its naïveté. He thought that the teacher community of the Grosse Pointe University School was identical with the "social structure" of Grosse Pointe; investigation could have told him, as it told me, that it's not. He thought that his parade of Thomas and Madeira students would please the jury. I strongly suspect it didn't—there's a significant social rift between the children of these jurors and the daughters of the rich, even between the daughters of the black jurors and the black student who stood for an integrated Madeira. He reported his client's travels all over the world to jurors who were sure to have been made a little envious of the favors she'd been shown. He didn't understand how academic prestige is established and judged, and that you don't crown someone with laurel by calling him a professor. Perhaps the jurors knew the difference between Ivy League and non-Ivy League better than the contending lawyers did—there was a wonderful moment in the trial when Bolen referred to other medical witnesses as Ackerman's "peers" and Ackerman courteously but promptly corrected him: "My colleagues."

But undoubtedly Aurnou's worst mistake was to assume that Mrs. Harris was so indisputably a "lady" that in itself this was virtually enough to win her case for her. Aurnou appeared to be convinced that no one could convict anyone as "classy" as Mrs. Harris of murder, and he was almost right. Very few people now know, as Scott Fitzgerald knew of his Daisy Buchanan, that her "classiness" wouldn't keep her from conspiring with her husband to cover a homicide—along with the ability and permission to make social distinctions we lose our ability to make moral distinctions. No one wanted to convict Mrs. Harris of murder. Obviously her class location, her appearance, her manners, her social connections had much to do with this reluctance, and she might indeed have been got off if she'd not been put on the stand and especially if the Scarsdale letter hadn't been read. Even without the Scarsdale letter, it was a miscalculation for Mrs. Harris to take the stand but with it in her lawyer's pocket it was a catastrophe—the prosecution had rested its case before a decision on its use had finally been handed down by the Court of Appeals and it's not at all certain that Bolen could have put the letter in evidence without Mrs. Harris's identification of it. I've spoken of Mrs. Harris's arrogance of manner, her quickness in retort, the sharpness of her wit, her imperious refusal to suppose that she had to answer questions like any other witness. It was not her considerable charm that was on display during her testimony but her least endearing qualities of character and personality. She stayed in one piece, to be sure, but she was less than wholly attractive. Who was to be impressed by a retentive memory or a commanding intelligence as self-serving as that of Mrs. Harris, and who would look for generosity of spirit in someone whose tears were always and only for herself? Long before Mrs. Harris took the stand her self-pity was apparent to anyone who was willing to see it. It ennobled her not at all to weep for herself under oath.

And there was the Scarsdale letter. If Aurnou had grown so accustomed to Mrs. Harris in all her fascinating complexity that he was no longer aware of the cutting edge of her personality, how could he yet have failed to see how destructive this letter was of the virtuous image he'd worked so hard to create? We'll never know, of course, if Mrs. Harris would have been convicted had the jury not been made acquainted with that unhappy document, but it's my surmise that without the Scarsdale letter she'd have had an even chance of acquittal and that if she'd not taken the stand her chance would have been better than even. After the decision several of the jurors said that they'd reached their verdict chiefly on their inability to re-enact Mrs. Harris's account of the struggle with Tarnower—it was Aurnou, incidentally, who had suggested that they re-enact the encounter, a procedure they followed in the jury room. I don't question that their difficulty in reproducing the scene was central to their decision. But what it is that finally influences us, and in what way, is always elusive: the jurors may have been far more affected than they know or care to admit by the obscene language of the Scarsdale letter and its coarse feelings, by its tone of smoldering hatred and its disconcerting juxtaposition of complaint and entreaty. Surely the letter exploded what I call Aurnou's class defense. The appearance of Mrs. Harris as a witness may have been meant to provide an impregnable social fortification of her case, but the Scarsdale letter robbed her of all social defense. It exposed her to the charge of having betrayed both her class and her education. Mrs. Harris wrote the letter. It was a bad part of herself that was exposed by it—we can't expect her to have seen that it was better to forgo telling her story than to have the letter read into the record. Was Aurnou so bedazzled by this "lady" or for whatever reason so dominated by her that it impaired his judgment of reality? I've never heard of a *folie à deux* between a lawyer and client.

Aurnou's multi-faceted defense of Mrs. Harris took everything into account except common sense. Where common sense demanded that someone in the situation that Mrs. Harris was in—humiliated, abandoned by her lover in favor of a younger woman—acknowledge that she was filled with bitter anger, Mrs. Harris undertook to persuade the world that her feelings for Tarnower had never altered and that she didn't think of Lynne as a rival. Knowing that the Scarsdale letter, with its cringing appeals for Tarnower's love and its harsh assaults upon Lynne, was about to be made public, common sense required that Mrs. Harris not be allowed her abrasive "superiority" to "Mr." Bolen. After the Scarsdale letter was read, probably the one thing Mrs. Harris could have done to lessen its impact was to admit its ugliness, weep in shame, not in self-pity, and beg the world for forgiveness: the letter had been written in terrible passion.

Mrs. Harris is not a simple subject for a book, not for a book of non-fiction. Without the armature of fiction she can all too easily become a clinical study. She belongs to imaginative writing where, as I say, Freud learned, as we learn, about character in conflict. Mrs. Harris was unable to bring her inner contradictions into reliable working agreement, but our interest in her derives precisely from the unresolved opposition between her conscience and her impulses. She belongs to the novel in the way that Emma Bovary does, or Anna Karenina. They too were characters in contradiction. Outside the novel, in a "report" of her case, she may not seem of a proper size for the company of these great sad ladies of literature. But what size—we may ask—would they have been if we'd met them in life instead of in art? Imagine Flaubert's heroine or Tolstoy's in a courtroom, testifying as a witness in her own defense, having to explain her actions and feelings so as to win the credence of a jury,

335

asked to conform to the rules of legal procedure or, even worse, having to speak to us in the voice of her lawyer. The human dimension of these characters depends on the fictional remove at which we meet them. In the old schoolroom phrase, these fictional women are bigger than life, which is why they enlarge our understanding of life. We're told that Flaubert said, "Madame Bovary, c'est moi"— Madame Bovary was himself. He meant by this that he had put his own powers of torturing phantasy at Emma's disposal, given her his own desire to overthrow the mean barriers of convention. She was his fictional surrogate. Tolstoy's was a different kind of autobiographical effort but Anna too was self-portraiture. Tolstoy hated whatever it was that impelled him to create Anna; she was too close a statement of what he disapproved of in himself. He was in the shady business of self-censorship and we can only be grateful that he so marvelously failed at it. Mrs. Harris is gifted and bright. She writes well; she has a kind of native literacy. But she isn't an artist; she couldn't have created herself as a character in fiction. She never had the capacity for externalization that would have made it possible for her to use herself as a subject. She was material asking to be written but with no one to write her. What is Emma without Flaubert? A silly girl who doesn't know the difference between daydreams and reality. And Anna without Tolstoy? A light-minded woman who thinks that passion is forever and who refuses to know when she's no longer wanted. The resemblances with Mrs. Harris are there but had we encountered Emma or Anna in real life as we have Mrs. Harris, would we have seen that they were "heroines" and that they proposed enough wonderful complication to excite the interest of many generations of readers? Perhaps so—instinctively I think we know when people are bigger, more various and engrossing, than they appear to be. It's all very well to say of Mrs. Harris, as I have, that what made her case so interesting to people was her place in society; it's a place where one is not supposed to act out one's murderous wishes. But finally this is not what made the fascination of the case: what we were caught by was the fact that while in Mrs. Harris we saw just such a person as makes a significant figure in fiction, we saw her in the raw state of life where we have only the making of art, without its seamlessness.

This was enough, however, to transform the Harris-Tarnower story into the Harris story. What had begun as the case of the Scarsdale diet doctor became Mrs. Harris's case. Even before she came to court, when we knew Mrs. Harris only through her first photographs in the newspapers and the scraps of information that were pieced together to provide a background for the shooting, she took the center of the stage, never to release it to anyone, not to her witnesses, not to the Judge or lawyers, not to Dr. Tarnower or Lynne Tryforos. There were long periods when one forgot about the doctor, and one's curiosity about Mrs. Harris's good-looking young rival was mechanical—the courtroom filled up because it had been rumored that Lynne would appear but she was not missed when she failed to appear. If there had been a moment in which the trial went on without Mrs. Harris, her absence would have been portentous. I am not suggesting that our understanding of her character was clear and steady, only that she steadily held us. In fact, from hour to hour my own judgment of her would drastically change—I'd swing from an extreme of sympathy to an extreme of disenchantment, from the wish to protect her to an extreme of distaste. When she was charming, I was charmed. When malice took over as it so often did without her being at all aware of it, I scarcely remembered that I'd ever felt anything but dislike of her—I would think, how can anyone fail to see that this woman is dangerous? Perhaps these swift shifts of feeling attest to her lack of a firm emotional core; certainly hers was a strange power for someone to exercise who sobbingly described herself in a metaphor of emptiness. I recall a long time ago being told that in painting there's a concept, or perhaps only that there used to be a concept, called "negative space": between any two objects represented on a canvas there had to be enough room or suggestion of enough room for the artist to have painted whatever would fit into that space in real life—it's a concept, I suppose, in the relation of reality and imagination. On the canvas of Mrs. Harris's personality there is much negative space, much room for what hasn't been painted in.

I never counted how many of us there were in the press rows but I'd guess there were no fewer than three dozen reporters who were in court either each day or with enough frequency to be regarded as regulars. It was a wonderful group of people; unusually so, I was told by the old court hands. We'd lunch together, talk through the interminable waits when it seemed as if nothing would ever again happen in our lives and that we'd just sit here forever in each other's pleasant weary company: it was our fate. In this press group we didn't talk very much about Mrs. Harris as a personality or character, except by indirection. We chiefly reacted to the developments of the day, tried to comprehend the testimony, but we did talk about what Mrs. Harris might have been up to in coming to Purchase that March evening. Was she telling the truth of her intent to commit suicide? Why had she let herself get so involved with a man like Tarnower? Further than that we didn't try to probe her character because there was too much to probe and too much inconsistency—it's hard to talk about the contradictions in another person's character without sounding self-contradictory. That we were all of us absorbed by her and that we were talking only about her when we were talking about evidence or testimony goes without saying. In court she was the one we wanted to look at, she was the one whose slightest change of facial expression we were watching for. Anyone of us would have got out of a sickbed as I did when she took the stand—maybe she knew this and it's why she wanted to testify. From the point of view of a legal verdict, it would have been better if we'd been left wondering about the unsaid, yet despite the revelations of her week as a witness, at the end of her testimony we were still left pondering about the unsaid: that was her private victory. One of the things we pondered was how this unprepossessing woman, whose life and love had been of such uninspiring quality, could create around her such an air of superbness.

People who work in the theatre talk a great deal about something they call "star quality": what is this mysterious ingredient that makes a person capture and hold the attention of an audience, stand out from everyone else on a stage? Is it the voice, the smile, a cast of countenance? Is it some grace of movement or stillness? Mrs. Harris has star quality. I doubt she knew it before her trial but I think she knows it now and even takes wistful pleasure in it. She draws strength from it. When Marilyn Monroe died, people said that it was Hollywood, in its greedy exploitation of her, that killed her. I believed just the opposite, that Hollywood had given her life. Just so the publicity of her case didn't destroy Jean Harris but sustained her. Had she had to stand trial for murder in some distant court, where there were no reporters or cameras or eager spectators, she'd long since have perished.

I put her in the company of large persons in literature and in life but it would be wrong to leave her without again emphasizing the ordinariness in which her extraordinariness begins. First, there's her physical smallness: Mrs. Harris's body is of no consequence, she's only neat, a tiny monument to biological orderliness. She's been twice a mother but there's no suggestion about her of maternal amplitude; she has the spareness of a snow maiden. Her movements are light, her voice is light, even her wit is light, if slashing. She's pretty without being beautiful, talented without having developed a specific gift, ambitious without having set her sights higher than Tarnower's Westchester, dedicated yet with no necessity to put her mark on life. She's naïve without innocence. Yet whoever has heard of her tragedy wants to hear about her and speak about her. Her elusiveness tantalizes, her personality is like a hall of mirrors: one loses one's way in it. She has become everyone's story. Everyone claims her, everyone claims to understand her, to have solved her mystery. But the mystery is of course not solved or to be solved. People aren't solved. Even women aren't to be solved though they sometimes act as if it were a desirable consummation. In one of the novels of Anthony Powell he has a character say, "When I read about *crimes passionels* in the papers, I am struck not by the richness of the emotions, but by their desperate poverty. On the surface, the people concerned may seem to live with intensity. Underneath, is an abject egotism and lack of imagination." Yes, this could be said of the Harris case too and of Mrs. Harris herself except . . . except that whatever the abjectness of Mrs. Harris and her self-boundedness, these are not the aspects of her character that, at the last, remain with us. I'm far from sure that Mrs. Harris is a worthy person, an admirable person, a lovable person, a person we would wish to see replicated in our society. Not any of these. But she's a person who for some reason sparks the imagination and who has her place in our imagination of this time.

As I write, Mrs. Harris is in the Bedford Hills Correctional Facility, pending appeal. Early report was that she had not only adapted to prison life better than anyone expected but that she was in excellent shape: in her first weeks she'd gained back the weight she'd lost during the trial and she was in good spirits. She'd found her quick firm way in the prison world; she'd organized a jogging group: several women ran with her in one of the prison corridors. If, before her arrival, the other prisoners had thought of her as in fact a special instance and awaited her with some tension, prepared to extrude her from their community, she'd apparently been able to make it plain that there was no reason for hostility—she would be one of them. She asked and received no favors. She wasn't the only middle-class woman, she wasn't the only woman of her age, who was imprisoned there for murder. Like Mrs. Harris, the other women also said they were innocent. Visitors learned to ask the inmates not "What did you do?" but "Why are you here?" The work to which Mrs. Harris had thus far been assigned was various: she assisted in the distribution of food in the prison hospital but she also worked in the library and tutored in high-school equivalency classes. She was said to be disturbed by the low level of education of many of the prisoners. She played bridge with them.

More recently she gave a television interview in which this early report was confirmed and enlarged upon. Mrs. Harris had gained fifteen pounds and looked blooming. She said she had never slept better in her life. She said she was discovering all sorts of new pleasures such as the stimulation of having only cold water to wash with in her cell. From her cell window she had a lovely view of the Bedford hills. She found relief in the fact that when the telephone rang it couldn't be for her and that when the prisoners were locked into their rooms three times a day to be counted, no one in the world could reach her.

I don't like to think of anyone in jail. If Mrs. Harris wins her appeal and is released, I'll have to be glad. And yet I'm not at all certain that the freedom to live her life in her old world is what best fits her needs and possibilities. The structure of prison life could turn out to be a better source of freedom for Mrs. Harris than her adorned but limitless normal world. She may also find much emo-